# ASIAN AMERICAN

# DREAMS

■ ■ ■

# ASIAN AMERICAN DREAMS

## The Emergence of an American People

### Helen Zia

FARRAR, STRAUS AND GIROUX

NEW YORK

Farrar, Straus and Giroux
19 Union Square West, New York 10003

Distributed in Canada by Douglas & McIntyre Ltd.
Printed in the United States of America
Designed by Lisa Stokes
First edition, 2000

Library of Congress Cataloging-in-Publication Data

Zia, Helen.
    Asian American dreams : the emergence of an American people / Helen Zia. — 1st ed.
        p.        cm.
    Includes bibliographical references and index.
    ISBN 0-374-14774-4 (alk. paper)
    1. Asian Americans—Cultural assimilation.    2. Asian Americans—Ethnic identity.
    3. Asian Americans—Social conditions.    4. Zia, Helen.    I. Title.

E184.O6.Z53        2000
305.895073—dc21                                                          99-026746

The author gratefully acknowledges permission to use excerpts from the following plays, song lyrics, and performance works:

*Yankee Dawg You Die*, by Philip Kan Gotanda, from *Fish Head Soup and Other Plays*, by Philip Kan Gotanda. Copyright © 1991, 1995 University of Washington Press, Seattle. Used with permission of the playwright.

"Go Hmong Boy, " by Tou Ger Xiong. Copyright © 1992 by Tou Ger Xiong. Used with permission.

"We Are the Children," written by Chris K. Iijima and Nobuko Miyamoto. Copyright © 1973 by Paredon Records. Used with permission.

"The Church of Born-Again Asian Americans," by Suz Takeda. Copyright © 1999 by Suz Takeda. Used with permission.

For my parents,
Beilin Woo Zia and Yee Chen Zia,

吳禧苓　　謝貽徵

And for the next generation:
Henry Dewey, Jr., Jennifer Camille, Frank Alexander, Emily Shizue, Beilin
Elizabeth, Rory Hajime, Grayson Alan, Marshall Teckyi, Madelaine Zia,
Mitchell Teck-zhang, and Devon Zia. Also Jarrin Kainoa, Erin Joy, Maya
Jialin, Kazumi Okahara, Masami Okahara, Alexander Tadashi, Maya Anne
Sachae, Nicholas Akai, and Peter Wen

# Contents

Introduction                                                    ix

### I    BEYOND OUR SHADOWS

1    From Nothing, a Consciousness                              3
2    Surrogate Slaves to American Dreamers                      21

### II    THE AWAKENING

3    Detroit Blues: "Because of You Motherfuckers"              55
4    To Market, to Market, New York Style                       82
5    Gangsters, Gooks, Geishas, and Geeks                       109

### III    UP FROM INNOCENCE

6    Welcome to Washington                                      139
7    Lost and Found in L.A.                                     166
8    For Richer, for Poorer                                     195

### IV    MOVING THE MOUNTAIN

9    Out on the Front Lines                                     227
10   Reinventing Our Culture                                    252
11   The Last Bastion                                           281
12   Living Our Dreams                                          311

Bibliography                                                    321
Acknowledgments                                                 329
Index                                                           333

# Introduction

In the early 1980s, a song entitled "Turning Japanese" jumped to the top of the charts and instantly thrust an otherwise obscure British group, The Vapors, into the limelight. New Wavers rocked to the musings of a singer who thinks he might be turning Japanese. Though many dancers added the quaint touch of pulling their eyelids taut as they pogoed to the beat, the song had nothing to do with becoming Japanese or Asian.

As an Asian American, I was intrigued by the notion that you could "turn" into or adopt another culture so vastly different from your own, and that you would be conscious of this transformation as it took place. When "Turning Japanese" was at the height of popularity, America was in the midst of a crushing depression that began with the collapse of the auto industry. Intense Japan-bashing characterized the times, and Asian Americans, too, came under fire. The song prompted me to ask, "What about 'Turning American'?"

It was the same question that many of the 10 million Asian Americans have been asking with increasing frequency in the last years of the twentieth century, an era marked by significant challenges and progress for us. But one question hadn't changed. Asian Americans were still wondering out loud, among ourselves and in public discourse, "What does it take to become American?"

The spirit of the question is not about the mechanics of becoming American, a process with which we are familiar: involving ourselves in our communities, gaining citizenship, participating in the political process by getting the vote out, running for office, and, yes, donating to campaigns. Nor is it about getting acculturated—most of us have been Americans plenty long enough to walk the talk and traverse the nuances of the rhyme, rhythm, and soul of this culture.

What we've really been wanting to know is how to become *accepted* as Americans. For if baseball, hot dogs, apple pie, and Chevrolet were enough for us to gain acceptance as Americans, then there would be no periodic refrain about alien Asian spies, no persistent bewilderment toward us as "strange" and "exotic" characters, no cries of foul play by Asian Americans, and no need for this book.

Instead, Asian Americans have been caught in a time warp that, every decade or so, propels us back to the nineteenth century, when congressional hearings debated whether we were too corrupt, too untrustworthy, too uncouth to be Americans. Only in the late 1990s the discussion was about campaign donations and alleged espionage.

Missing from the tons of newsprint and miles of videotape in this most recent round were the heartwarming stories of my universe, the tales of valiant women and men of Asian ancestry who struggled and sacrificed to make contributions to their country, the United States of America, and who wished to be seen as full Americans. I've been struck time and again by how little is really known about us and the America we are part of; how the rich textures of who we are, why we are here, and what we bring to America remain so absent from the picture.

But a community as large, diverse, and dynamic as the Asian American and Pacific Islander peoples cannot stay on the edge of obscurity, frustrated by images that have rendered us invisible and voiceless, while other American communities watch us and wonder why we are at the center of key issues of the day. This book was written with the hope of changing this condition. Its personal essays and broader chronicles reflect conversations and stories that Asian Americans tell one another, about the challenges we've met, the people we've encountered, and the lessons we've drawn. It's about the numerous and disparate Asian ethnicities that have come together in this land, evolving into an American people.

It is time for Asian Americans to open up our universe, to reveal our limitless energy and unbounded dreams, our hopes as well as our fears: to show what it means, at the dawn of a new century, for a people to be "Turning American."

# I

# BEYOND OUR SHADOWS

# · 1 ·
# From Nothing,
# a Consciousness

"Little China doll, what's your name?"

This question always made me feel awkward. I knew there was something unwholesome in being seen as a doll, and a fragile china one at that. But, taught to respect my elders at all times, I would answer dutifully, mumbling my name.

"Zia," they would cluck and nod. "It means 'aunt' in Italian, you know?"

To me, growing up in New Jersey, along the New York–Philadelphia axis, it seemed almost everyone was a little Italian, or at least had an Italian aunt.

One day in the early 1980s, the routine changed unexpectedly. I was introduced to a colleague, a newspaper editor. Making small talk, he said, "Your name is very interesting . . ." I noted his Euro-Anglo heritage and braced myself for yet another Italian lesson.

"Zia, hmm," he said. "Are you Pakistani?"

I nearly choked. For many people, Pakistan is not familiar geography. In

*The Zia family in 1957: Dad and Mom with (left to right) Henry, Hugo, Hoyt, and the author*

those days it was inconceivable that a stranger might connect this South Asian, Pakistani name with my East Asian, Chinese face.

Through the unscientific process of converting Asian names into an alphabetic form, my romanized Chinese last name became identical to a common romanized Pakistani name. In fact, it was homonymous with a much despised ruler of Pakistan. Newspaper headlines about him read: "President Zia Hated by Masses" and "Pakistanis Cry, Zia Must Go." I'd clip out the headlines and send them to my siblings in jest. When President Zia's plane mysteriously crashed, I grew wary. After years of being mistaken for Japanese and nearly every other East Asian ethnicity, I added Pakistani to my list.

I soon discovered this would be the first of many such incidents. Zia Maria began to give way to Mohammad Zia ul-Haq. A new awareness of Asian Americans was emerging.

■   ■   ■

The abrupt change in my name ritual signaled my personal awakening to a modern-day American revolution in progress. In 1965, an immigration policy that had given racial preferences to Europeans for nearly two hundred years officially came to an end. Millions of new immigrants to America were no longer the standard vanilla but Hispanic, African, Caribbean, and—most dramatically for me—Asian. Though I was intellectually aware of the explosive growth in my community, I hadn't yet adjusted my own sense of self, or the way I imagined other Americans viewed me.

Up until then, I was someone living in the shadows of American society, struggling to find some way into a portrait that was firmly etched in white and, occasionally, black. And there were plenty of reminders that I wasn't relevant. Like the voices of my 1960s high school friends Rose and Julie. Rose was black, and Julie was white. One day we stood in the school yard, talking about the civil rights movement swirling around us, about cities engulfed in flames and the dreams for justice and equality that burned in each of us.

As I offered my thoughts, Rose abruptly turned to me and said, "Helen, you've got to decide if you're black or white." Stunned, I was unable to say that I was neither, that I had an identity of my own. I didn't know the words "Asian American." It was a concept yet to be articulated.

Somewhere between my school yard conversation and the confrontation with my Pakistani namesake, Asian Americans began to break through the shadows. By then we had already named ourselves "Asian American" and we were having raging debates and fantastic visions of an America *we* fit into. But few outside of Asian America cared about our shadow dreams.

Gradually we began to be visible, although not necessarily seen the way we wished. Then we had to discover what it meant to be in the light.

When I was growing up in the 1950s and 1960s, there were barely a half-million Asian Americans in the nation. Of those, only 150,000 were Chinese Americans—not enough to populate a small midwestern city. We made up less than 0.1 percent of the population. Most of us lived on the islands of Hawaii or in a few scattered Chinatown ghettoes.

My parents met in New York City's Chinatown in 1950. They were among the new wave of Northern Chinese who fled China as a result of the Japanese occupation, the devastation of World War II, and the rise of the Chinese Communist Party. My father, Yee Chen Zia, was a poet and scholar from the canaled, garden city of Suzhou, known as the Venice of China. Like many Chinese of his generation, he had been a patriotic warrior against Japan, later becoming a newspaper editor and a member of the Chinese diplomatic corps in the United States. After the war, he decided to settle in New York, taking on various odd jobs—cabdriver, Fuller Brush salesperson, Good Humor ice cream truck driver.

My mother, Beilin Woo, was raised not far from Suzhou, in the metropolis of Shanghai. She fled its postwar chaos as a tubercular teenager aboard the *General Gordon*, the last American ship to leave Shanghai before the Communist government took power. Her first task upon arrival at the port of San Francisco was to find a husband who could not only ensure her continued stay in the United States but also help her repay her sister for the cost of the passage to America.

Finding marriageable suitors was not a problem for women from Asia. For more than half a century before World War II, several racially discriminatory laws prohibited Asian men from becoming U.S. citizens or marrying outside their race. The United States also barred women from China, India, and the Philippines from immigrating. The combined impact of these prohibitions created generations of lonely Asian bachelor societies in America. But World War II forced the United States to change such policies, so obviously offensive to its allies in Asia as well as to the thousands of Asian and Asian American GIs fighting for America. The shameful citizenship laws were eventually repealed and women like my mother gained entry into the country.

Among the many Chinese American men who courted my mother at her boardinghouse near San Francisco's Chinatown was a bank clerk who had come all the way from New York City in search of a wife. His jovial disposition and stable job appealed to her, even though he said he was forty years old. They were married in Reno, Nevada, on October 31, 1949. My twenty-year-old mother was on her way to New York as Mrs. John Yee.

Communicating with her new husband, however, was not easy. Like the vast majority of Chinese in America at that time, he was from Canton Province, a thousand miles away from Shanghai. The language, customs, and even facial features of the regions' peoples were different. Their local Chinese dialects of Shanghainese and Cantonese were unintelligible to each other. Cantonese people were considered more easygoing, light-hearted in spirit and darker in complexion, while Northern Chinese were taller and thought to be arrogant and hot-tempered. To get around in Chinatown, my mother had to learn some Cantonese. In the meantime she and her husband communicated in a mixture of pidgin English and pidgin Cantonese.

They settled into a dank tenement on Henry Street, where many new arrivals made their first home in New York. It stands today, with the shared bathroom down the hall and the bathtub in the kitchen, still home to new generations of Chinese immigrants. A year later, my older brother was born. They named him Henry, after the street. Had he been a girl, they planned to name him Catherine, after the nearby cross street. During the day, Henry's father worked a few blocks away in Chatham Square, at the Bank of China, while my mother found new friends. New York's Chinatown had only 15,000 residents in 1950, compared to more than 100,000 in 1990; a tiny but growing number came from Shanghai and its neighboring cities of Hangzhou, Ningbo, Suzhou, and Nanjing. Bound by their similar dialects and regional cuisine, which were so unlike those of the larger Cantonese community surrounding them, the Shanghainese speakers congregated at the curio shop of a Mrs. Fung, on the corner of Doyers and Pell. That's where my mother met my father.

When Henry was still an infant, his father suffered a massive stroke and died. From his death certificate my mother learned that her husband was ten years older than he had disclosed. The young widow was eligible for marriage again in the Chinatown society, with my father in pursuit. Months later they wed and moved to Newark, New Jersey, where my father was trying, unsuccessfully, to run a small furniture store. I soon came on the scene, another member of the post–World War II Asian American baby boom.

On a clear day the Manhattan skyline is visible from Newark, but the insular familiarity of Chinatown was worlds away. Outside of Chinatown it was rare to encounter another person of Chinese or other Asian descent. In Newark and the various New Jersey communities where we later moved, the only way to meet Asians was to stop complete strangers on the street, while shopping, or at the bus stop—anywhere that we happened to see the occasional person who looked like us. At an A&P supermarket checkout counter, my mother met her friend Sue, who came to the United States as a war bride, having married a GI during the postwar occupation of Japan. The animosity between China and Japan that brought both women to New Jersey was never an issue. Each was so thrilled to find someone like herself.

Auntie Sue and her son Kim, who was of mixed race, white and Japanese, were regular visitors to our home. Though our mothers bonded readily, it was harder for their Asian American kids to connect simply because we looked alike. Mom and Auntie Sue had the shared experience of leaving their war-ravaged Asian homes for a new culture, but Kim and I shared little except for our Asian features; we stuck out like yellow streaks on a white-and-black canvas. Outside of Chinatown, looking Asian meant looking foreign, alien, un-American. The pressure on us was to fit in with the "American" kids we looked so unlike, to conform and assimilate. Why would we want to be around other Asian kids who reminded us of our poor fit? At the tender age of six, I already felt different from the "real" Americans. I didn't feel comfortable with Kim and sensed his ambivalence to me. But the joke was on us, because no matter how hard we might try to blend in with the scenery, our faces gave us away.

Still, I was proud to be Chinese. Mom and Dad filled us with stories about their childhoods in China. Dad was born in 1912, one year after the founding of the Chinese Republic, and was imbued with a deep love for his native country. He was the second son of a widow who was spurned by her in-laws. His mother sold her own clothes to pay for his schooling. She beat my father every day so that he would study harder—this he told us proudly whenever we slacked off. Dad modeled his life after the ideal of the Confucian scholar-official: by studying assiduously he won academic honors and scholarships and achieved recognition as a poet and writer. China's system of open examinations was the foundation of the civil service—a Chinese creation, Dad pointedly reminded us as he turned the TV off. Studying hard, he said, was a time-honored route to advancement for even the poorest Chinese.

Mom grew up in Shanghai under the Japanese occupation. From the time she was a small child she lived with a fear and dislike of Japanese soldiers. Because of the war, her education was disrupted and she never went beyond the fourth grade—a source of regret that made her value education for her children. Mom's childhood memories were of wartime hardships and days spent picking out grains of rice from the dirt that had been mixed in as a way to tip the scales. Her stories taught me to be proud of the strength and endurance of the Chinese people.

Dad told us about our heritage. When other children made fun of us, or if news reports demeaned China, he reminded us that our ancestors wore luxurious silks and invented gunpowder while Europeans still huddled naked in caves. Of course, I knew that Europeans had discovered clothing, too, but the image was a reassuring one for a kid who didn't fit. My father wanted us to speak flawless English to spare us from ridicule and the language discrimination he faced. He forbade my mother to speak to us in Chinese, which was hard, since Mom spoke little English then. We grew up monolingual, learning only simple Chinese expressions—*che ve le*, "Come and eat"—and various Shanghainese epithets, like the popular phrase for a naughty child—*fei si le*, or "devilish to death." Dad also expected us to excel in school, since, he said, our Asian cranial capacities were larger than those of any other race. Pulling out the *Encyclopaedia Britannica* to prove his point, he'd make us study the entry, then test us to make sure we got the message. He told us about the Bering Strait and the land bridge from Asia to America, saying that we had a right to be in this country because we were cousins to the Native Americans.

These tidbits were critical to my self-esteem. In New Jersey, it was so unusual to see a person of Asian descent that people would stop what they were doing to gawk rudely at my family wherever we went. When we walked into a store or a diner, we were like the freak show at Barnum & Bailey's circus, where Chinese were displayed as exotic creatures in the late 1800s, along with the two-headed dog. A sense of our own heritage and worth gave us the courage and cockiness to challenge their rudeness and stare down the gawkers.

What Mom and Dad couldn't tell us was what it meant to be Chinese in America. They didn't know—they were just learning about America themselves. We found little help in the world around us. Asians were referred to most often as Orientals, Mongols, Asiatics, heathens, the yellow hordes, and an assortment of even less endearing terms. Whatever the ter-minology, the message was clear: we were definitely not Americans.

There is a drill that nearly all Asians in America have experienced more times than they can count. Total strangers will interrupt with the absurdly existential question "What are you?" Or the equally common inquiry "Where are you from?" The queries are generally well intentioned, made in the same detached manner that you might use to inquire about a pooch's breed.

My standard reply to "What are you?" is "American," and to "Where are you from?" "New Jersey." These, in my experience, cause great displeasure. Eyebrows arch as the questioner tries again. "No, where are you really from?" I patiently explain that, really, I am from New Jersey. Inevitably this will lead to something like "Well then, what country are your people from?" Sooner or later I relent and tell them that my "people" are from China. But when I turn the tables and ask, "And what country are your people from?" the reply is invariably an indignant "I'm from America, of course."

The sad truth was that I didn't know much about my own history. I knew that Chinese had built the railroads, and then were persecuted. That was about it. I didn't know that in the 1700s a group of Filipinos settled in Louisiana, or that in 1825 the first Chinese was born in New York City. I didn't know that Asian laborers were brought to the Americas as a replace-ment for African slaves—by slave traders whose ships had been rerouted from Africa to Asia. I didn't even know that Japanese Americans had been imprisoned only a decade before my birth. Had I known more about my

Asian American history I might have felt less foreign. Instead, I grew up thinking that perhaps China, a place I had never seen, was my true home, since so many people didn't think I belonged here.

I did figure out, however, that relations between America and any Asian nation had a direct impact on me. Whenever a movie about Japan and World War II played at the local theater, my brothers and I became the enemy. It didn't matter that we weren't Japanese—we looked Japanese. What's worse, by now my family had moved to a new housing development, one of the mass-produced Levittowns close to Fort Dix, the huge army base. Most of our neighbors had some connection to the military.

At the Saturday matinee, my brothers and I would sit with all the other kids in town watching the sinister Zero pilots prepare to ambush their unsuspecting prey, only to be thwarted by the all-American heroes—who were, of course, always white. These movies would have their defining moment, that crescendo of emotion when the entire theater would rise up, screaming, "Kill them, kill them, kill them!"—them being the Japanese. When the movie was over and the lights came on, I wanted to be invisible so that my neighbors wouldn't direct their patriotic fervor toward me.

As China became the evil Communist menace behind the Bamboo Curtain, and the United States was forced to deal with its stalemate in the Korean War, the Asian countries seemed interchangeable. Back when Japan was the enemy, China was the good ally—after all, that's how my mom and dad got to come to America. But now, quixotically, Japan was good and China was evil.

Chinese in America were suspected to be the fifth column of Chinese Communists, as J. Edgar Hoover frequently said before Congress and throughout the McCarthy era witch-hunts. In the 1950s, while Japanese American families attempted to return to normalcy after their release from American concentration camps during the war, the FBI switched its surveillance eye onto hundreds of Chinese Americans. My father was one.

Our mail routinely arrived opened and damaged, and our phone reception was erratic. I thought everyone's mail service and phone lines were bad. Polite FBI agents interviewed our neighbors, asking if my father was up to anything suspicious. What attracted the attention of the FBI was Dad's tendency to write letters to newspapers and politicians when he disagreed with their views on China or anything else. Nothing ever came of the FBI investigations of my father, nor was a ring of Chinese American spies ever found—but I later learned that the probes succeeded in intimidating the Chinese American communities of the 1950s, creating a distrust of and inhibiting their participation in politics.

The FBI queries hardly bolstered our acceptance in our working-class housing tract. Neighbor kids would nose around and ask, "So what *does* your father do?" It didn't help that my father had instructed us to say, "He's self-employed." This only added to our sense of foreignness.

Like so many Asian immigrants unable to break into the mainstream American labor market, my father had to rely on his own resourcefulness and his family's labor. In the back room of our house we made "baby novelties" with little trinkets and baby toys and pink or blue vases that my father then sold to flower shops. Every day, in addition to doing our schoolwork, we helped out in the family business.

Our home was our workplace, the means to our livelihood, and therefore the center of everything. This conveniently matched the Confucian notion of family, whereby the father, as patriarch, is the master of the universe. In our household it was understood that no one should ever disobey, contradict, or argue with the patriarch, who, in the Confucian hierarchy, is a stand-in for God. My mother, and of course the children, were expected to obey God absolutely.

This system occasionally broke down when my mother and father quarreled, usually about my father's rigid expectations of us. But in the end, God always seemed to win. Growing up female, I could see the Confucian order of the Three Obediences in action: the daughter obeys the father, the wife obeys the husband, and, eventually, the widow obeys the son. The Confucian tradition was obviously stacked against me, as a girl.

I found similar lessons in the world beyond our walls. Mom's best friend from the Chinatown Shanghainese clique had followed us to New Jersey, attracted by the low home costs and the fact that we already lived there. Auntie Ching and her husband opened a Chinese restaurant at a major intersection of the highway. In those days, there were few places outside Chinatown to get real Chinese food. After they had spent their own money to upgrade the kitchen and remodel the restaurant, business was booming. But Auntie Ching had no lease for the restaurant—and the German American owner, sensing an opportunity for himself, evicted the Chings and set up his own shop.

Our tiny Chinese American community was horrified that the Chings would be treated so unjustly. My cantankerous dad urged them to fight it out in court. But they chose not to, believing that it would be better not to make waves. Chinese cannot win, they said, so why make trouble for ourselves? Such defeatism disturbed my father, who would often say in disgust, "In America, a 'Chinaman's chance' means no chance." He felt that the Chinese way of dealing with obstacles—to either accept or go around them, but not to confront them directly—would never get us very far in the United States.

As a child, I didn't see Chinese or other Asian Americans speaking up to challenge such indignities. When my parents were denied the right to rent or buy a home in various Philadelphia neighborhoods, they had to walk away despite my father's outrage. We could only internalize our shame when my mother and her troop of small children were thrown out of supermarkets because we were wrongly accused of opening packages and stealing. Or when Henry was singled out of a group of noisy third graders for talking and he alone was expelled from the lunchroom for the rest of the year. Or when my younger brother Hoyt and the few other Asian boys in school were rounded up because another kid said he thought he saw an "Oriental" boy go into his locker.

Other times the discomfort was less tangible. Why did my fifth-grade teacher, a Korean War veteran, become so agitated when topics of China and Asian culture came up? Was there a reason for his apparent dislike of me and my brothers, who also had him as a teacher? After my Girl Scout troop leader asked all the girls to state their religions, what caused her to scowl in disgust at me when I answered Buddhist? My family didn't practice an organized religion, so I didn't know what else to say.

Absorbing the uncertainty of my status in American society, I assumed the role that I observed for myself—one of silence and invisibility. I enjoyed school and, following my father's example, studied hard and performed well academically, but I consciously avoided bringing attention to myself and rarely spoke up, even on matters related to me.

For example, there was Mrs. George. From second grade until I graduated from John F. Kennedy High School, Mrs. George was my physical education teacher. She was the aunt of Olympic track star Carl Lewis and was always kind to me. But for those ten years, Mrs. George called me Zi, as though it rhymed with "eye." One day, when I was in twelfth grade, she yelled over at me, "Zi, come over here." A classmate standing nearby said,

"Mrs. George, Helen's name isn't Zi, it's Zia." Mrs. George looked at me and let out a huge laugh. "Zi," she said, then corrected herself. "I mean, Zia, how come you never told me how to say your name after all these years?"

I didn't know how to answer. It had never occurred to me to correct my teacher. In the Confucian order of the world, teachers were right up there with parents in commanding respect and obedience. I simply had no voice to raise to my teacher.

Despite my deference to traditional Chinese behavior, the day finally came when I had to disobey my father. I had received several offers of full scholarships to attend college. Like the Chinese who lined up for the imperial civil service examinations in hopes of a new life, I viewed college as my means of escape from the narrow life of making flower shop baby novelties in our dull New Jersey town.

Though my father was proud of my educational achievement, he didn't want me to leave for college. He had already stated his desire for me to attend the closest school to home. When the time came for him to sign the college registration forms, he refused. "The proper place for an unmarried daughter is at home with her parents," he insisted. He wanted to keep me out of trouble until I found a husband to do the overseeing.

I could see the doors to my future slamming shut. At age seventeen, I had never knowingly disobeyed my father. I policed myself, turning down dates, invitations to parties, and even educational opportunities away from home, because I thought Dad would disapprove. I was caught between two conflicting Asian ideals. The Three Obediences demanded subservience from females, but the primacy of education taught me to seek advancement through study. My American side told me to heed my own call.

Somehow I mustered the courage to shout, "No! I'm going to college." I don't know who was more surprised by my outburst, my father or me. He said nothing more about the subject, and I continued my preparations to leave. I also finally learned that the world wouldn't end if I challenged authority, a lesson I would take with me to college.

My father was right on one account—I intended to look for trouble in the campus political and social movements that appeared on the news each night. The call for civil rights was all around me, beginning in my own high school. Women's liberation offered an alternative to the Three Obediences. Then there was the war in Vietnam, involving yet another

Asian enemy. My father was against the war because he saw U.S. involvement in Southeast Asia as a continuation of American domination over the people of Asia. At the dinner table my father lectured us about the immorality of the war; the next day I'd go to school and sit through government propaganda films and civics teachers condemning the Communist scourge and extolling the importance of the war effort to democracy.

For an Asian American kid, the worst part about the Vietnam War was watching the carnage on the news every night, with people who looked like my mom and dad machine-gunned from U.S. helicopters, scorched by American-made napalm, executed at point-blank range, igniting themselves with gasoline in protest, being massacred in their homes and ridiculed on TV shows. It seemed that we had killed the entire population of Vietnam many times over for all the dead who were reported in the body counts each night.

The constant barrage aimed at stirring up patriotic zeal against the Vietnamese enemy took its toll on Asian Americans, in the same way that the previous hostilities with Japan, China, and North Korea had. Many kids in my school had relatives fighting—and dying—in Vietnam. One classmate could barely look at me because I reminded her of the war that killed her older brother. Encountering her in gym class was awkward and sad. At the dry cleaner's and the doughnut shop where I worked in the summers, plenty of GIs would stop in, and some would have to comment. "They're everywhere, aren't they?" a soldier customer said to his buddy as I handed him his laundered and starched fatigues. I had become the local personification of a war nearly ten thousand miles away. Since I looked like the enemy, I must be the enemy.

At the same time, there was no place for me in the debates over national issues like the war or racial equality. People like me were absent from everything that was considered to be "American"—from TV, movies, newspapers, history, and everyday discussions that took place in the school yard. It was hard to feel American when I wasn't treated like one. Yet I didn't feel Asian, either: I couldn't speak Chinese and I hardly knew Chinatown, let alone China. The void left me with many questions.

In the spring of my senior year in high school, the small group of Asian American undergraduates at Princeton University invited me to an orientation meeting. My incoming first-year class had the largest number of Asian Americans ever—sixteen men and four women, nearly as many as the three upper classes combined. I was excited to be part of this tiny but growing Asian student body, coming to Princeton on a full scholarship, part of the wave that drove the university to open its doors to women for the first time in more than two hundred years. In the decades before my arrival, Princeton and the other Ivy League schools accepted only a few Asian students a year, most likely from Asia, not American-born Asians. Though I graduated from high school at the top of my class, I knew that I never would have been admitted to Princeton were it not for the civil rights movement. I was eager to find this movement, as soon as I could escape the watchful eyes of my parents.

The day of my orientation program happened to coincide with a massive student protest and strike at Princeton. The common areas were a sea of young people with placards, banners, and peace signs. Some were locked in earnest debate; others were simply playing Frisbee in the sun. Excited to have found my element, I headed to the Little Hall dormitory to meet the Asian American students.

When I and the handful of other visiting high school seniors knocked on the door that afternoon, we were shocked to find that our hosts were still asleep. About a half-dozen or so Asian American undergraduates were sprawled in various parts of the dorm suite. Strewn around them were beer cans, liquor bottles, ashtrays full of cigarette butts, and other paraphernalia. I was glad that my non-smoking, teetotaler parents had not come along, or I might never have made it to college after all. Our student mentors had been up all night, protesting, partying, debating the role that Asian American students should play in the Third World liberation movement and antiwar student strikes. They regaled us with tales of their lives as Asian American student protesters. I was on the road to discovering my own identity as an Asian American.

I wasn't alone in my quest. The Asian American baby boomers were all approaching college age. For the first time in American history, we were being admitted into colleges and universities in visible numbers as racial barriers began to come down. Some students were from immigrant families like mine, while others were multi-generation Americans.

The foreign-born Chinese students called us American-born types "jook sings," or "hollow bamboo"—Chinese on the outside, but empty inside. The kids from Hawaii were so much more secure in both their Asianness and their Americanness, having grown up in an Asian American majority; they called Japanese Americans from the mainland "katonks"—empty coconuts. The Chinatown kids seemed streetwise and hip, while students from places such as Phoenix, Buffalo, and Columbus were more like me, having grown up without seeing many faces like our own. Some Asian Americans I met called for Yellow Power, in the same spirit as Black Power advocates; others were so assimilated that they were called "bananas."

For the first time in my life, I heard about the internment of 120,000 Japanese Americans from third-generation—Sansei—Japanese American students. The experience of being incarcerated for presumed disloyalty was so painful that many of their parents refused to discuss it with them. I heard about Chinese "paper sons" who were "adopted" by Chinese men living in the United States after all immigration records were destroyed in the San Francisco earthquake of 1906. And about the Filipino "manongs"—old uncles—who worked the farms of California and the West, moving from harvest to harvest. We taught ourselves much of this information, using dog-eared mimeographed course syllabi gathered from Asian American courses in California and elsewhere like a new Holy Grail.

I began to make the connections between past history and my own life, understanding, for example, how the effort to deport my father in the early 1950s was linked to Chinese Americans of the 1800s. When the Immigration and Naturalization Service debated whether to permit my underemployed father to stay in the United States, the fact that he was the sole breadwinner for two infant U.S. citizens by birth swayed their decision. Henry and I were Americans thanks to an 1898 Supreme Court decision in response to a lawsuit by Wong Kim Ark.

I imagined people with Asian faces taking part in American life in a way that I had never before dreamed possible. A new generation of Asian Americans was injecting itself into national debates on civil rights, equality for women, poverty, workplace and labor issues, South African apartheid—we didn't limit the breadth of our vision. Just like the other baby boomers of all races in that 1960s and 1970s era, we knew we were making history. The excitement of that historical sweep added an element of grandeur to our activities; we weren't afraid to think big.

In the spring of 1971, a joint committee of the black, Latino, and Asian American students decided it was time to make the university address the racial inequities on campus. Princeton had very few students of color then, about a hundred in an undergraduate student body of nearly four thousand. We agreed that life at Princeton for students of color was akin to being stuck in a vast snowdrift, and it was time to thaw the university out. Our small numbers didn't deter us.

The leadership wanted to make a bold, definitive statement, so they decided that our loose grouping of minority students—Third World students—should seize and occupy Firestone Library and call for a massive rally at the University Chapel. We would denounce racism at Princeton and the racist war in Vietnam. We would demand an end to the war, as well as the creation of programs, courses, and a center for Third World students. To a first-year student from a sheltered Confucian home in New Jersey, this was the big time.

Princeton in 1971 was almost entirely male, having admitted its first women undergraduates in 1969. I was one of the half-dozen Asian American women students on campus, and the only one involved in this grandiose plan. Until then I assisted the guys by taking on useful "female" chores like learning to run a mimeograph machine. But this ambitious library plan caught us shorthanded, and somehow I was assigned the task of handling security for the takeover.

Firestone Library is bigger than most castles—and built like one. In my one previous attempt at security, I had installed a padlock on my bedroom door so my brothers wouldn't trash my room; that failed when they screwed the latch off the door. But I took my job very seriously and ran through all of Firestone, getting a good aerobic workout. Our little band of Third World men and a few women entered Firestone one afternoon and refused to come out. We secured the building and declared it occupied. I missed the main action, if there was any, because I was so busy running around and checking all the doors and windows.

The next day, we marched out of Firestone and declared victory before a huge rally at the chapel. My brush with student activism changed my life. Not just because of my successful tenure as security czar, during which I protected our sit-in from Princeton's wild squirrels, but because of the rally that followed. In the days leading up to our library takeover, it was somehow decided that several Asian Americans should speak about the racism of the Vietnam War. This was an important moment, because, as relative political newcomers, we would often defer to the more numerous black and Latino students. But we had a lot to say about racism and the war, and our Asian faces would make a powerful statement. It was also decided that an Asian woman should be among the speakers.

This idea posed a certain logistical problem, since there were so few Asian American female undergraduates. None of us would do it. I had never spoken to a group larger than my fifth-grade class, and the very idea made my stomach churn. Yet the thought that no one would talk about women of Vietnam and the war seemed terribly wrong. In the course of my patrol runs through Firestone the night before the rally, I decided that someone had to do it, even if it had to be me.

During our triumphant march out of the library and into the crowded chapel, packed with a thousand or more people, I fought nausea and panic. I had never met a Vietnamese woman, and what did I know about war? But my mother's stories rescued me: stories of the war that she had witnessed from her childhood spent fleeing Japanese soldiers, of the terrible brutality, of rape, torture, mutilation, and murder, and of the tremendous will to survive. I managed to walk through the long chapel without stumbling, and to speak of my mother's experiences and the inhumanity of this war.

After the rally, an undergraduate student from Vietnam thanked me. Marius Jansen, one of my professors and a distinguished scholar of Japanese history, gave me a puzzled look and told me I didn't sound like myself at all. His comment made me pause to think, for the first time, about the images I must project as an Asian American woman, and the images that might be projected back on me. Most of all, I was relieved and astonished that I, who a year earlier couldn't correct my teacher's pronunciation of my name, had spoken out loud. This Asian American movement was transforming me in a way such that I might transform others. Through it, I began to find my voice.

Finding my voice didn't always mean that my words were welcome, even among my Asian American pals. One day early in my second year, I was walking across campus with my classmate Alan, a street-smart Chinatown boy from California. We were headed to the newly established Third World Center—the prize from our student strike and occupation of the library. On the way, we argued over the relative importance of race and gender. "The revolution must fight racism first," Alan said to me. "Race is primary. Only after we eliminate racism can we fight sexism. Women will have to wait." It was like being at home with my brothers. I called Alan a male chauvinist; a pig, even.

Furious at such attitudes from our "revolutionary" Asian American brothers, the Asian American women at Princeton organized a seminar on Asian American women. Our numbers had grown enough to establish the first course on this topic on the East Coast, perhaps in the country. We didn't ask the men *not* to participate, but they didn't anyway. In our own space, we explored the social, historical, and political context of our mothers' and grandmothers' lives in Asia, their journeys to America, their experiences in sweatshops, on plantations, at home. We discussed our lives as Asian American women. I began to understand the Confucian hierarchy that forced women and girls into perpetual subordination. We, on the other hand, vowed never to accept being less than equal to our brothers.

But our class on Asian American women didn't explore the silences that our newly created Asian American "family" imposed on us. We didn't talk about sexual harassment or date rape within our own community. The language and the concepts didn't quite exist yet. But the incidents did. My academic adviser, a distinguished Chinese professor, gave unsolicited advice—about sex—to his female students during their faculty consultations. When the professor added such tidbits to the discussion of my thesis, my newly discovered voice failed me. I had run headlong into the quandary common to women of color and others from beleaguered communities: if we air our dirty laundry, we bring shame on ourselves and our community. With the status of Asian Americans so fragile, why drag down one of the few respected Asian American professors? Years later, I learned that another female student, a European American, had filed a report with the university. The esteemed professor had been disgraced—but, at least, not by one of "his own."

Women's liberation didn't offer much help at the time. I felt alienated after my visits to the campus women's center. The women I met were more interested in personal consciousness raising than social consciousness raising. I wanted to do both, but their lives as white women were so removed from mine, which was entwined with my life as an Asian American. Yet this distance didn't prove that race was primary, either. Other experiences made that clear, such as the time I met Gus Hall, a perennial candidate for president, on the ticket of the American Communist Party. He was speaking at Princeton with his running mate, Herbert Aptheker. Some Third World students were invited to a small luncheon for them; Alan and I went as representatives of the newly formed Asian American Students Association. Throughout the entire reception and luncheon, Hall and Aptheker, who were both white, spoke primarily to the African American students, pointedly ignoring Alan and me. To these American Communists, Asian Americans had no political currency; in their eyes, we didn't exist, or perhaps they assumed from our Asian faces that we were predisposed to support China, a bitter foe of the Soviets. It was the first time I witnessed such a blatant race ploy by political "progressives," but it wouldn't be the last.

A whole generation of Asian Americans was getting an education about our identity. We couldn't wait to leave the safe confines of our campuses, to share our lessons and our pride in this newfound heritage. Many of us went into Asian American enclaves as community organizers, intent on making changes there. Our campus experiences made it abundantly clear that if Asian Americans were to take our rightful place in American society, we would have to scratch and dig and blast our way in, much as the railroad workers had through the Rockies one hundred years earlier.

Few in America, or even in our own communities, paid much attention to these young Asian Americans. Among the separate—and expanding—Asian immigrant groups, the vision of pan-Asian unity was not compelling; survival was their main focus.

Still, a dynamic process was set in motion: we were reclaiming our stake in a land and a history that excluded us, transforming a community that was still in the process of becoming. We were following our destinies as Asian Americans.

# · 2 ·

# Surrogate Slaves to
# American Dreamers

In my childhood photo album, there is a tattered brown news clipping taped to the inside cover. It features me as George Washington, looking as earnest as a seven-year-old in shorts can. I'm pointing straight ahead across a make-believe

*The Asian Americans I saw in my youth: the driving out and murder of Chinese in Denver (*Frank Leslie's Illustrated Newspaper, *November 20, 1880)*

frozen river, leading other girls who are pulling imaginary oars. "Charades," the caption reads. ". . . Helen Zia, as Washington."

When the *Burlington County Times* photographed our tableau of George and the fateful crossing, no one seemed to care that this Revolutionary War hero was a Chinese girl, in a rice-bowl hairdo and razor-edge bangs. The role seemed natural enough to me. I was steeped in the stories of the ragtag Colonial Army and how it outsmarted the British and the Hessian mercenaries on Christmas night.

Each year, my history classes followed a predictable rhythm. September began with the Leni-Lenapes, the local Native American Indians who had vanished long ago. By midyear we were into Manifest Destiny, the Gold Rush, and the "settling" of the West. The Civil War came and went, and slavery was finally abolished. In the spring, we zipped through Woodrow Wilson, the League of Nations, and World War II. In this whirlwind treatment of history, there wasn't a single Asian American to be found. I hadn't a clue that people like me might have contributed to the building of America, the land of my birth.

The Second World War brought Asian faces into my textbooks, but that was hardly cause for celebration. My school chums would turn and squint at me, the face of the enemy. In American history texts, Asian people were either invisible or reviled. It was just like the real-life choice we faced, our Asian American dilemma. Was it better to choose invisibility and a life in the shadows than to be treated as a despised enemy? Or was acquiescent invisibility just another form of self-loathing?

My father wanted us to have a deeper understanding of history that included our Chinese heritage. As a young man he had translated and published several Western texts, including Georg Hegel's *Lectures on the Philosophy of History* from German into Chinese. His greater challenge was to imbue his American-born children with a similar devotion to knowledge. To accomplish this, he employed the teaching methods favored by many Asian immigrant parents: force-feeding and strict discipline. He also bought the *Encyclopaedia Britannica* from a door-to-door salesperson and assigned sections for my brothers and me to read. Then he'd quiz us with his own written and oral exams. Oral were worse. If we did well, we might be rewarded with a nickel, but the real incentive was to avoid the humiliation that came with failure.

Dad was not happy with the *Britannica*. He found the sections on China to be outdated and inaccurate; he bristled at the Western romanizations of important Chinese words and was driven to fury by Western arrogance toward Chinese people. He took issue with the title of Will and Ariel Durant's *Story of Civilization*, which in one volume covered five thousand years of Asian civilizations and devoted eleven volumes to European cultures. But he respected the knowledge they presented, and wanted us to study such books critically.

To supplement the shortcomings of Western texts, Dad lectured his children on China's glorious past. One of his favorite stories was about Cheng Ho, the Chinese explorer. Cheng Ho made seven voyages from Suzhou to Java and to various points around the Indian Ocean during the Ming dynasty. His enormous fleets of huge junks carried ten thousand armed men and were laden with fine silks. Cheng Ho's final voyage was launched in 1431, decades ahead of Christopher Columbus, centuries before the *Mayflower*. Dad always ended his lesson in frustration, saying, "If only Cheng Ho had turned left across the Pacific instead of turning right toward India, America would be Asian, not European."

Cheng Ho's wrong turn was Dad's link between Chinese and American history. Though he mused about the land bridge across the Bering Strait during the Great Ice Age ten thousand years ago, my father had little else to say about Asians in America. In spite of his great interest in history, there was no body of knowledge for him to teach his Chinese American kids.

One day Dad brought home an old book from a flea market, *The Pictorial History of the United States*. Of the four hundred pictures, one showed Asians in America: terrified Chinese, fleeing persecution from murderous white mobs in Denver, Colorado. A few pages later was a photo marking the completion of the transcontinental railroad. All the workers were white, as though there had been no Chinese railroad workers.

In college I found some of the missing stories—not in textbooks, but from young scholars and activists who launched a movement to find our lost history, to give faces and names to Asian American pioneers, and to place them in history books with George Washington, Columbus, and the *Mayflower*. From them I learned that Asian American faces had been deliberately obscured. As their American stories came to light, I found that I didn't have to choose between invisibility and revulsion. Instead, I discovered dramatic moments in the nation's history with Asian Americans at center stage, a history of which every American could be proud.

.    .    .

Long before the thirteen colonies declared their independence from Britain, Asian people could be found in the Americas. The first Asian Americans appeared as early as the 1500s. From 1565 to 1815, during the lucrative Spanish galleon trade between Manila and Mexico, sailors in the Philippines were conscripted into service aboard Spanish ships. A number of these seamen jumped ship for freedom, establishing a settlement on the coast of Louisiana; today, their descendants live in New Orleans.

In the 1600s, a thriving Chinatown bustled in Mexico City. The Chinese American success led Spanish barbers to petition the Viceroy in 1635 to move the Chinese barbers to the city's outskirts. Even then Asians were seen as a threat in the New World.

At the Continental Congress of the new United States of America in 1785, our nation's founders discussed the plight of some Chinese sailors stranded in Baltimore by their U.S. cargo ship, the *Pallas*, which had set sail for China. Meanwhile, the Reverend William Bentley of Salem, Massachusetts, wrote in his diary in 1790 that he spied a "tall, well-proportioned, dark complexioned man from Madras," India, walking about the town.

The first known Asian American New Yorker was born in 1825, the son of a Chinese merchant seaman who married an Irishwoman. In 1850, a young Japanese sailor was rescued at sea by an American ship; he learned English and became a U.S. citizen, adopting the name Joseph Hecco. He went to work in the office of a U.S. senator, met three U.S. presidents— Pierce, Buchanan, and Lincoln—and served as an important adviser in the establishment of United States–Japan relations. In 1854, a Chinese man by the name of Yung Wing graduated from Yale College and established an educational mission from China to the United States.

It is hard for most Americans to imagine Asian people on the scene in George Washington's day. Even today, prominent Asian Americans are thought of as foreign, alien. In 1984, Congressman Norman Mineta, a second-generation Japanese American who served in the U.S. House of Representatives for ten terms, was a guest speaker at the opening of an auto plant in his California district surrounding San Jose, the first joint venture between General Motors and Toyota. During the ceremony, a senior vice president of General Motors and general manager of Chevrolet said to the congressman, "My, you speak English well. How long have you been in this country?"

The real story of Asians in America is inextricably bound to several of the driving forces of American history—the westward expansion to the

Pacific and beyond, the growing nation's unquenchable need for cheap labor, the patriotic fervor of a young country in the throes of defining itself, and the ways in which race and racism were used to advance those ends.

Our Asian American migration begins with the Anglo-American moral dilemma over slavery. In 1806, one year before Britain officially ended the slave trade, two hundred Chinese were brought to Trinidad, a small offering to assuage the insatiable demand for plantation labor in the New World. Using the same ships that brought slaves from Africa, the flesh merchants rerouted to Asia. They indentured "coolie" labor from China and India to perform the same work, under the same conditions, as the slaves; in the case of Cuba, which continued the practice of slavery until the end of the nineteenth century, the Asian coolies worked alongside African slaves.

Despite the similar treatment, it is important to note that the Asian workers were not slaves; according to Professor Evelyn Hu-DeHart of the University of Colorado at Boulder, the coolies themselves insisted on the distinction between their status and that of the slaves. The Asians worked knowing that they would be free men after they served their eight-year contracts and paid off their indebtedness for their passage, food, clothing, and other necessities—which often extended their servitude for years. With China and India in political and economic chaos resulting from Britain's imperial expansion, a vast pool of desperate Asian workers became available as commodities. This reliance on Asia for cheap labor was the start of a global trend that continues to the present.

Over several decades beginning in 1845, more than 500,000 Asian Indians were shipped to British Guiana (now Guyana), the West Indies, and various French colonies. Importation of Chinese began in earnest in 1847, first headed to Cuba, where more than 125,000 Chinese eventually supplemented the shrinking African slave labor force. Peru and other parts of South America also became major markets for human cargo from Asia. Most of the laborers were men, setting a pattern of Asian bachelor societies for the next hundred years.

## The Pioneers from Asia

"Strangers from a different shore" is how historian Ronald Takaki, of the University of California at Berkeley, characterized the perception of immigrants from Asia, in his book by the same title. When gold was first discovered at Sutter's Mill in 1848, fewer than a hundred Chinese, mostly merchants and traders, were living in California. Plans to import Chinese labor to the territory were already in the works when news of gold reached China. Men from the villages near Canton in Southern China took off with dreams of making it in "Gold Mountain," their name for America. In 1850, some 50 Chinese arrived; the next year, 2,716. By 1860, some 41,000 Chinese had come to the United States. These Chinese were not coolies but "semifree" men who were deeply in debt from high-interest loans for their passage to America, according to K. Scott Wong and Sucheng Chan in *Claiming America: Constructing Chinese American Identities during the Exclusion Era.* By comparison, nearly 2.5 million Europeans immigrated during that same ten-year period.

Initially, the Chinese were welcomed to San Francisco, and some even participated in California's statehood ceremonies in 1850. The reception quickly turned cold, however, as new laws and taxes singled out the Chinese. A foreign-miners tax targeted Chinese miners, not Europeans. The tax gave way to complete prohibition of Chinese from mining. Laws forbade Chinese to testify in court, even in their own defense. Special zoning ordinances were selectively enforced against Chinese. Hair-cutting ordinances forced Chinese to cut off the braids, or queues, that the emperor required as proof of loyalty—ironically, making it harder for workers to return to China. In San Francisco, special license fees were levied solely against Chinese laundries.

The discriminatory treatment of the Chinese was overtly racist: the California state legislature declared that "Negroes, Mongolians, and Indians shall not be admitted into public schools." When the vote became available to African American men after the Civil War, citizenship was specifically denied to Chinese, because, it was reasoned, Chinese were neither black nor white.

Then came the killings. White gold diggers seized Chinese miners' stakes by beating, burning, and shooting the Chinese. Mass kidnappings and murders of Chinese took place, leading the *Shasta Republican* to report in 1856, "Hundreds of Chinamen have been slaughtered in cold blood during the last five years by desperadoes that infest our state. The murder of Chinamen is almost of daily occurrence, yet in all this time we have heard of but two or three instances where the guilty parties have been brought to justice and punished according to law."

Expelled from the goldfields, the Chinese miners found work with a railroad company hungry for workers. By 1865, Thomas Jefferson's dream of a transcontinental route was finally within reach. The Central Pacific Railroad was contracted to build the difficult half from the Pacific, through the Rocky Mountains; within two years, 12,000 Chinese were hired—about 90 percent of the company's workforce.

The Chinese workers shoveled, picked, blasted, and drilled their way through boulders, rock, and dirt, often suspended from mountain peaks high in the Sierras, even in the harsh mountain winters. It is estimated that one in ten Chinese died building the railroad. In return, they were paid sixty cents for every dollar paid to white workers. Chinese workers went on strike to protest the brutal conditions, going back to work only when Charles Crocker, superintendent of construction for the Central Pacific, cut off their food supply. In the meantime, the railroad made plans to ship several thousand black workers from the East in case the strike continued.

When the transcontinental railroad was completed in 1869, Chinese workers were barred from the celebrations. The speeches congratulated European immigrant workers for their labor but never mentioned the Chinese. Instead, the Chinese men were summarily fired and forced to walk the long distance back to San Francisco—forbidden to ride on the railroad they built.

## The Driving-Out Time

In the late 1870s, the anti-Chinese "Yellow Peril" movement gripped the West. Cities erupted in riots against the Chinese—homes, laundries, and shops were burned to the ground. Murders and lynchings of Chinese were commonplace. Chinese women—the very small number who were admitted to the United States—were molested by angry gangs of whites. In rural areas, white farm workers set fire to the barns and fields where Chinese lived and worked. These egregious acts established a particular brand of American racism that would be directed against Asian Americans into the next century.

The Chinese called this the driving-out time. The illustration of terrified Chinese men I had seen as a child stemmed from this period. The Workingmen's Party in California, a white labor party with a large Irish following, adopted the slogan "The Chinese must go!" One of its ideas was to drop a balloon filled with dynamite on San Francisco's Chinatown. The "Chinese question" framed the labor stance for Democrats and Republicans: while Democrats exploited the race hysteria to win the support of labor, Republicans supported the business ideal of an unlimited supply of second-class, low-wage labor. Caught between the racism of both political parties, the Chinese were used to inflame and distract white workers, frustrated by rising unemployment and an economic depression.

From Los Angeles to Denver, from Seattle to Rock Springs, Wyoming, Chinese were driven out. In Tacoma, Washington, hundreds of Chinese were herded onto boats and set adrift at sea, presumably to their deaths. Mobs burned all the Chinese homes and businesses in Denver in 1880. Newspapers from *The New York Times* to the *San Francisco Chronicle* stirred fears that the Chinese, together with the newly freed black population, would become a threat to the Republic. Years earlier, orator Horace Greeley had captured the sense of the intelligentsia: "The Chinese are uncivilized, unclean, and filthy beyond all conception without any of the higher domestic or social relations; lustful and sensual in their dispositions; every female is a prostitute of the basest order."

The anti-Chinese fervor led Congress to pass the Chinese Exclusion Act in 1882, not only barring Chinese from immigrating but forbidding legal residents from becoming citizens, a prohibition that would inhibit Asian American political development for decades to come. The ugly legislation was also the first ever passed by Congress targeting a group based on race.

Against this tide of Yellow Peril fever, Chinese Americans organized early civil rights groups—the Native Sons of the Golden State, later becoming the Chinese American Citizens Alliance, in San Francisco, and the Chinese Equal Rights League in New York. The Chinese Six Companies, formed in 1854, fought the Chinese Exclusion Act of 1882 all the way to the U.S. Supreme Court, which ultimately ruled against them in 1889. Seventeen lawsuits by Chinese Americans went to the Supreme Court between 1881 and 1896, with a few setting important civil rights precedents. In 1896 *Yick Wo* v. *Hopkins* established that "race-neutral" laws could not be selectively enforced against a particular group, as the city of San Francisco did against Chinese laundries, in violation of the Fourteenth Amendment of the Constitution. In 1898 the principle of U.S. citizenship by birthright was affirmed after native-born American Wong Kim Ark was denied reentry into the United States because he was Chinese. Through Wong's appeals, the U.S. Supreme Court ruled that all persons born in the United States are citizens by birth. Many of these cases became precedents that broke down barriers for African Americans and others during the civil rights movements of the twentieth century.

Nevertheless, after the Chinese Exclusion Act the population of Chinese plummeted to 71,531 in 1910. After building the West and contributing to the national economy, the Chinese men were confined to work as domestics, or in laundries and restaurants. The few crowded Chinatowns offered Chinese Americans some protection from racial terrorism and violence, but the numerous race restrictions prevented most Chinese from starting families and putting down roots in America.

## An Elusive Dream

Though the gates to America closed for Chinese, other Asian nations still offered a source of labor for the backbreaking work that white workers were unwilling to do. American labor brokers introduced in consecutive stages Japanese, Indian, Korean, and Filipino workers. Ethnic hostilities were used to pit the Asians against one another. Each successive immigrant group came with the expectation that *they* would avoid the problems of their predecessors and succeed in becoming American.

In 1888, the first 75 Japanese workers were brought in for the California harvest. Within two decades, more than 150,000 Japanese men and women immigrated. Like China, Japan was in deep economic crisis. Widespread starvation prompted many to take their chances as indentured laborers in America. By the 1920s, the Japanese American population reached 220,596—almost double the Chinese population. But the Japanese government, unlike China's, took an active interest in its citizens' welfare, viewing the emigrants as its representatives to the world.

The Japanese government was confident its citizens could avoid the fate of the Chinese, whom they thought responsible for their own misfortunes in America. "It is indeed the ignominious conduct and behavior of indigent Chinese of inferior character . . . that brought upon [them] the contempt of the Westerners and resulted in the enactment of legislation to exclude them from the country," the Japanese consul to the United States reported in 1884. The government of Japan screened all early émigrés.

Many were literate and more educated than their Chinese or European counterparts. Women were also encouraged to emigrate because of their stabilizing family influence.

In 1900, there were about one thousand Japanese women in the United States, but that number increased until 39 percent of Japanese immigrants were female. A "picture bride" system developed, allowing matchmaking to take place through photo exchanges, an imperfect system that frequently involved outdated or even fake photos, often to the great disappointment of the bride. The U.S. government refused to recognize the legality of the Japanese picture bride marriages, and the public derided Japanese women as immoral, even though photo matchmaking was common and tolerated among European immigrants. By 1920, more than 60,000 Japanese women were living in the mainland United States and Hawaii and 29,672 children had been born. American citizens by birth, these children—the Nisei, or second-generation Japanese Americans—made up the first Asian American baby boom.

The growing Japanese population on the West Coast and in Hawaii became a new target for the strong racial hatred directed against the Chinese only a few years earlier. While the racial slur "Jap" became part of everyday speech, Japanese immigrants also encountered the phenomenon of racial "lumping" of Asians: anti-Chinese slurs were routinely directed against them as if there were no difference between the two peoples. Despite the Japanese government's efforts to see that its overseas citizens would be treated equally, new laws were written against the Japanese.

The Japanese were condemned as more dangerous than the Chinese because of their willingness and ability to adopt American customs. Whereas the Chinese were attacked for not assimilating, the Japanese were reviled because they readily integrated. By 1913, a number of states west of the Mississippi River already prohibited Chinese and Asian Indians from owning land. The situation for Japanese immigrants in California was ambiguous until 1920, when a more comprehensive Alien Land Law was passed, preventing anyone of Asian ancestry from owning land.

In 1922, a Japanese immigrant who had become Americanized in every way but citizenship brought a challenge against the citizenship ban to the Supreme Court in *Ozawa* v. *United States*. Takao Ozawa attended high school in California and studied at the University of California for three years. He belonged to an American church and had no dealings with

Japan or Japanese organizations. He married a Japanese woman who, like him, had been educated in the United States. Their family spoke English at home and the children attended American schools. But the U.S. District Court rejected his application for citizenship in 1916, ruling that Ozawa was "in every way eminently qualified under the statutes to become an American citizen" but for his race. The U.S. Supreme Court upheld the decision that Ozawa was not entitled to citizenship because he was not Caucasian.

The decision was a big setback to the Japanese, who were caught in a cruel vise—under constant attack both for being "foreign" and for being "too ready to adapt." In the Kingdom of Hawaii, a number of Japanese had become naturalized citizens, but when Hawaii was annexed by the United States in 1898, becoming a territory in 1900, the territorial government refused to recognize them as U.S. citizens. Newspaper publisher V. S. McClatchy testified before Congress: "Of all the races ineligible to citizenship, the Japanese are the least assimilable and the most dangerous to this country . . . They come here . . . for the purpose of colonizing and establishing permanently the proud Yamato race. They never cease to be Japanese."

For the Japanese, the final blow came when Congress passed the Immigration Act of 1924, which was worded in a veiled way to sound applicable to all immigrants. It barred anyone who was "forbidden to be a U.S. citizen" from immigrating at all. The real intent of the law was to halt Japanese immigration, which had reached a total of 275,000 over a thirty-year span. While white nativists complained of the "huge waves" of Asian immigrants, by comparison, 283,000 Italians arrived in a single year, 1913–14.

With the population of Japanese immigrants increasing, plantation owners in Hawaii and labor brokers in the mainland United States feared that the growing community might organize for more money and better working conditions. To keep the workforce fragmented, the labor brokers looked to India for workers.

In 1900, some 2,050 Asian Indians resided in the United States. Most of these earliest Indian immigrants were professionals, students, merchants, and visitors in the northeastern states. However, between 1906 and 1908, nearly 5,000 Asian Indian emigrants from the Punjab region arrived in Canada, which quickly established regulations that would prevent "hordes of hungry Hindus" from entering the country. In reality only a small fraction of the Indians were Hindu, most being Sikhs and about one third Muslim, but the misnomer stuck. Discouraged from entering Canada, many of the Indians headed south to Washington and Oregon. Others ventured to the farmlands of California, where they were contracted specifically to counter the labor power of the Japanese workers. Intra-Asian hostilities arose between the Japanese and Asian Indian laborers working next to each other in the California farmland.

Prevailing race theories included Asian Indians with the Caucasian race. European Americans acknowledged them as "full-blooded Aryans." This led many Asian Indians to believe that they were a cut above the other Asian migrants and could avoid the prejudice that the others faced. Citizenship was actually granted to some sixty-seven Indians, in seventeen states, between 1905 and 1923. The 1790 Naturalization Law allowed "free white persons" to become U.S. citizens, and Asian Indians were thought to be part of the "Mediterranean branch of the Caucasian family."

Nevertheless, their dark skin and willingness to work for low wages made Asian Indians a threat to white society. The Japanese and Korean Exclusion League, established in 1905, later changed its name to the Asiatic Exclusion League to include the Punjabis. Agitating against the "Indian menace" and the "tide of turbans," they succeeded in barring Asian Indians from entering the United States between 1908 and 1920. A magazine writer of that time warned: "This time the chimera is not the saturnine, almond-eyed mask . . . of the multitudinous Chinese, nor the close-cropped bullet-heads of the suave and smiling Japanese, but a face of finer features, rising, turbaned out of the Pacific." Whites forced seven hundred Asian Indians from their community in Bellingham, Washington, across the border into Canada in 1907. A few months later Asian Indians in Everett, Washington, were rounded up and expelled. Indian immigration was short-lived, ending with the Immigration Act of 1917.

In an effort to tear down citizenship barriers for Asian Indians, Bhagat Singh Thind took the issue to court. Thind had been granted citizenship in 1920 by an Oregon court, on the grounds that he was Caucasian, but the federal government disagreed and appealed in 1923. Arguing his case before the U.S. Supreme Court, Thind reasoned that Indians are Caucasians, not Asians, and therefore should be accorded full rights of citizenship, including land ownership and suffrage. But the Court determined in *United States* v. *Bhagat Singh Thind* that it was not enough to be "Caucasian." It ruled that it was also necessary to be "white." Since Indians were not white, they could not become citizens, nor could they own land or send for their wives from India.

The decision in the *Thind* case was applied retroactively, and the citizenship of the naturalized Indian Americans was revoked. One Indian American committed suicide, writing in a note that he tried to be "as American as possible," but "I am no longer an American citizen . . . I do not choose to live a life as an interned person." The small Asian Indian population declined after the *Thind* decision, but a few thousand stayed on. A majority of the Asian Indian men in California married Mexican women and established successful farming communities. Other Sikhs, believing that discrimination was stronger against Asian Indians, abandoned their turbans and tried to pass as Mexican or black.

Korea offered yet another pool of cheap labor for the United States, as political and economic instability resulting from Japanese aggression sent many Koreans into exile. From 1903 to 1907, about 7,000 Koreans came to the United States, mostly to work as contract plantation laborers to Hawaii. Over 1,200 women and children also made the journey. Unlike the other Asian contract laborers before them, the first Korean immigrants came from cities, and were working, for example, as police officers, miners, clerks, even monks. Some 40 percent were Christians, encouraged to come to the United States by American missionaries.

Because their numbers were small, the Koreans didn't develop communities or settlements, as the earlier Asian immigrants had. Instead, they deliberately sought to become integrated into American society, learning English as quickly as possible, worshipping as Christians, and expressing their gratitude to America. Many Koreans felt that both the Chinese and Japanese were to blame for the hate they received from whites. They thought they could avoid the same fate. According to the Korean newspaper *Kongnip Sinmun*, "The reason why many Americans love Koreans and help us, while they hate Japanese more than ever, is that we Koreans gave up old baseness, thought and behavior, and became more westernized." Nevertheless, Koreans in America were subject to the same anti-Asian laws barring citizenship, land ownership, and equal access to education and housing.

Korean migration to America ended within a few years. Japan, which had occupied parts of Korea since the late 1800s, cut off Korean immigration to Hawaii in 1907, fearing that Korean labor would hurt the Japanese in Hawaii. The government also wanted to halt the overseas Korean independence movement. But this became moot when the Immigration Act of 1924 ended all immigration from China, Japan, India, and Korea. Although the Asian immigrants failed to connect with one another, U.S. policy and the prevailing anti-Asian racism subjected them all to the same treatment.

The last significant migration of Asians to the United States in the early twentieth century came from the Philippines. Because the Philippines was a U.S. territory and its residents were U.S. nationals, Filipinos carried U.S. passports and could travel freely within the States—they were the only Asians eligible for immigration after 1924. Hundreds of Filipinos came to the United States as college students beginning in 1903, on scholarships set up by the United States after it annexed the Philippines, ceded by Spain after the Spanish-American War. After 1907, more than 70,000 Filipino laborers arrived in Hawaii as contract laborers. Between 1920 and 1929, some 51,875 Filipino workers arrived on the mainland—many via Hawaii—to work in the fields and in other low-wage jobs on the West Coast, doing the same work as other earlier, excluded Asian immigrants.

Filipino immigrants, too, thought they could circumvent the troubles of the other Asians. In 1933, Filipino Salvador Roldan sought the right to marry outside his race by challenging California's 1880 antimiscegenation law that prohibited marriage between whites and "Negroes, mulattoes, or Mongolians." Roldan argued that Filipinos are actually "Malay," not "Mongolian," and therefore not subject to the 1880 law. The California Court of Appeals agreed that Filipinos were not Mongolian and allowed him to marry his white fiancée. The California legislature immediately voted to add the "Malay race" to the forbidden list. Once again, an attempt by one Asian group to separate itself from the others had failed.

Anti-Filipino prejudice continued to grow, with vigilantes attacking, even burning, the camps where the Filipino laborers lived, the very land that Chinese had made arable before they were driven out nearly two generations earlier. "This Is a White Man's Country" was the message on a sign in Salinas, California. With Filipinos, white nativists focused on the menace that a bachelor society posed to white women. Testifying before the House Committee on Immigration and Naturalization in 1930, newspaper publisher V. S. McClatchy, a consistent voice against the "Yellow Peril," said, "You can realize, with the declared preference of the Filipino for white women and the willingness on the part of some white females to yield to that preference, the situation which arises . . . California in this matter is seeking to protect the nation, as well as itself, against the peaceful penetration of another colored race."

The white exclusionists strategized that there was only one way to end Filipino immigration: the United States would have to grant "independence" to the Philippines. Their racially inflamed arguments persuaded Congress to pass another law specifically targeting Asians, the Tydings-McDuffie Act of 1934, converting the Philippines to a commonwealth. Immediately, all Filipinos were reclassified as aliens and prohibited from applying for citizenship because they weren't white. Only fifty Filipinos from any nation of origin would be permitted to immigrate each year, except for plantation labor to Hawaii. As with the Japanese in Hawaii, Filipinos were debarred from leaving the Hawaiian Territory for the mainland. Congress even offered to pay for workers' fare to the Philippines if they agreed never to return; the *Los Angeles Times* urged Filipinos to "go back home." Fewer than 5 percent took the offer—in spite of the elusiveness of citizenship, the rest wanted to stay in America, as Americans.

## *Working on the Fringes of America*

Of the approximately 489,000 Asians living in the United States when immigration from Asia was shut off after 1934, perhaps 99 percent had come to work as laborers, or were the offspring of laborers. Although these immigrants were overwhelmingly working-class, like those from Europe, they found no openings for solidarity with other workers in the burgeoning labor movements of the day. Rather, their status as "aliens ineligible for citizenship" who were neither white nor black turned them into objects of hostility and revulsion who could be used as a racial wedge by unionists and capitalists alike.

While Denis Kearney of the Workingmen's Party made driving out the Chinese his rallying cry, Samuel Gompers, founder and president of the American Federation of Labor, also maintained a special antipathy toward

Asian workers. He refused to issue a charter to an early effort at multi-racial labor organizing by the Japanese Mexican Labor Association with the admonition "Your union will under no circumstance accept membership of any Chinese or Japanese." When Asian Indians became a farm labor presence, in 1908 Gompers added them to his prohibited-from-membership list.

California's business leaders acknowledged in the late 1800s that the state's industries could not have developed without Chinese labor to build the railroads, to drain the delta swamps of the Sacramento and San Joaquin rivers, to build the vineyards and work in its main manufacturing industries of shoes, woolens, cigars, and sewing. But they found another purpose for Chinese workers: the low wages paid to them could intimidate both white and black workers. Using Asian workers as a racialized wedge set a powerful model for a future role that Asian Americans could play.

Businesses in other parts of the country tried to duplicate California's labor machinations. Southern plantation owners imported Chinese to Mississippi, Arkansas, and Louisiana in the 1870s to "punish the Negro for having abandoned the control of his old master." Chinese were also brought to factories in Massachusetts, New Jersey, and Pennsylvania to keep the wage rates down. The presence of Asian workers in Hawaii and the West served another function: they gave white labor the possibility of upward mobility by subordinating the Chinese. As railroad builder Charles Crocker observed, "After we got Chinamen to work, we took the more intelligent of the white laborers and made foremen of them . . . they got a start by controlling Chinese labor on our railroad."

In Hawaii, Asian workers made a special contribution to American labor history. With the Native Hawaiian population decimated by illnesses introduced by its colonizers, plantation developers relied on imported Asian labor. Hawaii was the first stop for many Asian immigrants to America. Labor contractors scoured Asia, Europe, and the Caribbean for cheap labor, bringing in Portuguese, Puerto Rican, and African American workers, but the vast majority were Asian. By 1920, the contractors had imported more than 300,000 laborers from Asia, who comprised 62 percent of the islands' population.

American business interests were busy creating a sugar plantation system that would turn Hawaii into an economic colony of the United

States. To do so, they embarked on a labor strategy of racial and ethnic antagonism. In *Strangers from a Different Shore*, Ronald Takaki chronicled the labor strategy of the plantation owners: "Keep a variety of laborers, that is different nationalities, and thus prevent any concerted action in case of strikes, for there are few, if any, cases of 'Japs,' Chinese, and Portuguese entering into a strike as a unit," advised one plantation manager. The Asian workers were mere commodities on supply manifests: "Bonemeal, canvas, Japanese laborers, macaroni, a Chinaman," read one plantation receipt. Foreign labor was imported to "set an example" for the Native Hawaiian workers; Chinese were hired to "play off" against Japanese, while Portuguese were brought in to offset the Chinese. As whites, the Portuguese were paid more than the Asians and took on the role of *lunas*, or overseers.

When Japanese workers organized for higher wages and better working conditions, plantation owners turned to Korea, sure that Koreans would never join any Japanese strike efforts. After Japan closed off Korean immigration, Filipinos were imported into Honolulu in order to put the Japanese "in their place." Inter-Asian resentments inevitably led to fights and even riots in the labor camps. The strategy of divide and conquer was effective, especially with newer immigrants who were less willing to risk changing the status quo. Despite the deliberate attempts to provoke ethnic friction, unity was eventually achieved. In 1920, Filipino and Japanese plantation workers decided to join ranks against the plantation owners; 3,000 members of the Filipino Federation of Labor and 5,000 Japanese workers went on strike after their demands for higher wages were rejected by the owners. Representing 77 percent of the plantation workforce, they brought sugar production to a halt, leading to a $12 million production loss. The strikers were joined by Portuguese and Chinese workers in the first united, interethnic labor action in Hawaii. Their action ultimately resulted in a 50 percent wage increase and paved the way for a strong trade union movement tradition that continues in modern-day Hawaii.

In the Western states, Filipino workers were in the vanguard of farm worker organizing, forming the Filipino Labor Union. They contributed significantly to the American labor movement, building interethnic solidarity with Mexican and white workers. In 1936, the Filipino Labor Union led a strike alongside Mexican workers. Their joint union received a charter from the American Federation of Labor—finally overcoming the barriers set by union founder Samuel Gompers against Asian workers in the unions. It is a little-known footnote to American history that Filipino labor activists initiated the United Farm Workers' grape pickers' strike that Cesar Chavez would build into a movement.

The labor and creativity of Asian Americans were responsible to a significant degree for developing the economies of California, Hawaii, Washington, Oregon, Alaska, and elsewhere in the growing nation. Many Asian Americans left the West Coast to find opportunities in less hostile locations in the Eastern and Midwestern states. Chinatowns and Japantowns sprang up as centers of commerce and social life, providing basic services to their separate and unequal communities. Even faced with the multitude of inhospitable barriers, Asian Americans found ways to build lives in America. They formed their own political and cultural organizations, and sometimes they were able to beat city hall—as they did in 1906 in Butte, Montana, where Chinese successfully fought a boycott aimed at driving them out of town.

In addition to their labor, the Asian immigrants made significant contributions to their adopted homeland. In 1875, Ah Bing developed the Bing cherry in Oregon, and in 1886, Lue Gim Gong produced the frost-resistant Lue orange, which became the foundation of Florida's citrus industry. In Hawaii, Japanese workers created irrigation systems throughout the islands. In 1921, two Koreans, Harry Kim and Charles Kim (not related), invented the nectarine, the "perfect, fuzzless peach," in Reedley, California, and opened a successful orchard business, Kim Brothers. In California's Central Valley, Asian Indians found that the region resembled the Punjab and used their expertise with irrigation methods and specialized crops to make the land productive. In Louisiana, the descendants of the Filipino sailors who escaped the Spanish galleons introduced the process of sun-drying shrimp to the region.

As the Asian immigrants had children, they were able to find ways around laws that forbade them to own or lease land. Japanese in particular were able to establish families because women had immigrated in significant numbers, but other Asians were also able to wed Asian women who made it into the country or women of other races. Their American-born children were American citizens by birth and therefore not subject to the "alien land" ownership prohibitions. Many immigrant Japanese parents bought farmland in their children's names. Farmers without children paid other families with Nisei—second-generation—children to use their names as fictitious landowners. In this way, Asian immigrants were able to create thousands of acres of productive farms across the West.

Although the American-born generations were entitled to the privileges of American citizenship, they continued to be treated as foreigners. Still subject to segregated housing and unequal treatment, young men and women who made it through high school and college could find work only as field hands and domestic workers, in the same limited occupations as their immigrant parents. Though the various Asian American ethnic groups experienced similar prejudices and were lumped together by other Americans as equally undesirable, each group suffered separately and in its own enclave.

## Infamy

World War II changed everything. Suddenly, the events in Asia and the political realignment of the United States and Asian nations dictated a new social order among the separate enclaves of the various Asian American groups.

Years before the bombing of Pearl Harbor drew the United States into war with Japan, the different Asian communities in America were engaged in war relief efforts. Many Korean Americans took part in a resistance movement against the harsh Japanese military rule of Korea, which had fallen under increasing Japanese control since the late 1800s until it was formally annexed in 1910. Japanese aggression against China that began in 1931 sparked demonstrations by Chinese Americans, who raised $56 million for China war relief between 1937 and 1945.

On December 7, 1941, Japan bombed Pearl Harbor, and seven hours later, Japanese planes turned the Philippines into a war zone. Suddenly China and the Philippines were important allies of the United States against Japan. Almost overnight, the much maligned Chinese and Filipino "rat-eaters," "monkeys," and "headhunters" were praised as though they were much beloved—especially compared to Japanese.

Two weeks after Pearl Harbor, *Time* magazine gave readers tips on how to distinguish between a Chinese "friend" and Japanese "enemy," complete with photos:

HOW TO TELL YOUR FRIENDS FROM THE JAPS

*Virtually all Japanese are short. Japanese are likely to be stockier and broader-hipped than short Chinese. Japanese are seldom fat; they often dry up and grow lean as they age. Although both have the typical epicanthic fold of the upper eyelid, Japanese eyes are usually set closer together. The Chinese expression is likely to be more placid, kindly, open; the Japanese more positive, dogmatic, arrogant. Japanese are hesitant, nervous in conversation, laugh loudly at the wrong time.*

*Time* magazine's Henry Luce was part of a powerful pro-China lobby—a prominent group that included public figures and other publishers. Chinese were resurrected from the depths of demonhood and elevated to sainthood—a switch so swift that Chinese Americans wondered how long it would last.

Knowing that Asians "all look alike" to most other Americans, the Chinese posted signs saying "This is a Chinese shop" and wore buttons that said "I Am Chinese" and even "I Hate Japs Worse Than You Do." Filipinos and Koreans did the same. Koreans, to their great horror and despite their own hostility toward Japan for occupying their country, were classified by the U.S. government as Japanese subjects and therefore "enemy aliens." In Hawaii, Koreans were required to wear badges designating them as Japanese; they retaliated by wearing other badges that read "I'm No Jap."

Many Asian Americans jumped at the chance to enlist as American GIs to demonstrate their patriotism. Their service offered another benefit: foreign-born GIs could become naturalized citizens. The demonization of Japanese Americans allowed other Asian Americans to become Americans. The nation's leaders worried about America's image in Asia, where the exclusionary laws were an obvious insult to the Asian allies—a point frequently made by Japan in its anti-American propaganda. India was also strategically important in the fight against Japan, and the same arguments were made for the Philippines. In 1943, the laws that excluded Chinese from immigration were finally repealed; Chinese could become naturalized. In 1946, the laws that barred Filipinos and Indians from citizenship were also overturned. For Japanese and Koreans, the ban would remain until 1952. Asian immigration was placed on a quota system, as European immigrants were, except that the Chinese quota was 102 Chinese from anywhere in the world and for Filipinos it was 50 per year. In contrast, 6,000 Polish and 65,000 British immigrants were allowed per year.

If the status of Chinese, Filipinos, and Indians improved somewhat as the United States went to war with Japan, the lives of Japanese Americans were destroyed. Japanese in America—including the thousands of Nisei youngsters who were native-born American citizens—became the personification of the enemy. On the day war was declared, hundreds of Japanese living on the West Coast were arrested by the FBI, including leaders of community groups, language teachers, Shinto and Buddhist priests and nuns, and journalists.

Using "confidential" Census Bureau survey reports, the FBI was able to compile addresses and information on all Japanese Americans along the Pacific coast. Those who worked for local, state, or federal government offices were summarily fired. Bank accounts were frozen. Japanese Americans already serving in the military were reclassified to menial duties; in Hawaii, Japanese American soldiers were disarmed and put to work digging ditches under armed guard. When politicians advocated that "all Japanese, whether citizens or not, be placed in inland concentration camps," some West Coast nativists admitted their eagerness to seize Japanese American–owned farmland for white farmers.

Even before Pearl Harbor, a secret report analyzing Japanese American loyalty was submitted to President Franklin D. Roosevelt. The report concluded that Japanese Americans posed no security threat; FBI director J. Edgar Hoover also stated in a separate report that a mass evacuation of Japanese was unnecessary. Lieutenant General Delos Emmons, who was in charge of Hawaii, was certain that the Japanese on the islands had nothing to do with the attack. But Lieutenant General John DeWitt, head of the Western Defense Command, concluded, "The Japanese race is an enemy race and while many second and third generation Japanese born on United States soil, possessed of United States citizenship, have become 'Americanized,' the racial strains are undiluted . . . Along the vital Pacific Coast over 112,000 potential enemies of Japanese extraction are at large today. The very fact that no sabotage has taken place to date is a disturbing and confirming indication that such action will be taken."

DeWitt's arguments were readily espoused by the media. Many newspapers throughout the West Coast, including the powerful Hearst chain, adopted the same tenor as this *Los Angeles Times* editorial: "A viper is nonetheless a viper wherever the egg is hatched—so a Japanese American, born of Japanese parents—grows up to be a Japanese, not an American." Even distinguished CBS news commentator Edward R. Murrow said, on January 27, 1942, "I think it's probable that, if Seattle ever does get bombed, you will be able to look up and see some University of Washington sweaters on the boys doing the bombing."

On February 19, 1942, President Roosevelt issued Executive Order 9066, which authorized the evacuation and internment of Japanese Americans. Soon after, all Americans of Japanese descent were prohibited from living, working, or traveling on the West Coast. Families were given no more than a week to somehow dispose of all their household goods and property before moving to points unknown with only what they could carry in clothing, bedding and linen, kitchen and toilet articles, and "personal effects."

With numbered tags tied around their necks, the Japanese Americans were packed onto buses and trains with blinds drawn down. They were sent first to racetracks and fairgrounds, which became makeshift assembly centers; they were forced to live in filthy animal stalls. There they awaited a more permanent incarceration at one of ten internment camps in the barren hinterlands of California, Idaho, Wyoming, Utah, Arizona, Colorado, and Arkansas. About half of the incarcerated were children. At the internment camps, the families were told they needed barbed wire and armed guard towers for their own protection—but the guns pointed inward. Families lived in prison-style blocks with communal latrines and showers.

Individual Japanese took up lawsuits and acts of civil disobedience to challenge the evacuation and various orders imposed on them because of their ancestry. At the Manzanar camp in California, protests and strikes led to the killing of two internees and the imposition of martial law; in Topaz, Utah, an elderly Japanese internee was shot and killed by guards. But most Japanese cooperated with the military to show that they were loyal Americans.

When the U.S. government required that the imprisoned Japanese Americans sign loyalty statements forswearing allegiance to the Emperor of Japan, bitter divisions broke out over how to answer. The second-generation Nisei—who were American citizens by birthright—had no such allegiance to disavow. If their first-generation parents renounced their Japanese citizenship, they would become stateless persons, since U.S. citizenship was prohibited. About 4,600 Japanese Americans resisted by refusing to give the expected yes to the loyalty tests; many were sent to federal penitentiaries, while other "troublemakers" were forced to move again to the harshest camp, Tule Lake, in the desolate mountains of Northern California. But the majority of internees answered yes to the loyalty tests, while thousands of eligible Nisei men responded to the recruitment drive for an all–Japanese American combat team. The loyalty issues drove a deep wedge into the Japanese American community that continues to this day, pitting internees against each other and tainting groups such as the Japanese American Citizens League, which many viewed as collaborating with the U.S. government.

All together, some 23,000 Japanese Americans served in the U.S. Army during World War II, the majority in the segregated 442nd Nisei Regimental Combat Team, the most highly decorated unit in U.S. military history for its size and length of service. In a 1944 battle to break the German ring in France, Japanese American soldiers in the 442nd incurred 800 casualties, with 200 deaths, in order to save 200 Texans of the 141st Regiment. Young Nisei men wrote home about their loyalty: "Sure we're called Japs—the more to fight to show them we're Americans . . . Prove to them and they'll change their minds! That's why I volunteered! Yes-sir! To fight for the rights of my parents, myself, and kid-brothers and sister."

Ironically, near the end of the war in Europe, the Japanese American GIs of the 442nd broke through the German defensive "Gothic Line" in northern Italy, and were among the first to liberate the Nazi concentration camp in Dachau, Germany. However, the U.S. military commanders decided it would be bad public relations if Jewish prisoners were freed by Japanese American soldiers whose own families were imprisoned in American concentration camps. As with the transcontinental railroad photographs seventy-five years earlier, the Japanese American soldiers who liberated Dachau were MIH—Missing in History.

When World War II ended, about 45,000 Japanese Americans were still interned. Many were unsure where to go, their homes and livelihoods lost and their communities poisoned by neighbors who had turned against them. Some followed children or relatives to the Midwest or the East Coast, while others received only train fare to go back to their old homes on the West Coast, which they often found dilapidated, vandalized, or destroyed, and farms wasted. The old racial hatreds were still alive and active, as American Legion outposts, anti-Japanese union leaders, and politicians agitated against them. When future U.S. Senator Daniel Inouye of Hawaii returned from the war as a hero in uniform with only one arm, a barber refused him service, saying, "We don't serve Japs."

Nevertheless, the thousands of veterans of Chinese and Filipino as well as Japanese descent returned home as bona fide American heroes. They made use of the GI Bill to attend college, and some were able to buy homes outside their ethnic ghettoes. They also returned from the war as citizens, which gave them the right to find a wife in Asia if they chose and to bring her to the United States—a right that had been denied to previous generations of Asian American men. The wives were not subject to the immigration quota restrictions, and for the first time in Asian immigration to the United States, more women arrived than men. The gender imbalance of the bachelor societies began to shift. In addition, several thousand war brides of non-Asian GIs were permitted to immigrate, a phenomenon that would continue in the subsequent wars the United States would fight in Asia.

In the years following the war, the newly created families brought a spirit of change—the notion that Asians could be part of America if they proved their loyalty as worthy Americans. This reinforced the flip side as well, that to stand apart from the American mainstream could be disastrous. The old Japanese adage "The nail that sticks out gets hammered down" was never felt to be more true.

## Menace and Democracy

It was not long before this sensibility would be tested. This time, the Communist revolution in China turned the newly beloved ally extolled in *Time* magazine only a few years earlier into a "Red Menace." In 1950, the Korean War, fought by the United States to "contain" Communism, raised the specter of two other Asian enemies—China and North Korea. The Chinese American population, under particular scrutiny from the FBI, became fearful that they, too, could be rounded up and incarcerated. Sharp divisions formed between Chinese Americans over the question of Communist rule in China—with a clear awareness of the trouble it might bring them in America. The more conservative community organizations mounted their own anti-Communist campaigns to prove, preemptively, that Chinese were loyal Americans.

Their fears were not unfounded. Congress passed a bill in 1950 authorizing another internment, the McCarran Internal Security Act, to lock up anyone suspected on "reasonable ground" that they would "probably" engage in espionage. The immigration service posted signs in Chinese in Chinatowns publicizing a "Confession Program," which encouraged people to inform on friends and relatives in exchange for legal immigration status; thousands participated, including more than 10,000 in San Francisco alone.

FBI director J. Edgar Hoover was convinced that Chinese Americans posed a domestic Communist threat. In 1969 he warned, "The United States is Communist China's No. 1 enemy . . . Red China has been flooding the country with propaganda and there are over 300,000 Chinese in the United States, some of whom could be susceptible to recruitment either through ethnic ties or hostage situations because of relatives in Communist China."

With hostilities directed toward the Chinese, citizenship exclusions for Japanese and Koreans were finally lifted in 1952, allowing many first-generation Japanese immigrants, now elderly, to become citizens. The Japanese American Citizens League actively sought to eliminate the laws that had impugned the loyalty of Japanese Americans, and tried to restore some of the property that they had lost. In 1956, Japanese Americans successfully led a ballot initiative in California to repeal all alien land laws that had for nearly a century prevented any Asians from settling down in America.

As the movement for racial equality swept the nation following the 1954 Supreme Court decision in *Brown* v. *Board of Education,* Asian Americans were inspired to civic consciousness and involvement, after having been so long forbidden to exercise the privileges of citizenship in a democracy. A contingent of Asian Americans from Hawaii joined the Reverend Martin Luther King, Jr., in Selma, Alabama, bringing him the lei he wore during the march. The first Asian American entered Congress when Dalip Singh Saund, an Indian immigrant, won election in 1956 in the mostly white district of California's Imperial Valley, ultimately serving three terms in the U.S. House of Representatives. He was soon joined by representatives from Hawaii, which was granted statehood in 1959 after years of opposition in the U.S. Senate. One of the primary concerns raised by Strom Thurmond and other senators from the South was the fact that

Hawaii's population was mostly "nonwhite," whose Asian ancestry posed an "impassable difference" with the European ancestry of whites.

Statehood brought a Chinese American senator, Hiram Fong, a Republican, under the Capitol dome. In 1963 he was joined by Daniel Inouye, a Democrat and decorated hero of the 442nd Japanese American Regimental Combat Team. For a time Fong and Inouye were the only people of color in the Senate. In 1964, Patsy Mink became the first woman of color to be elected to the House of Representatives. The presence of Asian Americans in Congress was a tremendous leap from the days of exclusion from American public life.

## A Myth and a Movement

In the 1960s, a new stereotype emerged on the American scene. As urban ghettoes from Newark, New Jersey, to Watts in Los Angeles erupted into riots and civil unrest, Asian Americans suddenly became the object of "flattering" media stories. After more than a century of invisibility alternating with virulent headlines and radio broadcasts that advocated eliminating or imprisoning America's Asians, a rash of stories began to extol our virtues.

"Success Story: Japanese American Style" was the title of an article that appeared in *The New York Times Magazine* on January 9, 1966. A few months later, *U.S. News & World Report* produced a similar piece entitled "Success Story of One Minority Group in the United States," praising Chinese Americans while making transparent comparisons to African Americans: "At a time when Americans are awash in worry over the plight of racial minorities, one such minority, the nation's 300,000 Chinese Americans, is winning wealth and respect by dint of its own hard work . . . Still being taught in Chinatown is the old idea that people should depend on their own efforts—not a welfare check—in order to reach America's 'Promised Land.' "

The radical attitude shift was a too familiar experience for Asian Americans who had seen many iterations of the "friend today, foe tomorrow" treatment. Nor was the link to urban uprisings an accident. Where Asians had previously been the economic wedge to distract labor unrest, in the 1960s they were refashioned as a political and social hammer against other disadvantaged groups. The "model minority" was born.

The new stereotype proved tenacious, surfacing like clockwork whenever the Westinghouse Science Talent Search winners or other scholastic prizes were announced, with tales of stunning accomplishment by Asian immigrant youngsters who had just learned to speak English. The "model minority" myth presented its own quandary: should Asian Americans accept, if not embrace, this "good" stereotype as an improvement over the "inscrutable alien enemy" image of the previous hundred years?

In the 1960s, a new generation of Asian Americans was preparing to reject all stereotypes, preferring instead to find its own self-definition. One of the unacknowledged consequences of the civil rights movement and the war in Vietnam was their impact on the consciousness of the postwar generation of Asian Americans—primarily the second- and third-generation Japanese, Chinese, and Filipino Americans. The call by African Americans for equality resonated among Asian American youth, appealing to their sense of justice as well as their own experiences as a racial minority.

The young Asian Americans, inspired by the movement for Black Power, declared "Yellow Power" and "Yellow is beautiful." They believed that the various Asian immigrant groups had common interests and experiences in America that transcended cultural differences and historical animosities from centuries of war and conflict in Asia. This was a radical departure from the views of the immigrant generations that identified more closely with "over there." It was a declaration that, for Asian Americans, our identities and futures held much in common with other Asians in the United States. The burgeoning Asian American student movement found a target in the Vietnam War. Asian Americans were outraged at the government's willingness to dehumanize and reduce Vietnamese people to mere body counts on the evening news.

Nineteen sixty-eight marked the coming out of this new movement, as Asian American students, along with other students of color, conducted militant student strikes at San Francisco State College (now University) and the University of California at Berkeley. In the course of the organizing, the words "Asian American" made their debut. At Berkeley, the pan-Asian cluster of students needed a name; they didn't want to use the word "Oriental," which was seen to represent the European colonialist view of Asia. Yuji Ichioka and Emma Gee, then graduate students, are credited with coining the moniker.

Among the demands the student strikers in San Francisco and Berkeley fought for—and won—were educational programs that taught their history in America. Out of these student movements, the first Asian American studies programs in the country were established as part of new ethnic studies departments at San Francisco State and Berkeley and, soon after, the Asian American Studies Center at UCLA. Other universities on the West Coast followed as Asian American scholars began to reclaim the rich history of Asians in America.

The Asian American esprit spread rapidly along the West Coast. Students at college campuses in the San Francisco Bay Area and Los Angeles founded groups under the same name, Asian American Political Alliance, to signal their unity. The following year, students on the East Coast established a network of Asian American Student Associations. The movement wasn't limited to students. In New York, two middle-aged Japanese American Nisei women, Kazu Iijima and Minn Matsuda, organized Asian Americans for Action in 1969 to protest U.S. imperialism in Vietnam.

As more young Asian Americans studied law and became public-interest lawyers, they began to fight discriminatory practices against Asian Americans in the courts. In 1972, the first class action suit brought for Asian Americans by Asian American attorneys was won by a San Francisco attorney named Dale Minami, against the Blue Shield insurance company for discriminatory employment practices. Minami and other Asian American lawyers founded the Asian Law Caucus, and went on to file other civil rights suits to stop the San Francisco police from making dragnet arrests of Chinatown youths; to end discriminatory hiring practices by the San Francisco Fire Department, which opened employment to minorities and women for the first time; and to restore jobs to Filipino American security guards who were fired because they spoke English with an accent.

The young activists created organizations that advanced a pan-Asian vision and have become community institutions: from the Asian Law Caucus in San Francisco to the Asian American Legal Defense and Education Fund and Asian Americans for Equality in New York, to the Asian American Resource Center in Boston and Leadership Education for Asian Pacifics in Los Angeles. Other ethnic-based organizations, such as Chinese for Affirmative Action, the Organization of Chinese Americans, and the Japanese American Citizens League, took on a more pan-Asian scope. Professional and business organizations followed suit, with the formation of national groups such as the National Asian Pacific American Bar Association and the Asian American Journalists Association. Even the federal government recognized the necessity for a statistical and programmatic category for Asian Americans.

Having their own pan-Asian organizations gave Asian American activists a base from which to launch campaigns against racism and discrimination. As new kids on the block, they coexisted uneasily—and at times conflicted—with the more established and conservative community groups. Old-time Chinatown organizations active since the exclusion years were staunchly anti-Communist and allied with the government of Taiwan; they opposed the younger groups that seemed, and often were, so radical and leftist. Among Filipino Americans, the older organizations supported the regime of Ferdinand Marcos, while many youths were seeking its overthrow.

Most of the efforts by the young Asian Americans were directed at grass-roots community issues: organizing sweatshop workers in Chinatowns, for example; or at bringing other issues into the Asian American community, such as opposition to apartheid in South Africa. Pan-Asian issues that linked the various Asian communities periodically caught fire. In San Francisco, efforts to evict fifty-five elderly Filipino American retired migrant workers from their home, the International Hotel, began in the late 1960s, as developers of the new financial district continued to dismantle the last pieces of what used to be a ten-block Manilatown. Asian American community activists fought the evictions with a broad multiracial coalition, mobilizing several thousands of protesters for tenants' rights and community control—a nine-year battle that finally ended in 1977 when police on horseback and in riot gear broke through the demonstrators' barricades.

A national Asian American campaign to win a new trial for death row inmate Chol Soo Lee, a Korean American immigrant, began in 1977 when Pulitzer Prize–nominated journalist K. W. Lee (not related) began to raise questions about the conviction. For the first time, a broad coalition was forged between Korean Americans and the multiethnic Asian American communities. They gathered more than 10,000 signatures on petitions and raised $175,000 in donations, resulting in a new trial and the release of Lee in 1983.

One of the most stunning civil rights victories was won in the early 1980s when the wartime convictions of three Japanese Americans were overturned. Gordon Hirabayashi, Fred Korematsu, and Minoru Yasui had resisted curfew orders for Japanese Americans and internment notices during World War II—and were sent to prison. Forty years later, re-searchers Aiko and Jack Herzig and Peter Irons discovered that federal officials had altered and destroyed evidence upholding the loyalty of Japanese Americans. With this new information, pro bono legal teams in three cities—San Francisco; Portland, Oregon; and Seattle—succeeded in getting the cases of the three men reopened on the grounds that funda-mental injustices had occurred. The lead attorneys—Lori Bannai, Rod Kawakami, Dale Minami, and Peggy Nagae—were all third-generation Sansei whose work vindicated their Nisei parents and Issei grandparents. Together with the findings of a congressional commission in 1983 that the internment was not justified but driven by "race prejudice, war hysteria, and a failure of political leadership," these various efforts paved the way for a national apology and federal legislation providing redress to surviving internees. Members of Congress Norman Mineta and Robert Matsui, both of California, led the legislative movement that culminated in the Civil Liberties Act of 1988, after a national campaign won the support of whites, African Americans, Christians and Jews, women, gays and lesbians, and many others. The young Asian American movement was providing a legacy for all Americans.

## The New Immigration Wave

Another profound transformation would drastically alter the demo-graphic underpinnings of Asians in America. In Congress, the tide of equal rights legislation included sweeping changes to immigration law. The Immigration Act of 1965 eliminated the quota system of preferences for whites, inexorably altering the complexion of America. A new generation of Asian immigrants, as well as Hispanics and Africans, began to arrive in unprecedented numbers. These Asians arrived from areas unfamiliar to most Americans—the Indian subcontinent, interior regions of China, Korea, the Philippines, Taiwan, and elsewhere.

Similarly, the U.S. involvement in Vietnam did more than ignite an antiwar consciousness among Asian Americans who identified with the plight of the Southeast Asians. The U.S. defeat in Vietnam triggered a mas-sive migration of war refugees, beginning with the Vietnamese and

Hmong who had been America's allies. In the frenzied evacuation after the fall of Saigon, 135,000 government officials, military personnel, and U.S. government employees were moved to the safety of the U.S. Seventh Fleet. This first wave of refugees was relocated to military bases in California, Arkansas, Pennsylvania, and Florida, then later resettled in communities throughout the United States.

As political persecution and economic conditions worsened in Vietnam, hundreds of thousands of people fled by boat across the perilous South China Sea. The "boat people" who didn't perish reached refugee camps in Thailand, Malaysia, Indonesia, and the Philippines. The flow of refugees from Cambodia surged after Vietnam attacked a weakened Khmer Rouge in 1978, allowing additional hundreds of thousands to escape the "killing fields." In Laos, numerous rural minority groups fled repression, particularly the Hmong, Mien, Khmu, and Thai Dam, as well as Lao, who had assisted the U.S. military during the "secret war" it waged outside Vietnam.

To address the refugee crisis, Congress passed the Indochina Migration and Refugee Assistance Act of 1975 and later the Refugee Act of 1980. For the first time, U.S. policy defined who could be admitted to the United States as a refugee and created a framework of assistance programs. In addition, about 100,000 Amerasian children—the offspring of American GIs—and their Southeast Asian mothers were also admitted under the Amerasian Homecoming Act of 1987. All told, more than one million Southeast Asians came to America after 1975—nearly doubling the existing Asian American population.

It is impossible to overstate the impact that the combined influx of the new immigrants and refugees had on Asian Americans and the nation as a whole. Initially, the changes to the American population were subtle. Many of the new Asian Americans were absorbed into the vast American suburbia, particularly those with the professional training favored by the new immigration laws, while the resettlement policies governing the refugees emphasized dispersal throughout the United States. The numbers of Asian Americans grew from 877,934 in 1960 to 1.4 million in 1970, 3.5 million in 1980, and 7.3 million in 1990, making Asian Americans the fastest-growing minority in the nation.

But flashpoints were inevitable when war-ravaged refugees unfamiliar with American culture, language, or people were placed in homogeneous rural and inner-city areas, where Asian Americans of any stripe were rare sightings. A report by the Massachusetts Attorney General's Civil Rights Division in 1983 noted numerous racially motivated assaults against Southeast Asian refugees: "Often, [they] cannot even walk along the public streets without being physically attacked and threatened because of the their race or national origin." In Davis, California, Thong Hy Huynh, a seventeen-year-old Vietnamese student, was stabbed to death in 1983 by a white student in a high school with a history of racial harassment of Southeast Asian students. Escaping the mainly African American section of West Philadelphia, a rickety car caravan of the entire Hmong community made a mass exodus out of the City of Brotherly Love in 1984 after suffering years of physical and verbal assaults. They hoped to find safe haven with other Hmong in Minnesota.

The existing Asian American community was unprepared to meet the multiple needs of the Southeast Asian refugee population, which was generally placed in areas far from Chinatowns, Little Tokyos, or other Asian communities. Violent clashes involving the Ku Klux Klan occurred along the Texas Gulf coast, where many Vietnamese were resettled in the 1970s. But occasionally the growing pan–Asian American movement intervened. When the Coast Guard began selective enforcement of a two-hundred-year-old law against Vietnamese fishermen off the coast of Northern California, Asian American attorneys of Chinese and Japanese descent in San Francisco took up their cause, and ultimately Congress passed legislation allowing the Vietnamese to operate fishing boats.

The convergence of these developments—an incipient Asian American movement, the creation of an Asian American infrastructure, and the burgeoning and increasingly diverse Asian American population—set the stage for an explosion of new organizations to meet the needs of the individual Asian ethnicities. On the other hand, the noticeable increase in our numbers would soon fuel a backlash that affected all Asian Americans. A broader Asian American consciousness and organization had yet to emerge in response to the new challenges. As Asian American scholars and historians reclaimed the past, Asian Americans were on the brink of another transformation.

# II

# THE AWAKENING

# · 3 ·

# Detroit Blues: "Because of You Motherfuckers"

I arrived in Detroit in 1976 with little more than my beat-up Chevy Vega, a suitcase, a few boxes, and about a hundred dollars. My first order of business was to find a job, preferably at an auto factory. I was on a mission, a grand adventure, to learn what it meant to be an American in America's heartland. I was finally doing what we had talked about endlessly in college—going to the grass roots, the workplaces and neighborhoods where we could learn from the people who were the real makers of history. This was not the road my ancestors had planned for me.

Like many Asian American immigrant parents, mine had instilled in me the virtues of education and scholarship. But our family's tiny baby novelty business offered little exposure to possible careers. My parents had few ideas of where my studies might take me. I was so unsure of what to do in my life beyond college

*Historic rally by Asian Americans in Detroit's Kennedy Square on May 9, 1983*

*(Victor J. Yang)*

that I did what any good Asian American child would do: I applied to medical school. Though I majored in public and international affairs, and minored in East Asian Studies and student activism, I also took a few pre-med courses—just to be safe. I even got accepted, and within days of starting on my M.D. I began to realize I had made a terrible mistake. But my filial obligation to my parents—and my entire line of ancestors—was a core part of my Chinese heritage, so I stayed on.

After struggling for two years, I finally mustered the courage to ruin forever my parents' dream—and that of nearly every Asian immigrant parent—to have an offspring who is a doctor, who will care for them in their old age. I quit medical school, spurning my path to respectability, wealth, and filial nirvana. But I was clueless about what to pursue instead. I still wanted to be part of the big social changes I discovered during the student protest years. My equally idealistic friends encouraged me to move to Detroit, which they viewed as the real America. My parents saw this as further evidence that I had lost my mind.

Almost immediately, I landed a job as a large-press operator at a Chrysler stamping plant, making car hoods, fenders, and other parts. I joined the United Auto Workers union. In a factory of several thousand workers, I was one of perhaps three Asian faces; I definitely stood out. I was a rarity on the streets of Detroit as well, with its 60 percent African American population and the rest mostly working-class whites, many from the South. At the time, Detroit had only 7,614 Asian Americans in a population of 1.2 million—not even one percent of the city.

I didn't go to Detroit to find a large Asian American population, but I had hoped to find some palatable Chinese food. I was unhappy with the restaurants in the diminutive and decaying Chinatown, whose residents seemed too old and fragile to move elsewhere. Desperate, I asked my co-workers at the stamping plant where to go.

"Stanley's is the happening place for Chinese food," the African American autoworkers unanimously told me. I wouldn't have been so trusting had I recalled that any dish more exotic than sweet and sour pork unnerved many of my black friends. At Stanley's, I wasn't surprised to find that the cocktails wore pink umbrellas. But I was stunned by the gigantic, flaky dinner rolls that accompanied my order. Rice was optional, and everything was smothered in heavy brown gravy. I didn't fault Stanley's—like Chinese everywhere in the diaspora, they had to survive and adapt to the environment. But if culinary influence was an indication of political status in Detroit, Asian Americans weren't even on the map.

Two years later, I was no longer a press operator. As easily as I found my job at the auto plant, I lost it, along with some 300,000 other autoworkers in the devastating collapse of the auto industry. I was learning more about "real Americans" than I ever imagined; my biggest lesson was that we were not so different. There was the occasional racial confrontation—like the drunken worker who pointed her finger in my face and said, "I don't care if you're from Jap-pan, the Philipp-eenes or Ha-wah-yeh, you're on my turf," but she was the rare exception. Standing together on the assembly line and the unemployment line, we shared our lives and recognized our common humanity.

In the midst of that social upheaval, I discovered journalism. I began writing for the *Detroit Metro Times* and other "alternative" news publications. I wrote about the auto industry and the labor movement for *Monthly Detroit* magazine, then joined the staff of a new city magazine, *Metropolitan Detroit*. I spent my days reporting on the life and trends that made Detroit dynamic. Asian American issues were not among them.

The last thing I expected to find in Detroit was an Asian American mandate that would compel the scattered groups across the nation into a broad-based pan-Asian movement. I was in for a big surprise.

∎   ∎   ∎

In the years leading up to the summer of 1982, Detroit was a city in crisis. Long lines of despair snaked around unemployment offices, union halls, welfare offices, soup kitchens. Men and women lost homes, cars, recreational vehicles, summer cottages, and possessions accumulated from a lifetime of hard work in a once-thriving industry. They were named the "new poor." For many, gloom turned to anger as they searched for the cause of their miseries.

At first, the companies blamed the workers for incompetence and malaise, for wanting too much in exchange for too little. The workers, in turn, pointed to decrepit factories and machines that hadn't been upgraded since World War II, profits that had been squandered and not reinvested in plants and people. The government was faulted for the usual reasons. Before long, however, they all found a common enemy to blame: the Japanese.

While Detroit had once scoffed at the threat of oil shortages, Japan's automakers were busily meeting the demand for inexpensive, fuel-efficient cars. In 1978, a new oil crisis and subsequent price hikes at the gas pumps killed the market for the heavy, eight-cylinder dinosaurs made in Detroit, precipitating the massive layoffs and a crisis throughout the industrial Midwest. The Japanese auto imports were everything the gas-guzzlers were not—cheap to buy, cheap to run, well made and dependable. They were easy to hate.

Anything Japanese, or presumed to be Japanese, became a potential target. Japanese cars were easy pickings. Local unions sponsored sledge-hammer events giving frustrated workers a chance to smash Japanese cars for a dollar a swing. Japanese cars were vandalized and their owners were shot at on the freeways. On TV, radio, and the local street corner, anti-Japanese slurs were commonplace. Politicians and public figures made irresponsible and unambiguous racial barbs aimed at Japanese people. Lee Iacocca, chairman of the failing Chrysler Corporation and onetime presidential candidate, jokingly suggested dropping nuclear bombs on Japan, while U.S. Representative John Dingell of Michigan pointed his fury at "those little yellow men."

Bumper stickers threatened "Honda, Toyota—Pearl Harbor." It felt dangerous to have an Asian face. Asian American employees of auto companies were warned not to go onto the factory floor because angry workers might hurt them if they were thought to be Japanese. Even in distant California, Robert Handa, a third-generation Japanese American television reporter, was threatened by an autoworker who pulled a knife and yelled, "I don't likee Jap food . . . only like American food."

I had lost my job at Chrysler in the first round of layoffs, four years earlier, but every time I drove my car I was grateful that it was American-made. The tension was an ominous reminder of dangerous times past. It seemed only a matter of time before the anger turned to violence.

That summer, a twenty-seven-year-old man named Vincent Chin was destined to become a symbol for Asian Americans. Vincent was a regular Detroit guy who happened to be of Chinese descent. Cheerful and easygoing, Vincent was a recent graduate of Control Data Institute, a computer trade school, and worked as a draftsman during the day and a waiter on weekends. He liked nothing more than spending a lazy afternoon fishing with his buddies. He hadn't been touched by the Asian American movement and knew little of the violence endured by past generations of Asians in America. But he had felt the sting of racial prejudice and witnessed the hardships of his immigrant parents, who worked in the laundries and restaurants of Detroit.

On June 19, 1982, a week before his wedding, Vincent's pals took him out for the all-American ritual the bachelor party. They went to Fancy Pants, a raunchy striptease bar in Highland Park, a tattered enclave of Detroit, near the crumbling mansions once home to auto magnates and Motown stars and only blocks away from the abandoned buildings where Henry Ford manufactured the Model T. Vincent, who grew up in that neighborhood, had been to Fancy Pants several times before.

That night, his mother admonished him, "You're getting married, you shouldn't go there anymore."

"Ma, it's my last time," he replied.

"Don't say 'last time,' it's bad luck," she scolded, conjuring up old Chinese superstitions.

At the lounge, two white men sat across the striptease stage from Vincent and his three friends—two white men and one Chinese American. Ronald Ebens, a plant superintendent for Chrysler, and his stepson, Michael Nitz, a laid-off autoworker, soon made it clear that they found Vincent's presence distasteful. The friends of the groom-to-be were paying the dancers handsomely to shower their favors on Vincent. According to witnesses, Ebens seemed annoyed by the attention the Chinese American was receiving from the nude dancers. Vincent's friends overheard Ebens say "Chink," "Nip," and "fucker." One of the dancers heard him say, "It's because of motherfuckers like you that we're out of work." Vincent replied, "Don't call me a fucker," and a scuffle ensued. Nitz's forehead was cut, possibly by a punch or chair thrown by Vincent. Both groups were ejected from the bar.

Ebens and Nitz hunted for Chin and the other Chinese man in his group. In the dark summer night, they drove through the area for a half hour with a neighborhood man whom they paid to help them "get the Chinese." Finally they spotted Vincent and his friend in front of a crowded McDonald's on Woodward Avenue, Detroit's main central thoroughfare. Creeping up behind the Chinese Americans, Nitz held Vincent Chin down while his stepfather swung his Louisville Slugger baseball bat into Vincent's skull four times, "as if he was going for a home run." Two off-duty cops who were moonlighting as security guards witnessed the attack. The impact of the blows broke a jade pendant that Vincent wore—to some

Chinese, a sign of bad luck. Mortally wounded, Vincent died four days later. His four hundred wedding guests attended his funeral instead.

The *Detroit Free Press* featured the bridegroom's beating death on its front page, telling of Vincent's life and hopes for his marriage, but offering no details of his slaying—none of the circumstances were yet known. Detroit's Asian Americans, unaccustomed to any media coverage, took notice. But they remained silent even though many believed that race was a factor in the killing. The community was small and unorganized. Conventional wisdom of the "don't make waves" variety admonished that visibility could bring trouble. Even if they wished to protest, they had no advocacy or watchdog group to turn to. It seemed that the matter would end there. I read the story with sadness and alarm, too aware of the racial tensions swirling around the region. I wondered how this Chinese American came to be killed, when there were so few Asian Americans in Detroit. As an enterprising young journalist, I clipped the story out and filed it, certain that there was a bigger story behind Vincent's death.

Nine months later, on March 18, 1983, new headlines appeared on the front pages of Detroit's two dailies: "Two Men Charged in '82 Slaying Get Probation" and "Probation in Slaying Riles Chinese." It seemed to be the courtroom conclusion to Vincent Chin's death. The two killers pleaded guilty and no contest to savagely beating Chin to death; each received three years' probation and $3,780 in fines and court costs to be paid over three years. The judge, Charles Kaufman, explained his reasoning: "These aren't the kind of men you send to jail," he said. "You fit the punishment to the criminal, not the crime." The lightness of the sentence shocked Detroit. Two white killers were set free in a city with a population more than 60 percent black, where African Americans routinely received harsher sentences for lesser crimes. The sentence of probation drew cries of outrage. Local pundits harshly criticized Judge Kaufman. "You have raised the ugly ghost of racism, suggesting in your explanation that the lives of the killers are of great and continuing value to society, implying they are of greater value than the life of the slain victim . . . How gross and ostentatious of you; how callous and yes, unjust . . ." wrote *Detroit Free Press* columnist Nikki McWhirter.

The *Detroit News* reporter Cynthia Lee, herself a Chinese American from Hawaii, interviewed members of the Chinese American community, who voiced their disbelief. "You go to jail for killing a dog," said Henry Yee, a noted local restaurateur who was described as the "unofficial mayor of Chinatown." Vincent's life was worth less than a used car, cried a distraught family friend.

The reaction within the Detroit area's small, scattered Asian American population was immediate and visceral. Suddenly people who had endured a lifetime of degrading treatment were wondering if their capacity to suffer in silence might no longer be a virtue, when even in death, after such a brutal, uncontested killing, they could be so disrespected. Disconnected, informal networks of Asian Americans frantically worked the phones, trying to find some way to vent their frustrations and perhaps correct the injustice.

I, too, was stunned. Here was the incredible ending to the story I had clipped out for future reference. I felt distraught, betrayed—and furious. The probationary sentences seemed to echo the familiar taunt, "a Chinaman's chance," that grim reminder of the days when whites lynched Chinese with impunity. The lessons from my Asian American student movement days came rushing back to me. After I read the articles, I telephoned the person named in the *Detroit News* article. Introducing myself to Henry Yee, whose common Chinese American name was the same as my older brother's, I offered to help in any way I could. Henry invited me to meet him and some others that afternoon. At Carl's Steak House, I met Henry Yee and Kin Yee (not related), president of the Detroit Chinese Welfare Council. A woman named Liza Chan, a Hong Kong–born attorney of my own generation, joined us. We talked generally about possible actions. The first step would be to conduct a larger meeting that could include more members of the Chinese and Asian American community.

The Chinese Welfare Council was the public face of the local branches of the Chinese Consolidated Benevolent Association and the On Leong Merchants Association, a tong, a form of Chinatown organization often associated with the seamier side of Chinese American ghettoes. In Detroit it served a social function. Both organizations had long histories in Chinatowns. The business association, also known as the Six Companies, began in San Francisco in the 1860s to provide public services denied to Chinese by local governments. The association arbitrated disputes, representing Chinese concerns to the city, state, and federal governments. The tongs, on the other hand, were alleged to conduct organized crime activities in Chinatowns, using their networks to run gambling, prostitution, drug-trafficking, and protection rackets. Some tongs performed legitimate community and civic functions; in Detroit, the Chinese Welfare Council and On Leong Merchants Association were well established, and both Henry Yee and Kin Yee were members.

Merchants were the Chinese pioneers in Detroit. In 1872, the first Chinese Detroiter, Ah Chee, arrived and set up a laundry business; subsequent arrivals did the same. The first Chinese restaurant opened in 1905. The Chinese business community hit its peak in the 1920s, when the city counted 300 Chinese laundries and 32 restaurants. Since that time, the Chinatown population and business base dwindled, becoming a mere shadow of its peak days.

Over the years, the Asian American population in the Detroit area changed considerably. The Immigration Act of 1965 had ushered in a new generation of Chinese immigrants, as well as those from Korea, the Philippines, and South Asia. Because the new immigration regulations heavily favored educated professionals, the newer Asian immigrants included highly trained scientists, engineers, doctors, and nurses. Many of the top researchers for the Big Three automakers were Ph.D.'s from throughout Asia. The professionals lived in the suburbs, far from Detroit's urban core and Chinatown. By the 1980s, Chinatown's shrinking base reflected the diminished role of the merchants. The children of the laundry and restaurant owners had gone to college and moved to the suburbs or to other cities. The family businesses in Chinatown faded.

The 1980 census reported only 1,213 Chinese in the entire city; while that is surely an undercount, the population was unquestionably small. On Leong ran the Chinese Culture and Recreational Center, offering activities for youth and English-language instruction to new immigrants. It also assisted the aging bachelor Chinese, settled disputes among immigrants, and maintained a cemetery plot for Chinese. If it had more nefarious pursuits, they weren't obvious, though the notorious Hong Kong–based chief of the national On Leong, Eddie Chan, was well known to the FBI and Interpol. The Detroit Chinese Welfare Council represented Chinatown interests to the city and at political functions. Both groups were run by the same aging elders who realized they needed to bolster their membership by attracting new, and younger, blood. The late Vincent Chin was one of their younger members.

Vincent's background was like that of many second-generation Chinatown Chinese. His father, David Bing Hing Chin, had worked in laundries all his life, from the time he arrived from China in 1922 at the age of seventeen until his death in 1981, the year before Vincent was slain. He had served in the Army during World War II, which earned him his citizenship and the right to find a wife in China. Lily came to the United States in 1948 to be married, like so many other Chinese women of her generation, including my mother. Lily knew her husband-to-be's family, and looked forward to joining him in America. Lily's father opposed the move because his grandfather had worked on the transcontinental railroad, but was driven out. He feared Lily might face similar bigotry. In Detroit, Lily worked in the laundries and restaurants alongside her new husband.

In 1961, Lily and David Bing Chin adopted a cheerful six-year-old boy from Guangdong Province in China. Vincent grew up into a friendly young man and a devoted only child who helped support his parents financially. He ran on his high school track team, but he also wrote poetry. Vincent was an energetic, take-charge guy who knew how to stand up for himself on the tough streets of Detroit. But friends and co-workers had never seen him angry and were shocked that he had been provoked into a fight.

For Chinese Americans, the identification with the Chin family was direct. The details of the Chins' family history mirrored those of so many other Chinese Americans, who, like Lily and David, came from Guangdong Province. So did the military service that made it possible for Chinese American men to get married, and their work in the restaurants and laundries. Vincent was part of an entire generation for whom the immigrant parents had suffered and sacrificed. Other Asian Americans also found a strong connection to the lives of Vincent, Lily, and David Chin. Theirs was the classic immigrant story of survival: work hard and sacrifice for the family, keep a low profile, don't complain, and, perhaps in the next generation, attain the American dream. For Asian Americans, along with the dream came the hope of one day gaining acceptance in America. The injustice surrounding Vincent's slaying shattered the dream.

But most of all, Vincent was everyone's son, brother, boyfriend, husband, father. Asian Americans felt deeply that what happened to Vincent Chin could have happened to anyone who "looked" Japanese. From childhood, nearly every Asian American has experienced being mistaken for other Asian ethnicities, even harassed and called names as though every

Asian group were the same. The climate of hostility made many Asian Americans feel unsafe, not just in Detroit, but across the country, as the Japan-bashing began to emanate from the nation's capital and was amplified through the news media. If Vincent Chin could be harassed and brutally beaten to death, and his killers freed, many felt it could happen to them.

After the news of the sentences of probation for Vincent's killers, his mother, Lily, wrote a letter in Chinese to the Detroit Chinese Welfare Council: "This is injustice to the grossest extreme. I grieve in my heart and shed tears in blood. My son cannot be brought back to life, but he was a member of your council. Therefore, I plead to you. Please let the Chinese American community know, so they can help me hire legal counsel to appeal, so my son can rest his soul."

As phone calls and offers of help from Chinese Americans and others poured in from all over the Detroit area, Henry Yee and Kin Yee called for a meeting on March 20, 1983, under the auspices of the Detroit Chinese Welfare Council at the Golden Star Restaurant in Ferndale, a working-class suburb just north of Detroit. Vincent had worked at the Golden Star as a waiter. The restaurant was three miles from the McDonald's on Woodward Avenue where he was killed.

One week after the sentencing, about thirty people crammed into the back dining room of the Golden Star. I had never been to the restaurant, but its familiar decor of red, black, and gold-speckled mirrors reminded me of Chinese restaurants everywhere. The lawyers stood at the front, fielding questions from the group. Barely a half dozen of them, they constituted the majority of Asian American attorneys in the entire state. Most were under thirty. None specialized in criminal law, but they agreed on one thing: once a sentence was rendered, little could be done to change it; the law offered few options. The impasse forced an uneasy quiet over the gathering, broken only by the low sounds of Lily Chin weeping at the back of the room.

Aside from Kin Yee, Henry Yee, and Liza Chan, whom I had just met, I knew no one at the meeting. At that moment I had to decide between being a reporter on the sidelines and being an active participant in whatever happened. I hesitated, then raised my hand. "We must let the world know that we think this is wrong. We can't stop now without even trying."

At first there was no response. Then the weeping stopped. Mrs. Chin stood up and spoke in a shaky but clear voice. "We must speak up. These men killed my son like an animal. But they go free. This is wrong. We must tell the people, this is wrong."

With Mrs. Chin's words as a moral turning point, the group decided to press forward. The lawyers recommended a meeting with the sentencing judge, Charles Kaufman. But who would accompany Mrs. Chin and Kin Yee to meet the judge? Some of the lawyers stepped back, explaining how such an act might jeopardize their jobs. In a community with so little political clout, to be "the nail that sticks out" was an invitation to disaster. After another pause, a woman spoke up. "I'll meet with Kaufman." It was Liza Chan, the only Asian American woman practicing law in Michigan. I took on the task of publicizing the news that Asian Americans were outraged and preparing to fight the judge's sentence. From the beginning, women would play a major role in the case.

In the next few days, Liza and Kin attempted to meet with the judge, who by now was flooded by angry phone calls, letters, and media inquiries, as Asian Americans and others challenged his sentence. He skipped their appointment. When I joined Liza and Kin for the next scheduled meeting, we were told that the judge had suddenly decided to go on vacation. On a pro bono basis, Liza began the work of finding and interviewing witnesses to reconstruct what happened to Vincent Chin that fateful night, so that Mrs. Chin and the community could assess their legal options. It soon became clear that there were failures at every step of the criminal justice process. The police and court record was slipshod and incomplete. The police had failed to interview numerous witnesses, including the dancers at the bar and a man the killers hired outside the bar to help them "get the Chinese"; when Liza and I visited the arresting officer, he had the murder weapon, the Louisville Slugger baseball bat, sitting behind his desk. The first presiding judge had set the initial charges against the killers at second-degree murder, which other legal experts determined to be too low. Almost as outrageous as the sentence itself was the fact that no prosecutor was present when Judge Kaufman rendered his sentence of probation.

After the community meeting at the Golden Star, I issued our first press release. We were flooded with numerous requests for information and offers to help. Without an existing advocacy group to manage the community response, we decided some kind of organization would have to be formed. The founding meeting was set for the following week, after we contacted the various community groups, which were mostly religious, cultural, and professional in nature. The meeting would be held at the Detroit Chinese Welfare Council building.

On the evening of March 31, more than a hundred solidly middle-aged and mainly middle-class Asian Americans from towns surrounding Detroit packed the dingy, low-ceilinged hall. The threat of a Michigan frost still lingered, but the topic under debate this night was hot and unprecedented among Asian Americans: whether to form a pan-Asian organization that might seek a federal civil rights investigation in the slaying of Vincent Chin. There had never before been a criminal civil rights case involving anyone of Asian descent in the United States.

Once again, the gathering was mostly Chinese American, with a few other Asian ethnicities offering a thin slice of diversity. The imagery was staunchly conservative: a faded portrait of Chiang Kai-shek at the front, flanked by the red-white-and-blue—not Old Glory but the flag of Taiwan, the Republic of China.

The main order of business was to create an organization that could file petitions and legal actions, raise money, and organize the outcry for a response. The idea was to form an umbrella organization to coordinate the efforts of the area's varied Asian American groups. Members of some twenty groups had come that night, mostly Chinese, from the Association of Chinese Americans and the Greater Detroit Taiwanese Association, to such professional associations as the Detroit Chinese Engineers Association; cultural groups like the Chinese American Educational and Cultural Center; church organizations from the Chinese Community Church to the Detroit Buddhist Church; and a women's group, the Organization of Chinese American Women.

Detroit had not seen such a broad gathering of Chinese since the China War Relief effort of the 1930s. Non-Chinese were also represented, including the Japanese American Citizens League, the Korean Society of Greater Detroit, and the Filipino American Community Council.

The pan-Asian intent of the group became clear as the group discussed what to name the new organization. "Citizens for Fair Sentencing in the Cause of Vincent Chin" and "Justice Committee of the Chinese Welfare Council" were rejected as too narrow. "Chinese Americans for Justice" limited the concern to Chinese. The vote overwhelmingly went to "American Citizens for Justice," which offered an inclusive base and a vision for justice beyond a single case. The founding of the American Citizens for Justice, or ACJ, marked the formation of the first explicitly Asian American grass-roots community advocacy effort with a national scope. Third-generation Japanese American James Shimoura was the first, and at the time only, non-Chinese to serve on the executive board. Japanese, Filipino, and Korean American groups joined in support, assured that they would be welcome. As word of our efforts spread, both white and black individuals also volunteered, making the campaign for justice multiracial in character.

That night, the new pan–Asian American organization drafted its statement of principles:

ACJ believes that:

1. All citizens are guaranteed the right to equal treatment by our judicial and governmental system;

2. When the rights of one individual are violated, all of society suffers;

3. Asian Americans, along with many other groups of people, have historically been given less than equal treatment by the American judicial and governmental system. Only through cooperative efforts with all people will society progress and be a better place for all citizens.

ACJ's first mandate was unambiguous: to obtain justice for Vincent Chin, an Asian American man who was killed because he looked Japanese.

Hard questions came quickly as the newly formed ACJ sought to gain supporters outside the Asian American community. Our first efforts at mounting a national media campaign were crude and amateurish as we learned the process of getting our news out; in the days before fax machines, each press release was hand-delivered, often by a retired Chinese American couple, Ray and Mable Lim. ACJ held its first news conference at the Detroit Press Club on April 15, 1983. The entire spectrum of local media appeared—it was big news to see Asian Americans coming together to protest injustice. To the reporters and the people of Detroit, Asian

Americans seemed to emerge from nowhere. Our task, and mine in particular, was to educate them quickly, in sound bites, about Asian Americans.

An appearance that Liza Chan and I made on a popular African American talk radio program drew numerous calls from black listeners. Some were pleased that Asian Americans would reach out to their community to talk about this injustice. Others asked if Asians were just trying to "ride the coattails" of African Americans, and still others accused Asian people of prejudice against blacks. We tried to answer questions frankly, acknowledging that anti-black prejudice exists among some, but not all, Asian Americans, and that ACJ was trying to address racial bias and injustice against any group, including attitudes held by Asians. The talk shows gave us an opportunity to point out the contributions of Asian Americans to the civil rights struggles. The listeners' comments also underscored the need for us to bring such discussions to the more recent Asian immigrants who had arrived after the 1965 Immigration Act with little awareness of the U.S. civil rights movement.

The growing prominence of the case gave Asian Americans our first direct entry on a national level into the white–black race dynamic with an Asian American issue. We tried to explain that we recognized and respected African Americans' central and dominant position in the civil rights struggle; we wanted to show that we weren't trying to benefit from their sacrifices without offering anything in return. On the other hand, many European Americans were hostile or resistant to "yet another minority group" stepping forward to make claims. Underlying both concerns was the suggestion, a nagging doubt, that Asian Americans had no legitimate place in discussions of racism because we hadn't *really* suffered any.

Still, many did welcome Asian Americans into the civil rights fold, as a new voice from a previously silent neighbor. As ACJ began to make its case, African American organizations such as the umbrella Detroit-Area Black Organizations quickly endorsed ACJ's efforts. Its president, Horace Sheffield, became a dependable supporter at ACJ events, and Asian Americans reciprocated. The Detroit chapter of the NAACP, the largest chapter in the country, issued a statement about the sentence. Several prominent African American churches gave their support, as did the Anti-Defamation League of B'nai B'rith and the Detroit Roundtable of Christians and Jews.

ACJ sought and won the support of other communities as well, including Latinos, Arab Americans, and Italian Americans. A diversity of women's groups from the Detroit Women's Forum to Black Women for a Better Society endorsed ACJ, as did a number of local political leaders from the president of the Detroit City Council to U.S. Representative John Conyers.

Many Asian Americans wanted to express their outrage, but were unsure how race fit in the picture. Their tentativeness about the issue of race was evident in ACJ's carefully crafted public positions. ACJ focused on Judge Kaufman's unjust sentence, deliberately not commenting on possible racial bias by the judge or the potential for a racial motivation in the killing of Vincent Chin. A few of us in the core organizing effort—attorneys Roland Hwang and Jim Shimoura, educator Parker Woo, and I—had an understanding of civil rights from the Asian American student movement days and felt that racism permeated the case on many levels. But we also knew that other Asian Americans would need to hear more conclusive evidence if they were to take a strong position on race.

ACJ waited to see if Liza Chan's interviews with witnesses would produce evidence of a racially motivated killing. I worded our press releases carefully to convey the context of our history with racism, while avoiding an outright accusation; one of the first ACJ press statements said: "This case has aroused the anger of the Asian community by recalling the days of 'frontier justice,' when massacres of Chinese workers were commonplace." News reporters, on the other hand, wanted ACJ to call Kaufman a racist. Journalists discovered that Kaufman had been held in a Japanese prisoner-of-war camp during World War II. ACJ refused the bait.

Soon the smoking gun the community needed appeared. A private investigator hired by ACJ to uncover the facts leading to Vincent's death reported that Racine Colwell, a tough blond dancer at the Fancy Pants, overheard Ebens tell Chin, "It's because of you motherfuckers that we're out of work." At a time when bilious anti-Japanese remarks by politicians, public officials, and the next-door neighbors spewed forth regularly, Asian Americans knew exactly what Ebens meant. A nude dancer with nothing to gain from her testimony had produced the link to a racial motivation that the community was waiting for. ACJ attorneys and leaders realized it was enough to charge Ebens and Nitz with violating Vincent Chin's civil rights. It was time to talk about race.

The next meeting of the ACJ was held at Ford Motor Company World Headquarters, in Dearborn. David Hwang, who had worked at Ford as a research engineer for thirty-six years, secured the use of the company cafeteria on a Sunday evening. More than two hundred people packed the cavernous room to hear updates on the legal efforts and to coordinate the grass-roots, volunteer work. A quick roll call identified Asian American employee groups from the top corporations of the Detroit area, from Burroughs and Detroit Diesel to General Motors and Volkswagen. The meeting's featured speaker from the U.S. Department of Justice explained the difficult process of getting the federal government to conduct a civil rights investigation. The FBI would need to show that there was a conspiracy to deprive Vincent Chin of his civil rights, he advised. The strong public outcry would also be a factor in its decision to investigate.

After the Department of Justice official left the meeting, a gray-haired engineer from General Motors raised his hand. In the clipped English of a native Cantonese speaker, he voiced the uneasiness of the crowd. "If we try to pursue a civil rights case," he asked, "is it necessary for us to talk about race?"

The simple question captured the race conundrum bedeviling Asian Americans. Should Asian Americans downplay race to stay in the "safe" shadows of the white establishment? Or should they step out of the shadows and cast their lot with the more vulnerable position of minorities seeking civil rights? Was there a third, Asian American way that would take sides with neither?

"We may alienate our supporters," argued an earnest-looking businessman, who voiced his fears that a stand on racism might affect an already fragile existence between black and white. "Could we win the NAACP but lose the FBI?" asked another.

Behind the discomfort of "talking about race" was the question of where Asian Americans fit in America, and, more important, where we wanted to be. Asian Americans had never been included in broad discussions on race, nor had we interjected ourselves. The questions were many. If race was such a volatile subject for whites and blacks, why should Asian Americans step in, to face potential wrath from one or the other, or both? Organizing over race might make us seem like troublemakers, as African Americans were often perceived, but we lacked the numerical strength and political power of blacks; if we stepped out of the shadows to make waves, wouldn't we risk becoming targets again?

One by one, people discussed their uncertainties. Those of us who had been involved with Third World movements knew the political theories about race and racism, but making the argument to struggling restaurant workers or comfortable professionals was another matter. Even in 1983, fifteen years after the term "Asian American" first designated a pan-Asian identity, civil rights and their importance to Asian Americans were simply not familiar at the grass-roots level of the Asian ethnic communities. We tried to give direct, even practical answers: yes, a civil rights suit would involve race, and if we wanted to pursue a federal case, we would have to get comfortable educating people—including ourselves—about our experiences with race. But remaining silent would not protect us from the anti-Japanese racial hostility all around us and we could all become targets anyway, the way Vincent Chin had.

Suddenly people began talking about the anger and frustration that brought them to this meeting, why they were touched and outraged by what happened to Vincent Chin. "I've worked hard for my company for forty years," said a computer programmer, his voice shaking. "They always pass me over for promotion because I'm Chinese. I have trained many young white boys fresh out of college to be my boss. I never complain, but inside I'm burning. This time, with this killing, I must complain. What is the point of silence if our children can be killed and treated like this? I wish I'd stood up and complained a lot sooner in my life."

The outrage overcame the fear. "We want to win this case, and we want equal justice for all, including Asian Americans," David Hwang reminded the group. In the end, we reached a consensus: to fight for what we believed in, we would have to enter the arena of civil rights and racial politics. Welcome or not, Asian Americans would put ourselves into the white–black race paradigm.

ACJ began to publicize its findings of racial slurs and comments made by Vincent Chin's killers and to call for a civil rights investigation. The backlash that some had feared was immediate. Non-Asians, most particularly those in a position to make policy on civil rights and race matters, openly resisted claims by Asians of racial discrimination and prejudice. Angry white listeners called in to radio talk shows to complain:

"What does race have to do with this?" and "Don't white people have civil rights?"

White liberals were the most skeptical. When Wayne State University constitutional law professor Robert A. Sedler met with Liza Chan and other ACJ attorneys about the legal issues in a civil rights case, he told them to forget it. In his opinion, civil rights laws were enacted to protect African Americans, not Asians. Asian Americans cannot seek redress using federal civil rights law; besides, he said, Asians are considered white.

Sedler wasn't alone in this view. The American Civil Liberties Union of Michigan initially dismissed the outcry from Asian Americans as a law-and-order, "mandatory sentencing" movement. Later, as the community outrage continued, Howard Simon, its executive director, issued a report absolving Judge Kaufman of bias and blaming the prosecutors for failing to prepare the facts of the case for sentencing. The Michigan ACLU wasn't interested in the civil rights aspects of Chin's slaying.

Nor did the Detroit chapter of the National Lawyers Guild, which defined itself as part of the political left, find any connection between Vincent Chin's killing and racism. But the Guild's West Coast chapters, more familiar with Asian Americans' history with racial violence, mustered the votes to give the national endorsement to ACJ's efforts. A near mutiny broke out in the Detroit chapter, but the national body prevailed.

To build a broad coalition of support, ACJ decided to approach the United Auto Workers union, and not just for its powerful presence in Detroit. We felt that if we could change some of its members' anti-Japanese rhetoric, we might be able to prevent future attacks on Asian Americans—and possibly save lives. The UAW department of fair practices was across from Solidarity House, the international headquarters, so it was impossible to avoid the racially inflammatory signs and bumper stickers adorning the parking lot entrance. "300,000 Laid-Off Autoworkers Say Park Your Import in Tokyo" proclaimed one large sign; Volvos, VWs, Saabs, and other European imports apparently presented no problem. I recognized Joe Davis, the fair practices director, from my days as a Chrysler press operator, when he was president of a militant UAW local. Davis told us that the UAW condemned the attack on Vincent Chin. "But if he had been Japanese," noted Davis, an African American, "the attack would be understandable, and we wouldn't give you our support." I had a similar encounter with Doug Fraser, the former president of the UAW, at a reception. I had just shown a city council member, Maryann Mahaffey, a supporter of ACJ, the photo of a poster at Auto World theme park in Flint, Michigan, that featured a buck-toothed, slant-eyed car dropping bombs on Detroit—an example of autoworkers' racial hostility. Mahaffey showed the photo to Fraser, who burst into gleeful laughter—until he saw me standing nearby. As a former UAW member, I was embarrassed and repulsed by the union's acquiescence in racism. I recalled the violent anti-Asian campaigns of Samuel Gompers and wondered when the chain would be broken.

In spite of the backlash, local, national, and international support for ACJ's efforts was growing daily. The legal twists and turns garnered steady local news coverage, and the mobilization of Detroit's Asian Americans was an interesting new phenomenon for reporters. The Vincent Chin case broke into national news by a strange twist of fate. I had rented a car while my American-made auto was in the shop; as I waited at the car rental agency, I stood in line behind a woman with a *New York Times* notebook and copies of the two Detroit daily newspapers, each open to a story about the Chin case. I happened to be carrying several ACJ press packets and asked her if she wanted more information. She turned out to be Judith Cummins, a *New York Times* reporter in town visiting relatives. She wrote a story about the killing and the controversy, even though the local bureau chief had shrugged us off. Perhaps Cummins recognized the story's importance because she was African American and the bureau chief missed it because he was white; in any case, the *New York Times* coverage brought other national media interest, including national network news, TV news magazine specials, and an appearance on the Phil Donahue show.

It was the first time that an Asian American–initiated issue was considered significant national news. Ethnic media from the Asian American community, as well as foreign-language news media from China, Hong Kong, Taiwan, and Japan, followed the case closely—sending to Asia images of Asian Americans raising political Cain over issues of race, racism, and racial unity. As the news of the case spread, groups from all over the country and the world contacted ACJ to extend their support. We developed an international following. Several Chinese Canadian groups offered assistance, as did the North American representative of Taiwan; ACJ politely declined Taiwan's help, deciding not to accept money from foreign governments. Families of other hate crimes victims reached out from afar; a representative for the family of Steven Harvey, an African American musician who was killed by whites in Kansas City, came to an ACJ meeting. Asian Americans and African Americans pledged mutual support.

ACJ was pursuing a three-pronged legal effort. It called on Judge Kaufman, who finally heard arguments by Liza, to set aside his own sentence, since it was based on incomplete information. ACJ filed briefs with the Michigan Court of Appeals to overturn Kaufman's sentence. The third approach was the civil rights case. Kin Yee and Lily Chin went to Washington, D.C., to meet with William Bradford Reynolds, President Ronald Reagan's civil rights chief, about a federal civil rights investigation. As the local and state actions turned sour, the FBI began to take an interest in the case. To capture the mounting frustration of the community, the ACJ decided to hold a citywide demonstration at Kennedy Square in downtown Detroit, the site of many historic protests. We had held a number of noisy picket lines in front of City Hall, but there had never before been a protest in Detroit organized by the broad Asian American community. This would possibly be the first in the country outside the larger Asian American centers of New York City and the West Coast.

The "demonstration committee" was headed by David Chock, Michael Lee, and Man Feng Chang, all senior scientists from the General Motors Tech Center. They enlisted the help of other engineers, and joked that this would be the most precisely planned demonstration in history. The outpouring of support was unprecedented. Waving American flags and placards that demanded equal justice, hundreds of professionals and housewives marched alongside waiters and cooks from Chinese restaurants across the region. The restaurant owners shut their doors during the busy weekday lunch rush to allow employees and their own families to participate in the demonstration. Children and seniors, hunched and wizened, walked or rode in wheelchairs. Chinese, Japanese, Koreans, and Filipinos marched in pan-Asian unity. Support statements were made by the city's major African American and religious organizations, local politicians, and even the UAW. At the rally's emotional end, Mrs. Chin appealed to the nation. Through her tears, she said haltingly, "I want justice for my son. Please help me so no other mother must do this." Finally, the demonstrators marched to the Federal Courthouse singing "We Shall Overcome," and hand-delivered to U.S. Attorney Leonard Gilman a petition with three thousand signatures seeking federal intervention.

ACJ used the demonstration to launch its call for a federal prosecution of the killers for violating Chin's civil right to be in a public place, even if that place was a sleazy nude bar. In his speech to the demonstrators, ACJ president Kin Yee read the group's carefully worded position on race: "Eyewitnesses have come forward to confirm something that we suspected all along: that Vincent Chin was brutally slain as a result of a racial incident. Ronald Ebens, a foreman at Chrysler, was so consumed with racial hatred toward Asian people that he started a fight, blaming Asians for the problems of the ailing auto industry. Even non-minority immigrant groups like the Irish and the Poles have faced violence from others who blamed them for their problems. This misguided view encourages attacks on Asian American people and it must be fought against by all who cherish justice and have respect for human dignity."

In direct yet subtle terms, ACJ showed the ways in which Asian Americans had been made scapegoats for the ills of the modern American economy, naming anti-Asian violence as a present-day phenomenon that should concern all people. This created a framework for Asian Americans to organize nationally, and was a first step toward placing Asian Americans in the center of domestic and international economic, political, and social policy contexts. Across the country, in Los Angeles, San Francisco, New York, and Chicago—cities with far greater Asian American populations than Detroit's—pan-Asian coalitions were being built to support the campaign and to address anti-Asian violence in the local community. Fundraising efforts nationwide encompassed the entire spectrum of Chinese American society, from the National On Leong Association and local chapters, the Chinese Consolidated Benevolent Association and the Chinese Hand Laundry Alliance, to overtly left-leaning groups like the Chinese Progressive Association and the Chinese Association for Human Rights in Taiwan. In between were civil rights groups like the Organization of Chinese Americans, Asian American Law Students Association, Chinese restaurants and business enterprises, and church groups. Dozens of chapters of the Japanese American Citizens League sent money, as did the Korean American Association of Illinois and the American-Arab Anti-Discrimination Committee. The broad cross section showed that the Vincent Chin case was able to overcome the forces of tradition and fear of the unknown, particularly in the arena of race politics. Asian Americans were finally joining together to correct perceived injustices.

Such unity was difficult to maintain. It was rare for the highly educated suburbanites who spoke the Northern Chinese Mandarin dialect to be aligned so closely with Cantonese-speaking Chinatown merchants and workers whose roots were in Southern China. In addition to differences in language, class, and kinship bonds, there was the political gap. Many business owners were Chiang Kai-shek loyalists and fervent anti-Communists, while the more left-wing groups openly supported Mao Tse-tung and the People's Republic of China.

Partly to avoid fractious conflict over "homeland" politics, the charter of the Organization of Chinese Americans, for example, expressly prohibited taking stands on international issues—a policy that is still in effect. ACJ's policy was to admit all who supported its goals, as long as they also maintained an open and tolerant policy toward others. Vincent Chin's story had struck such a raw nerve that Asian American groups were competing to be affiliated with ACJ. In San Francisco, with its rich profusion of Asian American groups, near warfare broke out among various factions. The first cracks appeared when the Chinatown business groups, a powerful constituency in San Francisco, withdrew their support of the case because leftist, pro–People's Republic groups were involved. They used their influence over several Chinese-language newspapers to criticize the fund-raising efforts.

Meanwhile, the leftists were at odds with one another. The Reverend Jesse Jackson's presidential campaign manager for Northern California, Eddie Wong, arranged for Jackson to stop in San Francisco's Chinatown to meet Mrs. Chin, who was attending local support events in California. Jackson became the first national political leader of any race to speak out against racial violence toward Asians. During Jackson's speech in front of a swarm of national reporters and TV cameras at Chinatown's historic Cameron House, where assistance had been provided to Chinese immigrants since 1874, the leaders of two rival leftist groups pinched and shoved each other, trying to elbow the other off the stage just beyond Jackson's view.

Despite the rumblings among the Chinese, ACJ continued to actively reach out to other Asian ethnicities. The second non-Chinese board member was Minoru Togasaki, a second-generation Japanese American. The

Chinese speakers on the board felt worried that they might insult Min by mispronouncing his polysyllabic name, difficult for Chinese speakers accustomed to single-syllable ones. A practice session was held, with a room full of Chinese Americans gingerly repeating the name "To-ga-sa-ki" until they got it right.

Detroit's growing Korean community was represented by two large groups: the Korean Society of Greater Detroit, and the Korean American Women's Association. The two groups had rarely worked together. The Korean women were the wives of non-Korean GIs and were often looked down upon by other Koreans—but their support for the Vincent Chin case brought them together. The Filipino and South Asian populations were larger than any of the others and had well-established connections with both Republican and Democratic parties. Their political savvy and access to politicians made it clear to other Asian American groups why they needed to get involved in politics, which many new immigrants tended to shun.

At ACJ's first fund-raiser dinner, a prominent local citizen appeared, the architect Minoru Yamasaki, designer of the World Trade Center towers in New York and other buildings of world renown. Yamasaki, then seventy-three years old, unexpectedly came to join the gathering as an ordinary citizen. Looking dignified but frail, he rose up slowly from his seat with the assistance of a companion. A hush fell over the banquet room as Yamasaki said in a strong, clear voice, "If Asian people in America don't learn to stand up for themselves, these injustices will never cease."

The civil rights investigations dragged on. In November 1983, a federal grand jury indicted Ronald Ebens and Michael Nitz for violating Vincent Chin's right to enjoy a place of public accommodation; the trial would take place the following June. During this period, other racial attacks drew the attention of the Asian American community. In Lansing, Michigan, a Vietnamese American man and his European American wife were harassed and repeatedly shot at by white men shouting racial slurs. In Davis, California, a seventeen-year-old Vietnamese youth was stabbed to death in his high school by white students, while in New York a pregnant Chinese woman was decapitated when she was pushed in front of an oncoming subway car by a European American teacher who claimed to have a fear of Asians.

In other cities, Asian Americans followed the Detroit Asian American community's example and organized to track such incidents. In Boston, a pan-Asian group called Asians for Justice was formed after an escalating number of anti-Asian attacks against Japanese Americans, Chinese Americans, and Cambodian Americans, as well as the stabbing death of a Vietnamese American man. As such new groups raised public awareness about the particular kind of racial hostility against Asians, they prompted more people to come forward to file hate crime reports. The growing list of cases underscored the existence of racism against Asian Americans.

ACJ expanded its civil rights work from anti-Asian hate crimes. It took on employment and discrimination referrals; successfully lobbied the governor to create a statewide Asian American advisory commission; campaigned against offensive media images, like the poster of the slant-eyed car displayed in Flint, Michigan, and a children's TV program whose host, Jim Harper, appeared in yellowface as a sinister Fu Manchu character with a phony Asian accent. To reach out to children and young people, ACJ members Pang Man and Marisa Chuang Ming sponsored a ten-kilometer Run for Justice, while Harold and Joyce Leon's three daughters, professional violinists and a cellist with the world's leading symphony orchestras, performed a special benefit concert for ACJ.

When the federal civil rights trial began on June 5, 1984, in the courtroom of Judge Anna Diggs Taylor, a dignified jurist who was one of the first African American women to serve on the federal bench, ACJ knew that the courtroom battle would be uphill. Many people had a hard time believing that Asian Americans experienced any kind of racial prejudice, let alone hate violence. What Asian Americans found to be racially offensive fighting words drew only shrugs from people who would otherwise never use racial epithets—at least not in public.

The words Racine Colwell, the stripper, heard—"It's because of you motherfuckers that we're out of work"—didn't contain a single racial slur. Asian Americans recognized that they were being singled out in that comment, but to others it was simply a true statement. Don Ball, the veteran *Detroit News* reporter covering the trial, wrote that such statements and the fact that Ebens and Nitz hunted for Vincent and his one Chinese buddy, while ignoring his white friends, were "flimsy evidence that Chin's slaying was racially motivated."

On June 28, the federal jury in Detroit disagreed, and found Ebens guilty of violating Vincent Chin's civil rights; Nitz was acquitted. The jury foreperson explained to filmmakers Christine Choy and Renee Tajima in their documentary *Who Killed Vincent Chin?* that Racine Colwell's testimony was the clincher—in Detroit, it was clear that "you motherfuckers" meant the Japanese, or people who looked like them. Ebens was sentenced to twenty-five years by Judge Taylor.

But the case won a retrial on appeal in 1986 because of pretrial publicity and evidentiary errors associated with audiotapes made of witnesses when ACJ was first investigating the case. It was a cruel irony that the very interviews that convinced Detroit's Asian American community and the U.S. Department of Justice of the killers' racial motivation would be used to grant Ebens's appeal. The new trial would be held in Cincinnati, where there was less chance that prospective jurors knew of the case.

Located across the Ohio River from Kentucky, Cincinnati is known as a conservative city with Southern sensibilities. Absent was the heightened racial consciousness of Detroit, with its black majority and civil rights history. If Asians were hard to find in Detroit, they were near-invisible in Cincinnati—but not completely invisible; on July 4, 1986, a gang of patriotic whites shot up the homes of Southeast Asian refugees in the city. When the jury selection process for the new trial began on April 20, 1987, potential jurors were interrogated on their familiarity with Asians. "Do you have any contact with Asians? What is the nature of your contact?" they were asked, as though they had been exposed to a deadly virus.

Their answers were even more revealing. Out of about 180 Cincinnati citizens in the jury pool, only 19 had ever had a "casual contact" with an Asian American, whether at work or the local Chinese takeout joint. A white woman who said she had Asian American friends was dismissed as though the friendship tainted her; also dismissed was a woman whose daughter had Asian friends, and a black man who had served in Korea.

The jury that was eventually seated looked remarkably like the defendant, Ronald Ebens—mostly white, male, and blue-collar. This time the jury foreperson was a fifty-something machinist who was laid off after thirty years at his company. This time the defense attorneys tried to argue that ACJ and the Asian American community had paid attorney Liza Chan to trump up a civil rights case; that argument was objected to by the prosecutors and overruled by the judge.

It was a terrible disappointment, but not a surprise, when the jury of this second civil rights trial reached its not-guilty verdict on May 1, 1987, nearly five years after Vincent Chin was killed. This jury, composed of people with so little contact with Asian Americans and knowledge of our concerns, couldn't see how "It's because of you motherfuckers" might contain a racial connotation.

Mrs. Chin was distraught. "Vincent's soul will never rest. My life is over," she said. She cried every day for Vincent, when she awoke in the morning and when she lay down at night. Soon after, she moved to New York, then San Francisco, to stay with relatives. Detroit had too many hard memories. Once the legal proceedings were over, Mrs. Chin, disheartened by the failure of the courts to bring her son's killers to justice, moved to her birthplace in Guangdong Province, China, after spending fifty of her seventy years in the United States.

In a civil suit against Ebens and Nitz for the loss of Vincent's life, a settlement judgment of $1.5 million was levied in September 1987 against Ebens, who later told documentary filmmaker Christine Choy that Mrs. Chin would never see the money. He stopped making payments toward the judgment in 1989. At no point did Ebens ever publicly express remorse for taking Chin's life; he never spent a full day in jail. He and his wife, Juanita, moved several times, leaving a trail in Missouri and Nevada en route to whereabouts unknown.

ACJ, however, vowed to continue in its mission of equal justice for all. After the Cincinnati trial, its president, Kim Bridges, a Korean American, announced that ACJ was founding a Midwest Asian American Center for Justice.

Losing the legal effort in its first national campaign of this magnitude after five years of intensive organizing did not devastate the Asian American community; instead, it had been transformed.

The legacy of the Vincent Chin case has lived on, in mainstream America as well as the Asian American community. The documentary *Who Killed Vincent Chin?* is a staple on college campuses, retelling the story to generations of students. Musicians from balladeer Charlie Chin to jazz artist Jon Jang have created songs and musical arrangements about the struggle for justice in the Vincent Chin case. The Contemporary American Theater Festival of Shepherdstown, West Virginia, near Washington, D.C., commissioned playwright Cherylene Lee to write the play *Carry the Tiger to the Mountain*; West Virginia Governor Cecil H. Underwood used the issues raised by the play to launch a statewide dialogue on race, modeled after President Clinton's Race Initiative. Consuelo Echeverria, a Latina sculptor at Carnegie Mellon University in Pittsburgh, welded a life-size installation from forged steel auto parts, portraying the baseball bat slaying, called *Because They Thought He Was . . .*

Los Angeles attorney and activist Stewart Kwoh, a MacArthur Fellowship "genius" award winner, attributes to the Vincent Chin case his inspiration for establishing the Asian Pacific American Legal Center of Southern California and the National Asian Pacific American Legal Consortium, which conducts an annual audit of anti-Asian hate crimes. New generations of Asian American activists, such as Victor M. Hwang, a civil rights attorney with the Asian Law Caucus in San Francisco, cite the influence of the Vincent Chin case on their desire to make a difference as Asian Americans.

Numerous scholars have studied the Vincent Chin case and its impact on the Asian American community. As Yen Le Espiritu, professor of Ethnic Studies at the University of California at San Diego, wrote in her book *Asian American Panethnicity*:

> *Considered the archetype of anti-Asian violence, the Chin killing has "taken on mythic proportions" in the Asian American community (W. Wong 1989a). As a result of the Chin case, Asian Americans today are much more willing to speak out on the issue of anti-Asianism; they are also much better organized than they were at the time of Chin's death . . . Besides combating anti-Asian violence, these pan-Asian organizations provide a social setting for building pan-Asian unity.*

After a century of seeking acceptance by distancing from one another, Asian Americans were coming together to assert their right to be American.

## · 4 ·

# To Market, to Market,
# New York Style

"Don't waste a single grain of rice," my mom would admonish at almost every meal. "You're lucky to be born in America, you don't know what real hunger is. In China . . ." She'd rattle off a string of "life in China" hardships. War. Starvation. Misery and death everywhere. No wonder she left. Dad chimed in, "When I was a boy, if I dropped a grain of rice in the dirty cracks of our old table, I had to pick it out and eat it or my mother would beat me."

This is America, I would say to myself. If I don't act like I'm from China, am I still Chinese? I eat Chinese food, but I eat Twinkies, too. Does that make me one—yellow on the outside, white on the inside, fluffy and artificial?

From my limited vantage point in New Jersey, New York was where the real Asian people lived. In those days, we were called "Orientals," not "Asians" or "Asian Americans." In New York, if you were Oriental, odds are you were

---

*Korean American shopkeeper Bong Jae Jang in his empty store, as boycotters picket outside in 1990 (Corky Lee)*

Chinese. Chinese Americans from New York were hip and confident. Kids spoke with ease in Chinese as well as their own "Chinglish"—Chinatown English. They spoke freely about *lo fan, bokwei,* and *hokwei*—the foreigners, white devils, black devils. Anybody who wasn't Chinese was some kind of devil. Posters and buttons shouted "Yellow Power!" My brothers brought some posters home and taped them on their bedroom wall.

New York Chinese Americans had real Chinese culture. They observed special days like the Lunar New Year and Ching Ming, the ancestral worship day. At weddings, brides wore, in turn, two gowns—a white Western gown and a red Chinese dress. They had their own newspapers to keep up with current events, in China as well as Chinatown.

Real Chinese food was what Mom and Dad missed most about New York. Bok choy and bean curd were too esoteric to be found outside of Chinatown—forget the thousand-year-old eggs! Periodically, we'd pile into the Chevy and head straight for Chinatown. Dad would make business calls to sell some of the pink and blue baby novelties we made, but first he dropped us off at Wing On, the biggest grocery in Chinatown, at the bend in Mott Street.

Wing On was dark, so crowded you could barely squeeze through the aisles without knocking down some of the indescribable food stuffs that were crammed into every conceivable space. Aromas of dried fish, pickled vegetables, and incense wafted about. Lines hung across the ceiling with crispy, dried intestine and tripe, and ducks pressed stiff and flat as boards. Mom took hours to choose her Chinese produce. I passed the time by poking at the baskets of live blue crabs, hoping to provoke a fight among the expensive delicacies.

Back at our suburban tract home, Mom stuffed the refrigerator and metal cupboards with her precious culinary treasures—jars of pickled cabbage and smelly fermented tofu, Chinese sausages, salted duck eggs, barbecued pork, dried mushrooms, steamed chicken, lots of Chinese vegetables, and special ingredients that she could find only in Chinatown, like the MSG she bought by the pound and kept handy in a thirty-two-ounce Hellmann's mayonnaise jar.

In the days after each trip to Chinatown, Mom prepared our favorite Chinese dishes—lo mein, wintermelon soup, butterfly shrimp, spare ribs, bean sprouts, stuffed tofu—gradually depleting her Chinese pantry. Soon it was back to hot dogs, beef stew, Shake 'n Bake, and frozen chicken pot pies, all much easier to prepare for her jook sing kids than the more labor-intensive Chinese dishes. Every supper, however, had abundant quantities of rice, in great heaping mounds, reassuring me that I was still Chinese.

When a new job brought me back to New York in the 1980s, its familiar "Chineseness" was no longer present. Outwardly, the landmarks were the same. Wing On was still there, as was the curio shop at Doyers and Pell where Shanghainese-speakers like my parents once congregated.

But Chinatown had exploded beyond its old boundaries. Across Canal, an infusion of gleaming Asian restaurants surrounded Little Italy, pressing it into a diminutive enclave of Chinatown. Shops with signs in Chinese characters could be found from West Broadway all the way east to the alphabet avenues. Nor was the script only in Chinese. An influx of new Asian immigrants to New York led to a myriad of signs in Vietnamese, Thai, Hindi, and Korean. A bustling Korea-town was growing in midtown, while Little India was ensconced in the East Village. Gas stations were run by Pakistanis, newsstands by Bangladeshis, green-grocers and nail parlors by Koreans. Across the East River in Queens, the once quiet neighborhood of Flushing was becoming the city's new Asia Central.

The exploding Asian diversity in New York meant an ever-expanding choice of Asian cuisines. Chinese food could no longer be described as merely "Chinese American"—it might be subtle Cantonese, spicy Hunanese, or sweet Shanghai-style Chinese food, or a variety of very different flavors, joined by Japanese sushi, Filipino lumpia, Indian tandoori, Korean bulgogi, Mongolian hot pot.

Suddenly anyone who looked Asian was expected to be an expert on all Asian cuisines. Total strangers would ask me for culinary advice. I was tempted to make up "food facts" for anyone foolish enough to think of me, the junk food queen, as an Asian gourmet.

Despite my gastronomic shortcomings, I knew there was one essential ingredient common to each of these Asian cuisines. So I dispensed this advice to my inquirers: don't waste the rice.

. . .

Late in 1987, in the months following the October stock market crash, Asian Americans began to notice a distinct New York edge toward people who looked Asian. After several boom years of soar-ing real estate prices and a long streak of mergers and acquisitions, the bust hit the city hard. Sliding real estate markets and a looming recession cast a pall over the region's economic future. Bloomingdale's and Abraham &

Straus's parent, Campeau Corp.; Resorts International; Seaman Furniture Co.; and the junk bond market itself teetered on the brink of collapse. As Wall Street wizard Michael Milken and savings and loan boss Charles Keating, Jr., came under scrutiny for wanton and excessive greed, the state budget had to be slashed to avoid a deficit. Tighter purses at corporate headquarters meant lighter wallets at corner grocery stores. Everyone was feeling pinched.

People were angry, ready to lash out at anyone. I noticed the change. One morning while I crossed the street to get to work, an elderly white man honked impatiently, then spit at me, shouting, "Hurry up, you Asian bitch." Beyond my agitation I felt surprise that he said "Asian," not "Chink" or "Jap." A few weeks later, as I pulled into an empty mall parking lot in New Jersey, a red-faced, white-haired man started yelling, for no apparent reason, "You can't park here. Go back where you came from!" On yet another workday during that same unpleasant period, a midtown Manhattan sales clerk snarled, "You people from Taiwan are all the same . . ." I could tell from his speech that he was from Eastern Europe. His tirade ended when I threw my cup of coffee at him.

By contrast, Japan's bubble economy continued to soar, with Japanese corporate raiders flaunting their megabucks the way New Yorkers used to, before the recession. In New York, the growing presence of industrious Asians who seemed willing to work at any price was a nagging irritation. Between 1980 and 1990, New York had taken in 854,000 immigrants, while at the same time losing almost a half million non-Hispanic whites. Many of the new New Yorkers came from the Caribbean, Latin America, and Asia, bringing an abundance of new cultures and languages. The number of black residents grew by 18 percent, Hispanics by 19 percent, and Asians—by 132 percent. In two decades, New York's Korean American community alone had grown from 30,000 to more than 250,000; many of the Koreans operated small businesses in the city's African American and Afro-Caribbean neighborhoods. With the volatile combination of a poor economy and swelling ranks of eager newcomers, sparks were bound to fly.

The first whiff of trouble came on August 27, 1988, in the Bedford-Stuyvesant section of Brooklyn. A scuffle broke out between two African American women and the Korean American proprietors of the Tropic Market. News spread quickly among African Americans that an elderly black woman and her daughter were "attacked, brutally beaten and threatened with a knife by the owners of the market," according to a flyer signed by a group called the December 12th Movement. (The group was formed in 1986 after a mob of whites killed an African American man whose car had broken down in the largely Italian American neighborhood of Howard Beach, Queens.) The Korean merchants countered that the two women stole a package of fish and refused to open their bags for inspection, then attacked the store owner's wife.

Robert (Sonny) Carson was the leader of the December 12th Movement. Carson viewed Korean-owned stores as part of a larger conspiracy. The group's flyers stated: "The Korean boycott must be seen as an overall campaign to control our community and not a campaign against the Korean people . . . Korean, Arab and Jewish owned stores in our community is economic warfare . . . The Korean merchants are agents of the US government in their conspiracy to destabilize the economy of our community. They are rewarded by the government and financed by big business." The December 12th Movement immediately set its sights on shutting down the Tropic Market and calling for a boycott of all Korean-owned stores, with the stated goal of forcing all Korean merchants out of black neighborhoods.

It was easy to single out the Koreans. By the late 1980s, Koreans owned some 1,500 vegetable markets, 500 fish markets, and 2,500 grocery stores, often in low-income, predominantly black, neighborhoods. The Korean shopkeepers operated at such a low margin that family members each put in sixteen or more hours per day, seven days a week, just to make a go of it. Their long hours meant that there was little time or energy left to develop a relationship with their customers and community. Many of the new immigrants didn't understand the importance of becoming a part of the neighborhood. For others, their limited ability to speak English added another barrier.

The call for a boycott of Korean stores gave release to the black community's simmering anger over economic and social dismemberment—a deep-rooted phenomenon that began long before Koreans came to Bedford-Stuyvesant. This most recent incursion by yet another outsider merchant group only added to the insult, worsened by the gulf between the cultures and the feeling that Koreans didn't show the proper respect or cultural sensitivity to African Americans. The Korean immigrants were not the same as the more familiar—and more acculturated—Chinese Americans and Japanese Americans.

The Tropic Market became a flash point for the discontent. A protest and boycott began outside the store immediately after the incident. Pickets with loudspeakers, led by the December 12th Movement, demonstrated outside the store almost daily. Amid chants of "Pass them by, don't shop, watch them die," community activist Coltrane Chimurenga told a crowd of more than a hundred that Korean merchants were controlling the economy of the black community and were disrespectful to blacks. "We want all Koreans to understand they do not control our community. We must drive them out," he said, and charged that the U.S. government hired Korean merchants to take over black communities. While such arguments usually went unchallenged, at another large protest gathering, a listener disagreed. "I really feel that there's some scapegoating going on here," said an Afro-Caribbean American woman, who noted that she had shopped at Korean stores for twelve years without a problem. Calling the complaints about Koreans "racist propaganda," she said Korean storekeepers provided a service by stocking foods popular with West Indian people.

As the racial animosity intensified, New Yorkers outside Bed-Stuy became increasingly concerned that the hostilities could spread. Bill Chong, a second-generation Chinese American who was then director of the Crisis Prevention Unit of the State Division of Human Rights, decided it was time to intervene. The first step was to bring the black and Korean communities together. Chong called New York State Assemblyman Albert Vann, an African American whose Brooklyn district included Bed-Stuy. "Initially," said Chong, "Vann didn't want to be seen with me because he was afraid some people might think I was Korean." But Chong's work on the Reverend Jesse Jackson's presidential campaigns bolstered his credentials as a potential mediator. Vann agreed to participate in discussions with Sung Soo Kim, executive director of the Korean American Small Business Service Center of New York and spokesperson for the Nostrand-Fulton Korean American Merchants Association in Brooklyn.

The efforts to negotiate a neighborhood peace marked the first time that the Korean storekeepers and African American community leaders came together in New York to resolve what seemed an unbreachable cultural divide. The groups met weekly over a period of three months, trying to reach some common insight on such fundamental issues as the particular significance of equal rights and economic justice to African Americans, or the hardships and problems faced by Korean American storekeepers. Most Korean storekeepers came to the United States after the civil rights movements of the 1960s and had limited knowledge of that struggle; some felt that Koreans were being used as racial cannon fodder in a black–white conflict. At the same time, many African Americans believed that Koreans disliked blacks, were rude, and received special government loans, or secret financing from the Reverend Sun Myung Moon's Unification Church, to open their stores. Each group was burdened with misinformed stereotypes of the other; each wanted recognition and respect.

Not all groups in New York's diverse African American community were willing to negotiate. "Korean merchants not only suck our blood, but they suck the blood of our children," declared one protest leader. The issue of disrespect and Korean stores tapped into a deep well of anger and, at times, ugliness. When a white reporter from the Chicago-based newsmagazine *In These Times* approached the picketers, he was told, "Jewish pig, Zionist dog. We will deal with white faggots who bring their AIDS into our community."

Four months after the initial incident, on December 21, the Korean merchants of Bedford-Stuyvesant agreed to all six demands from the African American negotiators. They apologized for the Tropic Market incident; they promised to open accounts at a black-owned bank, to participate in mutual cultural sensitivity training, and to donate money for scholarships and a program to build black entrepreneurship. Most amazing, the Korean negotiators also agreed to shut down the Tropic Market by helping the owner sell his business. In exchange, the African American negotiators would help end the boycott and in the agreement would acknowledge that Koreans receive no special financing from the U.S. government or the Unification Church for their businesses. This was an important point for Korean Americans, who mainly belonged to mainstream Christian churches and had scrimped over years to buy their businesses. The agreement explained that Koreans used a private investment and lending club system of pooling money with others, called "kye," to finance their businesses. The merchants agreed to assist African Americans in developing their own private credit pools.

By sacrificing the Tropic Market's owner, the other thirty-two Korean merchants of Bedford-Stuyvesant hoped to secure stability for their stores.

The concessions were made to generate some sorely needed goodwill with African Americans that would allow the other Korean American businesses in the city to operate without the threat of a boycott, which the Korean shopkeepers believed to be racially driven, in spite of the agreement.

When the pact was announced, both sides hailed it as a huge step forward. "The agreement ushers in a new era of understanding, respect, and cooperation between our two communities," said Assemblyman Albert Vann. For Korean Americans, the agreement marked the first time that they had established themselves as an organized force that could work with African American leaders and city and state officials. Sung Soo Kim, spokesperson for the merchants, said, "We are very happy to have a channel through which we can do things for the community." Not everyone concurred with their assessments. The December 12th Movement condemned the pact. Bill Chong, with the state's Crisis Prevention Unit, had mixed feelings. "We developed a process and a dialogue, but the store owner was forced out of business," said Chong. "If the other Korean merchants had supported him to stay in business, that might have made a difference later." The experience was a dress rehearsal for what was to come.

Even as the boycott pickets at the Tropic Market were dispersing, the new year of 1989 began with the obituary of the internationally renowned sculptor Isamu Noguchi, whose works graced numerous New York landmarks, from the rock fountain at the entrance of the Metropolitan Museum to the sunken garden at Chase Manhattan Plaza. Within months, the city's racial seismometer spiked again, this time involving the Japanese, over Mitsubishi's purchase of a stake in Rockefeller Center. Japan-born Noguchi's huge steel bas-relief of the five news gatherers had greeted visitors to the Associated Press Building in Rockefeller Center for fifty years, but a Japanese owner was unacceptable.

Another wave of anti-Japanese loathing was pulsing, this time with New York as its epicenter. "A stab in the back" by a "cruel, warlike race," wrote *Newsday* columnist Dennis Duggan. "Remember Pearl Harbor," declared Robert Reno, another *Newsday* columnist. Headlines screamed, "What Next? Will Geishas Replace the Rockettes?" To many Americans, Japanese investment in an American icon was a jarring reminder of the old enemy's resurgence. Sentiments of World War II veterans echoed in articles and letters to the editor: "The Japanese couldn't take us militarily but now they are taking us economically," wrote one *Newsday* reader. "We won the battle but they are winning the war," said another. "I was saddened and ashamed by the recent Japanese buyout of Rockefeller Center . . . things that make America truly American should be left in our own hands."

Mitsubishi's "buyout" of Rockefeller Center amounted to about 14 percent ownership, based on its 51 percent share of all the Rockefeller Group's holdings, but the facts were overwhelmed by the persistent symbolism of the Asian invader. British direct investments in U.S. properties were more than double Japan's, and two thirds of the foreign money in the United States came from Europe, including the other two Axis forces, Germany and Italy. Nevertheless, these foreign investors didn't elicit the same kind of protest. Mitsubishi's investment was compounded by news of a soaring trade imbalance with Japan, whose trade restrictions made it harder for American companies to enter its markets.

Old hostilities and wistful yearnings for days "when enemies were enemies" filled the city's newspapers and airwaves for months. Periodically CBS News and *The New York Times* conducted a joint poll of American attitudes toward Japan and found a marked increase in negativity. Talk shows and editorials, even cartoons maintained the steady drumbeat of ill feeling toward the Japanese. *Kudzu*, a nationally syndicated comic strip, featured a serial storyline about a Japanese company, "Sayonara," that was buying up a backwater southern town whose residents had acquired the inexplicable habit of slanting their eyes with their fingers. The cascading negative reports, commentaries, and columns became a regular agenda item for the Asian American Journalists Association's New York chapter, which struggled to determine what coverage crossed the bounds of fairness and how to get news organizations to address biased reporting.

The constant media imagery of Asians as rapacious intruders, combined with frustrations over the economy, had a violent impact on Asian Americans. In a two-week period in December 1989, at least nine Asian Americans were attacked on New York streets and subways. In Queens, a group of thirty to forty youths calling themselves the Master Race went on a hate rampage in a video arcade, sending five Asian American boys—two Korean Americans and three Chinese Americans—to the hospital. Across the Hudson River in New Jersey, the Dotbusters, whose name referred to the decorative bindi many Hindu women wear on their foreheads, waged a reign of terror against South Asians during the late 1980s. The Dotbusters violently assaulted several South Asian Americans, but in 1989 the youths who killed Navroze Mody, a thirty-year-old Citibank manager, were sentenced to probation. In a bizarre incident that took place on a crowded Brooklyn-bound N train, a man shoved an egg roll in the face of Chinese American Henry Lau, then stabbed him to death while shouting, "Hey, egg roll!" The New York and New Jersey police refused to prosecute any of these as hate crimes, on the grounds that no racial slurs were used. When the Committee Against Anti-Asian Violence, a New York group founded in 1986 by Monona Yin and Mini Liu, complained to the New York Police Department, the head of the bias crimes unit explained that hate speech or slurs had to be uttered *before* an attack; if slurs were made *during* an attack, the police didn't consider it a bias incident. Asian Americans already had difficulties in overcoming notions that they don't experience racism; the arbitrary time distinction only added to the victims' burdens.

The rash of violence against Asian Americans extended beyond New York. On January 17, 1989, in Stockton, California, a white man named Patrick Purdy donned military fatigues and a semiautomatic rifle, then drove to his old school, Cleveland Elementary, which had become 70 percent Asian American, mainly refugee children from Southeast Asia. Firing a hundred rounds of ammunition into the school yard where second and third graders were playing, he killed five children—one Vietnamese and four Cambodian; thirty others were injured. Purdy then killed himself. The police chief immediately rejected the possibility of a racial motive. That night, ABC's *Nightline* covered the shootings, but Ted Koppel didn't ask the obvious question: whether race might be a motive. After viewing the program, I called a colleague at ABC News and learned that the newsroom that night discussed the race factor, yet decided that Koppel shouldn't ask the question, in case the answer was no. But complaints by Asian Americans forced an investigation into the racial aspect of the killings. A special state commission discovered that Purdy often expressed his resentment of Asians—and that anti-Asian racism was most likely the motive for the attack.

With the continued antipathy toward Japan, the list of Asian American hate crime victims grew. Later in 1989, Jim Ming Hai Loo, a Chinese American college student in Raleigh, North Carolina, was killed after Loo and some other Asian American students were harassed at a billiards club. Two white brothers, Lloyd and Robert Piche, said that they didn't like "Orientals" and called the students "stupid gooks." They claimed that their "brothers" "didn't make it back from Vietnam"—when neither they nor any of their brothers had served in the war. The students tried to leave the club, but the Piche brothers went after them, killing Jim Loo. The criminal court found the Piches guilty; Robert was sentenced to thirty-seven years, but Lloyd received only six months, even though he had committed most of the racial harassment. This time, Asian American networks created during the Vincent Chin case succeeded in bringing a federal civil rights prosecution against Lloyd Piche. Finally, in 1991, a jury found him guilty of violating Loo's civil rights—making Piche the first assailant to be convicted in federal court of racially motivated violence against an Asian American. In an Op-Ed piece for *The New York Times* entitled "Another American Racism," I wrote, "Almost as distressing as the rise in such racism has been the failure to acknowledge the anti-Asian racial component of such attacks. Whether expressed by business leaders and politicians in their Japan-bashing, or more overtly, by hate groups, anti-Asian sentiment is rampant."

The violent incidents and the growing strain on Asian Americans went unnoticed in the constant churn of New York, still thick with recession-driven resentment over the sale of Rockefeller Center and other chunks of New York real estate to Japanese investors. A few Asian Americans attempted to force the city to respond to the wave of assaults. "It is outrageous that Asians returning from work [in Chinatown] are being preyed upon, menaced and assaulted. This dangerous situation needs to be addressed aggressively," warned the Committee Against Anti-Asian Violence in a letter to city and police officials.

A ray of hope that racial hostilities in the city might subside came with the election of David Dinkins, the city's first black mayor, who spoke of New York's "gorgeous mosaic" of ethnic groups in his election campaign. But less than three weeks after his inauguration, on January 18, 1990, tensions reignited between African Americans and Afro-Caribbean Americans, and Korean American grocers. Jiselaine Felissaint, a Haitian immigrant, filed a police report charging that she was beaten by the manager and employees of the Family Red Apple Market on Church Avenue in the Flatbush section of Brooklyn, after a dispute over three dollars' worth of plantains and limes. The store owner, Bong Jae Jang, was arrested and charged with third-degree assault.

Many residents in the Flatbush neighborhood were Afro-Caribbean immigrants from the West Indies. Korean grocery stores catered to West Indian tastes, selling mangoes, tamarind, salt beef, pig tails, and sorrel, a dark red root used to make a soft drink. As immigrants, the Koreans and Afro-Caribbeans had much in common—the hardships of adjusting to a new culture and sometimes a new language, as well as the drive to achieve the American dream. But in the complex racial dynamics of America, the gulf between the shopkeepers and their customers was too vast. Instantly, the situation turned volatile. The same issues that sparked the boycott in Bedford-Stuyvesant sixteen months earlier reemerged: that Koreans disrespected and exploited African Americans. Shoppers and passersby from busy Church Avenue rushed to Felissaint's aid and chased Red Apple employees into the street. People threw bottles at the store, prompting the police officer who arrested Jang to shut the store down, in fear of a riot.

Flatbush residents, members of the December 12th Movement, and others began a daily vigil of demonstrations outside the Red Apple. They not only picketed the Red Apple but included Church Fruits, the Korean-owned shop across the street, where a Red Apple employee had reportedly run for cover. The protesters demanded that both stores be shut down permanently; in addition, they wanted apologies from the Korean grocers and arrests of all involved in the alleged beating. Korean merchants in Flatbush offered to participate in sensitivity workshops and to provide more jobs and training for Flatbush residents—borrowing elements of the Bedford-Stuyvesant agreement in hopes of reaching a quick settlement. Both stores also temporarily shut down for a few days to create a cooling-off period.

Tempers continued to flare as the peace offerings made no difference. Raucous crowds of fifty to a hundred people gathered daily to protest the alleged Red Apple attack and the general disrespect black customers felt they were shown by Korean merchants. Each day, more than a hundred NYPD officers in riot gear lined Church Avenue, further aggravating the picketers, who saw the police as representatives of the racial disparities between blacks, whites, and Koreans.

The sketchy details of what happened to Felissaint kept changing, growing more elaborate. At first, it was reported that a Haitian woman was beaten by the manager and employees of the Red Apple. Flyers that came out the following week depicted a more extreme scenario: "Three Korean men assaulted her, kicking and beating her until she was bleeding and just about unconscious. The victim was taken to Caledonia Hospital where she sat for eight hours without any attention and was sent home where she is still suffering from internal injuries." Soon reports circulated that Felissaint had been beaten into a coma and sustained chronic internal injuries. The owners denied it all, claiming instead that Felissaint had refused to pay the correct amount for her items and began flailing about the store. When the manager asked her to leave, she lay down on the floor and began to scream as some other customers told her to stay on the floor.

NYPD's arrest of the wrong man added an element of absurdity. The owner, Bong Jae Jang, was at the barber getting his hair dyed when the incident occurred. But Felissaint and others identified him as the assailant, and he was hauled off to jail. It took months before police dropped charges and arrested his brother, Pong Ok Jang, the store manager, instead. Mistaken identity was also the concern of the owners of Church Fruits, the store across from the Red Apple, which continued to be swept in with the boycott of the Red Apple. "People think we are owned by the same person, but we are different," said Soo Chang, who worked at the store with her husband. The Changs put up large signs in their shopwindow, saying, "We have no connection to the Red Apple. We are being unfairly made party to a dispute." The sign only angered boycotters, and one punched Mrs. Chang in the face. She, too, filed charges, but this and other acts of violence experienced by Korean merchants failed to draw concern from public officials, the news media, or the boycotters, whose stated purpose was to seek redress for the violence against Felissaint.

Initially, the tide of public sympathy was for Jiselaine Felissaint, the injured victim. The Korean American population had burgeoned to an estimated 250,000 in New York, with more than 5,000 small businesses opened, yet a cultural understanding of Koreans was virtually nil. Nor had the Korean merchants done much since their experience in the 1988 Bedford-Stuyvesant boycott to break their isolation. The cultural differences with Americans—including other Asian Americans—were considerable. To Koreans, looking customers directly in the eyes was a rude affront; touching a stranger's hand when giving change, an inappropriate intimacy. The demeanor of Koreans was more abrupt and less self-effacing than Chinese or Japanese—other more familiar Asian American cultures. During those years I heard people of various races and ethnicities complain of experiences with Korean merchants; when I asked Korean American friends what made them so fierce, they said that hundreds of years of harsh colonial occupation made them curt and distrustful, even with each other. But to native-born Americans, the missing cues of friendliness were signs of rudeness.

At the same time, many of the grocers were well educated in Korea, trained as teachers or lawyers, or in other professional fields not marketable in the United States. About 78 percent had college degrees. Their lives as New York greengrocers involved sixteen-to-eighteen-hour days, seven days a week. Grocer Min Chul Shin of the Fresh N' Plus market in Manhattan began each day at midnight, picking up produce at the New York City Terminal Market at Hunts Point, unloading and setting up for the next day, until he closed his store at 10 p.m.; his only sleep would be stolen catnaps in his car. "It's a terrible life, but I have to do it," said Shin. The hours, the stress of the work, and changing family roles that included working wives and rebellious Americanized children took their toll on family life, mental health, and interpersonal relations. The constant occupational threat of robbery, assault, and death mixed dangerously with the prevailing racial stereotypes of African Americans as "crime-prone predators." Such images of blacks were imprinted even before Koreans left for the United States, from Hollywood's global presence and its pervasive representations of black people, to negative impressions of American GIs— many of them African American—after four decades of the U.S. military presence. But it was false to say that all Koreans harbored prejudice against blacks, or that all African Americans were biased against Koreans. Under these conditions, however, Korean Americans, like African Americans, were living inside their own pressure cookers, ready to explode.

For other Asian Americans, the rising antagonism toward Korean Americans was a sore that wouldn't heal. In the way that one Asian group's strife would inevitably spill over to other Asian ethnicities, the ill will toward Koreans was felt by all Asian Americans. Yet it was very different from the anti-Asian racism fostered by Japan-bashing, which involved a foreign Asian country with no link to Asian Americans except heritage. We could be neither held responsible nor blamed for the acts of a foreign government. In contrast, the situation with the Korean American stores seemed different. Privately Asian Americans asked themselves, what's going on with Korean merchants? Why is this happening so often? Besides Flatbush and Bedford-Stuyvesant, there were reports of flare-ups in Philadelphia; Washington, D.C.; Cincinnati; Oakland; Los Angeles; and elsewhere. The Chinese, Japanese, and Filipino Americans who were born in the United States were as ignorant of the Korean shopkeepers and their culture as everyone else; relationships between the American-born Asians and the immigrant Koreans were tenuous at best. If Asian Americans were hesitant to blame Korean Americans, they also found it hard to stand with them.

Within the Asian American community, there were reports that some black nationalist groups in different cities were fabricating incidents to exploit the provocative rumors about Korean businesses and the belief that all Koreans disrespected blacks. No one knew what to do with such stories. Asian business owners in enclaves like Chinatown didn't see the need to enter the quagmire of interracial conflict. Others who had business dealings with African Americans preferred to distance themselves from the Koreans, an echo of the "I'm not Japanese" days during World War II.

Asian American community activists, who saw themselves as allies with African Americans, were in a quandary. To support the Korean grocers could jeopardize the solidarity built over years of working together for civil rights, community empowerment, and other issues. Yet the virulent innuendo of the boycott bore an uncanny resemblance to other Asian-bashing times. "Asian American activists were caught in a dilemma," said Bill Chong, then with the New York City Human Rights Department. Chong himself had been politicized in the Asian American and Third World movements. "It was hard to deal with the idea of racism in communities of color. Neither blacks nor Asians were willing to fess up to prejudice."

Fears that all Asian Americans could be seen as enemies or targets in the way that Korean Americans had been stereotyped stymied Asian American activists. "We were paralyzed," said Manhattan resident Julie Azuma, a third-generation Japanese American community leader. "I grew up in Chicago with African Americans as close friends, closer than other Asians. Suddenly I was an enemy, a potential racist. I could no longer assume the alliances I had with African Americans would be there." Longtime activist and Harlem resident Yuri Kochiyama, the second-generation Japanese American who had cradled Malcolm X as he lay dying, was still respected for her unwavering support for African American causes, but the goodwill no longer extended to other Asian Americans. It seemed that decades of work by Asian American activists with the African American community—

against racism; supporting black liberation and Third World struggles; for ending apartheid in South Africa; for integrating trade unions; and in other areas of mutual work—had suddenly evaporated.

Asian Americans had become suspicious characters again—but this time cast as surrogate whites, a role that was not anticipated once we placed ourselves with African Americans in the black–white dialogue. At a time when we needed vision and fortitude, the old insecurities came flooding back.

In the months following the January 1990 incident at the Red Apple, Church Avenue became an encampment: angry, determined boycotters, the phalanx of police in riot gear, and the stony, entrenched shopkeeper standing amid his empty shelves. Over time, the image of the Korean storekeeper gradually changed: from the Asian immigrant interloper, the besieged Red Apple owner came to symbolize the racial frustrations and fears of both blacks and whites. Whites identified with the Asian American merchant as a target of black fury and accusations of racism, and they demanded that the newly elected black mayor step in to control the "unruly African American masses"; Alvin Berk, chairman of the polarized Brooklyn community board, called on Dinkins to end "lawlessness in the service of minority empowerment."

To many African Americans, the Korean stores represented the economic disenfranchisement at the hands of the white oppressors and their Asian surrogates. Charges by whites of black racism only further antagonized Sonny Carson and his supporters. Moderate Haitian community leaders, willing to negotiate with the Koreans, reported getting death threats from militant boycotters, who kept people from entering the stores by calling them "Uncle Tom" and other, more graphic expletives. Just as American-born Asians and the immigrant Koreans had divergent, even conflicting, concerns, African American groups with a larger political strategy were at odds with Afro-Caribbean immigrants who had a simple desire for peace in their neighborhood.

At the eye of the storm was Bong Jae Jang, the owner of the Red Apple. Although he was one of the two central characters in the conflict that started the mess, his story and persona were absent. The news media managed to avoid speaking to him even while relentlessly tracking the collapse of his livelihood; he was just another Korean grocer. At a reception for

Asian American journalists in August 1990 sponsored by *The New York Times* and hosted by Max Frankel, its executive editor, I asked the editors why they had waited months to interview the Red Apple's proprietor. One of the editors replied that the venerable newspaper wasn't able to find an interpreter in New York who spoke Korean, though that hadn't deterred reporters from other newspapers, since Jang actually spoke some English.

New Yorkers reserved a special antipathy for Mayor Dinkins, who remained silent about the turmoil as the weeks and months dragged on. To the boycotters, his silence was acquiescence to whites; Carson tarred him as "a so-called black man" and "a traitor to his people." Whites saw him as ineffectual, unwilling to criticize or control "his people" no matter how disruptive or dangerous the situation. To Korean Americans, the mayor was sacrificing them for his own political expediency. In editorials, speeches, and rallies, Flatbush residents as well as blacks, whites, and Asians across New York exhorted the mayor to do something.

Various government officials tried to find some way to defuse the conflict and address the black community's demands for economic empowerment, hoping to duplicate what had been accomplished in Bedford-Stuyvesant. A retinue of city officials, from Deputy Mayor Bill Lynch and Dennis deLeón, the city human rights commissioner, to the Mayor's Community Assistance Unit, struggled for a resolution. Korean merchants agreed to participate in ethnic sensitivity training and to provide jobs for Flatbush residents, but boycotters refused to negotiate. On the other hand, the city put no pressure on the NYPD to enforce a court order requiring pickets to stand fifty feet from the store entrances. Despite calls to the mayor from Jang's attorney to order the dozens of police standing idle at the picket line to enforce the law, they never did.

Without the mayor's visible involvement, there was no respite from the months of excoriating hostility. New York Human Rights Commissioner Dennis deLeón said the mayor deeply resented the notion that, as an African American, he should be accountable for the actions of all blacks. The mayor's resentment, said deLeón, kept him from assuming leadership and putting an end to the fray, as his constituents were demanding.

A bizarre turn of events came in May, at the start of Asian Pacific American Heritage Month. Pulitzer Prize–winning columnist Jimmy Breslin exploded in a raging tantrum at fellow *Newsday* reporter Ji-Yeon Yuh, a Korean American, who criticized one of his columns as "sexist." Storming into the busy newsroom, he shouted, "The fucking bitch doesn't know her place. She's a little dog, a little cur running along the street. She's a yellow cur. Let's make it racial. She's a slant-eyed cunt."

Yuh wasn't present for Breslin's display, but a few dozen shocked *Newsday* reporters were. New York's huge media corps began buzzing. Columnist Joe Klein wrote in *New York* magazine, "Even old friends seemed to be turning weird, like Jimmy Breslin."

In contrast to their paralysis over the Flatbush boycott, Asian Americans responded immediately to Breslin's string of racial slurs. I was then serving as president of the New York chapter of the Asian American Journalists Association, and we organized a joint press conference with the Organization of Asian Women and the Committee Against Anti-Asian Violence. Together, we demanded that *Newsday* fire Breslin. "Asian Americans are outraged by the racial and sexual slurs made by Jimmy Breslin against a Korean American reporter at *Newsday*. We must remind Mr. Breslin that violent hate crimes are increasing . . . There is no place for such poison in our multicultural society, and certainly not at a reputable news organization like *Newsday* . . . The last thing New York needs is a hate-filled bigot masquerading as the 'real' New Yorker," I said in my statement to reporters. Our stand was followed by similar statements by the National Association of Black Journalists and the National Association of Hispanic Journalists.

The extreme invectives and their prizewinning source became instant news across the nation, and for several days the trials of Jimmy overshadowed the main event in Flatbush. The city's close-knit circle of newspaper columnists rushed to defend Breslin and reassure New Yorkers that he was no racist; so did another pal, New York Governor Mario Cuomo. They chided the Korean American reporter for provoking Breslin. *New York Post* columnist Jerry Nachman used more refined language than the December 12th Movement's in Flatbush, but his conclusion was the same: he declared Ji-Yeon Yuh "an unwanted intruder" and warned that because she had hurled the race card at Breslin, no editor, presumably white, would ever hire a troublemaker like her. Nachman overlooked a minor detail: it was Breslin who made race the issue, not Yuh, who was leaving *Newsday* anyway to obtain a doctorate in history so that she could teach Asian American studies.

For Ji-Yeon Yuh, now a professor at Northwestern University, the episode was a turning point. "It forced me to be more honest about the pervasiveness of racism and sexism and the ways in which Asians and Asian Americans are dispensable to so-called liberals and progressives, and how Asian American women are dispensable to so-called white feminists, who didn't say a word in our defense. At the same time, I was thrilled to see such an active Asian American community, who understood that the issue was not about me or even about Breslin, but about racism and sexism in American society."

As the anger over Breslin's racial and sexual slurs raged on, more than five hundred people attending New York's Asian American Heritage Festival signed a petition demanding his dismissal. Columns and letters to the editors by Asian Americans appeared in newspapers around the country, all decrying the racial animus toward Asians that seemed to be flourishing with impunity. Breslin was eventually punished, not so much because of our efforts, but because of his own ignorance. Breslin called in to the Howard Stern show to joke about his outburst and exchange jabs with Stern about Koreans. This second act of racial insensitivity led *Newsday*'s managing editor, Anthony Marro, to suspend Breslin for two weeks. It was a victory for Asian Americans at a time of racial uncertainty and stress, when we needed all the affirmation we could find.

Everything changed when *The New York Times* ran an editorial on May 8, 1990, four months after the boycott began. It called Sonny Carson "a convicted kidnapper and racial provocateur" and exhorted "every fair-minded New Yorker, starting with Mayor Dinkins" to condemn the "tide of ugly, racist rhetoric." While other New York dailies had previously criticized the boycott, none had the impact of the *Times*'s strongly worded editorial, which propelled the conflict into the national limelight. With the prospect of a mass audience, the ranks of the boycotters swelled—and their noisome "Koreans must go!" rhetoric escalated into an endless stream of racial innuendo. Chinese American Peter Kwong, author of *The New Chinatown* and columnist for *The Village Voice*, had written a number of articles in support of the boycotters, arguing that Asian Americans could make a difference in race relations by backing African American economic interests to end financial redlining of inner-city neighborhoods, for example, as well as by calling for a speedy investigation of the Red

Apple Market incident. But when Kwong visited the picket line, he was told, "This is a black people's community. What the fuck are you doing here?"

In Flatbush and throughout the city, racial tensions were at a breaking point. News crews on location found themselves under attack, their vans and equipment destroyed. News photographers were rushing out to buy bulletproof vests. A City College professor, Michael Levin, set off a firestorm by claiming that blacks are inferior to whites and more likely to be criminals. The city's beleaguered mayor finally came out on May 11 with a public statement about the city's racial strife, imploring New Yorkers to help build a city of "peace and dignity" and to "learn understanding from our differences."

The ranks of the boycotters swelled to six hundred, forcing police to shut down Church Avenue. Adding to the volatility, a judge finally ordered police to clear picketers away from the store entrances. Inevitably, violence erupted, as Sonny Carson forewarned with his crude remarks: "In the future, there will be funerals, not boycotts." After midnight on May 13, less than forty-eight hours after the mayor's appeal for racial peace, black youths threw a beer bottle and smashed the window of some Vietnamese men who lived in a ground-floor apartment two blocks from the Family Red Apple Market. When occupant Tuan Ana Cao and two other men ran out to see what was wrong, they were met by a group of black teenagers who hurled bottles and racial insults: "Fuck the Chinese! Fuck the Koreans!" Cao was soon on the ground, bleeding profusely, his skull fractured by a baseball bat swung by one of the youths.

The assault on the Vietnamese was the result of the months of racial friction. The city anguished over the mistaken identity of the Vietnamese, attacked because they were thought to be Korean.

Stung by the apparent racial attack, Mayor Dinkins responded with a forceful statement condemning racial violence no matter what the color of the attacker or the victim. "Tuan Ana Cao is any one of the thousands of victims of lynch mobs in the Deep South in the years that followed slavery," said Dinkins, making his first public statement about black hostility toward Asians.

But the mayor's criticism of black violence against Asians was met with immediate defensiveness by black leaders, who tried to convince the public that the long boycott only targeted the two Korean stores, as opposed to all Korean merchants. They began to tone down slogans that called Korean Americans "bloodsuckers" and "monkeys." But there was no misconstruing the boycott's racially divisive content, with its demands— "Do not shop with people who don't look like us!"

The Reverend Herbert Daughtry, pastor of the House of the Lord Church on Atlantic Avenue in Brooklyn, also argued that the boycott was not racial. "Members of the community have singled out the store as a spot where abuses have taken place," Daughtry said. "Other Korean stores are doing quite well." After visiting the hospital to pray for Cao, Daughtry said the attack was a street confrontation that only coincidentally involved racial slurs—and therefore was not racially motivated. It was a surprising argument for a civil rights leader to make.

Taking their cues from the black community leaders, the police retracted their position that the attack on the Vietnamese was a bias incident, in spite of the mayor's antiracist message. Then Police Commissioner Lee Brown, an African American, sounded rather like the white columnists who had rushed to Jimmy Breslin's defense when he offered this reasoning: "In the heat of the moment, you may say many things. There is absolutely nothing to suggest they went to that location because of Asians being in that apartment."

If the police and city leaders didn't recognize the racism of the attack, the people of New York did. They had had enough; the attack on the Vietnamese in Flatbush proved that the animosities had gone too far, way beyond a neighborhood dispute with two stores.

Support quickly turned to Jang and his market. Members of the First Korean Church of Brooklyn held a prayer circle to end bigotry in front of the Red Apple Market the morning after Cao was hospitalized. Wiping tears from their eyes, they presented Jang with $200 collected from church members.

On May 14, the Monday after the attack, an African American teacher from nearby Erasmus High School, the rallying site for the boycotters, became the first black man to publicly defy the picketers. The teacher, Fred McCray, took fifty of his students on a shopping trip into the Red Apple after a classroom discussion of the boycott. "They want to put an end to this chaotic circus atmosphere," said McCray of his students. As they walked past jeering protesters, some shouted death threats and slogans like "What's the fortune cookie say? No money today!" The quiet schoolteacher was immediately reviled by boycotters, who branded him a race traitor for standing with the Koreans, and demanded that his teaching credentials be revoked. But in the news media he was lauded for his moral courage. His deed emboldened others to cross the picket lines to end the boycott.

In significant numbers, others from the community began to shop again at the Red Apple. A neighborhood teenager told reporters, "I'm buying an apple here, and I don't even like apples!" A man stopped at the Red Apple and dropped off a bag with an anonymous letter and cash. Jang cried when he read it, and taped the note to his empty shopwindow. It read:

> *To my brother Koreans:*
>
> *I am a Black American born in Brooklyn raised 20 years in Bedford-Stuyvesant. I cannot apologize for the treatment my brothers and sisters are giving to my Korean brothers. Instead I can only suffer. I can only feel pain as my Korean brothers and sisters feel. If any man has the authority to throw the first stone at his neighbor, it should be me. Instead I only feel LOVE.*
>
> *Please accept my small donation . . . along with these few words. "This is hard-earned money." I'm sorry and I only ask that you feel forgiveness in your heart. And please continue. Keep faith.*

The racial attack on the Vietnamese men forced other Asian Americans to confront their mute hope that silence would safeguard them from rancor. Now that African Americans began to defy the boycott, Asian Americans had no excuse for holding back. Paul Yee, the president of a major Chinatown organization, the Chinese Consolidated Benevolent Association, took a busload of Chinese Americans from Chinatown to cross the picket line and to shop at the Red Apple.

Yet even that gesture met with divided opinion. Peter Kwong reported in *The Village Voice* that at a gathering of Chinatown workers, the topic of the boycott came up. "We should not take sides, because both Koreans and blacks are minorities," said a woman garment worker. A waiter thought that it would be foolhardy to cross the picket line. "This kind of action will only inflame the blacks against the Asians, pushing the conflict to be even more racist than it is."

For Korean American storekeepers, the attack on Cao pushed them one step closer to the narrow edge of violence they faced daily—especially Red Apple owner Jang, who told reporters, "I feel very badly and I'm quite frightened for myself." He regularly received death and arson threats over the phone, and at one point the police removed several bombs from the rooftop of his store. "I came here with a lot of hope and promise and I'm not going back until that's broken, and it's not broken yet," Jang said. "I have every right to live and work in this country. I have eight years on my lease and until that's up I'm not going anywhere."

Finally, prodded by the fear that they, like the Vietnamese American men, might be targets, too, other Asian groups pressed the mayor for action. A few days after Cao's skull was fractured, about forty people representing twenty Asian organizations met at City Hall to discuss the rise in violent attacks against Asians. Store owner Bong Jae Jang also attended the meeting and stormed out abruptly, apparently angered by the sudden posturing of Asian Americans who had been absent over the many months of the boycott.

Chong Duck Byun, president of the Korean Association of New York, called on Mayor David Dinkins to act. In a strongly worded letter to *Newsday*, Byun wrote: "The mayor waited and tried to work things out. We waited. But now it is time to act. To fail to speak out every day is to allow racist bigots to gain credibility and to spread their poison."

If Asian Americans were concerned about losing ground with African Americans, it was already too late. In an effort to reach out, representatives of the Committee Against Anti-Asian Violence met with the boycott leaders, including the December 12th Movement. The encounter was discouraging. On May 23, representatives from CAAAV reported at a membership meeting that the boycotters resented the reference to anti-Asian violence, and harshly criticized a CAAAV member who mentioned "scapegoating," insisting that blacks were incapable of being "racist." They also accused CAAAV of being "nationalistic"—only interested in Asians.

Another Asian American activist group, the Asian American Legal Defense and Education Fund, participated in an interracial harmony march through Flatbush on June 23, singing "We Shall Overcome." The group's executive director, Margaret Fung, said at the rally, "We understand and acknowledge the frustrations and anger that African Americans have expressed over their lack of economic empowerment. As Asian Americans, we share these sentiments and emphasize that many of us are also struggling for our survival." The racial harmony march ended in a violent melee, as boycotters began a pushing and shoving match, injuring an elderly woman from the neighborhood who often shopped at the Red Apple. Neighborhood residents filed their own lawsuits against the boycotters to get them to stop.

Finally, Korean Americans took to the streets. In September, fully nine months after the boycott began, a coalition of Korean Americans organized a massive rally at City Hall. More than twelve thousand Koreans booed the mayor. The coordinator of the event, B. J. Sa, head of the Korean Produce Association, said most of the people who demonstrated had to close their stores in order to attend. More than half of the Korean American–owned businesses in New York shut down that day. "It was not a demonstration against blacks, but against the failure of leadership to help us end this boycott. We tried to change, to be closer to the black community for racial harmony, but they weren't interested," said Sa.

"It was the first time Koreans got together as a group," said Grace Lyu-Volckhausen, of Governor Cuomo's Asian American Advisory Council. "The message was sent that you will hear our response when you step on our toes. It created a momentum, especially among the young." The momentum pushed Korean Americans and African Americans to find their own ways to bridge their cultural differences, independent of government intervention. For example, Korean church congregations began to reach out to African Americans, sponsoring several cultural exchange trips to Korea for members of the black community.

Eventually Mayor Dinkins made the symbolic gesture of visiting the besieged shops and crossing the picket line to buy some potatoes, apples, oranges, and melons. "Let this boycott end so that the work of bringing this community back together can begin," he said. But it was too little, too late. His actions had no impact on the boycotters, who called him "Stinkin' Dinkins." By January 1991, on the one-year anniversary of the boycott, six hundred protesters held a rally, still insisting that the stores must go.

It seemed like the facts of what really transpired at the Family Red Apple Market would never be uncovered—and if they ever were, they wouldn't matter. By the time of the misdemeanor assault trial of Pong Ok Jang, the owner's brother, a year after the original incident, the presumed disrespect by Koreans toward blacks was etched in the minds of a city and a nation. The Korean storekeepers and Jiselaine Felissaint gave their radically conflicting and media-worn accounts in Brooklyn criminal court. But then a surprise witness, another customer, came forward and testified that Felissaint had not been beaten.

Alma Stein, an African American resident of Flatbush, told the courtroom that she was with her son buying some peppers when she heard Felissaint and the cashier argue in "broken English"—Haitian-Creole-English and Korean-English. She saw Felissaint throw some items at the cashier. When the store manager asked her to leave, the Haitian woman lay down on the floor and began to scream. Other customers began shouting at Felissaint to stay on the ground, that she could collect a lot of money. Stein said Felissaint was not slapped, knocked down, or kicked, as alleged.

When the six-member jury acquitted Jang of all charges after deliberating three and a half hours, the Korean American sank into his seat and sobbed uncontrollably. The Korean American community was vindicated and hoped that the verdict would bolster their claims that they were not abusive to customers. Celebrations were short-lived, however, as boycotters denounced the verdict and vowed to continue picketing the stores. Just hours after Pong Ok Jang's acquittal, ten boycotters entered the Red Apple, put their hands together in a pistol shape, pointed at Bong Jae Jang, and shouted "Die," pretending to pull the trigger. Said one Flatbush resident who supported continuing the boycott, "It has little to do whether the woman was hit or not. It's about the lack of respect Koreans have for blacks in general." Mayor Dinkins made a toothless plea for an end to the strife. The boycott continued for another few months, until Bong Jae Jang decided to give up and sold his store to a Korean couple. Even with the acquittal, his business couldn't recover. The new owners immediately put up a "New Management" sign and changed the name of the store at 1823 Church Avenue to Caribbean Fruits and Grocery. Two weeks later, the protesters disappeared.

After a seventeen-month boycott, the showdown between the Korean American merchants and the African American boycotters was finally over. Jiselaine Felissaint reportedly moved back to Haiti, dropping her $6 million civil suit against Bong Jae Jang. Fred McCray, the Erasmus High School teacher who crossed the picket lines to support the Red Apple merchants, was transferred to another school as a result of death threats he received after his shopping trip. His marriage fell apart because his wife disagreed with his stand.

Bong Jae Jang made a fresh start with another store in a different section of Brooklyn. He said he refused to succumb to the boycotters because he had done nothing wrong. Jang became a symbol to Korean immigrants of the discrimination and language handicaps they face and was named Small Businessman of 1996 by the Korean American Small Business Service Center of New York. "We honored him because of his bravery and courage to overcome his difficulties," said Sung Soo Kim, executive director of the group. "He did not lose his business although he was a victim of New York society."

Korean Americans in New York paid a hefty price to learn economic and political survival, American style. During the seventeen-month boycott, Jang's gross sales had dropped from $8,000 to a few hundred dollars a week, but he survived through donations from other Korean storekeepers and church congregations. "Before the boycott, if there was some problem, we'd say, 'That's not our house' and not worry about it," Jang said. "But then it came to the point where we didn't know who would be next."

Several Korean American groups worked to improve communications with African American and other communities, sponsoring scholarships, becoming involved in neighborhood events, donating five thousand turkeys to the needy on Thanksgiving, offering small-business workshops, conducting regular cultural exchange missions to Korea, and developing political ties. The Korean Produce Association issued a booklet to members, with such advice as "Don't speak Korean in stores," "Try to make eye contact with customers," "Make a personal touch when giving change," and "If there is a possible theft, don't chase after." "We tell our members, this is America, don't hold on to old customs," said executive director B. J. Sa, who was twice awarded the Martin Luther King Award by African American community groups for contributions made by his association.

One month after Jang's acquittal, a supermarket employee at a Korean-owned grocery store in Queens allegedly hit an eleven-year-old boy he suspected of shoplifting. This time, leaders of local community groups, the store's owner, and representatives of the Dinkins administration and the police department acted immediately to resolve the issue, to calm the neighborhood, and to keep outsiders who did not live in the community from entering the dispute. "We don't want this to be a

Brooklyn-type situation," said Ruby Muhammad, one of the community leaders.

In 1993, having lost the confidence of New Yorkers, David Dinkins, the city's first African American mayor, failed in his bid for reelection after serving only one term. Insiders cite his mishandling of the Family Red Apple Market boycott as the beginning of his downfall. "People wanted the mayor to control the 'savages,' " said Dennis deLeón, the mayor's chief negotiator during the boycott. "It cost him his office."

For the larger Asian American community, the prolonged drama marked two steps back. Not only did our political ambivalence mean that we failed to support Korean Americans against what some called racial extortion, but the rift of ill feeling had only deepened with many of the various African American groups. While some Korean Americans and African Americans attempted to build bridges, the young pan–Asian American organizations had far to go in building broad alliances with African Americans, Afro-Caribbean Americans, and other communities— including the more recent Asian American immigrants, such as Korean Americans.

Perhaps more disturbing, and potentially more damaging, was the relative ease in which Asian Americans could move back into the shadows, even with Korean Americans on center stage as the target of black discontent. The paralysis shifted Asian Americans back into a place of uncertainty over where we belonged in the landscape of a white–black society, afraid of stepping on the moving fault lines, looking to others for safety rather than taking our own principled stand. Hard questions remained from the Red Apple boycott: how could we build and maintain relations with African Americans and other people of color while safeguarding the equal rights of Asian Americans—whose interests may occasionally conflict with other communities of color? It was clear, however, that the answers would not be found back in the shadows.

# · 5 ·

# Gangsters, Gooks, Geishas, and Geeks

*Ching chong Chinaman sitting on a rail, along came a white man and snipped off his tail.*

*Ah so. No tickee, no washee. So sorry, so sollee.*

*Chinkee, Chink. Jap, Nip, zero, kamikaze. Dothead, flat face, flat nose, slant eye, slope. Slit, mamasan, dragon lady. Gook, VC, Flip, Hindoo.*

By the time I was ten, I'd heard such words so many times I could feel them coming before they parted lips. I knew they were meant in the unkindest way. Still, we didn't talk about these incidents at home, we just accepted them as part of being in America, something to learn to rise above.

---

*Demonstrators at the Broadway opening of* Miss Saigon *in 1991 (Corky Lee)*

The most common taunting didn't even utilize words but a string of unintelligible gobbledygook that kids—and adults—would spew as they pretended to speak Chinese or some other Asian language. It was a mockery of how they imagined my parents talked to me.

Truth was that Mom and Dad rarely spoke to us in Chinese, except to scold or call us to dinner. Worried that we might develop an accent, my father insisted that we speak English at home. This, he explained, would lessen the hardships we might encounter and make us more acceptable as Americans.

I'll never know if my father's language decision was right. On the one hand, I, like most Asian Americans, have been complimented countless times on my spoken English by people who assumed I was a foreigner. "My, you speak such good English," they'd cluck. "No kidding, I ought to," I would think to myself, then wonder: should I thank them for assuming that English isn't my native language? Or should I correct them on the proper usage of "well" and "good"?

More often than feeling grateful for my American accent, I've wished that I could jump into a heated exchange of rapid-fire Chinese, volume high and spit flying. But with a vocabulary limited to *"Ni hao?"* (How are you?) and *"Ting bu dong"* (I hear but don't understand)), meaningful exchanges are woefully impossible. I find myself smiling and nodding like a dashboard ornament. I'm envious of the many people I know who grew up speaking an Asian language yet converse in English beautifully.

Armed with standard English and my flat New Jersey "a," I still couldn't escape the name-calling. I became all too familiar with other names and faces that supposedly matched mine—Fu Manchu, Suzie Wong, Hop Sing, Madame Butterfly, Charlie Chan, Ming the Merciless—the "Asians" produced for mass consumption. Their faces filled me with shame whenever I saw them on TV or in the movies. They defined my face to the rest of the world: a sinister Fu, Suzie the whore, subservient Hop Sing, pathetic Butterfly, cunning Chan, and warlike Ming. Inscrutable Orientals all, real Americans none. With the exception of Suzie Wong, the prostitute, and Hop Sing, the house "boy," they weren't even played by real Asian actors. They were white actors in hideous "yellowface" makeup, playing cartoon characters created by non-Asian writers.

Real Asian culture had its own sinister characters. I got my first glimpse of an evil Chinese villain from a Chinese book when I was about six years old. My mother was an avid reader of Chinese pulp fiction: "storybooks," she called them. Many were illustrated with black-and-white line drawings and printed on cheap newsprint perfumed with incense and camphor. I'd spend hours on the bedroom floor, engrossed in the pictures. Unable to read Chinese, I guessed at the stories. One memorable book had a figure so malevolent that I could hardly look at the page: a hunched and wizened man whose narrow mustache snaked to the ground, draped in baggy black clothes that couldn't conceal his long, curling fingernails. In other words, he was the very essence of Fu Manchu.

But this guy was created in Hong Kong, not Hollywood. At night, he visited the homes of hapless men and women, who looked as normal to me as my own family. With his razor-sharp fingernails, he ripped open their bodies, slinking away with a gory blob in his clawlike hands. I asked my mother to tell me more. "This book is called *Monster Take Your Heart Out*," she translated. That was no comfort. I spent many sleepless nights guarding my heart against the monster.

Unlike the Take-Your-Heart-Out Monster, Hollywood's Fu Manchu never caused me to lose sleep. Even as a child, I found him utterly phony. Yet he provoked another kind of fear in me, the dread that this singular exaggerated image might stimulate a new round of unintelligible gobbledygook from my schoolmates. Worse still, some kids seemed to think that the fake Fu was real and that real Chinese people were just like him.

In my mom's storybooks, the old guy was the exception, a horrible "monster." There were plenty of other characters—everyday Chinese people who tended to their basic grooming needs. This offered a reassuring counter to the real-world confusion over Fu, even when I knew that the everyday storybook characters were destined for a monster of a heart attack.

.  .  .

In Philip Kan Gotanda's 1988 play *Yankee Dawg You Die*, two Asian American actors confront each other. Bradley, the fresh young actor, accuses Vincent, an experienced elder, of being an Asian American Uncle Tom, a yellow Stepin Fetchit. Vincent tries to explain. "That's all there was, Bradley. That's all there was! But you don't think I wouldn't have wanted to play a better role than that bucktoothed, groveling waiter? I would have killed for a better role where I could have played an honest-to-god human being with real emotions. I would have killed for it . . ."

Bradley retorts, "See, you think every time you do one of those demeaning roles, the only thing lost is *your* dignity. That the only person who has to pay is you. Don't you see that every time you do that millions of people in movie theaters will see it? Believe it. Every time you do any old stereotypic role just to pay the bills, someone has to pay for it—and it ain't you. No. It's some Asian kid innocently walking home. 'Hey, it's a Chinaman gook!' 'Rambo, Rambo, Rambo!' "

Gotanda's characters captured the very real conversations taking place among Asian Americans. Ever since the silent screen days, portrayals of Asians on stage, screen, and TV have fit into a narrow band of selections. Some, like the sinister alien spy, have become archetypal straitjackets for Asian American actors and audiences. Periodically, a particularly insulting film incites storms of protest by angry Asian Americans—the occasional outburst from a community that has grown accustomed, or perhaps resigned, to the meager set of offerings called entertainment.

The most visible of those protests was the rebellion against the Broadway musical *Miss Saigon*. Led by Asian American actors in New York and Los Angeles, the uprising reverberated from Broadway to London and Hollywood, and resulted, for a brief period, in the cancellation of the multimillion-dollar extravaganza.

What initially provoked the protest was not the play's hackneyed story line or its stereotypic characters but the notion that real Asian actors ought to have a chance to play Asian characters. At issue was the nameless Vietnamese character referred to simply as the Engineer. The brothel's conniving pimp and manager, he became the spark that set off the protest, pitting Tony Award winners—playwright David Henry Hwang and actor B. D. Wong—as well as the Asian American acting community and their union, Actors' Equity, against one of the theater's most successful and powerful producers, Cameron Mackintosh. Only later would Asian Americans take up the issue of the play's offensive content.

Britain's Cameron Mackintosh was the heavyweight in the rarefied air of theatrical producers. His three-hundred-some international shows included *Cats*, *The Phantom of the Opera*, and *Les Misérables*. *Miss Saigon* first opened at London's Theatre Royal, Drury Lane, in 1989. A box office smash, the show was sold out a year in advance, with scalped tickets going for as much as $150. The production was expected to be an even bigger hit in New York. When the controversy over the Engineer struck, advance ticket sales for the Broadway show had already reached an unprecedented $24 million.

Despite *Miss Saigon*'s popularity, its story was problematic. Set against the fall of Saigon in 1975, this version of the sacrificial Asian sex object featured a war-damaged American soldier boy who meets a Vietnamese virgin-whore at a Saigon brothel. As Saigon collapses, he leaves her behind, not knowing she is pregnant with their child. After she bears a half-white, half-Vietnamese son, she dreams of his future with his father. The unscrupulous, conniving pimp who brought the couple together tries to use the son as his ticket to America. Playwright Alain Boublil attributed his inspiration for Miss Saigon to a photo of a Vietnamese family he saw in *France-Soir* newspaper in 1985. But the theme was familiar and disturbing, a white male fantasy borrowed from Puccini's opera *Madama Butterfly*: sexy Asian woman falls for heroic white man; he uses, then abandons her; distraught, she kills herself.

Starring as the Engineer on the London stage was the acclaimed Welsh-born actor Jonathan Pryce. Tall and gangly, with long and decidedly British features, Pryce did not make a convincing Vietnamese, as the original libretto called for. This was remedied by declaring the pimp to be Eurasian, and applying heavy makeup to eye prosthetics to create an epicanthic "slant" to Pryce's Caucasian eyes.

In Britain, the use of eye prosthetics and yellowface makeup to "Asianize" white actors attracted little attention. But on the American stage and screen such practices were equated with racial mockery and had fallen into disuse since the days of the civil rights movement. In the way that African Americans rejected blackface, the use of yellowface in a major theater production in 1990 touched a raw nerve.

Until recent decades, the occasional Asian character in a leading role was routinely performed by a white actor attempting to interpret Asian qualities. Rarely did a real Asian play a major role, even if the role was for an Asian character. Since few American audiences before the 1970s had contact with any real Asian people, the actors' portrayals, no matter how inauthentic, were readily accepted. Real Asian actors were relegated to minor roles as servants, sidekicks, and teeming masses.

The list of white actors who have donned yellowface while playing Asian roles, compiled by actor Mary Lee, reads like a Hollywood and Broadway *Who's Who*: Loretta Young, Edward G. Robinson, Lana Turner, Fred Astaire, Lillian Gish, Helen Hayes, Bela Lugosi, Jennifer Jones, Angie

Dickinson, Shirley MacLaine; Mary Pickford in *Madame Butterfly*; Katharine Hepburn in *Dragon Seed*; Luise Rainer and Paul Muni in *The Good Earth*; John Wayne as Genghis Khan in *The Conqueror*; Mickey Rooney as the buck-toothed buffoon Mr. Yunioshi in *Breakfast at Tiffany's*; David Wayne, Burgess Meredith, and Marlon Brando in the Broadway and film versions of *The Teahouse of the August Moon*; Colleen Dewhurst in *The Good Woman of Setzuan*; Ricardo Montalban in *Sayonara*; David Carradine in the TV series *Kung Fu*; Boris Karloff and Warner Oland as Fu Manchu, and Oland as Charlie Chan.

These pseudo-Asian actors were often celebrated for their "interpretations" of "Orientals." In the nineteenth century, yellowface was used in *Ah Sin*, a play by Bret Harte and Mark Twain, which was promoted as "The Great and Original Creation of the Heathen Chinese." Reviewers praised its "truthfulness to nature and freedom from caricature"—this at a time when most information about Asians came in the form of Yellow Peril hysteria from publications like *The W.A.S.P.* Even in 1961, *The New York Times* lauded Mickey Rooney's yellowface performance in *Breakfast at Tiffany's*, saying, "Mickey Rooney's bucktoothed, myopic Japanese is broadly exotic"; Asian Americans would have described his portrayal as humiliating and degrading, the stuff of schoolboy racial taunts.

Anna May Wong (1907–61) and Sessue Hayakawa (1889–1973) were the rare Asian actors to appear as Asian characters. Wong's first major role was that of a Mongol slave girl with Douglas Fairbanks in the 1924 silent movie *The Thief of Bagdad*. As the mysterious Far East became a popular thematic venue, Wong set the standard for the conniving Asian temptress/villainess, whether as the "dragon lady" daughter of the evil Dr. Fu Manchu, or as a more contemporary version in *Shanghai Express*. In contrast to Wong's sexual seductiveness, Hayakawa's role as a wealthy Japanese sadist in *The Cheat* (1915) typified the image of Asian men as cunning sexual predators seeking to lure unsuspecting white women into depravity. In these Yellow Peril morality plays, Asian men were conduits to white slavery and the opium-crazed depths of Chinatown.

Wong's typecast role evolved with ease into the Suzie Wong/Asian prostitute character and even the Asian American dance hall floozy of *Flower Drum Song*, both memorably played by real Asian actors—Pat Suzuki on Broadway and Nancy Kwan in the film version. As American GIs married brides from Japan, Korea, the Philippines, and Vietnam, the tough dragon-lady edges were smoothed into the subservient, self-sacrificial, and eminently pliable geisha of *Madama Butterfly*. *Miss Saigon*'s Kim was the unimaginative heir to that archetype.

Television readily adopted the same limited Asian character types, so palatable to white artists and audiences of the stage and screen. Darrell Hamamoto, professor of Asian American studies at the University of California at Davis, spent thousands of hours watching archival tapes of TV episodes that included Asian actors or story lines. In his book *Monitored Peril: Asian Americans and the Politics of TV Representation*, Hamamoto analyzed the major Asian American racial themes in TV history. On television, real Asians found a niche as the subservient Asian household help of numerous TV programs, from Sammee Tong as John Forsythe's butler in *Bachelor Father* (1957–62) and Victor Sen Yung, who cleaned and cooked for the four Cartwright men on *Bonanza* (1959–73), to Miyoshi Umeki as the housekeeper, Mrs. Livingston, on *The Courtship of Eddie's Father* (1969–72). Asian servants for Richard Boone as Paladin on *Have Gun Will Travel* (1957–60 and 1961–63) didn't need names, with Kam Tong known only as Hey Boy; when his role ended, his replacement Lisa Lu was called Hey Girl. A *Gunsmoke* (1955–75) episode suggested why it wasn't necessary to give Asian characters names, with the line "Killin' Chinamen ain't really the same as killin' people."

Asian American viewers absorbed the steady diet of demeaning caricatures with embarrassment and shame. Many wished, as youngsters, to be another race, to be anything but the images that dominated them. The media portrayals were reminders of the ridicule they encountered from childhood, of closed minds of people who saw Asians in narrow, proscribed ways—the outsider, the foreigner, the gook.

For Asian American actors, internalized shame added another layer to the trauma of having to act as a caricature of themselves. As a young actor, Ming-Na Wen, the voice of Disney's Mulan, tried to deny her Asianness. "Acting was a way for me to get out of my own skin and be somebody else. Because for a while, my biggest obstacle was getting over the fact that I was Chinese. I kept denying it," she said to *A. Magazine* in 1998. Wen became proud of her Asian ancestry only after she played the role of the daughter, June, in the movie version of *The Joy Luck Club*, based on the bestselling novel by Amy Tan. The fictional daughter is an American-born Chinese, like the real-life Wen, who learns of the secrets and hardships her mother endured in China, and finally comes to accept her mother and herself. To film some of the movie scenes, Wen traveled to China for the first time, accompanied by her own mother, and in the process began to find a sense of pride in being Chinese.

Tony Award–winning actor B. D. Wong encountered similar feelings. "When I was young, I wanted to be an actor, but there were no parts for Asians," said Wong. "I consciously wished I wasn't Asian. Later, I told myself that I would be a different kind of Asian. It wasn't until I played an Asian in *M. Butterfly* that I could celebrate my Asianness. I became a better actor because I could relax within myself." *M. Butterfly*, which also won a Tony Award for Best Play in 1988 for playwright David Henry Hwang, was a fresh retelling of the *Madama Butterfly* story through Asian American eyes; Hwang's play revolved around a French diplomat and a Chinese opera singer and spy, Song Liling, performed by Wong. For many Asian American actors like Wong, the chance to play in a role that is reaffirming is a major turning point—an all too rare opportunity in the limited offerings of Hollywood and Broadway.

*The Joy Luck Club* and *M. Butterfly* were Asian stories told by Asian American writers and played by Asian American actors. But these were very much the exception to the rule. For the most part, whether Asian characters were played by whites or Asians, they were created and defined by white writers and producers who relied on simple images of Asians that could be traced to the Yellow Peril days. In the 1800s, newspapers and magazines like *The W.A.S.P.* and *The Saturday Evening Post* featured pen-and-ink drawings designed to provoke widespread fear of Asian hordes streaming into the West. The single illustration I saw in my youth, of hideous, terrified Chinese being beaten and killed by mobs of violent whites in the old West, was part of that genre.

In drawings, Chinese workers were depicted with baboon-like, subhuman features that coincided with the chinoiserie and Orientalist fads that swept the American and European middle classes into the 1800s. Household items took on what Western decorative artists imagined to be an Orientalized flair. In the lore of chinoiserie, a popular dishware or textile pattern might include Japanese pagodas mixed with Indian peacocks, Chinese scholars, and Persian animals. Monkeys dressed in "Oriental" garb often populated Orientalist patterns.

The curators of a special exhibit at Boston's Museum of Fine Arts, in

1997 described the phenomenon in this way: "Chinoiserie was the whimsical synthesis of fantasy and fact. As late as the mid-eighteenth century, most Europeans were quite ignorant of, or unconcerned by, the distinctions between different Asiatic countries and motifs."

This description is still apt, for most Americans are quite ignorant of, or unconcerned by, the distinctions between different Asian countries, peoples, and cultures. Characters in mass media often blend the wildly diverse traits from distinct Asian cultures into an unimaginative, one-size-fits-all Asian stereotype. Disney's high-budget and carefully researched *Mulan* features Chinese soldiers dressed in Japanese samurai outfits; Asian American audiences who recognize the Asian goulash can only wonder why.

The untrustworthy, sinister, evil, baboonish Chinese male laborer sketched in *The W.A.S.P.* in 1880 readily transformed, with slight changes, into Sax Rohmer's 1913 creation, Dr. Fu Manchu, the yellow peril incarnate. During World War II, Fu Manchu was replaced by the image of the "dirty Jap" kamikaze enemy, and soon after, the Chinese and Korean Communist hordes. The image survived intact as the sneaky "gooks" of the war in Vietnam; TV shows of the time such as *Laugh-In* and *That Was the Week That Was* spoofed the Vietnamese enemy troops and allied soldiers with skits on how they "all looked alike." Whether the gooks brandished bayonets or bamboo poles, daggerlike fingernails, karate-chop hands, or gangster machine guns, they had the same menacing character.

In the 1960s, a subtle transformation took place. In stories that created the "model minority" stereotype, news media began to distinguish between Asian Americans as the "good" minority that "strives to get ahead by dint of its own work," versus the "bad" minority that was "burning the cities and seeking to live off handouts." On the screen, less ominous, "acceptable" Asian characters appeared: the numerous hardworking, unobtrusive TV servants; the "chop suey" assimilated generation of *Flower Drum Song*; Rooney's buffoonish Mr. Yunioshi; Mr. Sulu, the hardworking, emotionless helmsman of *Star Trek*, played by George Takei. These Asian male characters were so unthreatening, they appeared to be asexual eunuchs. This was a switch from the days of Sessue Hayakawa, when Asian males were depicted as sexual predators.

With these roles, another monodimensional character was born: the geek, the industrious, unemotional, uncomplaining, emasculated Asian

American male who blends into the background. Whereas the gook emerges in times of U.S. conflict with Asia, the geek is the dominant image on the home front. Geeks are "model minorities" who never have problems, like racism or poverty, to contend with and never need assistance from government agencies or anyone else. Always the sidekick—the Green Hornet's Kato (Bruce Lee), the white/yellowface Charlie Chan's Number One Son (Keye Luke), Jack Lord's Chin Ho Kelly (Kam Fong)—geeks will happily accept playing second banana to whites without complaint, since they clearly seem to lack leadership abilities. Chinese exchange student and supergeek character Long Duk Dong in *Sixteen Candles* (1984), played by Gedde Watanabe, made passes at disdainful white girls using chop suey lingo: "Wassa happening hah-stuff?"

The movie *Year of the Dragon* (1985) incorporated every conceivable Asian American stereotype, earning it particular disdain and protest from Asian Americans. A sexy, hard-driving Chinese American reporter is violently "seduced" by an abusive white cop. This endears him to her and she becomes his girl; he saves her from other Chinese Americans in the cruel gangs of the amoral, off-kilter world of Chinatown, where numerous random, bloody encounters in restaurants and on the streets prove that Chinese have little regard for human life. The cop's ineffectual, bumbling Asian sidekick offers a comic contrast. Protests from an outraged Asian American community forced the studio, MGM-UA, to attach this tepid disclaimer to its footage: "This film does not intend to demean or to ignore the many positive features of Asian-Americans and specifically Chinese-American communities. Any similarity between the depiction in this film and any associations, organizations, individuals or Chinatowns that exist in real life is accidental."

For every disclaimer, new variations on the old themes developed, mutant strains more potent than their predecessors. Some of these same depictions have insinuated themselves into films and productions by other people of color, even as they attempt to create new images for themselves. Films like *Menace II Society* (1993), which repeatedly shows members of an African American youth gang blowing away a Korean American shopkeeper, portray Koreans as rude, inhuman carpetbaggers, gooks who deserve to be killed for sport. An unfortunate connection can be made between such thrill-kill treatment and the rash of real murders of Korean American storekeepers; no national figures are available, but in Washington, D.C., nine Korean grocers were killed in 1992, while in the first ten months of 1993, more than fifteen were killed in Los Angeles.

Geishas, gooks, and geeks have been the staples of the main characters of mass culture's Asian universe: the subservient, passive female; the untrustworthy, evil male; the ineffectual, emasculated nerd. As each stereotype gained a foothold in the popular culture, it brought on new prejudices that real-life Asian Americans would have to contend with. Those images and associated biases have been cited as the underpinnings of the glass ceiling by numerous Asian American organizations, such as the Asian Pacific American Women's Leadership Institute and Leadership Education for Asian Pacifics. For example, the U.S. Commission on Civil Rights cites the glass ceiling as one of the major types of employment discrimination faced by Asian Americans, while other reports found that, among all racial groups, Asian Americans have the worst chance of being advanced into management positions. For Asian American actors, there is also the danger that directors will accept the typecasting as truth, that Asian actors can play only characters that are either sinister and evil or passive and emasculated.

Slowly, the news of Jonathan Pryce's yellowface performance in the British production of *Miss Saigon* reached Asian American actors.

B. D. Wong was at a dinner party in 1989 with friends who had just seen the show in London. "They said how embarrassing it was to see this tall white man perform in yellowface," Wong recalled. "We were certain that the role would be recast when it came to New York." A highly publicized worldwide talent search was conducted to find an ingenue for the female lead role of Kim, the Vietnamese prostitute, in the American production. Many expected a series of auditions for the Engineer, but none took place. When it was announced in 1990 that Cameron Mackintosh would bring Jonathan Pryce over for the New York run the following year, Asian American actors were stunned. "We were so innocent," said Wong. "We just assumed that Asian American actors would have a chance to be auditioned."

Wong contacted Actors' Equity to see if the union, whose imprimatur was required on all work visa applications by foreign actors, was aware of the casting news. The Committee on Racial Equality, a group within Actors' Equity, was discussing the matter, and Wong was invited to a committee meeting. Most of the more than twenty actors present at this special meeting were Asian American; others were African American and Latino. But they all shared the experience of rarely getting the chance to play major characters of their own ethnic background, let alone whites or characters of other races, while white actors have always had opportunities to play people of color. "We discussed how hurtful it was that Asian American actors weren't even auditioned, that it would be assumed that no Asian actor would be good enough to play an Asian man," said Wong.

The Committee on Racial Equality's meeting at Actors' Equity Association was the start of a collective spirit among actors of Asian descent. As they began exchanging experiences with one another and with black and Latino colleagues, their frustration turned into a momentum for change. Asian American actors from New York to Los Angeles began to call attention to the lack of opportunities for Asian actors, even to portray Asian characters. "*Miss Saigon* was the straw that broke the camel's back," said actor Kim Miyori, one of the organizers in Los Angeles, where a flurry of weekly meetings took place at the Japan Center in Little Tokyo. Miyori had worked in movies, on television, performing as a regular on *St. Elsewhere* and *Hard Copy*, and in the theater, including the Broadway production of David Henry Hwang's *Golden Child.* "Everything about the way [producer Cameron] Mackintosh handled it was offensive . . . For the first time so many Asian Americans—actors and community members—came together to say we're deeply offended and we're mad as hell."

The actors formed a new group, calling themselves the Asian Pacific Alliance for Creative Equality (APACE). In New York, they met with actor Colleen Dewhurst, president of Actors' Equity, and Alan Eisenberg, the executive director, to persuade their union to reject Jonathan Pryce's work visa request. They argued that a white actor in yellowface should not play the role of an Asian, particularly when Asian American actors had not even been asked to audition for the part. B. D. Wong sent letters to Dewhurst and other members of Actors' Equity, imploring them to act. He wrote: "There is no doubt in my mind of the irreparable damage to my rights as an actor that would be wrought if Asian actors are kept from bringing their unique dignity to the specifically Asian roles in *Miss Saigon*, and therefore to all racially specific roles in every future production which will look to the precedent *Miss Saigon* is about to set . . . We may never be able to do the real work we dream [of doing] if a Caucasian actor with taped eyelids hops on the Concorde."

*The New York Times* printed portions of Wong's letters, and asked *Miss Saigon*'s casting director, Vincent Liff, for a response. In the *Times* report, Liff said that there were no Asian actors in the world capable of playing the role of the Vietnamese pimp. In a lengthy, handwritten letter on a yellow notepad, he listed every Asian actor he knew of and why each was unsuitable for the part. The Asian American actors were stunned.

Citing the limited number of Asian-themed shows on stage and screen, Liff wrote: "There has been no professional venue for the development of the Asian actor or Asian actor/singer on the Broadway stage between *Flower Drum Song* and *The World of Suzie Wong* in 1958 and *M. Butterfly* in 1988, a 30-year span. With the exception of the original and revival companies of *Pacific Overtures* and two Broadway revivals of *The King and I,* there was nothing in between. The bottom line is there was just no product to provide Asian actors with successful, financially viable acting careers in the mainstream venues of Broadway, film and television."

The *Times* article evoked considerable rancor from the Asian American actors for publishing Liff's assessment as if it were fact, without substantiation or balance. The productive and talented Asian American theater companies in Los Angeles, New York, San Francisco, and elsewhere—where playwrights such as David Henry Hwang and Philip Kan Gotanda first showcased their work—were completely ignored by Liff. The article failed to note the careers of the handful of actors who had managed to achieve success despite the limited roles for Asians in "mainstream venues." Randall Duk Kim, for example, a classical Shakespearean actor, co-founded the American Players Theatre in Spring Green, Wisconsin. Also dismissed without consideration was the extensive performance work over the years in Asian American film and video.

"There is a generation of Asian American actors and writers who have been forged in the crucible of Asian American literature, theater, and politics," said David Henry Hwang. "Most of the Asian American theaters around the country arose around the flowering of Asian American identity. It's part of our aesthetic legacy."

As early as 1965, a group of Asian American actors in Los Angeles founded the East West Players, initially to provide a stage for Asian American actors to perform in Western plays. In the 1970s, a movement of actors, writers, producers, and directors came together to create an Asian American performance genre. In 1971, the Kumu Kahua repertory company was formed in Honolulu, followed by the Asian American Theater Company in San Francisco, in 1973; the Pan Asian Repertory Theatre of New York, in 1977; and the Northwest Asian Theater Company in Seattle, in 1976. The talent from these stages had won many accolades. Yet to Mackintosh, Liff, and the news media, it was as though they didn't exist.

Most infuriating to Asian American actors was the insinuation that hundreds of Asian American actors had been auditioned for the role of the Engineer but were not good enough. Liff stated in *The New York Times*: "We have overall auditioned hundreds more Asian performers in the continental United States and Hawaii than we have Caucasian performers . . . We have conducted endless totally open calls in New York City (many), Los Angeles (3 occasions), Hawaii (3 occasions), San Jose (once), Orange County (once). We are currently on our way to Daly City (California), Vancouver and Toronto continuing our quest for Asian talent in these Asian centers of population . . . I can say with the greatest assurances, that if there were an Asian actor of 45–50 years, with classical stage background and an international stature and reputation, we would surely have sniffed him out by now. Furthermore, if we hadn't found him, he certainly would have found us."

Weeks later, Cameron Mackintosh admitted that those extensive auditions cited by Liff were to find the female lead, the ingenue who would play Kim, the virgin prostitute. No auditions were held for the male lead role of the Engineer-pimp. But, for the Asian American actors, the harm was done. The misrepresentation set a news spin in motion without any Asian American sources. The news story became focused on "less qualified" Asian actors who were insisting that they should get the part held by a white male star, solely because they were Asian and he was white. "Acting Silly About Color" was the headline of one *New York Times* editorial, which asked, "If the race test were applied to American shows . . . who on earth would have played the King of Siam? . . . If [Pryce] is no affront to Britain's substantial Asian community, why should he offend America's Asians?"

With the disapproval of the New York theater establishment and literati mounting against them, the Asian American actors took their case to Mayor David Dinkins, hoping that he might intervene. "We explained that it was not just about yellowface, but that nobody was ever auditioned for the Engineer. Yet they said they did audition us—and we weren't good enough," said B. D. Wong. "They thought we were docile, that we would go away. Nobody expected us to speak up." Life mimicked myth as the actors were boxed into the well-behaved, "model minority" role. In response, Mayor Dinkins sent a letter to Actors' Equity president Colleen Dewhurst, stressing the concerns of minority artists while also supporting artistic freedom.

The volume and tone of the news, editorials, drama critics, and columnists angered the actors and fueled their desire to right an injustice. In an open letter appealing for public support, Tisa Chang and Dominick Balletta of the Pan Asian Repertory Theatre wrote: "In a *New York Times* editorial, Equity's protests are deemed 'silly.' Would any protest on a similar Black issue be deemed 'silly'? We are asking you to join us and protest that in 1990 we will absolutely NOT tolerate 'taped eyelids and Yellowface' on a Caucasian actor in an Asian role. We will absolutely NOT allow continued perpetuation of demeaning stereotypes and that we will NOT be cowed or silenced by the financial power or the international clout of Cameron Mackintosh and the 'Miss Saigon' producership."

With the help of the union's Committee on Racial Equality, the Asian American actors continued to push the Actors' Equity council to reject Jonathan Pryce's work visa application. They sought the support of stars performing on Broadway. Actors Tyne Daly, Patrick Quinn, and Charles Dutton came to a meeting and listened to their accounts of how decades of hiring whites to play Asian roles had limited their creative horizons as actors. Saying, "This is ridiculous," Dutton stood up and encouraged the Asian American actors to fight on.

The issues raised by *Miss Saigon* dominated several meetings of the seventy-nine-member council of Actors' Equity. Finally, on August 7, 1990, it was time for the council to vote. More than one hundred members of the actors' union packed the council room on West Forty-sixth Street. With Colleen Dewhurst and Alan Eisenberg heading the meeting, people stood to speak, pro and con. Several actors openly wept as Asian American members gave statements, while others fumed. "Lots of older Equity members spoke against us," said B. D. Wong. "Nobody understood; they asked us, 'Why are you embarrassing our union? What about blacks playing Othello, or Morgan Freeman playing Petruchio in *The Taming of the Shrew*?' We explained that we support color-blind casting, but we want to be able to play ourselves, too."

The union's council members went behind closed doors to vote on Cameron Mackintosh's application for Pryce. They returned with a vote to reject Pryce, stating that the union could not appear to condone the casting of a Caucasian as an Asian. "We were overjoyed," said Wong.

The Asian Americans' joy was soon squelched by the torrent of reaction. The union's phone lines immediately lit with calls from Charlton Heston and other angry members, who vehemently opposed the vote.

In rendering the decision to bar Pryce, Actors' Equity leaders said they were taking a moral position. They acknowledged that their position was not likely to be upheld in arbitration, which they anticipated to be show producer Mackintosh's next step.

But Mackintosh didn't intend to go to arbitration. In a statement responding to the Actors' Equity vote that would presage later arguments against affirmative action policies, Mackintosh said: "We passionately disapprove of stereotype casting, which is why we continue to champion freedom of artistic choice. Racial barriers can only undermine the very foundations of our profession. Indeed, Equity has rejected our application solely on the grounds that Mr. Pryce is Caucasian. By choosing to discriminate against Mr. Pryce on the basis of his race, Equity has further violated the fundamental principles of federal and state human rights laws, as well as of federal labor laws."

Mackintosh announced the cancellation of *Miss Saigon* on August 9, and placed an ad in *The New York Times* instructing ticket holders how to get refunds for the $24 million in advance sales. News reports ridiculed the union's position. Stung, Jonathan Pryce announced that he would refuse to play the role even if the show made it to Broadway; but the actor also ceased wearing prosthetics to "slant" his eyes in his London performances. Petitions began circulating among Equity members to reconvene the council and reconsider the vote. Even the Anti-Defamation League of B'nai B'rith weighed in against the Asian Americans.

A whirlwind of media surrounded the Asian American actors, accusing them of using reverse discrimination. "Union Bars White in Asian Role," read the headline in *The New York Times*. "Racism, stage-front," declared the *New York Post*'s editorial, which congratulated Cameron Mackintosh's stand as a besieged white male who did not cave in to racist demands by Asians. Jonathan Pryce accused B. D. Wong of raising his protest in order to promote his own self-interest in possibly landing the role. While the controversy centered on Asian American actors, the intensity of the discussion reflected national tensions, frustration, and anger over issues of race and affirmative action.

"I was surprised by the speed and the ferocity of how the issue was reduced from a complex question into 'Us vs. Them,' " said David Henry Hwang. "In a country divided by race, this Asian context was a more comfortable territory to play out the black–white thing. The issue had a lot of other baggage associated with it. It triggered an emotional reaction that encompassed the nation way beyond Asian Americans. What we wanted to show was there is a consequence for offending Asian Americans. An important point had to be made."

The personal attacks took their toll on B. D. Wong and Hwang, who had also strongly criticized the use of yellowface. Hwang responded to the critics with his 1994 Broadway play *Face Value*. Wong worried about reprisals from casting directors. "My friends warned me, 'You'll never get another job.' And I thought, 'Oh no, I'm not an actor anymore, I'm a political activist.' But as an actor, I had to speak up. I was being told, 'You're not good enough to play this part, you'll never be good enough.' If Asian American actors aren't good enough to play Asian roles, what are we good for?"

In his column for *The Oakland Tribune*, essayist William Wong wrote: "The reaction against the union's positions—which reflects the Asian American theater activists' sentiments—has been vehement. Those who denounce Equity's stance don't understand the pain felt by Asian American actors who, in effect, are being told again that they aren't any good. How long can Asian American actors be treated like houseboys and whores?"

Some significant allies stepped forward in support of the Equity stand. The AFL-CIO, with its 14 million members, hailed Actors' Equity for its "heroic stand." So did Joseph Papp, who headed the New York Shakespeare Festival and Public Theater. "There's something maybe foolish, but brave, about Equity's position," said Papp. "I think in the final analysis their position will mean more employment for Asian American actors. As a producer, I have a certain resistance to their position, but as a citizen, and because of my commitment to minority casting, I think they did the proper and heroic thing." Papp himself was the target of a similar complaint when yellowface was used in the play *New Jerusalem*, which was part of the Shakespeare Festival in the late 1970s. After playwright David Oyama brought the issue to Papp's attention, the festival chief immediately began to encourage Asian American playwrights to bring material to him. David Henry Hwang and Philip Kan Gotanda credit Papp for bringing their work to a wider audience. "In that sense I benefited from the affirmative action and 'non-traditional' approach that resulted from these previous struggles," said Hwang.

Only two days after the council meeting, more than 150 actors had signed petitions demanding that the union reconsider its decision, well beyond the 100 signatures required by union rules; by the time the petitions were turned in, several hundred had signed on to rescind the council vote. To kick off the drive, petitions were first circulated backstage at six Broadway productions, three of which were produced by Cameron Mackintosh.

To counter the negative media storm, the newly formed Asian Pacific Alliance for Creative Equality frantically organized support in New York and Los Angeles. The Asian American theater companies—Pan Asian Repertory Theatre, headed by Tisa Chang, and East West Players in Los Angeles, with Nobu McCarthy as artistic director—provided a base for the actors. Such established Asian American stars as George Takei, Kim Miyori, B. D. Wong, and Tamlyn Tomita were joined by other artists of color. The Association of Asian/Pacific American Artists and twenty other organizations placed ads in *Variety*, criticizing the casting of *Miss Saigon* and raising other issues encountered by Asian and Pacific actors. Numerous Asian American groups, including the Asian American Legal Defense and Education Fund and its executive director, Margaret Fung, assisted the actors.

The New York chapter of the Asian American Journalists Association, during my tenure as its president, organized a joint Asian American community press conference to provide a venue for the Asian American actors to articulate their position in the face of a media juggernaut. Up until then, the pack of reporters and columnists had shown little initiative in interviewing Asian American actors, yet at the same time had misstated their position to be that no whites could play Asians. On August 15, the day before the Equity vote, representatives of more than fifteen organizations in the Asian American community met with the major New York news media and theater journals to show support for the actors, and to criticize the media's failure to balance their reporting. By assisting with the press conference, the New York AAJA chapter opened up a major controversy in the national AAJA organization over whether we had gone too far as a journalists' organization to help the community on a live news issue. The New York group came under considerable criticism from the national body, but a dialogue was launched that moved us from asking *whether* Asian American journalists have a responsibility to the larger Asian American community, to *how* we can meet our responsibilities both as journalists and as members of a community. It was a dialogue that mirrored the very questions that many Asian American actors were beginning to ask themselves: What responsibility did they have for the roles they were fighting so hard to play?

Cameron Mackintosh had called Equity's bluff, and the union flinched. The Actors' Equity council had never intended to block *Miss Saigon* from Broadway. The council had expected its symbolic vote to be appealed by Mackintosh to arbitration, and to be overruled. They would have made their moral stand and the show would go on. Mackintosh's ultimatum tested the council's convictions, which quickly crumbled. Even among Asian American actors, there was great ambivalence over the possibility of losing a show that offered so many Asian roles on a stage otherwise barren for Asian Americans and other actors of color.

The Actors' Equity council reconvened and in a quick vote, on August 16, rescinded its earlier vote to bar Pryce. Actors' Equity issued a lengthy statement to clarify its position. It noted that in 1990 not a single actor of color was cast in 33 shows representing 504 roles, out of nearly 100 shows produced under the agreement between Equity and the League of American Theatres and Producers; an additional 12 shows included only one or two ethnic actors.

On the issue of nontraditional casting, Equity's statement read:

> *For years, minority actors were denied access to roles that were not expressly written for the ethnic performer. As a result, ethnic actors were largely excluded from working in the theatre. The concept of nontraditional casting was established to achieve the goal of having the American theatre reflect the multi-racial reality of*

*American society. Non-traditional casting was never intended to be used to diminish opportunities for ethnic actors to play ethnic roles.*

*Since this debate began, the meaning and purpose of non-traditional casting has been distorted and misconstrued. Much mention has been made of Morgan Freeman's casting as Petruchio in "The Taming of the Shrew." What is ignored in those arguments, and the reason Equity applauds this casting, is the fact that Mr. Freeman played Petruchio as a man who happens to be black and was not asked to play a role, usually reserved for whites, as a Caucasian. The fact that Mr. Freeman's name has been mentioned so frequently is indicative of how few true examples there are of non-traditional casting.*

*Comparisons between the casting of Morgan Freeman and Jonathan Pryce also overlook the once common practice of Caucasian actors using make-up to darken their skins to play people of color, while, at the same time, other actors were barred from roles solely because of the color of their skin. To further suggest that Equity advocates the narrow-minded view that Jews can only play Jews, or Italians can only play Italians, or any similar casting that is drawn strictly along racial or ethnic lines, totally distorts the issue. Jews have always been able to play Italians, Italians have always been able to play Jews, and both have always been able to play Asians. Asian actors, however, almost never have the opportunity to play either Jews or Italians and continue to struggle even to play themselves.*

Equity noted that Mackintosh had expressed his intent to seek Asian actors as replacements or understudies on Broadway, and to assist in the vocal training of Asian actors for consideration of those roles. The statement ended with: "Actors' Equity welcomes Jonathan Pryce and wishes Cameron Mackintosh's production of 'Miss Saigon' a long and prosperous run."

Equity's words were intended to appease the Asian American actors, but its actions only further infuriated them. Equity entered into an unusual private contract with Mackintosh, who was coyly noncommittal about returning to Broadway. The private agreement allowed Mackintosh to import two non-American, Asian actors per year for principal roles in

*Miss Saigon*, further eroding the potential opportunities for Asian Americans to land jobs playing one of the show's six principal characters. The actors took to the picket lines in New York and Los Angeles to protest the Equity-Mackintosh agreement. They found a sympathetic reception in the New York Commission on Human Rights, which initiated public hearings on racial discrimination in the theater industry.

The battle over *Miss Saigon* was over. Cameron Mackintosh's show, with Jonathan Pryce, sans eye prosthetics, was coming to Broadway. The actors continued their protest. Pryce called B. D. Wong to ask him if there would be lingering hard feelings toward him in New York.

After Pryce left *Miss Saigon* in 1992, every successive Engineer has been played by an actor of Asian descent. Despite Mackintosh's initial argument that no Asian Americans were capable of acting the major roles, the play has successfully cycled several generations of Asian performers through its ranks—a direct result of the actors' protest. "We may have lost the battle, but we won the war," said B. D. Wong. Theater critics had insisted that only Jonathan Pryce could do justice to the role of the Engineer, but several of his Asian male successors have performed to rave reviews. Other principal roles that were previously held by white actors, including Kim's Vietnamese fiancé, have since been cast with Asian American actors. The chorus was also opened to Asian performers. Lea Salonga, the ingenue discovered after the much publicized worldwide search, paved the way for a number of Asian, particularly Filipino, actors. "Most Filipino actors get to Broadway through *Miss Saigon*," observed Marlina Gonzalez, executive director of the Asian American Renaissance, an arts organization in St. Paul, Minnesota. "That's the 'advantage' of being colonized by the Spanish and the Americans over five hundred years—you can play Asian parts but you can also play the other roles. In Brazil, there is a phenomenon known as *anthropophagia*, where the dominant culture eats up the minority culture, the way tacos or pizza become as acceptable as hamburgers. In *Miss Saigon*, we were fighting to play a role that we would end up protesting."

The impact of *Miss Saigon* reached beyond Asian Americans. African Americans and other actors of color were also hired for roles that previously went to whites in *Miss Saigon* and in other plays. The harsh glare of attention on the theater's hiring practices exposed its biases and lack of creative casting. For the first time, the spotlight shone on nontraditional casting—the theater's form of affirmative action—and opened a space for change. Other Broadway shows, such as *The Will Rogers Follies, Les Mi-sérables,* and *The Phantom of the Opera,* were forced to examine why they weren't hiring ethnic minority actors in their shows. As a result of these changes, audiences, regardless of their race, could benefit from the fresh hiring approaches and creativity that arose out of the controversy.

Ultimately, the battle over *Miss Saigon,* which began over yellowface and painful stereotyped images of Asians, ended as a struggle over jobs, casting, and creative expression. The discussion raised the consciousness of many. "When we first spoke up, people didn't understand what we were talking about. 'Yellowface? What's that?' " said B. D. Wong. "They didn't even expect us to speak up. We changed a lot of people's misconceptions about us, and we changed ourselves." Some Asian American actors would end up rejecting such roles, like the actors quoted in Josephine Lee's book *Performing Asian America*: "I will never play Suzie Wong or a Vietnamese whore again. I want to play Blanche and Nora, Medea and Desdemona. I have a lot to contribute."

The content of *Miss Saigon* would prove the more problematic issue for Asian Americans, but at the time few Americans had seen the Mackin-tosh production on the London stage.

"The casting debate came up first—it was just so off the wall that they were thinking of doing yellowface, we were shocked," said David Henry Hwang. "The deeper debate is the non-ironic retelling of *Madama Butter-fly*. I always thought that the ideal way to handle the *Miss Saigon* content debate would be for Asian women to refuse to perform in it. Asian male performers aren't critical to the show—they need the authentic 'exotic erotic' in order to succeed commercially. This idea may just be a fantasy."

With so few jobs available to Asian American actors, there was no crit-ical mass of actors who felt confident enough to reject participation in a racially demeaning show; in the case of the male lead, the part wasn't avail-able for actors to reject. But the protest over jobs was a first, incremental step forward in creating a voice that could speak from the inside of the entertainment business.

As *Miss Saigon* prepared to open at the Broadway Theatre, the Asian American community got a closer look at the content and characteriza-tions of the show. The glowing reviews gave a good indication of what we would see. *Newsweek* critic Jack Kroll wrote: " 'Miss Saigon' sounds only two true emotional chords. One is the sweetness and gallantry of Salonga, the young Filipina who sings and acts with remarkable power. The other authentic feeling is the sheer lust for 'The American Dream' of the Eurasian pimp called The Engineer, played with Brechtian brilliance by Jonathan Pryce (whom Actors' Equity tried ill advisedly to bar from Broadway, insisting the role should be played by an Asian). Hands slithering like snakes, eyes darting like a jackal's, Pryce sings his show-stopping anthem of evil entrepreneurship . . . and then makes lubricious love to a white Cadillac carrying a bimbo dressed as the Statue of Liberty."

Such reviews sounded remarkably like the praise for the "truthfulness to nature" of Bret Harte and Mark Twain's Ah Sin and Mickey Rooney's "broadly exotic" Mr. Yunioshi. The sweetly self-sacrificial prostitute and the pimp's cynical, sinister lust for the American Dream were the kinds of stereotypes that had plagued Asian Americans for more than a century.

Asian Americans began to organize a community response to the play's content. A letter by a Chinese American man to WNET, New York's public television station on Channel 13, protested the offer of tickets to *Miss Saigon* as a fund-raising premium:

> I am writing to you to protest your choice of "Miss Saigon" as one of your premiums . . . This is one of the most offensive shows ever written. I feel that Thirteen should not be associated with it. Many of the lyrics, from the libretto, are blatantly racist: The G.I. chorus sings about "these slits" who might become Miss Saigon. The Asian women "prostitutes" offer to "melt [their] brass" while propped against a wall, stuck with pins in the "ass." The Engineer declares that his race thinks only about rice, but he laments that "greasy Chinks" are "sleazy."
>
> This is not a call for censorship. In the context of violence against women, a show that presents Asian women as sex objects and whores, whose passivity is underscored by their willingness to commit suicide for a white god of a visiting G.I., affects Asian women and women in general by inciting harassment and even rapes against them.

Several Asian American groups prepared to set up pickets as The Heat Is On Miss Saigon Coalition. Led by the Committee Against Anti-Asian

Violence in New York, the coalition called for a boycott because of the "racist and sexist images that fuel violence," and citing the 680 percent increase in violent acts against Asians in New York between 1985 and 1990.

Hundreds of protesters demonstrated on opening night, especially targeting the Lambda Legal Defense and Education Fund, a gay and lesbian civil rights group, which was using *Miss Saigon* as a fund-raiser. The demonstrators pointed to the sex tourism industry in Southeast Asia and the market for "mail order brides" among men who are seeking docile wives. "These women are often brutalized by their husbands," said Veena Cabreros-Sud, a spokesperson for the coalition. While their pickets had little impact on the show itself, they again brought visibility to the frustration felt by Asian Americans over their portrayals in the media.

The link between the depiction of women in popular cultural works such as *Miss Saigon* and the real treatment that many Asian American women face has been a source of continuing outrage for Asian American women. In 1990, *GQ* magazine published "Oriental Girls: The Ultimate Accessory" by Tony Rivers. "Her face—round like a child's, . . . eyes almond-shaped for mystery, black for suffering, wide-spaced for innocence, high cheekbones swelling like bruises, cherry lips . . . When you come home from another hard day on the planet, she comes into existence, removes your clothes, bathes you and walks naked on your back . . . She's fun, you see, and so uncomplicated . . . She's there when you need shore leave from those angry feminist seas. She's a handy victim of love or a symbol of the rape of third world nations, a real trouper." In her essay on racialized sexual harassment, Sumi Cho, a professor at DePaul University College of Law in Chicago, critiqued the *GQ* article and noted: "Given this cultural backdrop of converging racial and gender stereotypes in which the model minority meets Suzie Wong, so to speak, Asian Pacific American women are especially susceptible to racialized sexual harassment."

So strong is this pervasive image of the sexually exotic, available Asian woman that, at the time when the fight over *Miss Saigon* was raging in New York, Christopher Barnes, an African American man in Los Angeles, was scamming thousands of other men by duping them into corresponding with him, under the ruse that *he* was an Asian woman. In one nine-month period, he conned at least $280,000 from four hundred men who thought he was their Asian pen pal sweetheart. Soo-Young Chin, a professor of anthropology at the University of Southern California, researched the evidence found by the postal inspectors, who convicted Barnes of mail fraud for a second time in 1992. She found that he received over a thousand letters per week from new and continuing correspondents by pretending to be Song, an eighteen-year-old student; Tess, a twenty-six-year-old nurse; Velma; Pearl; and others. His computer database held over 8,500 men from every state in the nation, from truck drivers to doctors, lawyers, and college professors, who paid money to get letters from his Asian women characters—some exchanging letters for more than a year. Catering to men who want to meet Asian women, he created a pay-for-mail-and-porno operation called Crossroads International, which featured a glossy brochure stating: "To know her is to love her . . . Each year millions of American and European men flock to the Orient in search for an Oriental woman. Why? Because they know Oriental women make ideal lovers. From birth they are raised to love, honor and respect their man. Unlike so many other women, the Oriental loves only one man. In their eyes, you are a god. You are her lord and master. She will never betray you." The willingness to believe in another man's fake correspondence offering his imagined ideal of an Asian woman is amply documented by Barnes's success. In fact, when postal inspectors contacted some of Barnes's "boyfriends," they became furious with the inspectors for casting doubts on their "Oriental girl."

Not all "sellers" and "buyers" of the Asian women stereotype are harmless participants, however. At Ohio State University, Asian women students in the late 1980s were targets of rape by a fraternity in a "game" called "Ethnic sex challenge." In 1985, two months after *Penthouse* magazine featured pictures of Asian women in various poses of bondage and torture, including hanging bound from trees in deathlike poses, an eight-year-old Chinese girl named Jean Har-Kew Fewel was found raped and lynched in Chapel Hill, North Carolina. At his trial, the killer admitted that pornography played a significant role in his attitudes. Though it wasn't determined whether the *Penthouse* feature influenced him, pornography shops and, now, Internet sites are replete with material featuring Asian women.

Asian American men encounter another treatment. Because they are seen as gangsters, gooks, and geeks, they have trouble getting depicted realistically even when they are key to the story. During the devastating fires in the hills of Oakland, California, in 1991, Filipino American Fire Captain Ray Gatchalian valiantly rescued numerous trapped people. He later agreed to sell his story to a movie studio on the condition that his character be portrayed as an Asian American. When the made-for-TV movie was released, Gatchalian, the Asian American hero, had become a Hispanic firefighter.

In 1992, a new organization formed in Los Angeles to take on such images of Asian Americans, in response to the movie version of Michael Crichton's novel *Rising Sun*. The Media Action Network for Asian Americans was organized by Guy Aoki and George Johnston to "create an environment free of racism through accurate, balanced, and sensitive Asian American images." Though Crichton had spent little time in Japan, *Rising Sun* depicted a country full of corrupt Japanese men, lusting for white women and bent on destroying America. "Japanese have invented a new kind of trade—adversarial trade, trade like war, trade intended to wipe out the competition—which America has failed to understand for years," wrote Crichton. The movie promised even more explosive material; after someone in the studio sent MANAA a copy of the script, the group began talks with studio executives of Twentieth Century-Fox about the film's more volatile racial content. When talks broke down, MANAA and several other Asian American organizations organized demonstrations in Los Angeles, San Francisco, New York, Chicago, and Washington, D.C. At a news conference, Aoki stated that the film depicted the Japanese as "ruthless, aggressive people intent on getting their way in business through blackmail, extortion, and even murder," depictions, he said, that could contribute to escalating hate crimes against Asian Americans. MANAA did not call for a boycott or criticize the Asian American actors who appeared in the movie, but instead pursued its mission to educate the entertainment industry and the public about portrayals of Asians and Asian Americans.

Months after the controversies over the casting of *Miss Saigon* had quieted, the Asian Pacific Alliance for Creative Equality, the newly formed actors' group, organized a forum called "Gangsters, Gooks, and Geishas" at the Public Theater to discuss what had emerged. (This chapter's title is adapted from that event's.) George Takei, the veteran Asian American actor best known for his role as *Star Trek*'s Lieutenant—later Captain— Sulu, spoke about the joint responsibility of Asian American actors and the Asian American community to define ourselves as Asians and Asian Americans. "It is up to us to change the notion that suicide is an Asian trait, or that Asian male actors don't have the talent to portray ourselves," he said. "It is the responsibility of Asian American actors to learn how to portray Asians well, and it is the responsibility of the community to support the shows created by talented Asian American playwrights. Actors can't do it alone."

Jessica Hagedorn, author of *Dogeaters* and editor of *Charlie Chan Is Dead*, spoke of the ever present stereotypes. "Suzie Wong. Flower Drum Song. Dragon Lady. Madame Butterfly. China Doll. Tokyo Rose. Fu Manchu. Charlie Chan. Mr. Moto. Ming the Merciless. Little Brown Brother. Savage. Mysterious. Inscrutable. Sinister. Exotic. Submissive. Diminutive. Indolent. Insolent. Sexless. Sexy. Mail Order Bride. Model Minority. I could go on and on, listing familiar and not so familiar stereotypes, drawing from the abundant arsenal of dehumanizing images that assault us daily in America, as we sleep and dream, as we eat, work and study. What is this ghastly sickness all about? The heart of darkness?" she asked, in an essay she wrote for *Newsday*.

Philip Kan Gotanda, whose play *Yankee Dawg You Die* dramatized the very issues that arose with *Miss Saigon*, said, "Asian American actors have to ask themselves, 'What is the context of the role?' As Asian actors become politicized, leaders will emerge who will say, 'No, I won't accept that role.' But the hour is getting late. It's not just an Asian American issue, either. There's an emerging perspective in this country that we need to move our consciousness forward on issues of color or we're in trouble."

Out of the turmoil that began as a protest over one role in a single play, Asian Americans brought into the open the pernicious impact that deeply imbedded stereotypes have on all aspects of Asian American life. In assessing the issues opened by the *Miss Saigon* showdown, community activists pointed out that many more individual acts of courage and bravery would be necessary to tear down our prisons of gangsters, gooks, geishas, and geeks.

# III

# UP FROM INNOCENCE

# · 6 ·

# Welcome to Washington

In kindergarten, I learned the Pledge of Allegiance. Or rather, I learned to imitate it. The words spilled out of my mouth in one long jumble, all slurred and sloppy. I'd stand tall and put my right hand over my heart, mumbling proudly, like a five-year-old on a drunk. Even then, I understood that " 'Merica" was my home—and that I was an American.

Still, a flicker of doubt was ever present. If I was truly American, why did the other American people around me seem so sure I was foreign?

By the time I was a teenager, I imagined that I was a "dual citizen" of both the United States and China. I had no idea what dual citizenship involved, or if it was even possible. No matter, I would be a citizen of the world. This was my fantasy, my way of soothing the hurt of being so unacceptable in the land of my birth.

---

*Labor activists Silme Domingo (left) and Gene Viernes (right) with union organizer Claro Eugenio, by their union hall in 1981 (Rick Furukawa/ILWU/IBU Region 37)*

When I got to college, I decided to learn more about "where I came from" by taking classes in Asian history. I even studied Mandarin Chinese. This had the paradoxic effect of making me question my Chineseness. Other students, and even the teachers, expected me to spout perfectly accented Chinese. Instead I sounded like some hick from New Jersey, stumbling along as badly as the other American students next to me. Still my fantasy persisted; I thought I might "go back" to China, a place I had never been, as rude detractors so often urged.

President Richard Nixon's historic trip to China in February 1972 made a visit seem possible for me. That summer, China cracked open the "bamboo curtain," allowing a small group of Chinese American students to visit the country as a goodwill gesture to the United States. I desperately wanted to be one of them, and I put together a research proposal that got the support of my professors. With a special fellowship from Princeton, I joined the group and became one of the first Americans, after Nixon, to enter "Red" China.

In China I fit right in with the multitude. In the cities of Shanghai and Suzhou, where my parents were from, I saw my features everywhere. After years of not looking "American" to the "Americans" and not looking Chinese enough for the Cantonese who made up the majority of Chinese Americans, I suddenly found my face on every passerby. It was a revelation of sameness that I had never experienced in New Jersey. The feeling didn't last long.

I visited my mother's eldest sister; they hadn't seen each other since 1949, the year of the Communist revolution in China, when my mother left with their middle sister on the last boat out of Shanghai. Using my elementary Chinese, I struggled to communicate with Auntie Li, who seemed prematurely wizened from the years of hardship. My vocabulary was too limited and my idealism too thick to comprehend my family's suffering from the Cultural Revolution, still virulently in progress. But girlish fun transcended language as my older cousins took me by the hand to the local "Friendship Store" and dressed me in a khaki Mao suit, braiding my long hair in pigtails, just like the other young, unmarried Chinese women.

All decked out like a freshly minted Red Guard in my new do, I passed for local. Real Chinese stopped me on the street, to ask for directions, to ask where I got my tennis shoes, to complain about the long bus queues, to comment on my Shanghai-made blouse, to say any number of things to me. As soon as I opened my mouth to reply, my clumsy American accent infected the little Chinese I knew. Suddenly the speech that, in English, drew compliments in America brought gasps of fear and disapproval in Chinese. My questioners knew immediately that I was a foreigner, a Westerner, an American, maybe even a spy—and they ran from me as fast as they could. I had an epiphany common to Asian Americans who visit their ancestral homelands: I realized that I didn't fit into Chinese society, that I could never be accepted there. If I didn't know it, the Chinese did: I belonged in America, not China.

When I got back to the States, I took my new appreciation of my Americanness and went to Washington, armed with a degree in public and international affairs and a minor in East Asian studies. After a lengthy application and interview process that included months of FBI security checks, I landed my dream summer job as an intern on the China desk at the State Department, created as a result of President Nixon's historic visit. As one of the first Americans to visit the People's Republic of China, I was eager to contribute to the efforts of my country—the United States—to rebuild diplomatic relations.

When I reported to work on the designated day at the State Department monolith in Foggy Bottom, the personnel officer greeted me with "We have no job for you." He offered no explanation about the job I had worked so hard to get. I was stranded in a strange city with no money, a scholarship student whose livelihood depended on summer earnings. The urgency of my financial situation forced me out of shock and into action. I walked to Congress and found the offices of the two senators from New Jersey, Harrison Williams, Jr., and Clifford Case. Their staff members kindly listened to my plight and went into action for their young constituent.

With this congressional assist, I learned why the job had suddenly vaporized. I was told that the State Department had a policy that no persons of Chinese descent should work at the China desk, no matter how many generations removed from the ancestral bones. This would protect America in case some genetic compulsion twisted my allegiance to China.

I was incredulous. Hadn't they noticed earlier that I was Chinese American? Surely the FBI agents and State Department folks hadn't missed that minor detail. I was terribly disappointed that I wouldn't have a chance to do the one job I felt perfectly qualified to do. At least the senators managed to extract another internship offer from the State Department. My anger and disappointment gave way to practicality, and I went to work at my first writing job: researching and writing State Department briefs, reports, and various propaganda.

As I became more certain of my Americanness, my government again asserted its ambivalence to me. But I understood what the Pledge of Allegiance meant—that America was my home.

■ ■ ■

The clear arctic waters of Alaska's 33,000-mile tidal shoreline are far from the hot, bountiful fields of California's Central Valley, and farther still from the halls of Congress. For Filipino Americans, the latter journey began with a lawsuit filed in 1973 against Alaskan salmon canneries over the most overt kind of segregated working conditions that were once typical of plantations. The workers' fight would take them all the way to the U.S. Supreme Court, and then to a massive pan-Asian and multiracial effort in Congress that would enhance the civil rights of all Americans. Except for their own.

For much of the twentieth century, Filipino Americans were part of a parallel migration to Alaska that takes place each summer, between the spring planting and the fall harvest, along the West Coast in the lower Forty-eight. The first migration was shaped during the Great Ice Age of the Pleistocene Epoch, when ancient salmonlike fish began to venture from fresh inland waters to the salty ocean deep, which imprinted for the next million years the salmon's epic breeding ritual. The other migration is of the human variety: thousands of seasonal workers make their way upcoast and upstream to harvest the salmon as they journey to their freshwater spawning grounds.

Seafarers from the Philippines first made their way to the Americas in the 1500s, but it wasn't until about 1911 that they ventured to Alaska, as replacements for Chinese and Japanese workers who were shut out by the various anti-Asian, white nativist exclusion movements. The Philippines, however, was annexed by the United States in 1898 after the Spanish-American War, allowing for the free migration and importation of Filipino labor, until 1934, when Filipinos, too, were excluded.

By the 1920s, there were more Filipino workers in Alaska than any other ethnic group except for Native Alaskan Indians and whites. At the height of their cannery employment in the 1970s, thousands of Filipinos made the annual trek up the Alaskan coastline, to work the long summer days cleaning, processing, and canning the approximately 100 million salmon caught each year. In those days there was hardly a Filipino American man who hadn't worked in the Alaskan canneries, including the dapper college men who came from the Philippines to study. Calling themselves Alaskeros, they were lured by the promise of better pay than they could get elsewhere. But the Filipinos found themselves doing the work that no one else would do.

Even under the continuous light of the Arctic summer solstice, there's no glamour in working at a salmon cannery. When the boat tenders—large, floating fish warehouses—pull up to the cannery dock, the "beach gang" hustles to unload cargo holds full of murky brown brine and large dead fish, which must be processed within days of being caught. A greenish sheen tags the older catch. Big vacuum pumps suck out the fish, dumping them onto conveyor belts that carry the fish to sorting bins. Machines cut the heads and tails off the salmon and eviscerate the guts. The egg sacs are carefully pulled from female fish and sent to the egg house to be hand-packed for shipment to Japan. The salmon roe has become the most valuable commodity in Alaska's $185 million salmon industry.

A constant stream of cold water moves the fish carcasses along circular metal tables to the "slime line," where most of the Filipino labor force works, scooping the entrails from the fish by hand. The slimers cut, dress, wash, and trim the fish for freezing. Fish marked for canning move on to the hopper and the chopper, to be boned, skinned, and trimmed to fit into cans, which are then cooked in large machines called retorts. Slimers clean fish day after day for weeks, getting only a few hours of sleep; using knives and scoops, their hands are constantly soaked in icy water, cuts infected with fish slime and a stink that won't leave.

In exchange for their hard work and long hours, the Filipino Americans found themselves caught in a segregated plantation economy similar to that of the antebellum South. The Filipino workers were housed in decrepit wooden barracks; the white workers had modern housing. Filipinos and whites ate at different mess halls, with different menus. Stuck in the most tedious and lowest-paying jobs in the canneries, the Filipinos had no chance of getting promoted out into non-cannery jobs. White workers earned more than twice the pay and received the opportunities for better jobs.

For decades, immigrant Filipino American workers accepted the unequal conditions. Some six thousand to seven thousand people a season work on the slime lines and freezers and chutes of the canneries, earning little more than the minimum wage—which becomes more attractive when multiplied by long hours and overtime. But by the late 1960s, a new, American-born generation of Filipino Americans went to work at the canneries. This generation came of age at a time when civil rights was at the top of the national agenda—and in keeping with the mood of the times, they rebelled.

The salmon canneries, like the California grape growers, were resistant to making changes for their migrant workforce. Since its earliest days in the late 1800s, the salmon industry has depended on an abundant supply of cheap labor that could be deployed at a moment's notice, or discharged if the salmon run was weak. The workers had to be willing to do grueling work under harsh conditions; they had to be dependable but expendable. Asian immigrants, a captive workforce with a tenuous status in America, were considered ideal and preferable to Native Alaskans, who could easily leave the canneries for home if conditions became intolerable.

The first group of Asian workers hired for Alaska duty were Chinese, beginning the era of the "China crew" in 1872. Canneries hired Chinese labor contractors who became successful merchants by procuring and selling the labor of their fellow Chinese. They transported, fed, and paid the workers. Unscrupulous contractors exploited their fellow Chinese, who were sometimes kidnapped and imprisoned in the locked, crowded, unsanitary hulls of Alaska-bound ships. The less the contractor paid his labor gang, the more he kept for himself.

Once in Alaska, the workers were housed in barnlike hovels called China houses and fed meager rations. Stranded in Alaska, they had no choice but to work in the canneries. Chinese workers were so essential to the salmon industry that a machine invented in 1903 to mechanize salmon processing was named the Iron Chink. The racial slur for the machine's name is still commonly used in Alaska; it is labeled as such in government-funded museums without reference to its offensive nature.

With the Chinese Exclusion Act of 1882 and the violent driving-out time, salmon canneries switched to Japanese immigrant labor, and renamed the work gangs the Oriental crew. Japanese labor contractors took the place of the Chinese bosses. When the anti-Asian backlash soon halted Japanese immigration, the canning companies began hiring women, Mexicans, and Filipinos.

Many of these Filipino Americans first came to the United States as college students, part of Teddy Roosevelt's legacy to help "our little brown brothers" in the Philippines. But even with their college diplomas, the Filipino men could find work in the segregated American labor market only as seasonal migrant workers. In winter and spring they tended the California asparagus and lettuce fields; later, they moved on to the fruit orchards and the searing heat of the vineyards to pick grapes. In Oregon and Washington, they worked the hop fields. As the last major group of Asian immigrants prior to the 1965 Immigration Act, many Filipinos ended up working as laborers for Japanese American farmers. Few Filipino women could immigrate to the United States because of exclusionary policies against Asians, forcing most of the 54,747 Filipino Americans who immigrated between 1920 and 1930 to form a migrant bachelor society. Living close to the fields in tents, barns, and boxcars, they made pennies a day and were under the constant threat of racist harassment and violence from white mobs. Every June, there was the salmon harvest in Alaska. Soon Filipino Alaskeros became the dominant cannery workforce; in 1928, 3,916 Filipinos journeyed north, compared to 1,065 Chinese, 1,445 Japanese, and 1,269 Mexicans.

Cannery companies tried to force down the cost of labor by getting the different groups to bid against each other. As unions sought to organize the cannery workers in the 1930s, they, too, used racial and ethnic competition to win votes. A federal labor official of that era noted that the Asian ethnic groups in the cannery labor market "will probably never be assimilated into the American strain at any time . . . this element is always going to cause trouble."

Frontier anarchy and corruption were commonplace in both the salmon-canning companies and the unions. Workers hoping to land union jobs in Alaska had to buy heavily marked-up goods at company stores and to participate in gambling rings run by the unions and organized crime before they would even be considered for employment. Sometimes they had to pay bribes up front to contractors and union dispatchers. Cannery unions often ignored union seniority and hiring rules to favor their own group.

In the late 1930s, an alliance between Chinese, Japanese, and Filipino immigrant and Asian American cannery workers emerged, writes historian Chris Friday in *Organizing Asian American Labor*. They held the potential of developing a united front among Asian cannery workers across ethnic lines, but it broke down with changes in the salmon industry and the wartime internment of Japanese Americans. In its place, ethnic-specific unions competed. Because Filipinos were the main source of the cannery labor pool, their labor organizations, run by Filipino officers, emerged as the most powerful. Among them was Local 37 of the Inland Boatmen's Union of the International Longshoremen's and Warehousemen's Union (ILWU).

Little had changed at the canneries in 1970 when American-born Silme Domingo followed in his father's footsteps to Alaska for a summer job after graduating from high school in Seattle and before heading to the University of Washington. That summer, at the salmon cannery owned by the New England Fish Company on Uganik Bay, Kodiak Island, Silme found his father's name carved into one of the bunks: "Nemesio Domingo, 1927"; back then, his father had been one of the college students from the Philippines who was unable to find other work.

In college, Silme found the growing Asian American student movement and became a political activist, organizing with other Filipino Americans so they wouldn't be overshadowed by the dominant Chinese Americans and Japanese Americans. When Silme and his brother, Nemesio Jr., returned to work at the canneries the following summer, they became shop stewards for Local 37.

Unlike the white workers, who slept two in each room in their own bunkhouses, up to eight Filipino workers were crammed in a single room. "The Filipino bunkhouse was still leaning toward the water, the doors didn't shut, and there were cracks in the walls; open to the elements, it hadn't been painted in forty years," said Nemesio Jr. To add insult, the Filipino housing was commonly referred to derogatorily as "the Flip bunkhouse."

Food was another sore point. In some mess halls, partitions separated white workers from Filipinos. At the Red Salmon Cannery in Naknek, on Bristol Bay, owned by the Wards Cove Packing Company, the "white mess" served different food from the "Filipino mess." In 1971, Gene Viernes, a Filipino American friend of Silme Domingo, got his start as a labor organizer when he argued with white mess cooks over a chocolate cake. The cooks made the cake for white workers and refused to serve any to Filipinos. Viernes insisted that the Filipino workers should be allowed to have cake. As food quality declined for the Filipino mess, Viernes took up the issue with the cannery management, without result. Finally, Viernes organized a hunger strike with nine other young workers, an action that didn't improve the food but infuriated both the company and union representatives.

When Viernes and the Domingo brothers returned to Seattle at the end of the salmon harvest, they found that they were blacklisted by their union, which dispatched workers to jobs in the canneries. Silme Domingo suggested that they sue the canneries, an idea he picked up from a burgeoning Third World workers' movement that was fighting exclusion from the high-paying construction trades in the building of Seattle's Kingdome. Construction workers of color had successfully filed lawsuits against discriminatory hiring practices in several cities around the country. The young cannery organizers wanted to end the unequal conditions and to open up the ranks of higher-paying, higher-skilled jobs to Filipinos and Native Alaskans so that they would not be stuck in the worst cannery jobs. But their union, Local 37 of the Inland Boatmen's Union, was reputed to be corrupt and was then closely allied with cannery management. Since their union wasn't interested in changing working conditions at the canneries, Viernes, the Domingo brothers, and other Filipino and Asian American activists organized their own labor organization, the Alaska Cannery Workers Association (ACWA), modeled after the United Construction Workers Association. The organizers managed to get hired back into the canneries as members of Local 37 by threatening to sue the canneries for retaliating against them. Once they were back in Alaska and in the canneries, they found other workers who would be plaintiffs in their legal actions.

In 1973, the ACWA filed three class action lawsuits under Title VII of the 1964 Civil Rights Act, citing discriminatory treatment in working conditions and denial of higher-paying jobs, against some of Alaska's largest salmon canneries: New England Fishing Company; NEFCO–Fidalgo Packing Company; Wards Cove Packing Company; and Castle & Cooke (Dole). They worked with the Northwest Labor and Employment Law Office, which had also successfully taken similar legal actions for minority workers in the construction trades. It was the first time that class action discrimination suits had been brought on behalf of a migrant workforce. Silme and Nemesio Domingo, Jr., were among the plaintiffs in the first suit, while Gene Viernes was a plaintiff against Wards Cove and Dole. "We saw the law as a tool that workers could use," said Nemesio Jr.

The lawsuits took years to wind their way through the legal system. The first case was decided in 1977, when a federal district court judge ruled that the New England Fishing Company was guilty of racial discrimination in housing and employment. In 1981, the second suit was decided when another federal judge ruled that the NEFCO–Fidalgo Packing Company also discriminated in housing and hiring. Eventually, financial settlements were reached between the companies and the affected workers. The ACWA hoped that the court would order an affirmative action plan with 50 percent of all higher-level jobs to go to Filipinos or Native Alaskans. But the court didn't follow through, and the NEFCO–Fidalgo company filed for bankruptcy five years later.

Meanwhile, the labor activists turned their focus on other pursuits— reforming the cannery union and supporting efforts to end the military dictatorship of Ferdinand Marcos in the Philippines. The young radicals saw a parallel between the harsh treatment of workers by the canneries in the United States and the oppressiveness of martial law in the Philippines. But their anti-Marcos views stood in opposition to the politics of many Filipino Americans, who were conservative Marcos loyalists and staunchly anti-Communist. In Asian American immigrant communities, politics "back home" are a source of great internal community tension, often splitting family and friends into bitterly divided camps, and sometimes leading to violence. Silme Domingo's opposition to U.S. government policy placed him squarely against the views of his father, a veteran of World War II and an active member of the Veterans of Foreign Wars. But the ACWA's commitment to improving working conditions for the cannery workers won support for the activists. Their lawsuits had shown workers what could be done to force the canneries to change. In 1980 Silme Domingo was elected Secretary-Treasurer, and Gene Viernes elected Dispatcher, on a reform slate for Local 37 of the International Longshoremen's and Warehousemen's Union, with its 1,200 Filipino cannery worker members. One of their campaign promises was to enforce such union rules as seniority in dispatching workers on jobs—something that hadn't been done in years.

But inside the union, the labor activists' stand against corruption infuriated the Filipino gangsters who ran the gambling rings in the Alaskan cannery towns—which depended on getting their gang members sent to Alaska. Viernes and Domingo had also introduced a resolution at the ILWU convention to oppose the martial law restrictions against workers and labor unions in the Philippines—a resolution that Marcos supporters called Communist. The union leaders became subjects of death threats and surveillance. On the evening of June 1, 1981, two Filipino men with long police rap sheets entered the Local 37 ILWU office and opened fire on their targets, Silme Domingo, twenty-eight years old, and Gene Viernes, twenty-seven.

Gene was dead at the scene, but Silme was able to name the killers before he died the next day. In the trial that followed, prosecutors won convictions against the hit men who had conspired to execute the Filipino American activists. Winning a major political victory against the Marcos government, the families of Gene and Silme obtained a $15 million civil suit against Ferdinand Marcos for the role his government and agents played in the conspiracy to kill the two men. Gene's and Silme's survivors eventually received a much lesser amount from the Marcos estate.

Under the slogan "Turn anguish into anger," a shaken Filipino American community resolved to carry on the work of the fallen union leaders. The lawsuits against the canneries were now stained with the martyrdom of two plaintiffs and initiators of the lawsuits; for the cannery workers in Local 37, there was no turning back. Other union reformers recommitted themselves to the work that Silme and Gene had started. Silme's widow and fellow activist, Terri Mast, was elected to lead the reform of the cannery workers' union; Mast became the first woman president of an ILWU local. Silme, Gene, and the other Filipino American activists could not foresee that their lawsuit would get caught in the shifting political sands over a span of three decades—or that their struggle in Alaska would lead to the nation's capital.

The workers succeeded in their first two class action discrimination lawsuits against the canneries. But the last case, involving the Wards Cove Packing Company, dragged on, with two adversaries who couldn't have been more different. On one side were the Asian American seasonal workers: among the name plaintiffs were Frank Atonio, a Samoan American; a

Japanese American; some Chinese Americans; and several Filipino Americans, including Gene Viernes, the murdered union leader.

On the other side was the Brindle family, owners of Wards Cove Packing Company, one of the few family-owned canneries left in Alaska. The politically influential Brindle clan, led by Alexander Winn Brindle, company president and son of the company's founder, took great umbrage at the charge of racial discrimination. At every opportunity, the Brindles filed motions that delayed the trial, even arguing for dismissal of the suit because Gene Viernes, one of the name plaintiffs, was dead. As the two thousand Filipino and Native Alaskan cannery workers covered by the lawsuit discovered, Wards Cove was just as determined to win as they were.

Class action discrimination suits are notorious for their long and tedious discovery processes. This case was no different, but the delays worked decidedly in Wards Cove's favor. Though the suit against Wards Cove began in 1974, it didn't come to trial until 1982. By then Ronald Reagan was president and the political pendulum had swung away from civil rights and claims of workplace discrimination. "When we first brought the case, we saw the law as an ally," said Diane Narasaki, the former executive director of the Northwest Labor and Employment Law Office, which oversaw the class action suits. "But that changed with the appointment of a new set of conservative federal court judges." Unfortunately for the cannery workers, theirs became the test case to revise and roll back the legal proof of workplace discrimination.

When the cannery workers first filled their lawsuit, they used a statistical procedure that the Supreme Court had previously established in its 1971 landmark ruling *Griggs* v. *Duke Power Company*. Duke Power had used a battery of written tests to screen out applicants, even for janitorial jobs. In that case, the Supreme Court said that covert discrimination was unlawful: "practices that are fair in form but discriminatory in practice" which caused a disparate impact were prohibited—for example, a complicated written test for janitorial jobs, or height requirements unrelated to job performance that kept women and many men from being hired as police officers, firefighters, and so forth. The Court specified the statistical analysis necessary for a complainant to establish a "disparate impact" case. In the Griggs ruling, the Court also said that if disparate impact was shown, then the burden of proof shifted to the employer to show a business necessity for the seemingly illegal practice.

If the employer could not prove a business necessity, it would be in violation of federal antidiscrimination law and it would have to change its practices.

The attorneys for the cannery workers used such a statistical analysis to make their case against Wards Cove. They claimed that company practices prevented Filipinos and Native Alaskans, who made up more than half the cannery workforce, from getting jobs such as cook and forklift operator, which were held almost entirely by whites. Numerous class action lawsuits had been won by workers using the procedures set forth by the 1971 Griggs ruling.

But in the course of sixteen years, nine hearings and eight decisions by federal district court, appeals court, and, ultimately, the Supreme Court, the lawyers and judges used the Wards Cove workers' case to reconsider the use of the statistical analysis and whether the workers' suit had applied it appropriately. Through it all, the Filipino American and Native Alaskan workers continued to press their claim, receiving encouragement and support from black and Latino workers in the Northwest to continue their legal battle.

By the time the *Wards Cove Packing Company* v. *Atonio* case was decided by the Supreme Court in 1989, the majority of justices had been appointed by Presidents Reagan and Bush. In a five–four split, the Court handed down a ruling on the cannery workers' suit that changed the statistical standards required to show disparate impact, and shifted the burden of proof from the employers to the employees. As a result of this landmark decision, workers would have a far more difficult time establishing disparate impact. In his dissenting opinion, Justice Harry A. Blackmun said that the court had taken three major steps backwards: by putting the burden of proof on the workers, by barring the use of company workforce comparisons, and by requiring proof of discrimination for each employment practice at issue.

The decision devastated employees who, like the Filipino migrant cannery workers, had spent years on their court cases to fight workplace discrimination. Women or minorities who were shut out of jobs as construction workers or firefighters, for example, would have a harder time in court. The newly configured Supreme Court had battered a number of other civil rights cases, but Wards Cove dealt a mortal blow. Filipino American and Native Alaskan cannery workers became the whipsaw to reverse a civil rights standard that had been in place for nearly twenty years.

The nation's lawyers might previously have been unaware of the marginal existence of Asian American immigrant low-wage workers who defied the model minority image. Now the Supreme Court decision of *Wards Cove Packing Company* v. *Atonio* turned them into a law school case study. On behalf of the four dissenting Supreme Court justices, Justice John Paul Stevens wrote that "some characteristics of the Alaska salmon canning industry described in this litigation—in particular, the segregation of housing and dining facilities and the stratification of jobs along racial and ethnic lines—bear an unsettling resemblance to aspects of a plantation economy." Justice Blackmun added, "The salmon industry described in this record takes us back to the kind of overt and institutionalized discrimination we have not dealt with in years."

But the Supreme Court's majority ruled otherwise in its 1989 landmark decision, throwing the lawsuit of the Filipino cannery workers and several other pending class actions into turmoil. Those pending cases had followed one set of rules, but the rules had changed. The Northwest Labor and Employment Law Office knew the battle would have to shift to the legislative arena. "As soon as the Supreme Court decision was handed down, Nemesio [Domingo, Jr.], Tyree Scott [head of the construction workers' association], and I began strategizing about the legislation necessary to reverse the decision and to restore the workers' rights," said Narasaki. For the Filipino workers who endured this tortuous legal saga, it became clear that the courts could no longer be relied on to remedy racial injustice. Instead, the workers turned to Congress and the political arena for a solution. They broached the idea of new civil rights legislation to Senator Edward M. Kennedy and other members of Congress, who said they were already working on it.

Within months after the Supreme Court's *Wards Cove* ruling, Democrats in Congress, led by Senator Kennedy, proposed a new, comprehensive civil rights law. The bill aimed to stop the steady erosion of civil rights law in the very courts that had defined that legal ground only a generation earlier. The *Wards Cove* decision's crippling effect on all vulnerable workers spurred Congress to try to codify for the first time nearly three decades of courtroom measures prescribed to reverse the effects of discrimination.

In Washington, the Leadership Conference on Civil Rights rallied civil rights advocates around the country to push for a new civil rights law. Several Asian American groups, particularly the Japanese American Citizens League and the Organization of Chinese Americans, were active in the coalition efforts. Fresh from their legislative victory in gaining redress for Japanese Americans with the Civil Liberties Act of 1988, Asian Americans were eager to continue their involvement in the national political arena. But the GOP was divided over affirmative action, and conservative Republicans assailed the legislation as a "quota bill." The Democrat-controlled House and Senate passed the 1990 civil rights bill, but President George Bush's veto killed it.

With the opening of the 102nd congressional session in 1991, the Democrats came back for another try. In a bipartisan effort, Republican Senator John Danforth of Missouri co-sponsored the civil rights bill with Senator Kennedy. By late October, after the rancorous confirmation hearings of Supreme Court nominee Clarence Thomas and the long months of racially divisive attacks on civil rights by conservatives such as avowed racist David Duke, the GOP candidate for governor of Louisiana, several moderate Republicans swung over in support of the legislation. But to overcome another Bush veto, the Democrats needed support from two more Senate Republicans.

As co-sponsor of the civil rights bill, Danforth came under sharp criticism from the White House. But after Danforth led the GOP efforts to get Clarence Thomas confirmed to the Supreme Court, another Republican senator, Ted Stevens of Alaska, stood up to defend Danforth at a White House meeting. "How can you do this to Danforth after he got Thomas confirmed?" Stevens reportedly asked, adding, "You can't count on my vote to sustain a veto against the Civil Rights Act."

The Alaska senator's outburst suggesting that he might switch his vote in favor of the civil rights bill triggered a flurry of late-night horse trading between Senate Republicans and Democrats outside Senate Minority Leader Bob Dole's office, just off the Senate floor. To get the necessary Republican votes, Danforth was adamant in his demands to Kennedy, his Democratic co-sponsor. "I need something for Stevens," he said.

That night, with Kennedy and his chief counsel, Jeff Blatner, leading the charge, the senators began to hammer out a compromise amendment to the civil rights bill. They cinched the votes from the two Alaska senators and thereby secured the bill's passage. On October 25, 1991, an agreement was announced; on October 30, the Senate approved the bill, and within a matter of days, the House voted its approval. Finally, the Civil Rights Act of 1991 was passed after nearly two years of wrangling; among its many provisions, the new law removed the onerous changes that the Supreme Court had made in its 1989 *Wards Cove Packing Company* v. *Atonio* ruling.

As champagne corks popped in celebration of the new civil rights law, no one paid much attention to the obscure language that had swung the Alaska senators' votes and won the compromise. Buried deep in Section 22(b) of the bill was this odd amendment, introduced by Senator Frank Murkowski of Alaska: "Notwithstanding any other provision of this Act, nothing in the Act shall apply to any disparate impact case for which a complaint was filed before March 1, 1975, and for which an initial decision was rendered after October 30, 1983." Senator Murkowski himself explained what this language meant in a Dear Colleague letter to his fellow senators: "To the best of my knowledge, *Wards Cove Packing Co.* v. *Atonio* is the only case that falls within this classification."

In other words, the only case in the nation that would not be covered by the new law was the very case that inspired it—the lawsuit initiated by the Filipino American salmon cannery workers. Only one group of workers in the United States would fail to benefit from the new law; only one company would be spared its provisions for their 1974 lawsuit.

"This is like saying everyone can sit in the front of the bus except for Rosa Parks," declared Gloria Caoile of the Philippine Heritage Foundation and the Asian Pacific Heritage Council.

This was no chance break for Wards Cove but the result of its dogged persistence. The company, a large employer in Alaska, spent $175,000 on a high-powered Washington lobbyist and an estimated $2 million to fight the cannery workers' discrimination suit over the years. Its owners, the Brindles, were active in Alaska politics and big-time political campaign contributors. Beyond the campaign pursestrings, the Brindles were personal friends of Senator Murkowski. Alec Brindle, the son of the company president and grandson of its founder, was employed by Murkowski as a legislative aide on Capitol Hill when the senator introduced this amendment.

Where the Brindles had connections in high places, Asian Pacific Americans had a different experience. Neither of the two Asian American senators from Hawaii—Daniel Inouye and Daniel Akaka—nor the three Asian American representatives—Robert Matsui, Norman Mineta, and Patsy Mink—were consulted when the deal was struck by Kennedy, Danforth, Stevens, and Dole. Nor were the D.C.-based Asian American groups who were working to support the civil rights bill informed of the true meaning of the camouflaged, disingenuous language of the compromise. Other civil rights leaders knew what happened to the Wards Cove workers, but no one bothered to inform the Asian Americans on Capitol Hill. Asian Americans were simply not considered players in the civil rights arena; they didn't need to be consulted, nor were there fears of political repercussions from the Asian American community.

Washington Senator Brock Adams's staff caught the amendment and notified the Asian American labor activists in Seattle, who clearly understood the intent of the obscure language and began making urgent appeals. Several of the plaintiffs were constituents of the senator, including Frank Atonio, the name plaintiff in the *Wards Cove* suit. Atonio wrote to Adams: "Few workers in the country are as economically disadvantaged as non-white migrant, seasonal workers, a group which comprises the class in our case. Yet the special exemption in the bill will now make it harder for us than anyone else to prove discrimination against our former employer . . . I do not see how a law which was designed to overturn the Supreme Court decision in our case can exclude only our case from coverage. I would appreciate your asking the sponsors (both Republican and Democrat) how they can justify this special exemption."

It was too late to put the brakes to the civil rights bill; the Senate vote had already been taken and the exemption for Wards Cove was part of the deal. Asian Americans had worked for the new civil rights bill to assist all people seeking civil rights remedies, including the Filipino American Wards Cove workers whose case inspired the legislation. Instead, they found themselves betrayed.

The cannery workers' saga might have ended with the stealth provision, but in a strange twist of fate, the Murkowski amendment exempting the Wards Cove suit was inadvertently omitted from the civil rights legislation by a drafting error. The amendment had to be reintroduced in Congress and voted on as a technical correction. Such a vote was usually pro forma, but not this time. When the Senate was asked for its unanimous consent to put the exemption back in, Senator Brock Adams stood up and protested, bringing attention to the backdoor maneuver. Adams himself had worked in the canneries and witnessed the segregated work environment.

By chance, a national convention of Asian American lawyers, the National Asian Pacific American Bar Association, was meeting in Seattle the week of the vote that passed the civil rights bill. It would have been hard to find another gathering more familiar with the Wards Cove case. In addition to the many NAPABA members who had entered the legal profession to be advocates for the Asian Pacific American community, representatives from other national Asian American organizations were present. With leaders of key Asian American groups already assembled at the convention, they sprang into action as soon as they got wind of the Wards Cove exemption and the imminent vote on the technical correction.

The Senate's drafting error gave Asian Americans a chance to block the injustice to the Wards Cove cannery workers. NAPABA, the Organization of Chinese Americans (OCA), and the Japanese American Citizens League (JACL)—the major national Asian American groups then with offices in Washington, D.C.—began a flurry of press conferences, phone calls, and visits to members of Congress in a frantic effort to block the amendment.

"This effort is nothing but an attempt to again relegate Asian Pacific Americans and Native Alaskans to second-class citizenship," said Dennis Hayashi, the national director of JACL.

"Why should the special interests of one employer outweigh the civil rights of all Asian Pacific Americans?" asked Daphne Kwok, executive director of OCA.

Besides the anger, there was a clear sense of betrayal by their own civil rights partners. "I am dismayed and outraged—how did the Democrats, 'the party of the people,' allow all of this to happen?" wondered Caoile of the Philippine Heritage Foundation. It was a rude awakening to Asian Americans who thought of themselves as equals in the civil rights coalition.

The Democratic leadership and civil rights establishment who had approved the compromise were stunned by the criticism. "A lot of people were shocked that this became a national issue, they were surprised that

Asian Pacific American groups would take such a stance," said Lindsay McLaughlin, Washington, D.C., representative for the International Long-shoremen's and Warehousemen's Union, who worked on mobilizing support. "Asian Americans are not seen [to be] as important as other groups with a history of being discriminated against. Very few people think of Asian Americans when they think of civil rights. The dealmakers didn't even think of it, or else they might have thought again."

The Asian Americans first lobbied the Senate, meeting with Senators Edward Kennedy and John Danforth, as well as Daniel Inouye and Daniel Akaka. On the Senate floor, Akaka, Brock Adams, and Paul Simon of Illinois argued against the exemption, but few senators were willing to vote against the deal with Murkowski. The Senate approved the exemption, 73–22.

Next the vote would be taken in the House, and Asian Americans focused particular attention on members of the Rules Committee and the House leadership, Speaker of the House Thomas Foley and Majority Leader Richard Gephardt.

Members of Congress who supported the cannery workers voiced their anger. At a weekly leadership meeting for House Democrats, Representative Norman Mineta railed against the Senate deal, noting in an oblique reference to Senator Kennedy that a lawsuit involving two thousand Irish Americans in Massachusetts would never have been exempted. Massachusetts Representative Joseph Kennedy II rushed to his uncle's defense; when Mineta returned to his office, Senator Kennedy was on the phone, trying to explain the need for the exemption. Mineta called the compromise "special-interest legislation at its worst."

When the vote for the rule allowing the technical amendment came up in the House, several Democratic members of the House spoke against it. Representative Jim McDermott of Washington declared, "Someone has let a skunk into the garden."

"Do you think for a second that this is a compromise? This is extortion," said Representative Neil Abercrombie of Hawaii. Other members of Congress, including Patsy Mink (Hawaii) and Patricia Schroeder (Colorado), Robert Matsui (California), Norman Mineta (California), Don Edwards (California), Craig Washington (Texas), and Alan Wheat (Missouri) also spoke against the exemption.

To quell the revolt, Speaker of the House Thomas Foley made a rare appeal for votes for the civil rights bill compromise, promising to see that the exemption would be struck down at a later date. "I say to the Members . . . who are concerned with the Wards Cove case in particular that I will cooperate with them in advancing legislation to place that issue squarely before this Chamber and the other body, and I will exercise every effort on my part to see that this matter is corrected." House Majority Leader Richard Gephardt similarly pledged "to bring up the issue of the Wards Cove exemption in separate legislation as soon as humanly possible . . . so that that issue can be dealt with. My view is that it should not have been exempted. I am sorry that it was."

With the promise of corrective action, the technical amendment sailed through the House, 327–93. Immediately after, the House approved the Civil Rights Act of 1991, 381–38. Patsy Mink and Neil Abercrombie, the representatives from Hawaii, felt so strongly about the exemption that they crossed their own party and voted against the Civil Rights Act.

If the advocates for the Asian American cannery workers were unable to slow the rush to approve the Civil Rights Act of 1991, they were not about to forget the commitments made to them by House Speaker Foley and House Majority Leader Gephardt. Their promises were joined by Senator Edward Kennedy's. At a post–Civil Rights Act party in the Rayburn Building he also publicly announced his resolve to rectify this unfinished business.

Senator Brock Adams and Congressman Jim McDermott, both from Washington State, wasted no time introducing the Justice for Wards Cove Workers Act in November 1991 to delete the offending exemption. Asian American groups assembled their forces and embarked on a new round of hard work to win votes for the bill. A new national Asian American organization also joined the effort, the Asian Pacific American Labor Alliance (APALA). This time around, they marshaled the broad coalition support of the Leadership Conference on Civil Rights; legislative directors from the AFL-CIO and the ILWU; and key staff members from supporting members of Congress.

But what had seemed clear-cut, given all the promises, sank into a deep political abyss, an ugly maw of excuses that exposed a lack of will to support an Asian American cause.

First, there was the political stonewalling in the House and the Senate. In spite of Foley's and Gephardt's promises, House Judiciary Committee Chairman Jack Brooks (Texas) wouldn't move the bill because he viewed it as the Senate's problem. The Senate version of the bill was stuck because it was seen as violating a private deal between two senators, Kennedy and Murkowski. Meanwhile, various scandals didn't help: Senate sponsor Brock Adams was immobilized by sexual harassment charges, while House Speaker Foley had his own distractions with the House Post Office and banking investigations. On top of all that, there was another rationale that made Kennedy and civil rights groups hesitate: the Wards Cove exemption had to be maintained as a sacrificial offering to bolster the Democrats' claim that the Civil Rights Act of 1991 was retroactive. They hoped that all pending civil rights suits that had been initiated before 1991 would be covered by the new law—all except the Wards Cove workers' case. But this hope never materialized. With so much political detritus, the proposed Justice for Wards Cove Workers Act didn't even make it to the House or Senate floor. The bottom line: the injustice involving Asian Americans—and Filipino American migrant workers at that—just wasn't worth the political capital it would take to go back on a deal and right the wrong.

But Asian Americans were not giving up. After all, they weren't strangers to the labyrinthine legislative process. Only a few years earlier, the Civil Liberties Act of 1988 was won by Japanese Americans with the aid of numerous non-Asian civil rights groups. The multiracial effort garnered an official apology and monetary redress for the surviving Japanese Americans who had been imprisoned during World War II solely because of their ancestry. That legislation was first proposed within the Japanese American Citizens League in 1970. Congress finally took action in 1979 and established a commission to investigate the wartime relocation and internment of civilians. It took yet another ten years of hearings around the country, the unearthing of more evidence and testimony, individual lawsuits, and outreach to other communities before the apology and redress were won. That victory was a testimony to the resolve and tenacity of Japanese Americans, particularly third-generation Sansei, who forced history to alter its judgment of their parents and grandparents.

The lessons of persistence and dogged determination from the redress effort were not lost on the Asian Americans in Washington, who focused their energies on getting the Wards Cove exemption removed. The workers themselves had been waiting for their day in court for nearly twenty years. Some, like Gene Viernes, had died; others had long retired from the grueling cannery work. The canneries had also changed, upgrading their facilities and working conditions so that they didn't need to rely on Asian migrant workers. But none of those changes undid the harm that the Filipino American workers had suffered while working at Wards Cove.

Representative Jim McDermott reintroduced the Justice for Wards Cove Workers Act on March 2, 1993, for action in the 103rd Congress. With a long list of co-sponsors in both the House and the Senate, the Justice for Wards Cove Workers Committee was prepared to make a full-court press. This time, they even had the support of the White House. On the day that the bill was reintroduced, newly elected President Bill Clinton stated, "It is contrary to all of our ideas to exclude any American from the protection of our civil rights laws . . . I am committed to removing this exemption."

A national Asian American presence in the District of Columbia began to emerge through the systematic lobbying efforts of Daphne Kwok of OCA; Karen Narasaki, then the JACL Washington representative; Stephen C. Chin of NAPABA; and Matt Finucane of APALA. Following their lead, Asian American organizations from around the United States rallied in support of the bill; so did the more than 185 national civil rights organizations of the Leadership Conference on Civil Rights, representing minorities, women, people with disabilities, older Americans, and labor and religious groups. In Houston, Texas, city council member Martha Wong got a resolution passed against the exemption. The American Bar Association backed the removal of the exemption. Rallies and demonstrations were held periodically in Seattle, Washington, organized by the Justice for Wards Cove Workers Committee. The national effort was built on a pan-Asian, multiracial coalition, as the years of organizing in Seattle that preceded the Washington effort had been. Even Senator Kennedy allowed his name to be added as a co-sponsor of the Senate version of the bill with Senator Patty Murray, who had been elected to Adams's seat for the state of Washington.

But as the end of the 103rd session approached in 1994, the bill was still stuck in the Senate Committee on Labor and Human Resources—a committee that happened to be chaired by Ted Kennedy. Kennedy had given his name to the bill, but little else. There were plenty of reasons for him to sit on the bill—the condemnation by Republican senators of reneging on a done deal, and the argument that sacrificing the cannery workers again would assist other pending lawsuits to be covered retroactively by the new civil rights bill. There was also the fear that a debate on the exemption might be a Pandora's box to revisit other parts of the civil rights act. The arguments on behalf of fairness for Filipino and Asian Americans weren't enough to budge the bill or even to get answers from Kennedy's staff on the bill's lack of progress.

No Senate Republicans would vote against Murkowski for the bill, and the stalling by the Democrats gave the senator from Alaska and the Wards Cove lobbyists time to mount their counterattack. They sent out numerous "Dear Colleague" letters to members of the House and Senate who supported the Filipino American workers, aggressively trying to discredit their position, and succeeded in getting a few members of Congress to withdraw support. They sent stern letters to newspapers they believed to be sympathetic to the effort to remove the exemption.

Some of Murkowski's encounters turned nasty. When Stephen C. Chin of NAPABA wrote an editorial critical of Wards Cove and the exemption, Murkowski published letters accusing Chin of deliberate misinformation, innuendo, personal attacks, and "politically motivated rubbish." At a Washington, D.C., conference of the Committee of 100, a group of prominent Chinese Americans, a heated argument took place between Senator Murkowski and Representative Robert Matsui. The two members of Congress had appeared on different panels earlier and happened to be in the audience during a discussion of the Wards Cove legislation. Murkowski rose to justify the exemption, and Matsui took issue, challenging the senator. "They started shouting at each other and it quickly became a personal thing—the animosity was intense," said Henry Tang, the group's chairman.

In September 1994, at the end of the 103rd Congress, the Justice for Wards Cove Workers bill finally moved out of Kennedy's committee, with the Democrats voting for and Republicans against. Again, the cannery workers were defeated.

"This was such an easy piece of legislation, no one should have cared except Wards Cove and Murkowski," said JACL's Narasaki. "Everyone agreed that what happened to the Wards Cove workers was horrible, but the political dynamics kept the bill from moving forward. Asian Americans got the short end of the stick, and we didn't have a big enough stick to beat it back."

The following year, in 1995, Representative Jim McDermott again reintroduced the Justice for Wards Cove Workers Act. But with a Republican majority in both Houses of Congress, the bill went nowhere. It hasn't been reintroduced since.

At a convention of the Inland Boatmen's Union that represents many of the Filipino American cannery workers, the news reached Richard Gurtiza, regional director of the union and a former cannery worker, that the 1995 effort was dead.

Gurtiza, a Filipino American, stood up on the convention floor and made an impassioned speech to his fellow unionists, a multiracial group, still with many Filipino faces. "We have a moral obligation to see that justice is done for our brothers and sisters at Wards Cove who had to work under terrible plantation conditions. Now I've been told that the legislation is dead as a doornail." Everyone in the room rallied behind Gurtiza, vowing to fight on to the end.

Each year, at the start of the salmon harvest, Gurtiza makes the long trip up to Alaska, visiting several canneries in a nonstop membership blitz. Most of the run-down bunkhouses of twenty years earlier have been replaced by modern, weatherproofed buildings; at the Wards Cove Packing Company Cannery in Ketchikan, a building is dubbed the Holiday Inn. Mess halls like the log-cabin-style A. W. Brindle Dining Hall at the Red Salmon Cannery in Naknek are no longer segregated. Western and Asian foods are available to all workers. The changes are surely in part a result of the lawsuits filed by the Filipino workers.

Now that the living and working conditions have improved, the companies no longer rely on migrant immigrant workers. This may be the unkindest cut to the Filipino Americans—thanks to their efforts, conditions have improved so much that they are no longer needed, since a "higher class" of workers are willing to come in. On the other hand, it is also true that the Filipino American population has changed significantly since the days when Filipinos could find jobs only as laborers. Most of the post-1965 Filipino immigrants are educated, working as professionals and office staff. These days, college students outnumber

the Filipino workers: the canneries used to be more than 80 percent Filipino; now they're 65 percent white college students. The canneries are
no longer closed shops in which a union membership is a prerequisite
for a job. As a result, the union's cannery membership is below 2,000, less
than half of what it used to be. Gurtiza has the difficult task of persuad-
ing college students to become union members. Unlike the Filipino
workers who came back to the salmon canneries year after year, students
don't see themselves as workers who can benefit from union representation.

There are reminders of the past, too. The yellow clapboard Filipino
mess hall where murdered union leader Gene Viernes led a hunger strike
decades ago still stands at the Red Salmon Cannery, though no longer in
use. The canneries persist in using the racial slur "Iron Chink" to refer to
the automated butcher machine, but the unions only recently began to
strike the term from the union contracts. And the weathered, creased faces
of aging Filipino cannery workers silently ask: When will they be treated as
equal under the law to every other American?

With the business of the Wards Cove workers still unfinished, the
twisted courtroom saga and the legislative farce stand out to Asian Americans as lessons in unequal justice at best, betrayal at worst.

In October 1999, after sitting on the workers' last appeal for five years,
District Judge Justin Quackenbush—the original presiding judge who
ruled against their case in 1974—finally dismissed the Wards Cove workers' case—again. The Northwest Labor and Employment Law Office filed
another appeal on behalf of the aging workers. Judge Quackenbush will
preside. And there is still the possibility that the Justice for Wards Cove
Workers legislation will be revived one day to strike the offending exemption—though such an act would be symbolic only. "I've seen the issue for
Wards Cove workers narrowed down from the substance of outright segregation and discrimination, to a legal issue, and now to an empty symbolic gesture with no substance," said Diane Narasaki, formerly of the
Northwest Labor and Employment Law Office, which initiated the lawsuit.

Washington insiders who were part of the Senate compromise leading
to the Wards Cove exemption vehemently assert that it was simply "politics" that led to the deal, that two senators' votes were needed, and it
wouldn't have mattered who had to lose. Those close to Ted Kennedy

rejected the notion that the senator was insensitive to Asian American concerns or that a particular group was singled out in the exemption. But hardball politics is all about who wins and who loses; the efforts to obtain justice for the Filipino workers became emblematic of how little power Asian Americans could muster in Washington.

In the office of Jeff Blatner, Senator Kennedy's chief counsel during the 1991 legislation, hangs a plaque commemorating the passage of the 1991 Civil Rights Act, with a handwritten message from Senator Kennedy thanking him for bringing the bill into law; it seems as if a thank-you plaque should go to the Filipino American cannery workers, too. As Richard Cohen, columnist of the "Congressional Chronicle" for the *National Journal*, wrote of the Wards Cove plaintiffs, "Welcome to Congress, Mr. Atonio."

The disappointment over Wards Cove did not embitter Asian Americans, but the experience made it clear that the moral high ground is not enough in American politics. To become players in the rough and tumble of national politics, Asian Americans would have to bulk up in the traditional arena of electoral politics: by registering voters and getting the votes out, by encouraging Asian Americans to run for office, and by contributing to political campaigns. At the same time, the Wards Cove effort demonstrated the strength of pan-Asian cooperation and multiracial coalition-building. Asian Americans became tempered in the work of Washington lobbying, and numerous Asian American groups developed organizing drives, separately and together, to get their communities involved in mainstream politics. "I've seen Asian Americans in Washington grow from a subdued force to a politically astute and effective voice," said Wade Henderson, executive director of the Leadership Conference on Civil Rights. "They are becoming significant players by following a well-worn political path."

The Wards Cove experience proved the necessity of learning to be loud, combative, and punitive when necessary, across the nation, and in Washington as well as the local community. When the Voting Rights Act came up for reauthorization in 1992, the Asian American community's interests in having bilingual ballots seemed destined for the congressional chopping block in another backroom deal. "We thought, remember Wards Cove," said Chris Strobel, former Representative Norman

Mineta's legislative director. "We didn't want people to think they could get away with selling out Asian Americans. If we lose, at least let's fight. We want people to realize there will be consequences from Asian Americans."

The sacrifices of the Filipino American cannery workers, and those of union leaders Gene Viernes and Silme Domingo, galvanized Asian Americans. They offered another Asian American contribution to civil rights and American democracy. Asian Americans found betrayal, but also discovered a new level of political involvement.

# · 7 ·

# Lost and Found in L.A.

At some point in my childhood a rumor took hold that those "Chinese Zia children" were "so very well behaved." It was my first lesson in cultural mythology because in truth my brothers and I were wildly undisciplined. Our main entertainment was chasing after one another and bombarding the sibling target of the moment with any available unsecured object. We were so unruly that while I was still in elementary school, my parents imposed a rule of silence at the dinner table and reassigned seats according to who was least likely to pummel his or her neighbor.

Dad and Mom used the enforced quiet to lecture us on various topics. Most often these contained some Confucian parable on the eternal obligation children have to their parents. My father had a special fondness for the tale of the boy whose mother beat him soundly with a stick every day, even after he had grown

*Los Angeles store owner Hwa Ja Kim (background) jokes with customers in August 1993; two weeks later she installed a Plexiglas partition after the security guard was shot to death during a robbery attempt (Chang W. Lee)*

into manhood. Never did he raise his voice or hand in response. One day, his mother didn't hit him. The man-boy began to cry and brought the stick to his mother, begging her to strike him. "Mama," he cried, "please don't stop beating me. When you hit me I know you are strong and healthy." He realized his mother was too old and frail to beat him anymore, and his heart was filled with sadness.

Since Dad's own mother beat him daily and he was quick to anger himself, the story seemed a bit self-serving to his skeptical ABC—American-born Chinese—kids. But Dad carried his own sorrow, his failings in his filial duties. During Japan's invasion of China, Japanese soldiers occupied his home province of Jiangsu, raping and pillaging wherever they went. My father was stationed in Chongqing, a member of Chiang Kai-shek's staff. As he learned of the massacres in Nanjing and neighboring Suzhou, his home, he desperately tried to get news about his mother and elder brother. Finally, a courier brought word that their bodies had been sighted along a roadside, where they had apparently tried to flee to safety. He brought back a ring that my grandmother wore, convincing my father that his mother, brother, and sister-in-law were killed during the rampage at Nanjing. He was never able to retrieve their bodies. Dad often recounted this story during an otherwise silent dinner, his voice breaking.

There was no escaping the message of our own unspecified obligations, as Mom, too, exhorted us with many such stories of Chinese kids who willingly, enthusiastically, sacrificed body and soul for their parents. Over our evening meal, she'd tell us about the less fortunate families who had nothing to eat. How, in China, the truly dutiful daughter would cut off a piece of her arm and cook it for her parents, rather than watch them starve. Or the good son who used the warmth of his own body to melt a hole in a frozen pond, so that he might catch fish for his ailing mother.

I'd sit unconvinced, trying hard not to roll my eyes, repressing the urge to make some disrespectful comment. But it was impossible not to absorb the lessons in filial obligation: much was expected from us. My parents didn't have to tell us that they sacrificed for our sake; every day we could see how hard they worked in our family business to make ends meet. And we were expected to do our share.

Each kid had assigned tasks. When I was five years old, I tied ribbons and attached plastic white horses to the pink and blue merry-go-rounds my father sold to flower shops. As I grew older, I took on more challenging tasks. Henry, the oldest, made miniature bassinets and night lamps decorated with yellow ducks, while Hoyt assembled the merry-go-rounds. Hugo painted and wrapped the pieces, while the two toddlers, my only sister, Humane, and baby brother, Haddon, entertained us. Mom usually stayed up way past midnight, cutting and sewing the satin tops of the carousels. The work took on a dreary monotony.

I'd pass the time listening to the Top 40 Pop/Rock Hits on the radio. Dad recited classical Chinese poems while he worked, telling us about his days as a rising young scholar in China, but how in America his education was worthless. He spent hours scheming to sue the government of Japan for reparations, to hold Japan accountable to families like ours, who had lost loved ones during the Japanese occupation. His anger and bitterness toward Japan was deep. Then he'd load up the family car with the merry-go-rounds, lamps, bassinets, and other "baby novelties" to sell to flower shops. Occasionally I went along with Dad on his deliveries. I loved to breathe the heavy, green smell of the flower shops, to admire the colorful flowers organized in their refrigerated showcases. If I was lucky, I might see one of our merry-go-rounds or bassinets filled with flowers, waiting to be delivered to a new mother. But it was painful to watch my proud father kowtow and scrape to his customers, making small talk and chitchat in strange fawning tones that he didn't use at home.

We never complained about the tedium—it was how we survived. But I knew this life making baby novelties wasn't for me. Dad's stories about the Chinese system of scholarships for bright students from poor families suggested a way out of an uninspiring existence. I studied hard—not out of filial obligation to my parents, but as a means of escaping the life they were consigned to.

When I finally left for college, I felt joyously liberated from my parents' Confucian sensibilities. But I also felt a sense of guilt, that I was no longer around to help carry the family load. No one said it out loud, but it was understood: one day my siblings and I would support our parents, when they couldn't work at the baby novelty business anymore. My first-generation immigrant parents had no pension plans, health coverage, life insurance. We were their future in America.

As I involved myself in issues that touched the various Asian American communities, I came to know many other Asian American immigrants like my parents. They are a self-selected group of pioneers, high-risk takers who made the difficult passage to America to satisfy a hopeful but uncertain vision. Once here, they navigate between two worlds, processing their American lives through an Asian filter, sifting the land of their past with the America of our present.

With time, my parents' connection to their American reality grew perceptibly stronger. Their future was so obviously here, with us. Their stories began to change, with different endings. Dad's voice still broke whenever he told the story of his family's wartime slaughter. He unsuccessfully pursued a lawsuit against the government of Japan—he even studied the Japanese language to better make his case. But at some point his rancor toward Japan ended when it came to Japanese Americans. When the campaign to seek justice for Vincent Chin was under way, he told me he was glad I was involved, that it was a good thing for Chinese Americans and Japanese Americans to work together for the common good. After all, he'd say, this is America.

.    .    .

It's 8 a.m. at the busy street corner of Vernon and Arlington, in the heart of South Central Los Angeles. Outside of L.A., this mainly Latino and African American enclave is most known for the urban uprising centered here in 1992 following the not-guilty verdicts on four white police officers in the beating of motorist Rodney King.

The intersection is alive with parents walking their children to the nearby elementary school. Commuters wait at the bus stop by the steel-grated tire shop, across from the New Orleans Oyster Loaf House and a run-down motel. On the northwest corner is the newest building for blocks around: the One Stop Market, neat and trim in eye-pleasing pastel shades of green, yellow, and pink.

The parking lot is empty, closed off by a sturdy black metal fence whose gates are firmly anchored and padlocked. The textured cinderblock walls are capped by a fireproof tile roof that sports a matching black metal fence and coiled barbed wire around the perimeter, interrupted only by strategically placed floodlights. Heavy-gauge metal security doors cover all the windows and doors. Even the bottled water refill machine, a ubiquitous feature of Southern California, has a metal security gate to protect it.

Within minutes, a modest white two-door sedan pulls up. Jae Yul Kim, the stocky owner of the One Stop, gets out to unlock the various gates, while Pedro, his Latino son-in-law, picks up the bundles of newspapers for the day. Nina, Jae's diminutive wife, goes in first to open the side entrance. Their movements are stiff, slow with the weary anticipation of another long day, still tired from the one that ended less than eight hours before.

Jae looks much older than his fifty-four years. His face is creased by deep furrows. The decades of building—and rebuilding—a livelihood that is low on profit, long on hours, with constant safety concerns, has taken a toll. Jae first arrived in the United States in 1974 as a university graduate, with $20.22 in his pocket and no knowledge of English. He went to work for a Korean wig manufacturer, then moved on to pumping gas. He later got a job as a carpenter and an air-conditioning mechanic. He saved some money and, with the help of a Small Business Administration loan, in the mid-1980s bought a store with 600 square feet of space in the Hollywood area. The previous owner, who was Jewish, showed Jae how to run the store. "He told me, 'Don't worry, it's small, but I raised two lawyers and two doctors. You can, too,' " says Jae. A few years later, Jae moved to a larger store in South Central.

This new version of the One Stop was built in 1995. Its bunker design is typical of the stores built since the riots. When the Kims' shop was looted and torched on April 30, 1992, they lost not only a business but their extended family's income. In that one fiery moment, Jae's entire life changed—the externals of his family's livelihood, the business and their home, but also the internals, their hopes and dreams, the expectations they had for themselves in America. In the three years it took to secure the city approvals and financing to rebuild on the old site, the bank foreclosed on Kim's home; they survived on food stamps.

Inside the store, the tidy rows of shelves are filled with a variety of goods, from the usual canned foods and snacks, soft drinks, beer and wine, to pantyhose and jewelry, and hula hoops and toys for the kids. Fresh produce and meat are in the deli section, while the hard liquor and cigarettes are enclosed in a booth with the cash register behind thick bulletproof Plexiglas walls.

Before tending to his first customers of the day, Jae goes to the back and loads a clip into a 9 mm pistol. He wears it around his waist, along with a pair of handcuffs and a canister of Mace—mandatory paraphernalia for a licensed security guard, which he is. Jae covers it all with a cheery red *Forest Gump* apron. The city wouldn't permit him to reopen the One Stop unless he hired a security guard. He couldn't afford to hire a guard, so he obtained a license to be one himself. As he holsters the gun, he shrugs. One of his friends, he says, refused to keep a gun at his shop and was stabbed to death there. Until last week, Jae didn't wear a gun either, but an armed robbery attempt brought a change of heart.

One week ago at 3 p.m., a man came up to the cash register and flashed a gun under his T-shirt. Jae dived under the counter, but Nina screamed and ran for the back room. The man reached through the merchandise window cut out of the Plexiglas and began shooting at her. Jae was pinned under the counter, unable to reach the .32 near the cash register, or the shotgun in the back office. The shooter missed Jae and Nina, but struck several bottles of Seagram's Extra Dry Gin before running out of the store. A few of the bullet slugs remain imbedded in the Plexiglas, a silent reminder that Jae and Nina might have joined the other Korean store-keepers killed in their stores each year. In the year following the riots, fifteen grocers were killed in Los Angeles County alone.

A stream of customers pours in and Jae keeps up a cheerful banter. "Good morning—what's good for you about this morning?" he asks a regular. "It's good that I'm alive to say good morning to you," she shoots back. A Latina shopper approaches and, in the July heat, Jae teases, *"Feliz Navidad."* When she asks about some prices, he answers in Spanish. After a while, Jae tends to the deli section. A customer requests four slices of cheese; Jae runs the slicer and wraps the cheese, then stops to talk with her little girl, enfolding her in an affectionate hug. A hand-lettered sign says no deli orders under a dollar can be filled, but many orders are not much more than that. Jan, a rail-thin African American woman, saunters over to Jae and gives him a peck on the cheek. Jan asks if he can help her out today, and he slips her a couple dollars, saying he'd rather give money than deal with extending credit. "Before the riots, I never talk with my customers. They don't like me. Now we make jokes, we like each other. I learn to change—I have to."

Everything about life changed for Korean Americans on April 29, 1992. When the smoke cleared from the three-day uprising in Los Angeles, 54 people had died and some 4,500 shops were reduced to ashes. More than half of the destroyed or damaged businesses were Korean-run. Each shop represented at least one extended family. Tens of thousands of Korean Americans lost their livelihoods and years of sweat equity that day. Countless others who provided services to those businesses were also caught in the downward suction of the sudden impoverishment. Nearly half of the city's total financial loss of more than $1 billion in damages was suffered by a single group: the Korean American mom-and-pop storekeepers. The staggering devastation of that date became known by Korean Americans as sa-i-gu, pronounced "sah-ee-goo," or April 2-9.

The angry fracture lines and bitter divisiveness over those three days are evident from the divergent terminology that describe the event. To some observers, sa-i-gu was an urban rebellion, an expression of protest against the economic disenfranchisement of blacks and Latinos—with Korean merchants cast as the oppressor class. Other called it a food riot, a conflagration of inner-city poor and their frenzied plundering of all shops in striking distance, many of which happened to be Korean-owned. Still others, preferring a more subdued description, referred to the riot as a civil unrest, an upheaval that marked all Angelenos.

Most Korean Americans reject such references. To them, it was a SCUD missile attack with a very definite target. "An American pogrom" is how K. W. Lee, the venerable Korean American journalist, described the events beginning April 29. "Koreatown was a war zone. For us it was like the Jewish last stand in Warsaw, or the internment of the Japanese Americans. Sa-i-gu was a convenient way for mainstream America to deflect black rage," said Lee, who was editor in chief of the *Korea Times* English Edition at the time of the riots.

Sa-i-gu has become the reference point for Korean American life in the United States, in the way that the mass imprisonment of Japanese Americans during World War II was a defining moment for that community. Sa-i-gu has become the point at which all dreams, hopes, and illusions were stripped bare and burned to their essence. How real was their American dream? Was the image of the multicultural society and pan–Asian American unity just another myth? In the aftermath of sa-i-gu, a transformed community and leadership would emerge from the ashes, with a vision based on a cold new reality.

Before sa-i-gu, Korean Americans were invisible, subsumed in the generic Asian American landscape, blurred in with the more established Chinese Americans and Japanese Americans. After sa-i-gu, Americans discovered Koreans in their midst. They found a different breed of Asian —more confrontational, less accommodating. Before sa-i-gu, Korean Americans, like most immigrants and most Americans, saw themselves as individuals on their own quests for their personal dreams, bystanders to American society. Those Asians who accepted the model minority myth found it easy to believe that hard work and a low profile would reap their eventual rewards. Sa-i-gu exposed the myth. After sa-i-gu, Korean Americans were isolated and deeply hurt by the unspoken but widely held sentiment that they somehow deserved what they got. Starkly visible and alone on center stage, Korean Americans were forced to reevaluate their place and assert themselves in America.

If Korean Americans have been profoundly changed by sa-i-gu, the impact felt by other Asian Americans is no less significant, but less clear. Sa-i-gu compelled other Asian Americans to reconsider their own status in America, to alter the relationships between the various Asian American ethnicities as well as with communities of other races, even to recast who Asian Americans are. But sa-i-gu has not taken on the symbolism for Asian Americans of the Japanese American internment—at least, not yet. It took fifty years for Asian Americans to begin to see the concentration camps as emblematic for *Asian* Americans, beyond *Japanese* Americans. Where Korean Americans could not miss the implications of sa-i-gu for their community, many other Asian Americans have managed to avoid considering the broader meaning of that unpleasantness in L.A. Sa-i-gu was a hard teacher with lessons that have yet to be learned.

The warning signs of approaching cataclysm were evident in Los Angeles for months, even years. Before most Americans even recognized that Koreans existed in America as a growing and vital population, Korean Americans and many other Asian Americans were acutely aware of the explosive potential surrounding them. Two years before sa-i-gu, the divisive, year-long boycott of the Family Red Apple Market in New York City's Flatbush section sent shivers through Korean Americans across the United States, especially in states where Koreans had settled in large numbers— California, New York, Illinois, Texas, Colorado, Ohio, and Minnesota. In Los Angeles, unlike New York, Korean Americans and Asian Americans in general were better organized. But better organization did not offer solutions to the deepening tensions. Korean newspapers and grocers' associations in Los Angeles monitored the New York Red Apple situation closely and tried to learn from the incident, especially as African American newspapers such as the *Los Angeles Sentinel* ran numerous articles warning that Koreans were "taking over" the black community.

L.A.'s Korean American population increased from 8,900 in 1970 to 145,431 in 1990. In Koreatown, just north of the inner-city core of South

Central, their numbers had grown from 1,099 to 23,995 in two decades. Some 80 percent of the burgeoning Korean American community were immigrants who had arrived following the passage of the Immigration Act of 1965. In 1990, only half had been in the United States more than ten years. Though the majority of men and women had graduated from Korean colleges, the largest employment category for Korean Americans was "self-employed."

Not all Korean storekeepers had shops in black neighborhoods. In his research, Professor Edward T. Chang from the University of California at Riverside found that only about 10 percent of Korean merchants in Southern California were in neighborhoods servicing a primarily African American clientele. But high-profile conflicts between Korean merchants and black customers drew greater attention to their presence. To many African Americans, the Korean American storekeepers were a maddening reminder of chronic poverty and economic injustice in the black community, while yet another immigrant group was advancing, at their expense. In their pursuit of the American dream, the new immigrants seemed oblivious to the African Americans' long history of struggle for their unfulfilled dreams. In Los Angeles as well as New York and other cities, black people bristled over incidents of disrespectful treatment and false accusations of shoplifting.

Some of the tensions spilled into violence. In 1986, in a single month, four Korean storekeepers in L.A. were shot to death by African Americans in separate incidents. Both African American and Korean American communities recognized the danger signs. That year, with the assistance of the Los Angeles County Human Relations Commission, they tried to bridge their differences by creating the Black-Korean Alliance.

One of the first efforts of its kind in the country, L.A.'s Black-Korean Alliance (BKA) was to maintain an ongoing dialogue, even though conflicts had sparked between the two communities in several other cities. Discussions began with a group of black ministers, representatives from a few Korean American groups, and two consultants with the Los Angeles County Human Relations Commission—Larry Aubrey, an African American, and Jai Lee Wong, a Korean American. But problems beset the BKA from the start. Though the alliance came together initially to address racial tensions and the death toll among Korean shopkeepers, some of the merchant groups didn't want any publicity about the killings, fearing that attention would cause more trouble. The compulsion to "not make waves" presented a familiar quandary to Asian Americans, offering the tantalizing notion that if they kept quiet, they might escape further misfortune. At the same time, African American groups were also ambivalent about the BKA, as interracial relations with Koreans were a low priority among blacks. If the BKA's purpose was to encourage multicultural understanding, it was off to an inauspicious start.

As tensions escalated, the Black-Korean Alliance pulled in representatives from the NAACP, the Southern Christian Leadership Conference (SCLC), and, significantly, merchants and storekeepers from both African American and Korean communities. The reluctance of Korean storekeepers to speak to the media presented a problem. One of the BKA's goals was to draw the media's attention to positive efforts at interracial relations between blacks and Koreans, rather than the constant focus on conflicts. The BKA recruited Chung Lee, owner of the Watts Market, as the first Korean merchant to join the dialogue between the two communities. Lee was proud of his relationship with the black community of Watts, where riots were centered in 1965. He hired local workers, was involved in the Watts community, and, unlike other Korean shopkeepers, was willing to talk to the media. Seen as a positive role model, Lee and his work in Watts were often profiled in the *Korea Times*. However, some Korean merchants resented the publicity Lee received, and he drew criticism from Koreans for his visibility. After several months, Lee resigned from the BKA and another Korean storekeeper took his place.

The BKA continued with its mission to improve black–Korean relations. Other Asian Americans who worked with the L.A. County Human Relations Commission supported the Korean Americans and the BKA, but they treated the efforts as a Korean and black problem. When one of the former African Americans on the BKA, Mark Ridley-Thomas, ran for a seat on the L.A. City Council, Korean American grocers supported his campaign with enthusiasm and raised donations for his successful bid. Compared to other cities, Korean American immigrants in Los Angeles were taking positive steps to become involved in mainstream political life and a multiracial, multicultural alliance. As part of the BKA, Korean Americans met with key political leaders, including Mayor Tom Bradley, and city, county, and state officials. Both Korean and African American members of the BKA warned that unless substantial proactive measures were taken, there could be dire consequences for Los Angeles. Few heeded their warnings. "Then the Soon Ja Du shooting blew everything apart," said Jai Lee Wong, of the Human Relations Commission.

Soon Ja Du was minding the cash register of the Empire Liquor Market on South Figueroa Street in South Central L.A. when fifteen-year-old Latasha Harlins came into the store on Saturday morning, March 16, 1991. It was only thirteen days after Rodney King had been beaten by four white LAPD officers, their assault captured on videotape that aired repeatedly on the TV news. Racial tensions were high—and that was why forty-nine-year-old Soon Ja Du happened to be at the store that day. Her son Joseph was normally at the store on Saturdays, but members of the violent Crips gang had threatened him because he agreed to testify against them after another robbery attempt. To relieve Joseph from the stress and fear at the Empire Liquor Market, she took his place.

Something went terribly wrong when Harlins approached the cash register to pay for her orange juice. She had the money in her hands, and had already placed the juice in her backpack. Du grabbed the backpack and accused Harlins of stealing—a provocative charge that underscored persistent complaints of disrespect and scrutiny of African Americans by Korean merchants. Harlins punched Du, knocking her down twice, then turned to leave the store. As Du got up, she grabbed the gun that was under the counter. She fired the gun, and Latasha Harlins crumbled. Soon Ja Du's husband, Billy Heung Ki Du, who had been resting out back in their van, ran in and called 911. But it was too late for Latasha, killed by a bullet to the back of her head.

The entire episode was captured on the store's security video camera. Jan Jung-Min Sunoo, a federal mediator and then president of the L.A. County Human Relations Commission, reviewed the video with another federal mediator, who was African American. "I watched the video and saw a frightened Korean American woman whose gun went off accidentally. My black colleague watched and said, 'That settles that. She shot the girl in cold blood.'"

The Black-Korean Alliance issued a statement signed by the NAACP, the SCLC, and several Korean American organizations urging people to come together. "One case does not paint a true picture for everyone," said

Dennis Westbrook, the African American co-chair of the Black-Korean Alliance. "This incident is not indicative of the overall general relations between Korean merchants and their customers."

Though the BKA and the Human Relations Commission exhorted the police not to make the videotape of the Harlins shooting public because they feared it would further inflame racial tensions, the police released the tape to the news media anyway, a move that some believed was intended to draw attention away from the tape of the police beating of Rodney King. Their fears were justified: TV news programs repeatedly aired the tape of Soon Ja Du shooting Latasha Harlins. "The news media ran the story, 'Girl killed over $1.79 bottle of juice,' over and over again. The coverage was irresponsible—we knew it could lead to a riot," said Jai Lee Wong. Many merchants were so angry with the *Los Angeles Times* for depicting the killing as a racially motivated incident representative of all Korean grocers that they refused to sell certain issues at their stores.

It wasn't the first time that the grocers had exercised their economic power. When African American rap singer Ice Cube came out with "Black Korea" almost a year before Latasha Harlins was killed, Korean American political groups launched a boycott of his CD. His rap warned that if store-keepers did not respect blacks, their shops would be burned to a crisp. The consumer boycott had little impact. Then members of the Korean American Grocers Association (KAGRO) decided not to sell the malt liquor brand that was endorsed by Ice Cube, and the liquor manufacturer persuaded the rapper to offer an apology. But conflict resolution is not reconciliation, as University of Hawaii law professor Eric Yamamoto noted in his book *Interracial Justice: Conflict and Reconciliation in Post–Civil Rights America*. He cited an editorial in the *Los Angeles Sentinel* by Sheena Lester describing the Korean grocers as "poison-pushing merchants, who are apparently more outraged about being called names than they are about a dead Black child." The presence of so many liquor stores in South Central L.A. angered African Americans; some 682 liquor licenses were issued there, ten times more per square mile than elsewhere in the county, with about 30 percent of the independent liquor stores owned by Koreans. Conflict resolution without "action on underlying grievances, by both racial communities, seemed to inflame rather than heal racial wounds," wrote Yamamoto.

The killing of Latasha Harlins pushed an already charged atmosphere to the brink in Los Angeles and other cities, where African Americans and Asian Americans were following the events closely. Soon Ja Du in particular and Korean merchants in general became the angry focus of pickets and media events organized by an African American group called the Brotherhood Crusade. Led by a media-savvy leader named Danny Bakewell, their aim was to shut down Korean-owned stores, then take them over at drastically reduced prices. "I can put any one of them out of business," Bakewell told author Itabari Njeri in her book *The Last Plantation: Color, Conflict, and Identity: Reflections of a New World Black.* "If I got thirty organizations committing to twelve days a year [picketing a designated site], that means you out of business [*sic*]. That means, your number comes up, you're gone. You're history. You can't survive that. I only need to do that once or twice and I will have absolute, major control of this community." Bakewell initially picketed the Du family's Empire Liquor Market, but the store never reopened after the shooting. The Brotherhood Crusade hung a banner across the door: "Closed for Murder and Disrespect of Black People."

Every Korean American store was a potential target. The Watts Market of Chung Lee, the outspoken former member of the Black-Korean Alliance who was considered to have a model relationship with the black community, was surrounded by pickets. A baseless rumor circulated that Chung Lee's sister-in-law was related to Soon Ja Du. The market's black employees tried to dissuade the pickets without success. "He's being picketed because he's Korean," said one black employee; "they don't care if the rumor isn't true." Even if it were true, why should other Koreans take the blame for Soon Ja Du?

But other Koreans were blamed. Shortly after the killing of Latasha Harlins, two more Korean grocers were killed. A Korean girl who was in her parents' store was shot and critically wounded; the attacker reportedly said, "This is for Latasha." In the year following the shooting, 48 murders and 2,500 robberies were reported in L.A.'s Koreatown, and the number of hate crimes against Korean Americans topped all other anti-Asian incidents.

The situation went from bad to worse. Two and a half months after Soon Ja Du shot Latasha Harlins, an African American man named Lee Arthur Mitchell was killed during an apparent holdup attempt at Chung's Liquor market in South Central. Mitchell was shot to death by the store's owner, Tae Sam Park, who incurred several broken ribs in a scuffle at the cash register. Police ruled it a justifiable homicide. A daily picket went up outside the store, which the Brotherhood Crusade was determined to shut down. As the tense communities awaited the outcome of the prosecution of Soon Ja Du, violent incidents against Korean Americans increased.

Tensions wore through the bonds within the Korean American community. Some Korean Americans were angry with Soon Ja Du. They felt that her tragic act placed their entire community in jeopardy. "We should not lose our tempers over a bottle of orange juice," said Young Kyu Yi, owner of a store in South Central. "Even if we are victims of theft many times over, we must control our temper and be patient." Another Korean American told the *Korea Times*, "I'm hard-pressed to find some justification for someone to shoot another person over orange juice." Still, some felt empathy for Du. Korean Americans identified with the great stress she apparently faced. Like many Korean immigrants, Du was deeply religious. A Seventh-day Adventist and a church deacon, she spent more time at church and supporting various charities than at the store. A hundred members of her church packed the courtroom at her arraignment.

Other Asian Americans were reluctant to act on a problem they saw as internal to the Korean community. But the strain was wearing down the threads of pan–Asian American unity. The Red Apple Market boycott in New York had exposed the inability of the old-style multiracial coalition to act in a 1990s conflict between communities of color. The influx of a more diverse population of Asian immigrants after the 1965 Immigration Act brought new sets of interracial dynamics and issues that Asian American activists had still not confronted. When I brought up the issues of black–Korean tension and black–Asian violence at one of the few meetings of the ad hoc National Network Against Anti-Asian Violence in November 1991, there was almost no discussion, as though no one knew what to say.

Even under the best conditions, the organizational and structural ties between the different Asian American ethnic groups were tenuous and informal. Asian Americans who had any access to the political system tried to bring attention to the impending crisis. Stewart Kwoh, executive director of the Asian Pacific American Legal Center, one of L.A.'s main Asian American advocacy organizations, was then serving as president of the Los Angeles City Human Relations Commission. After years of trying to get Mayor Bradley to hire a director and activate some kind of program, the commission finally hired a director, nine months before sa-i-gu. "We issued a report saying that South Central was ready to blow up," said Kwoh. "We recommended that multicultural teams go into the community to work on the tensions." It never happened.

In October 1991, only months before sa-i-gu, Soon Ja Du was found guilty of voluntary manslaughter in the killing of Latasha Harlins. Judge Joyce Karlin suspended Du's sentence, placing her on five years' probation and ordering 400 hours of community service, $500 in fines, and funeral costs for Latasha. Explaining her sentence, the judge noted that the gun's firing mechanism had been altered to have a hair-trigger touch, and said that Du, who was inexperienced with guns, would otherwise not have shot Harlins. She then advised the parties to use the tragedy as an opportunity to fight "intolerance and bigotry." The probationary sentence for Soon Ja Du stunned a nation, much as probation for Vincent Chin's killers had. For Asian Americans, the parallels were unavoidable. Though there were fundamental differences between the cases, it was hard to advance justice for Vincent Chin without also advocating justice for Latasha Harlins. But for Asian Americans to do so would be seen as a slap in the face of an already battered Korean American community, while to concur with the sentence would draw further wrath from African Americans. Any public statement might be misconstrued by the media, taken out of context in a volatile situation. The safest route was to say nothing. This was the course that many Asian American leaders took.

The Black-Korean Alliance offered a slim hope for Korean Americans and African Americans to defuse a racial explosion. Stepping up its efforts, the BKA changed to weekly meetings to keep up with the various pickets and the intensity of the media attention. Months before the riots, the BKA began to fragment. "We were spending too much of our time in constant battle with the media," said Bong Hwan Kim, a member of the BKA and executive director of the Korean Youth Cultural Center. "Reporters seemed satisfied to portray the matter as race hatred between two communities of color, rather than looking at the forces that brought them into conflict." The BKA ended up working more with the news media than its communities, trying to get the news to show more of the history and context of racism and the causes of poverty and economic disenfranchisement. Its members hoped that a greater understanding would inspire some constructive approaches, but the momentum toward collision was too strong.

As the extreme positions of both the black and the Korean communities became more polarized and vocal, advocates of conciliation were attacked and BKA members of both groups were labeled race traitors. "No African American was willing to risk standing in front of a camera with a Korean American for fear of being called out as an apologist and sellout, and vice versa," said Bong Hwan Kim.

Kim himself came under heavy criticism from Koreans when, at a BKA press conference, he suggested that justice would have been better served had Soon Ja Du received jail time. Mainstream news media didn't find it newsworthy to report that a Korean American leader challenged the shopkeeper's sentence, but the Korean news media picked up the story and accused Kim of betraying his community. Kim's stand was a courageous one, when even Asian Americans outside the Korean community were silent on the subject of probation for the killing.

Under this pressure the fragile Black-Korean Alliance disintegrated. Jai Lee Wong recalls that an African American minister came to a BKA meeting and likened Koreans opening stores in Los Angeles to Europeans opening America with guns. "Everyone was pissed off. Korean Americans were at the table, but they were always on the defensive, having to prove they were worthy," said Wong. "It was as though the African Americans were doing Koreans a favor by meeting. The BKA had no unified voice, and the Korean community didn't have the sophistication or clout to say, Don't fuck with us. Some Korean Americans wanted to declare the killings of Korean merchants racially motivated hate crimes. African Americans disagreed—to do otherwise would be to admit that blacks could have prejudice," said Wong.

On the other hand, few Korean Americans would admit that prejudice played a role in the insensitivity to blacks that they were so often accused of. The Black-Korean Alliance finally disbanded, with bitterness on both sides, after six years of meetings.

Then sa-i-gu erupted. On April 29, 1992, a jury in suburban Simi Valley pronounced four white Los Angeles police officers not guilty of assault in the beating of Rodney King. The verdict uncapped all the pent-up anger over police brutality that was routine in Los Angeles, over the years of empty talk about economic and social inequities, over the racial injustices that never got righted. Outrage and fury rushed onto the streets.

Much of that anger found a target: the neighborhood Korean-owned stores. "Our worst nightmare come true," said Jan Jung-Min Sunoo, of the L.A. County Human Relations Commission. As stores were looted and torched, Korean Americans desperately called 911 for assistance. But the LAPD let South Central, Koreatown, and the inner-city core burn. When the police did show up, they did little to stop the violence. Store owners like Yong Hwan Sul and his partner tried to keep looters from carting off their wares. As looters turned to beat his partner, Sul called to a line of thirty police who stood across the street and merely watched; Korean Americans suspected that the LAPD was relieved that the rage over police brutality had found another outlet.

Anxious Korean American families sat transfixed by news on Radio Korea, nervously listening to damage reports. A call went out for volunteer security brigades from the community, to protect itself where the police and the government would not. Both men and women tried to keep looters at bay. Korean American men, many of whom had served their mandatory time in the U.S.-supported Korean military, ringed their shops with barricades of shopping carts, cars, and refrigerators and other items that hadn't been carted away. Some shopkeepers took up arms and exchanged fire with arsonists. The jarring image of Korean American merchants with guns shocked an American public that knew little about the Koreans in their midst. Among the individuals who answered the call for volunteers on Radio Korea was an eighteen-year-old Korean American college freshman named Edward Lee. He was killed, apparently in crossfire from other Koreans; dozens of shopkeepers and their family members were wounded.

"Cry Koreatown" read the banner headline of the *Korea Times* English Edition, which served as the English-language window on Koreatown. Businesses and property owned by all races and ethnicities were destroyed. The looters were also multiracial in composition, with some Koreans even participating in the spree. But Korean Americans overwhelmingly bore the brunt of the riot's devastation. With nearly 2,500 Korean-owned stores destroyed and more than $500 million in damages to the Korean community alone, it was hard to recall a more devastating punishment meted out to a single group.

It didn't matter whether or not the Korean shop owners had good relations with their neighborhood. Chung Lee, the Watts Market owner and former co-chair of the Black-Korean Alliance, saw his store burn to the ground in spite of fifteen years of strong relations with the Watts community. Several of his customers tried to keep arsonists away, but they were outnumbered.

If Korean Americans had been invisible in America before, they were now in the full limelight. Asian Americans consider the riots to be the moment that America took notice of Korean Americans. Journalists did not know what to make of this Asian American population that suddenly emerged in their headlines. Even when news reports were quick to label the riots a black–Korean problem rather than one of police brutality, replaying images of Korean Americans with guns, few reporters ventured to Koreatown or bothered to interview Korean Americans. A post-riot survey of Angelenos conducted by the *Los Angeles Times* queried more than a thousand people on their feelings about the riots; the front-page results reported the views of "Whites, Blacks, Hispanics and Others." In explanation, Shelby Coffey, editor of the *Los Angeles Times*, said that Asians were not statistically significant enough to include, even though they made up 11 percent of the Los Angeles population, roughly the same percentage as African Americans. Ted Koppel of ABC News dedicated two weeks of *Nightline*'s programs to on-site coverage in Los Angeles, visiting with African American gang members and discussing black–Korean tensions. But Koppel didn't speak to Korean Americans. Finally, after complaints of bias by Asian Americans in Los Angeles, attorney Angela Oh was brought on *Nightline* for a few minutes as a lone Korean voice. Oh's strong appearance brought her instant prominence as one of the very few Asian Americans to speak on national television about the riots.

On May 2, as the embers of what used to be their livelihoods smoldered, more than thirty thousand Korean Americans marched through Koreatown, calling for peace and denouncing the police and criminal justice system in the Rodney King trial. The demonstration was historic, the largest protest ever held by Asians in America. "Why are Korean Americans the fall guys for social injustice?" read one sign that captured the crowd's sentiments. A special ire was reserved for the news media and their failure to present a Korean American view, even as some portrayed Korean Americans as a cause of the riots. "Media: Report the Tragedy of Koreatown," demanded a protester. But the news media barely covered the historic march and rally.

Bitterness was not directed only toward the news media. Korean Americans noticed a striking absence of other Asian Americans. At the rally, besides Korean Americans, there were a few African Americans, Latinos, and Asian American individuals. But leaders of other Asian American groups were nowhere to be found. Only one, Lily Lee Chen, the former Chinese American mayor of Monterey Park, came out to support the Korean American demonstration. "I remember wondering, 'Where is everybody, for God's sake?' " said Brenda Paik Sunoo, then news editor of the *Korea Times* English Edition. Sunoo had spent years as an activist for Asian American causes. To find her community abandoned by the pan–Asian American spirit she espoused was a devastating blow.

In 1992, more than two decades after the Asian American student movement first gave a name to this new unity, some Asian Americans were trying hard to dissociate themselves from Korean Americans. As with the Red Apple Market boycott in New York, some Asian Americans did not want to be forced to take sides with Korean Americans against African Americans. Others didn't want to be perceived as the "bad guy" and to become a potential target themselves. A few, like Elaine Woo, an editor with the *Los Angeles Times* and the sister of city council representative Michael Woo, were honest enough to fess up. In an essay for the *Times*, she wrote, "I was afraid of being mistaken for Korean." The public revelation was a painful validation of what Korean Americans sensed from their Asian American brethren.

"Suddenly I understood the isolation that Japanese Americans must have felt when they were interned during World War II. Such a sense of cosmic sorrow," said journalist K. W. Lee. Lofty images of a pan–Asian American "family" in a multicultural America now seemed to be empty rhetoric.

Asian Americans had lost something, too. In a way, the "model minority" was taking a beating from blacks, whites, and Latinos who seemed only too glad to deliver their comeuppance. The extreme severity of the punishment meted out to Korean Americans suggested that sa-i-gu was not just for Latasha Harlins and Rodney King but also for Rockefeller Center, for Toyota, and for being the "success story." Korean Americans had taken the hit for all Asian Americans.

The wrongness of it added to the Korean Americans' *han*, their collective sense of bitterness. "Every Korean generation has acquired a sense of *han*, accumulated grievance and unquenched woe," explained Lee. "*Han* is a part of the collective psyche of Koreans, the grievance against external forces, like the Japanese subjugation of Korea, or the chauvinism of hundreds of years. And now this. The *han* is deeply imbedded." Yet *han* is also intrinsic to the Korean will to survive, through centuries of occupation by foreign rulers, and even the pervasive U.S. military presence for the last fifty years. Other dreams and ideals would have to be forged.

The riots precipitated a leadership crisis in the Korean American community. As in other Asian American immigrant communities, the mantle of leadership for Koreans unequivocally rested on the senior men of the immigrant first generation, following traditional hierarchical lines of age, gender, and class. Traditional leadership offered stability to itinerant populations far from home. At the time of the riots, Jae Yul Kim, the owner of the One Stop Market at Vernon and Arlington, and others like him were still in their prime, some not even in their fifties, hardly ready to hand over the reins to their inexperienced twenty- and thirty-something progeny.

Yet the rubble of Koreatown testified to the inability of the first-generation immigrants to lead the Korean American community out of crisis. Communicating their needs to politicians and the media in clear and persuasive English posed a problem. So did their schizophrenic "old country/new country" reality, with some storekeepers more ready to call the Korean government than to contact American local, state, and federal authorities. But the main problem was that the shops and grocery stores of the first generation were destroyed in the riots, and men like Jae Yul Kim had to put every ounce of energy into restoring their family's livelihood.

After sa-i-gu, Jae Yul Kim and his wife, Nina, lost their home. Nina cried every day. She stopped using her Korean name, Soon Ja, which might remind people of Soon Ja Du. They moved into a $600-a-month apartment with two of their grown children, their children's Latino spouses, and their grandchildren. They relied on food stamps for the three years that Jae was out of work. In 1995 they finally reopened the One Stop Market, with $500 in cash and only a few shelves stocked. They depended on their older son, a graduate of UC Berkeley, to work at the store, as well as on their daughter's husband. During that time, Jae volunteered at a Korean relief organization for riot victims. Eventually he became involved with the Korean American Grocers Association, serving on its board of directors. But with his store opening like a new business, Jae no longer had time to be involved in groups like KAGRO.

The extreme duress of sa-i-gu forced a sudden transfer of leadership from the first-generation immigrants to the more acculturated 1.5 and 2.0 generations. The "1.5 generation," a designation coined by Korean Americans and sometimes used by other Asian groups, refers to those who came to the United States as children, while the "2.0 generation" was born in America. Unlike their parents, both were fluent in the ways of America. After sa-i-gu, in the historic demonstration of thirty thousand Korean Americans, the first-generation immigrants could march to City Hall and wave placards, but they could not convey their needs to the politicians and the media. It would be up to their young adult children, the 1.5s and 2.0s, to appeal to the hearts and minds of the American people.

Among the American-educated 1.5- and 2.0-generation Korean Americans who stepped up to the plate was Bong Hwan Kim, a member and executive director of the Korean Youth Cultural Center, who was thirty-four years old at the time of the riots. Kim took many strong public stands. He criticized attempts by some African American leaders to mobilize blacks by scapegoating Koreans and the failure of other black leadership to take a stand—in addition to his own questioning of Soon Ja Du's sentence. After sa-i-gu, he worked with other Asian Americans to convert burned-out liquor stores to alternate uses, such as Laundromats. Their effort was overshadowed by a broad movement to drive out the liquor stores without offering the owners any compensation for their businesses—and Bong Hwan Kim was again called a collaborator and a traitor to Koreans. Nevertheless, his leadership skills are still recognized and called upon by the community. "I was seen as a young upstart who wasn't sensitive to the needs of the first generation," said Kim. "But leadership is about taking risks."

Another of the community's leaders who emerged forcefully after sa-i-gu was attorney Angela Oh, celebrated for her strong commentary on national TV after the riots. She later became the only Asian American appointed to serve on the President's Initiative on Race during the Clinton Administration—and the Korean press criticized her for "benefiting" from the riots. A member of the 2.0 generation, Oh was born in Los Angeles, the Korean equivalent of a Chinese jook sing, or hollow bamboo. Without speaking Korean, and presumed to lack an understanding of the culture, she has had to reach out to the first generation while facing the disdain of some of her elders. Even worse, Oh is female and outspoken, a hard combination for the more Confucian-bound elders to accept. "Her gutsiness grates on their chauvinism," says K. W. Lee. "In Korean culture, the Korean woman is lowest on the food chain. The gender *han* is the deepest grievance of all." For Oh, the criticism was not unexpected. "It's part of the deal: if you open your mouth, you will be criticized. But younger Koreans were excited to see that they might be able to play a role in the community and the nation. The riots woke them up," said Oh.

To younger Korean Americans, Angela Oh and Bong Hwan Kim are revered as role models. After sa-i-gu, twenty-something Krystene Park went to work in Koreatown. Park joined the Korean American Grocers Association as its director after finishing college. She sees herself as a link to the "American system" for people like her father, who runs the family's liquor store. "Being from the 1.5 generation, I know more of what's going on politically outside the community. I attend hearings on ordinances that will affect the grocers, who are too busy running their shops to follow what the government is doing," said Park. "I am a bridge for our community."

Other young Korean Americans such as Do Kim see an opportunity to serve their community and develop as leaders. A tough street kid from Koreatown whose mother worked in garment shops and whose father pumped gas, Kim came to the United States when he was three years old. He grew up speaking Korean and inner-city slang, but won a scholarship to Harvard. Kim saw the riots on TV in his dorm in Cambridge, feeling angry and helpless as he watched looters being interviewed only three blocks from his parents' home. "I had to do something," he said. Even before the riots, Kim wanted to make a difference, and he majored in African American studies. At Harvard, Kim got black and Asian students together to raise money for riot victims of all races. When he returned to L.A., he sought out community advocates such as Bong Hwan Kim and Jai Lee Wong to learn how he could become one, too.

"The 1992 riots served as a catalyst to bridge the gap between first- and second-generation Korean Americans," said Edward T. Chang, professor at UC Riverside. A specialist in black–Korean relations who came to the United States from Korea as a teenager, Chang is often asked by reporters to give a Korean perspective on the riots, but he says that a

Korean voice is often still lacking in the coverage because few of those interviews are ultimately used. "After the riots the 1.5 and 2.0 generations became much more aware and proud of what their parents went through, and the immigrants were grateful to the young Korean Americans who spoke up for the community. There's a new sense of Korean American ethnic identity and activism, and many younger Koreans have come back to the community," said Chang. "But the first generation still holds on to the traditional hierarchy and way of doing things. Whether the 1.5 and 2.0 generations stay in Koreatown in spite of the frustrations remains to be seen."

Some younger Korean Americans, like Do Kim, are certain that they will stay in Koreatown. "This is where the fight is. I wanted to be in on the fight," he said.

After sa-i-gu, the Asian American leadership had to undergo its own soul-searching and metamorphosis. Asian American history is rife with examples of one Asian ethnic group separating itself from another—each hoping that it will be the one that is accepted into American society, or that it can avoid being brushed by racism. While many Korean Americans felt abandoned by the rest of the Asian American community, "other Asians expressed an initial resentment toward Koreans, blaming Korean Americans for the increased racial tension they experienced," said Edward Chang.

Some Asian Americans worried that they might be targeted because they looked like Koreans—and some indeed were. Hundreds of stores owned by other Asians—among them, Chinese, Cambodians, Japanese, Indians, and Filipinos—were also destroyed, possibly because they were believed to be Korean-owned, or simply because they were Asian. Close to L.A., in the neighboring city of Long Beach, numerous shops of Cambodian Americans were torched. Deborah Ching, director of the Chinatown Service Center, recounted hearing Chinese say it's a Korean problem, not a Chinese problem. A Japanese American man was severely beaten during the riots, mistaken for Korean; the incident was caught on camera, but the Asian American community was silent about this and other attacks.

Years after sa-i-gu, there is still bitterness over the ambivalence revealed by Asian Americans in the face of the Korean American community's greatest crisis. Brenda Paik Sunoo, then news editor of the *Korea Times* English Edition, was still angry about Asian American silence on the targeting of Korean stores. "For all the work on anti-Asian violence, the Asian American community didn't formulate the destruction of two-thousand-plus Korean American stores as hate crimes. Instead, we let the major media define the events," said Sunoo, a third-generation Korean American who grew up in L.A.'s Crenshaw area near South Central. "Asian Americans should have stood up and said these anti-Korean attacks are not acceptable."

Some Asian Americans did take stands, behind the scenes, sending letters to the mayor, submitting position papers to numerous officials and government agencies. In the months leading up to the riots, Stewart Kwoh of the Asian Pacific American Legal Center wrote columns published in the *Los Angeles Times* in which he called for an end to anti-Asian rhetoric. Part of the problem, said Kwoh, is that all Asian Americans have been invisible, not just Korean Americans. As a result, Asian Americans were often as ignorant of one another's actions as non-Asians. The more fundamental problem was that Asian Americans as a whole, despite totaling 11 percent of the city's population, lacked political clout and recognition in Los Angeles.

Another consideration is that there was no single Asian American organization or national leadership that could have offered support. Still, many Asian American activists recognized they could have done more as individuals. "There's a good element of truth to the Korean American feeling that Asian Americans didn't step up," said Warren Furutani, a fourth-generation Japanese American who was president of the Los Angeles Board of Education in 1992. But part of the problem was not only Asian Americans' lack of power but their inability to reach other people in power. "We had the same glaring problem when the Japanese American internment happened: no one was on the inside, where the decisions were being made, to represent our interests. Korean Americans expected more support and were shocked to find there was none. Asian Americans didn't have the political foundation to make it happen."

Sa-i-gu forced Asian Americans to take a hard look at their own status and lack of power. "1992 was a defining event for Korean Americans, and it was a wake-up call for Asian Americans," said Ron Wakabayashi, executive director of the Los Angeles County Human Relations Commission.

"For a lot of us it was the hardest lesson to experience. We thought we had been making progress, but we were not," said Deborah Ching, who, as head of the Chinatown Service Center, chaired the Asian Pacific Planning Council, a pan-Asian coalition linking some fifty Asian American social service groups.

What the pan-Asian American groups couldn't do politically they tried to provide in the form of organization and social services to the victims of the riots. The Asian Pacific Planning Council took on the crisis management task of locating and coordinating services for the thousands of Korean and other Asian Americans who were hurt by the riots. Disaster relief; emergency food and clothing; processing of claims to insurance companies and local, state, and federal governments; unemployment assistance; job placement and training; legal aid; health services and counseling—all were needed urgently, and in multiple Asian languages. "Assistance to our communities is often overlooked by government and private agencies because they don't perceive Asian American populations as needing the help," said Ching.

If the pan-Asian groups did not speak up loudly on behalf of Korean Americans before sa-i-gu, it became a necessity after the riots. "Some political leaders were unsympathetic, even antagonistic to Korean Americans," said Stewart Kwoh, founder and chief executive officer of the Asian Pacific American Legal Center. When Ron Brown, Secretary of the U.S. Department of Commerce, announced a large federal grant to Los Angeles after the riots, he noted, "Not a penny will go to the Koreans." Kwoh's group had to sue about one hundred insurance brokers whose carriers declared bankruptcy or otherwise failed to make good on the insurance policies purchased by many of the Asian American store owners. The legal center's staff increased from fifteen to twenty-five overnight in order to expand its services. Because of its pan-Asian mission, the center also served as a liaison between the larger social and political institutions and the Asian American community. "We tried to bring Asian Pacific Americans together to support the Korean community," said Kwoh. He met with the *Los Angeles Times* editorial board about the depiction of Korean Americans as greedy, gun-toting merchants and urged it to hire some Korean American journalists—an effort that contributed to the hiring of a veteran reporter, K. Connie Kang.

After sa-i-gu, Asian Americans had to confront the issue of obtaining real political power. The human suffering from the riots magnified the cost of not doing so.

Beyond the issue of political empowerment, Asian Americans also had to reconsider their own conceptions of "Asian Americans." In the 1960s, most Asian Americans were American-born Chinese and Japanese, as well as some Filipino Americans. But the millions of Asian immigrants and refugees who arrived after 1965 brought profound changes to the Asian American population and its relationships with other communities. The new Asian Americans brought a diversity of cultures and sensibilities that the old-guard Asian Americans had not previously grappled with. Sa-i-gu forced leaders of the pan-Asian American ideal to accept a new understanding of diversity and inclusion.

For example, in Long Beach, just south of Los Angeles, the shock of sa-i-gu compelled the Cambodian American community to emerge as a vocal Asian American community. The fifty thousand Cambodian Americans of Long Beach found themselves caught in the destruction of Korean American businesses, as hundreds of Cambodian American businesses were looted and burned. The riots in Long Beach nearly shut down the United Cambodian Community agency of Long Beach, which depended on the financial support of local businesses for its survival. "Not only were community people hurt, but this agency almost collapsed," said Sovann Tith, its director. Tith, a 1.5-generation Cambodian, became executive director three years after sa-i-gu, at the age of thirty-two. In Long Beach, the community elders have turned over leadership to a younger generation that can be more effective in dealings with the American mainstream, learning from the changes occurring among Korean Americans. In turn, the pan–Asian American community is also evolving.

The young, outwardly focused leadership of people such as Sovann Tith brings a very different set of experiences and concerns to the Asian American movement. When Tith came to the United States, he was a fourteen-year-old refugee who had lost his parents and three older brothers in the "killing fields." "The life of the Cambodian people in the United States is unlike other Asians'. We are the Asian poor, the very poor. Most Cambodians here are farmers with only four years of education; now they live in urban America. I am the in-between generation, the bridge generation— old enough to have memories of the Communists, but also familiar with the American way. My generation has to be flexible with the culture of our elders, but we have to bring our community into the American rule of law, or we won't survive."

After sa-i-gu, Kwoh organized a new coalition, Asian Pacific Americans for a New Los Angeles, to unify Asian American communities into a collective force. The linking of Cambodians, Chinese, Filipinos, Japanese, Koreans, Vietnamese, and other Asians from private, nonprofit, and public sectors had never happened in Los Angeles before.

Seven years after sa-i-gu, few Korean American storekeepers had fully recovered. Many were still pursuing government disaster relief loans or trying to collect from unscrupulous insurance companies. Some shopkeepers never recovered. Chung Lee, who owned the popular Watts Market, closed down his business for good.

According to Professor Edward Chang, the interaction between African Americans and Koreans hasn't changed much since the riots, though individual merchants have worked hard to improve relations. The spirit of the ill-fated Black-Korean Alliance has been resurrected in a new and broader coalition called the Multicultural Collaborative that, this time, includes Latinos, Asian Americans, whites—as well as blacks and Korean Americans. Such an approach, involving the entire Los Angeles community, may work better when new sparks fly, but there has yet been little resolution over the events of April 29, 1992. "Interethnic relations between blacks and Koreans are not a high priority. On a policy level, nobody wants to talk about it," said Chang, who has written a popular Korean-language book on African Americans and is thinking of writing another on Latino Americans. "But Koreans can never forget this. It is the worst situation that ever happened to Korean Americans in Korean American history. In the meantime, Korean Americans are moving on, to closure, away from being victims."

Driven by their collective *han*, Korean Americans have been building on their strength and moving outward with considerable momentum. Since the riots, several new Korean American community organizations formed. Community members launched a fund-raising drive to create a Korean American History Museum. Business leaders have been trying to reshape their image, raising banners that effused: "Experience Koreatown: Smiles on our faces, love in our hearts."

Some groups, such as the Korean American Coalition (KAC), are guided by a new vision that includes a working partnership with other Asian American organizations. That coalition is based on practicality and common goals, not simply on an Asian American ideal. "I don't blame any other leaders who didn't come forward after the riots," said Charles Kim, the group's founder and president. "We weren't ready ourselves. But next time we will be. We had always been saying that Korean Americans can't be an isolated island, but nobody listened. Then came the L.A. riots—the first generation suddenly realized they have to be a part of this society." In 1992, the KAC had two staff members; six years later, it had a staff of eleven and an office in Washington, D.C.

Pointing the way is a youthful new leadership, cued in direct response to sa-i-gu. Do Kim, the college student who went to work in Koreatown after graduation from Harvard, now runs a leadership training program for high school and college youth. One study found that 15 percent of college-age Korean youth had dropped out of school because of the riots. Several of Kim's graduates have gone to work in jobs that benefit the community. "I wanted to train leaders so that sa-i-gu wouldn't happen again. My generation is going to have to move things ahead," he said.

Through their trial by fire, Korean Americans have forged an intergenerational bond in their community with a younger leadership that is bent on projecting its voice in America. Their transformation has rippled through other Asian American groups, shaking up notions of who and what is Asian American.

At Jae Yul Kim's One Stop Market, his customers became worried after word spread through the neighborhood about the shooting and attempted robbery. Several customers called to inquire, "Is Ma and Pa okay?" says Jae, adding that, before sa-i-gu, nobody would have cared.

After he installed additional Plexiglas to prevent would-be shooters from firing through the windows, his customers asked if he didn't trust them. "I point to the bullets in the Plexiglas, they don't ask no more."

When Jae opens his shop at 8 a.m. each day, customers are already waiting. One early morning customer, an Afro-Latino man from Belize, tells Jae that he drives past seven or eight other stores to come to the One Stop because Jae is so friendly. Business has been picking up. In a good month, the store will clear about $7,000 to $8,000, before taxes. From that sum Jae pays his son and son-in-law, his loan, and the electricity. Jae estimates his own pay is less than $2.50 per hour. But he has his livelihood again, and his dignity.

Jae says he doesn't like to carry a gun, but he sees firearms as an occupational necessity to defend his life and his livelihood. He has a grim reality about life, despite his cheery disposition.

"I'm still scared," he says. "When you run a business, people complain. I don't know what they might do." From his vantage point behind the meat counter, Jae observes the dynamics of American society. "I live here and I see that people count color," he says. "White people are together, black people are together. Latino people are together, too." Jae points to the pictures of his three grandchildren, stuck to the bulletin board, and notes that they are all half-Latino and half-Korean. His son and daughter met their spouses in school and are part of a wave of Korean–Latino alliances. Their children speak English and Spanish, not Korean.

For the present, Jae's dreams are about survival. But he is also thinking about how life could be different in his home, Los Angeles. "If Asian people could stick together, we could have more power," he says. "We Oriental people think we are all different, but we look the same. The Chinese, Koreans, Japanese, Cambodians—everyone must learn cooperation. Otherwise we cannot have the things that are important to us."

# ·8·

# For Richer, for Poorer

A few times each year, Mom received a special letter in the mail. The tissue-thin paper and the deliberate, spidery lettering that looked drawn, not written, announced that it was a letter from China. Mom's face would light up with excitement. Using her sharpest scissors, she would gingerly cut the folds to avoid

*Taxi driver and labor organizer Javaid Tariq, at the wheel of his cab (Alan Raia/Newsday)*

tearing the delicate missive. Then she'd sit quietly on the sofa, absorbing the news from back home, Shanghai.

I'd look over Mom's shoulder, waiting for her rough translation while futilely trying to decipher the Chinese script. Because China was Communist and an avowed enemy of the United States, the news was invariably sketchy but vaguely positive, written to pass the censors of both Chinese and U.S. governments, real or imagined. It was as incriminating for us to get mail from the People's Republic of China as it was for our relatives to correspond with Americans. Telephone contact across the Bamboo Curtain wasn't possible. The fragile letters and their meager news were our only link to Mom's mother, eldest sister, and numerous cousins.

Occasionally a small black-and-white photo was tucked in the letter. Stiff and formal in their studio poses, my grandmother, aunts, and other relatives were enigmas to me. Their serious faces, etched with hardship, were so far from my life as an American-born Chinese in New Jersey. I could hardly guess at their lives in China or how my grandmother and other Chinese suffered as part of Mao's Cultural Revolution.

One day when I was home from college, a letter from China arrived. Mom unleashed a mournful wail: my grandmother, her mother, was dead. Mom hadn't seen or spoken to her mother in twenty years, and the prospect of never seeing her again filled Mom with anguish. Disconsolate, she lay down in bed and cried for days. I had never seen my energetic, attentive mother like this and was unsure how to comfort her for the loss of a grandmother I never knew.

But changes in federal law brought some of my unmet relatives closer. The 1965 Immigration Act allowed family members of long-ago immigrants who were now U.S. citizens to come to America. Some of my relatives responded. My Auntie Betty in Queens, Mom's elder sister, asked if I would apply to sponsor one of my cousins to come to the United States. As a young adult just starting out on my own, I felt queasy about accepting full financial and legal responsibility for a relative I had never met, but knowing the importance to Mom and Auntie Betty, I agreed.

Soon my cousin Ziyoung was in New York, staying at Auntie Betty's little apartment. Ziyoung, a kindly man in his fifties, was the son of Mom's and Auntie Betty's eldest sister. In China he was an accountant. To finance his visit, he began looking for work in New York. The only job he could find was washing dishes and unloading boxes in a Chinese restaurant. At night he'd lie down and moan, his body sore from his grueling days. After a few months, Ziyoung decided to return to China. Like many immigrants from China, Ziyoung had found that life in the United States, despite its gilded image and high standard of living, was a harsh place for those with little money and limited English—so harsh that life in China looked a lot better, and Ziyoung happily returned to Shanghai.

Not long after Ziyoung's short stay, a new set of visitors moved in with Auntie Betty: Bebe and her husband, Goh. As the daughter of a family friend who was a longtime American citizen, Bebe was eligible to become a permanent resident of the United States. In her early fifties and already a grandmother, Bebe was eager to make a new life here.

Auntie Betty, though, was disturbed by the stubborn Chinese habits of Bebe and her husband. They washed their laundry in the sink each day, and hung their clothes to dry throughout the small apartment. This drove Auntie Betty to the edge of madness. She couldn't understand why they wouldn't spend fifty cents to use the dryer. This is America, not China, she'd say. But my seventy-year-old auntie put up with their ways and their damp, ubiquitous laundry because she needed the extra money they paid her each month to supplement her own meager Social Security income.

One day, while talking with my mother, I learned some details about Bebe's life. I was writing an article for *Ms.* magazine on the resurgence of sweatshops in America when Mom informed me that Bebe and her husband were working at one in Queens. Through Mom and Auntie Betty, I contacted Bebe. We communicated in our pidgin Chinese-English and she let me accompany her to a stark, gray factory complex near Shea Stadium.

Each day, locked behind a sturdy chain-link fence and a steel door with hundreds of other polyglot newcomers, Bebe and Goh worked sixteen, eighteen, twenty hours a day for days, toiling every day for a Chinese immigrant owner, as long as the work lasted. They earned a dollar or two an hour, way below minimum wage, off the clock and under the table, producing clothes for some of the most popular mall labels. It was the only work new immigrants with little English could find. Despite the long hours of tedious work, at night my tired cousins would trudge the few miles back to Auntie Betty's rather than pay for the bus. Too tight, Auntie Betty would say, but for them each penny was precious.

The reality of Bebe's life brought me closer to the grim margins of the American economy, filled with such people as my distant cousin. While I grew up in the immigrant landscape and was well aware of the sweatshop underbelly of the nation, this close connection disturbed me. Though I might breeze through my comfortable world amid the gleaming skyscrapers of midtown Manhattan, I wondered if my kin toiled nearby, locked up in one of the many illegal sweatshops that dotted the city.

Bebe came to America seeking a life like mine—or at least the life she imagined mine to be. She never expected to end up in an American sweatshop that was no better than one in China. But if she couldn't live the American dream, she hoped that one day her grandchildren might, if they ever came to America. I hoped that my story for *Ms.* might, in some small way, help Bebe and other immigrants like her by shining another light on the American practice of sweatshop labor.

Many months after the story appeared, I went to the posh Waldorf-Astoria Hotel in New York to receive an award from the National Women's Political Caucus for that article. I couldn't help thinking how far I was from Bebe at that moment. In spite of our connection of family, spirit, and empathy, we remained worlds apart. Powerful forces of language, culture, class, and immigrant generation kept us distant. Yet something intangible, perhaps the threads of a shared history or wisps of an old dream of a place called America, still bound us together.

· · ·

On a cold January night in 1998, a lone twenty-something Asian American woman could be found wandering Manhattan's yellow cab dispatch garages and coffee shops where taxi drivers hang out. Wearing a loose-fitting Indian shalwar kameez under her overcoat, Bhairavi Desai made small talk with cabdrivers about their families, their lives in New York—and the need to organize for safer and better working conditions. Even on the coldest nights, Desai found that 1 to 2 a.m. was the best time to reach night-shift cabdrivers, a slow period in their 5 p.m. to 5 a.m. shifts.

"Driving a cab is depressing," said Javaid Tariq, whose long graying hair is pulled back into a ponytail. A cabdriver whom Desai met in an early foray, Tariq has been driving a cab in New York City for four years. He came to the United States in 1990 to escape political persecution in Pakistan. In his off hours he photographs life from behind the steering wheel and volunteers with Desai and the New York Taxi Workers Alliance to organize other cabdrivers. "We're like turtles in a pond for twelve hours every day. After we pay for the car and the gas, all we make is a few dollars an hour, if we're lucky." The drivers' backs hurt from sitting in a car all day, the exhaust fumes are bad, and the threat of robbery is constant. With the job pressures comes the stigma of the lowly cabdriver, layered onto negative attitudes toward immigrants. "People hate us and treat us like slaves. To them we aren't even human."

The taxi drivers' workforce includes recent immigrants from Asia, Russia and Eastern Europe, Africa, Latin America, and the Caribbean—just about everywhere. But South Asians, mainly from Pakistan, Bangladesh, and India, make up the majority of the 45,000 people licensed to drive cabs in the city: 25,000 South Asians hold licenses in New York. They often are objects of derision—along with Apu, the brown-skinned convenience store clerk on *The Simpsons*, and David Letterman's soda-slurping Bangladeshi newsstand operators, Sirapul and Mujibur.

In May 1998, the South Asian cabdrivers and the fledgling New York Taxi Workers Alliance stunned the city and embarrassed its mayor by accomplishing the unthinkable: they staged a successful one-day strike, unifying the more than twenty thousand unorganized, seemingly unreachable cabdrivers who were to work that day. They lacked a common language, offices, phone contacts, or basic organizing tools. No longer just the butt end of a joke, the cabdrivers forced a surprised city, at least for a moment, to recognize their concerns and their humanity.

The victory of the underdog immigrant workers against New York Mayor Rudolph Giuliani made grist for the news. Previously invisible South Asian American faces began to headline the city's dailies and television news programs. *New York* magazine named the strike one of the year's ten top stories. *The Village Voice* profiled the India-born Bhairavi Desai as a defiant and proud immigrant. *George* magazine featured her in its list of "100 Most Fascinating Political People"—placing Desai ahead of Hillary Clinton. Not only were these labor organizers South Asian but they were working-class, contrary to the stereotype of South Asians as successful professionals and entrepreneurs. Despite the coverage, Desai mused that "the story of the 'brown masses rising' wasn't told."

The sudden news spotlight on the successful strike leaders, who happened to be Pakistani and Indian Americans, did not seem to interest other South Asian Americans. Their apparent disregard drew scornful shrugs from the taxi driver organizers. "Middle-class South Asians with no connection to working-class South Asians just don't have compassion for the cabdrivers," said Desai, whose mother worked in a factory and whose father ran a convenience store after they came to the United States in 1979, when she was six years old. "None of the Indian or Pakistani papers said our communities should be proud of us," added Tariq. "We never saw any support from the professional or upper-class Indians or Pakistanis. To them we are a bad symbol because we are doing labor." Yet the dynamic interplay of class and generational change among the immigrants who came after 1965 would also offer some surprising linkages.

The vast majority of South Asians, like the majority of Asian Americans, came to the United States after the 1965 Immigration Act. Within three decades, the total Asian American population surged from less than a million to 10 million, a number that included more than a million refugees from Southeast Asia and almost 900,000 from South Asia. The sizable population of new Asian Americans could maintain their attachments to homeland languages, classes, religions, ethnicities, castes, and cultural traditions in ways that the much smaller earlier Asian migrations could not. South Asians emigrated from India, Pakistan, Bangladesh, Sri Lanka, Bhutan, Nepal, and the Maldives. For some the United States was a secondary or even tertiary point of a migration that began in Africa, the Caribbean, or Britain generations earlier as part of the South Asian diaspora.

This wave of South Asian immigrants was not the first to reach the United States. In the early 1900s, a few thousand Sikh farmers from the Punjab region came to California to work the fields when white nativist hysteria shut down immigration from China, Japan, and Korea. Many of these Punjabi bachelor farmers settled in California's Sacramento Valley, marrying Mexican women and establishing their own communities. The family of Jane Singh, who teaches South Asian American history at the University of California at Berkeley, was among those early farmers, and one of the few where both parents were from South Asia. "If you took a poll, most South Asians wouldn't even know that there was an early migration. Our numbers were so sparse—the critical mass came after 1965," said Singh.

The new immigrant groups brought unfamiliar levels of diversity to the Asian American sensibility, particularly where South Asians are concerned. Even American-born second-generation South Asian Americans debate whether to consider themselves Asian American. The predominance of Chinese, Koreans, Japanese, and Vietnamese from East Asia often makes South Asians feel like outsiders in pan–Asian American settings—a situation made worse by East Asians who fail to recognize South Asia as part of Asia. Differences in physical features also come into play when, in archaic racial parlance, brown-complexioned South Asians are "Caucasoid" while yellow-toned East Asians are "Mongoloid." Some South Asian Americans cite this racial distinction as a reason not to consider themselves Asian American. This was argued by the Punjabi immigrants in the Supreme Court case of *United States* v. *Bhagat Singh Thind* in 1923. For several decades after the *Thind* decision, South Asians were classified by the federal government at varying times as "Hindus," "Whites," and "Other." Then, in 1974, the Association of Indians in America successfully lobbied Congress to be counted as "Asian American" rather than "White." Their purpose was to obtain for "Asian Indians" the governmental and social benefits that Asian Americans were receiving as minorities, according to Lavina Dhingra Shankar in *A Part, Yet Apart: South Asians in Asian America*.

Given this historic ambivalence and the widening diversity of Asian Americans across class, ethnicity, religion, and other significant markers, new generations ask whether Asian Americans could ever truly claim to have a single identity. But then, who would have thought that taxicab drivers from Pakistan, India, and Bangladesh could unite and lead a motley army of global migrants?

In the bone-grinding hustle of New York City, where hard knocks are part of the daily ethos, cabdrivers get little sympathy. Nearly everyone has a few "taxi from hell" stories that portray cabbies as rude, manic drivers who don't know the city; don't speak English, or, equally irritating, speak English with an accent; drive funky-smelling cabs; wear unfamiliar clothing, such as turbans; and commit a host of other offenses. Cabdrivers have also been cited for refusing to pick up black passengers or drive to black neighborhoods, a charge that points to their own prejudices.

But changing their public image, however unfair, was not a pressing concern for the drivers, who were burdened by the work itself, with grueling twelve-hour shifts spent scrambling to find enough fares to cover the cost of leasing the cab for the shift and paying for gas. Taxi drivers had no health insurance, no benefits—only traffic jams, air pollution, and demanding passengers. Their work is a virtual sweatshop on wheels, the most dangerous job in the country. Cabbies and limo drivers are more than twice as likely to be killed on the job as the next group—sheriff employees and bailiffs—according to a report by the National Institute for Occupational Safety and Health.

The public's attention was on the rising number of accidents involving yellow taxicabs, which pick up fares in the street, and vehicles of car services and other livery operations. These accidents shot up 41 percent between 1990 and 1996, according to the New York Taxi and Limousine Commission, which regulates the industry. In 1997, 28 people were killed and 21,617 injured in 14,063 accidents involving taxis, livery cars, limousines, and unlicensed, illegal cabs. Some news reports indicated that livery drivers and unlicensed cabs were responsible for the soaring accident rate. But several highly publicized incidents did involve yellow taxicabs—for example, the cab that jumped the curb onto the sidewalk, ripping off a pedestrian's right leg and crumpling a baby stroller that had carried a little boy, breaking his legs.

"Reckless," "lawless," and "terrorists" was how Mayor Rudolph Giuliani described the taxi drivers. A *Daily News* headline read: "Crazed Cabbies Run Down the City." Bhairavi Desai, of the New York Taxi Workers Alliance, was one of the lone voices trying to counter the rhetoric. "There has been a consistent bashing of the taxi drivers by the media and the politicians, until the public feels the taxi driver is a bad person who can be punished and punished," she said.

Mayor Giuliani proposed a seventeen-point plan to rid the city of reckless cabdrivers. The new rules included requisite annual drug tests, at the cabbies' own expense; a defensive driving course, also at their expense, required before they could renew their taxi license; increased fines that would climb to $1,000. Most severe was the proposal that after six penalty points accumulated within an eighteen-month period, a driver would be suspended for thirty days; for ten points, the driver's license would be revoked. A driver could amass six points for following another car too closely or for having a burned-out roof light. The proposed rules would push even good drivers, already living on the economic edge, over the brink and out of work.

It was difficult for the hundreds of small taxi associations and informal affinity groups to respond to the mayor. Taxi garage owners had their own group, as did companies that leased out their taxis. Another group existed for drivers who owned their cabs. At the bottom of the heap were the thousands of independent contractor taxi drivers who individually leased one of the city's 12,187 yellow cabs for a twelve-hour shift each day. Though they lacked a unified organization to represent their interests or even a common language, they had their own smaller networks and groups, too, which were mostly organized by language and ethnicity—a Pakistani drivers' brotherhood, another of drivers from Bangladesh. They communicated with one another via CB radio networks and cell phones. Sometimes they were just a handful of friends or acquaintances who split shifts as a cooperative, or referred fares to each other.

In this eclectic mix was the Taxi Workers Alliance. A few hundred strong, with a core of about twenty driver organizers like Javaid Tariq, and non-drivers like Desai, the alliance had evolved from a project that began with the Committee Against Anti-Asian Violence (CAAAV), one of New York's most visible pan–Asian American advocacy groups. The committee itself grew out of the Asian American movement against hate violence associated with the Vincent Chin case. To reach out to South Asians, the committee took up taxi driver organizing in 1991, at the instigation of four South Asian American women who had just graduated from college.

The young South Asian American organizers made late-night visits to cabbie hangouts, leafleted the taxi dispatch lines at the garages and the airports, and plugged into the CB channels, according to former CAAAV staff member Tamina Davar. They participated in a protest demonstration by several thousand cabdrivers in October 1993, after three Pakistani cabdrivers were killed in separate incidents during a twenty-four-hour period. They also assisted cabdrivers who were contesting unfair tickets and harassment by police and the Taxi and Limousine Commission.

When cabdriver and organizer Saleem Osman, a former lawyer in Pakistan, was beaten and jailed by a New York cop in a racial incident, the Committee Against Anti-Asian Violence quickly mobilized its network among cabdrivers and within the Asian American community. But the drivers who came to support Osman were all Muslim, Punjabi-speaking Pakistani drivers; no Indian or Bangladeshi drivers demonstrated. In addition, East Asian activists—mostly Chinese Americans and Korean Americans—far outnumbered the Pakistani cabdrivers, who ended up carrying

Chinese- and Korean-language placards. "There was not a single placard in Bengali or Punjabi, and a mere few in Urdu . . . this reflected an inability to mobilize bilingual South Asians in the day-to-day running of the organization," wrote Anuradha Advani, former director of the committee, referring to the main languages of India and Pakistan, in an essay on taxi driver organizing in *Making More Waves: New Writing by Asian American Women.*

Bhairavi Desai and other taxicab drivers and organizers created the New York Taxi Workers Alliance after a split from CAAAV in 1997 over differences in organizing strategies. Without an office or money, they continued their outreach to cabdrivers. A newly formed Indian American group called the Forum of Indian Leftists (FOIL), made up of college professors and intellectuals, offered assistance of volunteers and resources. Within a few months, this collection of South Asian immigrant taxi drivers, 1.5- and second-generation community activists, and college professors would be organizing and leading a citywide taxi strike. Their vision was to reach out and give voice to those who didn't fit the class and ethnic stereotypes of Asian Americans.

The spacious storefront office of The IndUS Entrepreneurs (TIE), comfortably nestled in the heart of California's Silicon Valley, is far from the sweaty grit of a taxi steering wheel. Jaguars, Mercedeses, and other luxury sedans fill the parking lot. Inside the modern offices, there are few visible cultural markers; the most dominant feature is the group's red, white, and blue logo.

The entrepreneurs represent the wealthy extreme of the complex class spectrum of the 4.5 million immigrants from all Asian countries who came to the United States between 1970 and 1990. While the entrepreneurs of TIE are mainly South Asian, they have counterparts in the wealthy emigrants from Taiwan, Hong Kong, Singapore, and elsewhere.

At the other end are the immigrants from Vietnam, Laos, and Cambodia who arrived as refugees, beginning in 1975, in the aftermath of the war in Southeast Asia. The rich and poor immigrants live and work in close proximity in Silicon Valley, where former refugees and more recent migrants work along the acid vats that etch the circuit boards and on the computer parts assembly lines, in factories often owned by other Asian immigrants, producing the technology created by The IndUS Entrepreneurs.

TIE's charter membership reads like a *Who's Who* of the high-tech industry. Suhas Patil, the founder of Cirrus Logic, and Kanwal Rekhi, once Novell's chief technology officer, were founding directors and presidents of the group, which formed in 1992 after a chance encounter of Patil, Rekhi, and other prominent Indian American businessmen. The "I" in TIE is a proud reference to the Indian subcontinent, birthplace of much of its membership. But the group's focus is decidedly American, with such stated objectives as "To help members integrate with the mainstream community" and "As recent immigrants in the United States, the Indus people recognize that they have benefited by the efforts of the pioneers and earlier waves of immigrants over the centuries. They now have a desire to discharge their responsibilities towards the next generation and the community at large. TIE is one manifestation of this desire."

In the years immediately following the Immigration Act of 1965, a highly educated and professional elite came to the United States from India and elsewhere in Asia. They were part of the "brain drain" targeted and encouraged by U.S. immigration policy. The decade between 1960 and 1970 was the first census period in which immigrants from throughout Asia rose above 10 percent of the total immigration to the United States.

Most of the 450,000 Indian Americans who immigrated between 1965 and 1990 came from the educated elite and middle class of India. This pattern was true for the middle-class and elite professionals who left Taiwan, Hong Kong, China, the Philippines, and Korea—and the earliest wave of refugees from Vietnam who came from the country's leadership and intelligentsia. For example, an entire stratum of health care professionals emigrated from the Philippines. Many of these doctors, scientists, and engineers from Asia had a relatively smooth transition finding their places among the educated elite and middle class of the United States.

The timing of this migration of highly skilled professionals coincided with the spread of the model minority myth, first presented in 1966 in *The New York Times* and *U.S. News & World Report* as a contrast to African American urban unrest. The post-1965 immigrants had no historical reference to civil rights or the way that Asian Americans were vilified in the previous decades. For them, being the "model minority" seemed to capture their aspirations and the belief that through hard work and individual merit they could achieve the American dream for themselves and their families.

Less well-to-do classes of immigrants followed that first wave after 1965, when Asians from the middle and laboring classes came, many of whom were relatives of the émigré intelligentsia. In the 1970s, the Indian elite was joined by a solidly middle-class, mercantile migration, largely from the western Indian state of Gujarat and other coastal regions. Many South Asian motel owners, diamond jewelers, and other small-business entrepreneurs entered the United States in this period.

By the 1980s, a working-class migration began. Among the immigrants from South Asia were many farmers, particularly from the Punjab and Bengal regions of India and Pakistan, as social, political, and religious turmoil displaced populations; people from Sri Lanka and elsewhere in South Asia added to the migration. Some first went to the Middle East as temporary guest workers in oil refineries, or to Europe, before coming to America to work in newsstands, in gas stations, and as cabdrivers. A similar pattern of secondary migration occurred with other Asian American ethnic groups. In the Chinese American community, the population also grew as desperate individuals fled China via smuggling rings aboard ships like the *Golden Venture*, which ran aground on the outskirts of New York City.

After the 1960 Census, the Asian American population began to double in each decade. For South Asians and other more recent immigrants, the groups grew at staggering multiples. The numbers of "Asian Indians" were first recorded in the 1980 Census, at 387,223. The 1990 Census reported that the Indian American population increased by 125 percent, to 815,447, while Pakistanis numbered 27,876, with about 10,000 each from Bangladesh and Sri Lanka, as well as Indians from Fiji and Guyana.

The middle- and working-class Asian immigrants of the 1970s and '80s were joined by more than a million people who fled Vietnam, Laos, and Cambodia by boat or across mountains and jungles into countries that offered asylum. The U.S. refugee resettlement efforts placed many of the Southeast Asians in rural locations or in urban ghettos, often far from the limited resources of existing Asian American support networks. According to Ngoan Le, former president of the National Association for the Education and Advancement of Cambodian, Laotian and Vietnamese Americans and a former refugee from Vietnam, the initial resettlement policy was to disperse people as thinly as possible throughout America to

encourage assimilation. Later policies settled refugees in clusters to facili-
tate the creation of mutual support networks.

Because most refugees arrived with little more than the clothes they
were wearing, very limited English, and few marketable skills, many were
completely dependent on public assistance programs. Cambodians, Lao,
and Hmong have had a particularly hard time adjusting and becoming
independent of welfare. In 1990, more than 60 percent of Hmong Americans and 40 percent of Cambodian Americans were living below the
poverty line, and a significant number had not completed the fifth grade—
54.9 percent of Hmong Americans, 40.7 percent of Cambodian Americans, and 33.9 percent of Laotian Americans.

Not all Asian American poor are Southeast Asian, not by a long shot.
In contrast to the superachiever image, an estimated 30,000 South Asian
Americans rely on public assistance. They are among the 169,000 Asian
American families who lived in poverty in 1990, comprising 11 percent of
the Asian American population. With each successive wave of Asian immigration, income levels and educational attainment have dropped, while
poverty rates have risen, according to a 1998 study by the Asian Ameri-
cans/Pacific Islanders in Philanthrophy. The report also noted that while
42 percent of Asian Americans have a bachelor's degree, which is almost
double the percentage of the general population, 9.8 percent of adult Asian
Americans had not gone beyond the eighth grade, compared with 6.2 percent of whites.

For those Americans more familiar with Asian American success stories of The IndUS Entrepreneurs variety, reports of Asian American
poverty simply don't register. Where poor Asian immigrants have garnered
public notice, it is usually to celebrate the exceptional individuals who
overcome all odds, such as the refugee or immigrant child who becomes
an Intel (formerly Westinghouse) Science Talent Search winner. Asian
Americans often express frustration with assumptions that Asian Americans don't need public assistance or culturally specific programs, don't
deserve private foundation support, and don't need educational help.
Asian Americans/Pacific Islanders in Philanthrophy reported that Asian
American and Pacific Islander organizations received only 0.2 percent of
all philanthropic and charitable dollars from foundations between 1983
and 1995, despite the doubling of the population and the significant
poverty rate. Even some educated people incorrectly believe that Southeast

Asian refugees get "special" welfare benefits, or that the U.S. government bought the fishing boats for enterprising Vietnamese American shrimpers and fishermen—just as urban poor have sometimes wrongly concluded that Korean American merchants must be receiving "special" bank loans for their businesses. None of those special-benefit rumors is true, yet they have become the stuff of modern legend and are still widely believed.

Between the extremes of wealth and poverty, there is a significant Asian American middle class, both immigrant and American-born. The 1990 Census data showed that the median household income of Asian Americans was $36,784, compared with $30,056 for all households. But per capita income of Asian Americans compared to all others was lower— $13,638 versus $14,143 nationwide. Juanita Tamayo Lott, in *Asian Americans: From Racial Category to Multiple Identities,* attributes this disparity between the oft-touted high household incomes of Asian Americans and the lower per capita income to several factors: larger households with more workers per household, longer hours worked, and a higher cost of living where the majority of Asian Americans reside. Others point out that Asian Americans in the workforce hold a greater number of advanced educational degrees compared to co-workers in like positions.

In a report in the LEAP Asian Pacific American Public Policy Institute and UCLA Asian American Studies Center's *State of Asian Pacific America: A Public Policy Report, Policy Issues to the Year 2020,* Sucheta Mazumdar noted that 35.5 percent of Indian American women and nearly 70 percent of the men had completed college, according to the 1980 Census. In this first wave, 47 percent of Indian Americans were employed as managers, professionals, and executives—mainly as engineers and physicians. The Association of American Physicians from India claimed about 26,000 doctors of Indian descent—just behind Filipino Americans in foreign-born medical personnel.

Yet the credentials and middle-class incomes have not brought Asian Americans the career progression of their white and black colleagues. Joyce Tang, Queens College (New York) assistant sociology professor, examined the National Science Foundation's database of 38,000 U.S. engineers and scientists to track Asian Americans. She found that Asian Americans do better in obtaining entry-level jobs, but they are significantly behind whites and blacks in reaching management positions. A *Los Angeles Times* analysis of 1993–97 census earnings data found that in California Asian American college graduates in management jobs earned 38 percent less than white college graduates in such professions.

Disaffected Asian American professionals make up the ranks of business entrepreneurs. Frustrated in their careers by job discrimination and the glass ceiling, some prefer to strike out on their own as motel or convenience store owners. In the high-technology industry, Asian Americans are estimated to be one third of the workforce, yet almost all the high-ranking management positions are held by whites. Those who started high-tech businesses formed the base of The IndUS Entrepreneurs—for example, Raj Jaswa, an electrical engineer with an M.B.A., who quit his high-tech firm when he wasn't allowed to manage the business unit he led. Jaswa started his own semiconductor business, which was valued at $180 million when it went public in 1993.

The considerable Indian American elite and middle class has had little connection to the working class, in America or India—in the same way that the Chinese American elite has few ties to sweatshop workers. Though the later waves of South Asian immigrants in the 1980s and '90s were more working-class in background, with new immigrants finding their way to truck stops, gas stations, and taxicabs, Sucheta Mazumdar concluded that very few South Asian community organizations have been interested in building alliances across class lines. Professional associations like The IndUS Entrepreneurs focus on their memberships, who are unlikely to have much contact with the likes of cabdrivers. "TIE is strictly for entrepreneurs and business professionals. Our by-laws prohibit us from getting involved in political or social concerns," said Saddique Imam, executive director of The IndUS Entrepreneurs. "Discrimination is not a concern of our organization. Women's issues are not a concern. It is not our role to get involved in unfair practices. We stay away from making political statements. But because we are powerful and our members are extremely educated and extremely rich, the community expects us to." While conscious efforts to eschew politics or certain political topics, like foreign policy, are not uncommon in predominantly immigrant organizations, TIE's disavowals are ironic, considering that many of their members became entrepreneurs as a result of the discrimination they faced in their professions.

Lack of recognition of these middle-class Asian Americans is mirrored in society. "If it weren't for the Indians and Chinese in Silicon Valley, the whole U.S. high-tech industry would collapse." Rendering his assessment in matter-of-fact tones, Narayan Keshavan expressed a widely held notion among Asian Americans that seems to have gone unnoticed by mainstream America. Television shows featuring hospital emergency rooms with no South Asian, Filipino, or other East Asian American staff members provoke similar scorn. An estimated 50,000 computer professionals of Indian descent are working at high-tech firms in Silicon Valley alone, while some 25 percent of doctors and other health workers are Asian American—many South Asian. Keshavan, the special assistant to the Congressional Caucus on India and Indian Americans for U.S. Representative Gary L. Ackerman (New York), pointed to a rumor that Microsoft's Bill Gates threatened to move his operations to Asia if Congress didn't increase the special visa program for highly skilled foreign workers.

Microsoft, Intel, and the nation's most influential high-technology companies lobbied hard to raise the cap on these special H1-B visas from 65,000 to 115,000 in 2001 for foreign high-tech specialists to work "temporarily" in the United States for up to six years. 44 percent of those visa holders are Indian, 9 percent Chinese, with the remainder divided among British, Filipino, Canadian, Japanese, German, Pakistani, and French nationals.

This 1990s wave of highly skilled professional H1-B visa holders may have more in common with the taxi drivers than they would like to imagine. Those who end up at established companies often find that they are treated like "temps" and paid far less than other programmers. Many others end up in "bodyshops"—high-tech sweatshops—pounding out code from one place to the next, arranged through high-tech labor agencies. Their drive to follow the path of Suhas Patil and Kanwal Rekhi and other Silicon Valley first-wave immigrant successes comes at a cost. "The foreign-born professionals are trading in their cultures to be accepted in their companies," said Monica Mehta, who wrote about the high-tech immigrants in *Mother Jones* magazine. Their fluency in English and several programming languages hasn't helped them advance in their companies. "They're taking classes to learn American accents and American slang and how to hang out with American co-workers. They're trying to assimilate as quickly as possible by enrolling in cultural training courses to learn the attitudes, accents, and auras of Americans. But one day they might wonder if it was worth the price."

The hopes and expectations of the first generation of immigrants differ considerably from the lives and concerns of their Americanized children, who must grapple with all the issues associated with growing up Asian in America. For some 1.5- and second-generation South Asian Americans, the awareness of their own struggles is creating an empathy for and affinity with the taxicab drivers, a triangulation that is leading them to involvement in social issues, sometimes in spite of their parents.

What the first-generation Indian American middle class is most concerned about, to the edge of obsession, is the seeming paradox of ensuring that their children succeed in the mainstream yet retain traditional cultural values.

"The most important task for the second generation, in my mind, is assimilation," asserted Saddique Imam of The IndUS Entrepreneurs. Imam is not a high-tech high flyer but an avuncular sixty-year-old who took an early retirement from the planning department of American Airlines in Dallas before becoming executive director of TIE. "The first generation brings in the baggage—all the traditions, the religion. The kids want to do things the American way. That process cannot be stopped—we want them to understand America, to be a part of it, to assimilate. But in the back of our minds we want them to know where their mother and father came from, and to pass it on.

"This problem comes up all the time for the people around me, my friends, family, among TIE members. We're all in the same boat."

Like other first-generation Asian American immigrants, Indian American parents expect—and often demand—that their children achieve the requisite standards of success: outstanding grades, acceptance into a top-tier college, a high-status job that is both secure and well-paying. "It appears that young people have interiorized their parents' expectations and put themselves under severe pressure," Professor Rosane Rocher of the University of Pennsylvania reported, basing her conclusions on papers written by South Asian students. "Many students have come to accept an 'A' as a norm, and failure to achieve it as a matter of shame or, worse, guilt. Young South Asian Americans report in droves that the reason why their parents emigrated was to afford their children the best education. [They are even] convinced that men who emigrated as young bachelors . . . did so not for better opportunities for themselves, but for the benefit of their yet unborn children. Such a conviction fosters a notion that they owe their parents extraordinary levels of achievement to compensate them for the trauma of emigration."

But superachievement is not enough. Maintenance of cultural traditions is also required. South Asian Americans today expect their children to adhere to homeland traditions in ways that earlier immigrants could only wish for. The middle class has built religious temples and schools and can afford to send their American-born children to visit India or other parts of Asia. In addition, the profusion of Hindi movies and videos from India's "Bollywood" studios aids in reinforcing tradition and cultural continuity.

"There are parents who literally force their children to act as though they are in India or Pakistan, telling their kids when and whom to marry. I don't agree with those parents," said Imam. "I try to be subtle—I take my twenty-five-year-old daughter to the mirror and say, 'Look, is this an Anglo face? Let us go find a husband for you.' My daughter just laughs. At this rate she'll end up a spinster."

As the 1.5- and second-generation children of the first- and second-wave immigrants have become young adults in colleges and careers, many feel caught between their parents' conflicting demands to assimilate and yet to stay traditional. It is a familiar conflict in Asian American immigrant communities. In the same way that American-born Chinese are negatively referred to as jook sings, South Asian Americans are called ABCDs—"American-born Confused Desis."

"Not a conversation goes by where there isn't talk about some kid getting disowned because of the intergenerational clash in values," said Minal Hajratwala, a twenty-six-year-old Indian American poet and journalist who was born in San Francisco. "Every family anguishes over kids not marrying as their parents wish." Her nineteen-year-old cousin was disowned and kicked out of the house because she was dating a Bengali boy not approved by her parents. Hajratwala points to issues that have gripped South Asian Americans, like the highly publicized case of a twelve-year-old Indian American girl in Michigan who was impregnated by her older brother. "Indian parents don't want their kids to know anything about sex. That's not reality," she said.

The clash in values includes attitudes toward life in America. After Hajratwala's father, Bhupendra, completed his master's degree in pharmacy at the University of Colorado at Boulder in 1965, he traveled across the country looking for a job, only to be refused everywhere he turned. He was finally offered a job in Chicago, but then couldn't find a place to live because no one would rent to him. "I'm outraged, but he's not," says Hajratwala. "Rather than conclude that America is a racist country, he would say that if you try hard enough, you can overcome anything. It's very Hindu."

Her father accepts that the second generation will be different. "It is hard for Minal's generation to relate to Indian culture and values," said Bhupendra Hajratwala, a retired professor of pharmaceutics. "They are totally aware of being Indian, but find it impossible to identify with. The traditional culture won't be lost with the second generation, but it will be altered."

Maintaining the traditional culture and strong family ties falls most heavily on the female members of the household. "South Asian daughters are expected to uphold the culture, to remain chaste and not bring in the pollution of outside people's cultures," said second-generation Sayantani DasGupta, a writer and physician. "While heterosexual South Asian men are out pursuing and preserving the model minority myth, the women are told, 'Leave your business shoes at the door, put your chappals [sandals] on and do puja, the traditional prayers.' This is the dominant theme for the second generation. Issues of dating, sexuality, and marriage are really code for controlling women's sexuality."

Second-generation girls are taught by their parents, especially their mothers, to reject dating and accept the traditional practice of arranged marriage, which is seen as essential to the preservation of "Indian" ways, according to Shamita Das DasGupta, a professor of psychology at Rutgers University, and the mother of Sayantani. In *A Patchwork Shawl: Chronicles of South Asian Women in America*, DasGupta recounted what her father told her about the folly of choosing one's own partner: "Family and parents are the most important parts of one's life. After all, the feelings of love are created by one's family." She knew then that her marriage would have to conform to her parents' wishes.

It is the same lesson that DasGupta's generation is trying to teach its American daughters. "The first generation has the siege mentality that the larger culture is going to subsume us," said DasGupta. "So they try to indoctrinate the younger generation that everything is beautiful about India, and their role is to preserve that beautiful culture." But the "traditional culture" that the first generation is attempting to inculcate in their children no longer exists, if it ever did. India has changed. Second-generation Indian Americans who visit relatives "back home" find that their parents' teachings are outmoded.

Many daughters rebel by ignoring their parents' wishes, dating behind their parents' backs, or leaving home altogether. But the considerable volume of matrimonial ads in American community-based newspapers such as *India Abroad* and *India West* suggest that a high proportion of second-generation Indian Americans accept parental involvement in their marriage: "North Indian Hindu parents invite correspondence including those on H1-B visa for their 28 years/5'2" M.S. Electrical engineer daughter. Please send biodata with photo." Or: "Parents invite correspondence for their fair, handsome son, MD, from women who are Gujarati, professional, slim, fair, beautiful." Such ads create further pressures on young Indian American women by reinforcing impossible standards of beauty and fair skin, according to a study of matrimonial ads by Himanee Gupta, doctoral candidate at the University of Hawaii.

Occasionally the burden of safeguarding the culture and satisfying the first-generation parents spills over into family violence. Some daughters who refused to accept an arranged marriage and the responsibility of carrying the culture have encountered parental violence. In 1985 DasGupta and four other South Asian women founded Manavi, the first South Asian women's group in the United States to address violence against women. But it is a myth that it is the arranged marriages that lead to increased spousal abuse, warned DasGupta. Rather, the abuse reflects the problems faced by immigrant women who are isolated in a foreign country. The wife of a high-tech immigrant on an H1-B visa, for example, is prohibited by federal immigration law from getting a job—rendering her completely dependent on her husband financially as well as for her immigration status in the United States.

A proliferation of South Asian women's organizations in the United States may be a sign that the cultural demands are too much. Since Manavi was founded in New Jersey, a number of other South Asian women's groups have formed around the United States, including Sakhi in the New York area, Narika in the San Francisco Bay Area, and Apna Ghar in Chicago. These women's groups are leading the efforts to reach out to all parts of the South Asian community, as well as to build coalitions with other Asian American and mainstream women's groups.

Tension between a broader social vision and traditional expectations may link the children of middle-class South Asians to the working-class and poor. In 1995, progressive South Asian Americans, including women's groups like Sakhi, the South Asian Lesbian and Gay Association, and the New York Taxi Workers Alliance, became targets of the Federation of Indian Associations. The federation, as the umbrella agency for the India Day Parade in New York City, barred from participation all groups that used the term or concept of "South Asian" in name or purpose. Any group that included ethnicities beyond Indian Americans couldn't march. The exclusion affected the very groups that were actively seeking to build coalitions on issues affecting South Asian Americans across boundaries of class and ethnicity. Such tradition-oriented groups as the Federation of Indian Associations evidently found the cross-class collaboration of the South Asian groups to be threatening.

None of the subtleties of the South Asian American community were captured when a writer for the *Chicago Tribune* attempted a satire about a fictional Indian cabdriver, published on August 20, 1997. The sports columnist, Gene Wojciechowski, wrote in the cadence he imagined an Indian immigrant might use. "Yes, yes, you may enter my cab," the column began. "Please partake of the complimentary curry chips and pay no attention to my sister (woman in hooded shawl nods) or to Uncle Shankar (old man grunts while reading New Delhi newspaper)." When the taxicab driver realizes he failed to recognize Kevin Garnett of the Minnesota Timberwolves basketball team, the driver exclaims, "I should be trampled by a thousand diseased yaks for such stupidity. At the very least, please accept as a humble gift my cellular phone and this small television set that I often watch while driving at high speeds on Expressway of Kennedy."

Chicago's Asian American community sprang to action. A Filipino American who saw the column notified the Indo American Democratic Organization. Its president, Ann Kalayil, a second-generation Indian American, and secretary, 1.5-generation Selma D'Souza, fired off a stinging letter to the *Tribune*, which was printed two days later:

> Mr. Wojciechowski seems to have trouble distinguishing between various ethnic groups, so we thought we should provide him with some

*helpful information the next time he decides to insult South Asians or Middle Easterners. First, Indians, Pakistanis, Bangladeshis and Sri Lankans are from South Asia and Iranians and Arabs are from the Middle East and North Africa. Whereas Afghans, Tajiks, Turkoman and many others are from Central Asia . . . There are no date trees in India but they are found in the Middle East. Yaks are not found in India but in Central Asia. And what in the world are "curry chips" and "curry jars"? Also, Indian women do not generally wear hooded shawls, because this is not part of any religious custom or tradition. Only conservative Muslim women cover their heads, but not all Muslim women . . .*

*[B]efore you write a satire using an ethnic group, you must be well informed about the ethnic group. You probably would have been more successful had you poked fun at your own ethnic group. Although the article was meant to be satirical and is a column of the writer's opinion, that is no excuse for using such negative stereotypes of any ethnic group. Furthermore, Mr. Wojciechowski, please apologize to the Asian Indian community and set your karma straight.*

Kalayil and D'Souza didn't stop with the letter. They contacted several other Asian American organizations in the Chicago area, including the Japanese American Citizens League, and the Asian American Institute, a pan-Asian non-profit. With a 1990 population of 39,225, the South Asian American community in Cook County not only was one of the largest in the United States but could build effective coalitions both inside and outside the community. When Indian American immigrants created the Indo-American Center in 1989 in the heart of Chicago's South Asian community, they intended for the center to serve the newer waves of immigrants from Pakistan and other parts of South Asia, as well as India. "The early 1965 immigrants were truly midnight's children, idealists who were born in the aftermath of the independence movement of India," said Padma Rangaswamy, president of the center.

The Indo American Democratic Organization and other Asian American groups met at the *Chicago Tribune* offices with its editors. In addition to asking for an apology from the *Tribune*, the group sought an ongoing dialogue between the newspaper and the Asian American community.

Within the week the newspaper took the unusual step of printing an apology to its readers and the Asian American community. It was only the fifth apology by the *Chicago Tribune* in more than thirty years.

The Chicago protest was a significant victory for Asian Americans and a model of pan-Asian coalition-building. It also served as a bridge between the first and second generations of South Asian Americans. "The college students were outraged," said Kalayil. "I never imagined such a reaction—they felt violated, that this image was so far from the truth." But the South Asian community's own attitudes toward the working-class taxicab drivers and the poor were still unclear. It was one thing to fend off defamation and ridicule from the outside, but quite another to examine internal attitudes and class dynamics.

In New York, real-life taxi drivers didn't attract the attention of the broad middle class of South Asian Americans the way the *Tribune*'s imaginary cabdriver did in Chicago. In April 1998, only a few weeks before the taxi drivers' strike would take place, *The New York Times* also ran an article with a reference to South Asian taxi drivers. This one was written by Tunku Varadarajan, the India-born New York bureau chief of *The Times* of London.

Varadarajan recounted a conversation at a dinner party with several successful and rich Indian American couples. "You know, we're really thought of as whites here," an Indian woman said to the *Times* reporter. His host interjected, "Not for long. Soon they'll think we're all cabdrivers." Varadarajan recounted their concerns: "These cabbies were 'ruining our image' in America. 'In just five years they've undone all the good work. These uncouth chaps, straight out of Punjab, can't even speak proper English—can't even drive. I don't know how they got here. Must be through Mexico or something. I don't know why they let them in.' "

From their side of the Plexiglas, cabdrivers couldn't fail to notice that many of their more successful brethren not only had assimilated into American culture but also had adopted and internalized the model minority status. "Sometimes the rich Pakistani or Indian doctors will speak to me in Urdu. But plenty of them just look away and speak in English," said Rizwan Raja, who came to the United States in 1996, when he was twenty-three years old. Raja worked as a bank teller during the day, a cabbie at night, studied computer science, and volunteered for the Taxi Workers Alliance in between. "I look right back at them and answer in Urdu."

Between steady puffs on a cigarette, Javaid Tariq shrugged off thoughts of the middle-class South Asians. "They look down on laborers. We have a saying, 'Anybody can catch a big bird of gold.' They are not so special." A cabdriver interviewed in *Taxi-vala/Auto-biography*, a video documentary about New York cabdrivers by Vivek Renjen Bald, summed it up: "They think they're American now and we are not."

Even as the *New York Times* article hit the newsstands, the New York Taxi Workers Alliance was preparing a response to Mayor Giuliani's unwillingness to negotiate over the Taxi and Limousine Commission's seventeen-point proposal that would drive them out of their jobs.

The NYTWA had no intention of seeking support from the broad South Asian American middle class, in part because of the familiar attitudes expressed in the *New York Times* article. But the middle-class intellectuals of the Forum of Indian Leftists proved crucial to the strike's success. Biju Mathew, a professor of information systems at Rider University in New Jersey, joined Bhairavi Desai and the Taxi Workers Alliance in 1997. When he wasn't teaching, he was helping staff the desk space they sublet from the US-China Peoples Friendship Association at the Brecht Forum. Students and other volunteers recruited online by FOIL helped print and distribute flyers— 25,000 copies per flyer—handing them out at dispatch garages, airport and hotel taxi stands, and Pakistani and Indian restaurants frequented by cabdrivers. Because of their access to college campuses and the Internet, FOIL's members were instrumental in reaching the college-age second generation.

With their taxi driver members simmering over Mayor Giuliani's plan, the Taxi Workers Alliance decided to call for a citywide strike on May 13. No one believed the strike could succeed—the politicians dismissed the cabbies while the news media downplayed their potential impact. Mayor Giuliani called the drivers "taxi terrorists," and accused them of demonstrating "for the purpose of being able to drive recklessly."

The NYTWA and the drivers, however, knew the strike would be big. One hundred to two hundred taxicab drivers were coming to their meetings, which were sometimes conducted in three different languages—Bengali, Punjabi, and Urdu. As the 5 a.m. shift began on May 13, there was hardly a yellow cab to be found.

More than 11,000 of the leased cabs sat idle in their garages, with 95 percent of the taxi drivers on both shifts, of all races and ethnicities, forgoing a day's worth of fares to prove their point. Even the garage owners, who lost hundreds of thousands of dollars in lease fees, supported the drivers. Hard-boiled New Yorkers were glad for the reduced congestion on the city's streets, but it was impossible not to notice the impact that the taxi drivers had. The cabbies finally got the public's attention and even their respect.

"Everybody was surprised by what happened," said Mathew. "We were not surprised at all." The taxicab drivers, particularly the South Asian organizers, were ebullient. "We did it, and oh, it felt great," said Rizwan Raja, eyes lighting up. "We showed big, big unity with our strike. I was on Wall Street and there wasn't a single cab. The media said there would be lots of cabs around. Everybody said we couldn't do it, we would fight each other. I felt so proud. We might be new immigrants, but we showed people that we are a part of the city, too."

Despite the many potential fracture lines among the widely diverse cabdrivers, their differences did not get in the way of their class solidarity. Nor did the often violent clashes in their countries of origin come between the South Asian drivers. "It doesn't matter if we are Jews or Muslims, Hindus or Christians, as workers we have common interests," said Javaid Tariq. "We don't talk about homeland politics. If we talk about politics, it's New York politics."

If strikes by working-class Asian Americans don't ruffle middle-class aspirations to success, hate crimes have been a jarring reminder that complacency is dangerous. With disturbing frequency, such incidents have affected every segment of the Asian American community, including more affluent groups of South Asian Americans. Since it began auditing hate crimes against Asian Americans in 1993, the National Asian Pacific American Legal Consortium has reported a continuing increase in reported incidents. Many of those attacks have elicited a strong public outcry, and a few, like the Vincent Chin case, have catalyzed a sustained, organized response capable of transforming community consciousness.

On Sunday, September 20, 1998, Rishi Maharaj, a nineteen-year-old American-born Indian, was attacked by three white men in his neighborhood. Maharaj was walking two female cousins home after dinner from his uncle's house in South Ozone Park, New York, a solidly middle-class section of Queens, when the men set upon him with baseball bats, shouting anti-Indian epithets: "Get the Indian motherfucker" and "This is never going to be a neighborhood until you leave."

Maharaj was hospitalized in critical condition with blunt-trauma injuries to his head. When his uncle ran to his assistance, he, too, was beaten. Their attackers were arrested and initially charged with assault and harassment and released on bond.

The next day, *New York Times* reporter Somini Sengupta was on duty, wading through police crime lists, when the note about an attack on an Indian man caught her eye. She followed up and wrote about the incident for the next day's paper, placing the Maharaj family in the context of a steady migration of Indo-Caribbean people from Trinidad and Guyana to the South Ozone Park area. The story immediately electrified a broad spectrum of the South Asian American community, as well as other Asian Americans and New Yorkers. That night, Sengupta's story was reported on every major television news station in the city.

Sengupta, then the only South Asian American reporter at *The New York Times*, attributed her ability to recognize the story to her own background as a 1.5-generation Indian American. "I knew nobody else would pick up the story," she said. Two weeks later, she and Vivian S. Toy wrote a follow-up story on how the incident had galvanized a fragmented South Asian community—and about the prejudices that some of the Indian Americans from India had toward the Indian immigrants from the Caribbean. Where Sengupta was hailed by Indian Americans for breaking the story, she was criticized for reporting on their divisions. But the internal differences made the unified community response all the more noteworthy.

The response to the attack on Maharaj was led by Sumantra Tito Sinha, a 1.5-generation South Asian American attorney with the Asian American Legal Defense and Education Fund in New York, which had taken on numerous civil rights lawsuits in its pan-Asian advocacy work. When Sinha read Sengupta's news report in *The New York Times*, he contacted the Maharaj family. "We are an unassuming family, Indian by way of Trinidad, who came to the United States in the 1960s," said Chandra Maharaj, Rishi's eldest sister. "The attack was a crisis for our family. Then an amazing thing happened—Tito called out of the blue. He helped us with a public response and brought all these groups of activists. They took a lot of stress off us."

Through his network of pan–Asian American contacts, Sinha, who grew up in Queens, helped organize community meetings, petition drives, and protests that had the support of more than thirty different groups—pan–Asian American, African American, white, Caribbean, gay and lesbian, and a wide range of South Asian American organizations. Pan–South Asian groups such as the Taxi Workers Alliance, South Asian Youth in Action, Sakhi, and the South Asian Lesbian and Gay Asociation were visible participants. Significantly, the Federation of Indian Associations joined in—the very group that had banned these South Asian–oriented groups from the India Day Parade in 1995.

As a result of their efforts, charges against Maharaj's attackers were changed to attempted murder, and bail was raised from $20,000 to $100,000 to match the seriousness of the crime. Rishi Maharaj's condition improved as his multiple skull fractures healed. But Sinha emphasized, "What happened to Rishi Maharaj is not an isolated incident within the Indo-Caribbean, South Asian, and Asian American communities." Only two days after the attack on Maharaj, a Pakistani gas attendant was beaten to death on Long Island, also with a baseball bat. Ten years before, the Dotbusters violently terrorized the Indian American community in northern New Jersey, creating the climate of racial hostility that led to the killing of Navroze Mody in Hoboken, New Jersey, in 1987. Only four of Mody's eleven attackers went to trial; the four, who were teenagers at the time of the assault, were charged as juveniles and received sentences of probation. In contrast to the Mody case, at least Maharaj's assailants would face a real prosecution.

Organizing among South Asian Americans took place on a national level as offers for support poured in. It was the first time anyone could recall that Indian Americans and Indo-Caribbean people came together, along with pan–South Asian groups, to address racism. They made linkages with other communities as well; in New York State and Washington, D.C., for example, South Asian Americans called for stronger hate crimes legislation that would include protections for sexual orientation hate crimes. "In coming together, everyone's consciousness was changed. By building bridges within our own community, we also built bridges with others," said Sinha.

The coalition to support Rishi Maharaj also demonstrated the power of pan–Asian American cooperation, in spite of the hesitancy of many South Asians to come under the Asian American rubric. "For me it's an academic issue," said Sinha. "You have to work with other groups. Being 'Asian American' gives us a certain credibility and expertise in working in multiracial coalitions." He also admonished, "Asian American leadership needs to make a more concerted effort if we're really concerned about diversity and democracy."

Building broad unity among South Asians is particularly challenging, according to Debasish Mishra, the executive director of the India Abroad Center for Political Awareness, a Washington, D.C.–based national advocacy organization that helped mobilize national support for the Maharaj case. Mishra has gone on record advocating that South Asian Americans should resist separatism and actively participate in the pan–Asian American community, an opinion he has had to defend many times in debates before college student audiences. "We share all of the issues Asian Americans face as the 'perpetual foreigner.' We can mutually benefit with our combined numbers and resources. In addition, 'Asian American' is a governmentally defined racial category," said Mishra. But an alliance won't relieve the dominant Asian American groups of their responsibilities to the less recognized Asian ethnicities. "Asian Americans as a whole must re-evaluate what it means to be Asian American in order to finally stop the cycle of concentric exclusions," he wrote in A. Magazine, a monthly magazine for "Asian America." "The alternative is that Tamils will continue to feel ignored by Sri Lankans, who are in turn tokenized by South Asian Americans, who feel marginalized by Asian Americans, who are invisible to Americans because they aren't black or white."

First-generation immigrants who hesitate to call themselves "Indian American" or "Pakistani American" because they identify more closely with their country of origin are unlikely to accept Mishra's Asian American vision. Knowing this, the India Abroad Center for Political Awareness and other organizations are setting their sights on the second generation. The center works closely with campus groups for its popular summer internship program, which places college students, mostly of the second generation, in public service jobs in Washington, D.C. "If we can reach the kids, we'll reach the parents," said Mishra.

Indian American and South Asian college student associations are burgeoning across the United States, some choosing to remain ethnically separate, while others are pan–South Asian American or pan–Asian American in outlook. The South Asian Students Alliance (SASA) formed in

1989 "to unite the growing population of South Asian students" and "to prepare for [their] growing role in American society." SASA's goal: to make an impact on the political, social, environmental, and legal arenas through community service and action.

Their parents' emphasis on retaining traditional South Asian values did not go unheard. In ways that their first-generation parents never imagined, this next generation of South Asian Americans is joining its South Asian cultural traditions and historical past to its American heritage. When African American civil rights leader and former U.S. ambassador Andrew Young addressed their Atlanta conference in 1998, he told them how Mahatma Gandhi's 1930 protest march to the sea was the inspiration for the 1963 march on Washington. "We followed Gandhi, and we learned from Gandhi and we sought to make changes that would make Gandhi's tactics more relevant to the United States," Young told the attendees. The appeal to South Asian American students was picked up by the India Abroad Center for Political Awareness, which launched a National Gandhi Day of Service at colleges across the United States to encourage Indian American youth to reach out and participate in American society.

Young South Asian Americans are taking up the very community causes that their elders of The IndUS Entrepreneurs so assiduously avoid. A distinct political leadership beyond Chinese American and Japanese American is emerging from South Asian Americans as well as other Asian ethnic communities, consciously making linkages across class and other boundaries. These leaders are stepping forward as the outspoken and empowered children of post-1965 immigrants, eager to take their place in America.

# IV

# MOVING THE MOUNTAIN

# ·9·

# Out on the Front Lines

It was difficult for my parents to accept that I quit medical school to become a community organizer. I could hardly explain it myself, but I finally concluded that medicine was not right for me. The hardest part of my decision was letting

---

*The couples who sued the state of Hawaii for the right to marry: (clockwise) Joseph Melillo and Patrick Lagon; Genora Dancel and Nina Baehr; Antoinette Pregil and Tammy Rodrigues (Tania Jo Ingraham and Lambda Legal Defense and Education Fund)*

my parents down. My mom said softly, "I hoped you would take care of me when I got old." My father stopped speaking to me for a time, which spared me from having to break the additional news that I was working as a construction laborer in the South End of Boston, at a site only a few blocks from my apartment.

In my new life, I was part of a fellowship of Asian American, black, and Latino community and labor organizers working to integrate the highly paid construction trades, a tight fraternity long open only to white men. We saw ourselves as sisters and brothers on a journey toward a noble goal. Beyond the idealism, there was another upside: paid at union scale, I made ten times more as a laborer than I had as a highly trained medical student. I could finally send some money home to my family, allowing me to make a small contribution toward my filial obligations.

Construction work and union organizing were male-dominated arenas, as was medicine. The dynamics reinforced my belief that women should not have to wait in line for our liberation, no matter what Confucius or my Americanized cohorts said. I became deeply involved in Boston's burgeoning women's movement. Hundreds of women came to each meeting we organized that linked women's lives with freedom struggles everywhere. I found a community of sisters, some of whom were openly lesbian. As I learned from the widely diverse range of women about their paths to self-awareness, I began to explore feelings that I'd had for a long time, that I was a lesbian.

Soon I was invited to a special meeting by my fellow Asian American and black community activists. When I arrived at the meeting, I was seated at one side of the room, and my friends sat in a semicircle facing me. It slowly dawned on me that I was the subject of the meeting.

Tariq, a soft-spoken African American man who lead a collective of activists in the Roxbury neighborhood of Boston, started the discussion. "Helen, we've noticed that you're spending a lot of time with lesbians. We need to know if you're a lesbian, because you would harm our organizing efforts. We would have to break off ties with you and the other Asian Americans." It seemed wrong that my sexual orientation would reflect badly on everyone who looked like me, but my Asian American friends nodded in agreement. The leader of our Asian American group hastened to reassure Tariq. "Homosexuality is not part of our community," he said. "It's a symptom of white, middle-class self-indulgence. We could not have a lesbian working with us." The meeting became more like a trial as they amassed the charges and the evidence. Together, they asked how I would plead. "So tell us, Helen, are you a lesbian?"

I couldn't believe my ears. These friends, my extended family, were asking me to choose between my Asian American self and another intrinsic part of me. Feeling their stares as they awaited my response, I felt unsure. I hadn't acted on my impulses. Was I really a lesbian? I didn't know the answer, but I was certain of one thing. My Chinese upbringing taught me to value my family above all. Suddenly my extended family, my community, was threatening to disown me. Was I a lesbian? I answered, "No, I'm not."

Tariq and the others were relieved not to lose one of their energetic young organizers. The meeting was over and everyone went on to business as usual. Except for me. I had stepped into the closet and slammed the door shut. Rather than face my lesbian friends, I gradually stopped going to the women's gatherings. When friends in Detroit suggested I move there to discover America's heartland, I jumped at the chance.

In Detroit, what I found seemed to fill the void. As an autoworker at Chrysler, I experienced the essential humanity of people, across differences of race, culture, and class. I discovered my voice and my calling as a journalist. I embraced a vibrant Asian American community that went far beyond my fellowship of well-meaning activists. My work on the Vincent Chin case cemented a deep relationship with my extended family of Asian Americans. Even my mother and father were proud of me—my shortcomings as a daughter and medical school dropout were forgotten.

Yet something wasn't right with me. I was still searching for a way to make my whole self welcome in my community of Asian Americans. After nearly a decade in Detroit, I moved back east to New York—to pursue my career as a magazine editor, to be closer to my family, and to find the person I had run away from.

There was no lack of Asian American activity in the New York I returned to. While I had been stamping out car parts and writing about the local Detroit scene, bustling communities of South Asians, Koreans, and Filipinos had sprung up. There seemed to be more new Vietnamese restaurants in Chinatown than Chinese. Hate crimes against Asian Americans were on the rise, as were boycotts of Korean American markets. I became part of a support network of Asian American women activists; I joined a growing effort to fight domestic violence in the Asian American community by volunteering with the New York Asian Women's Center. An exciting organization of Asian American journalists was starting in New York. My own career flourished—I was the editor in chief of a travel magazine, and later the executive editor of *Ms.* magazine.

In another, separate part of my life, I had met someone to make a home with—and she was a woman. I came out as a lesbian. My life was full and happy, but it took on that strange bifurcation that many gay people experience. I was an Asian American and I was a lesbian, but in those days I couldn't be both in the same space. It was easy to maintain a façade in a world that presumed all Asian Americans to be heterosexual, and all gays to be white and generally male. Yet my commitment as a journalist and activist was to bring forward communities struggling for visibility. The contradiction grew increasingly intolerable.

When I came out to my family, they were loving and supportive, glad that I found happiness in a home life of my own. Mom talked about gays in old Shanghai and encouraged me to raise a family anyway. Auntie Betty in Queens continued trying to match me with Mr. Right. "So what if you're gay? You can still find a man," she said with a shrug. The remaining challenge was to come out to an Asian American community whose kinship meant so much, when memories of my lesbian trial and the threat of ostracism were still fresh.

An opportunity arose when I was to deliver a speech on Asian Americans and the media to the annual convention of the Asian American Journalists Association in 1992. It was a time when anti-gay campaigns were under way across the country, and Asian Americans seemed irrelevant to the national debate. I wanted to acknowledge that Asian Americans had a stake in the issue, but try as I might, I couldn't work sexual orientation into my short speech. So I asked Hayley, the emcee and a friend, to add this minor detail to her introduction. Fine, no problem, she said. As Hayley addressed the national gathering of journalists and the live C-SPAN cameras, she said, "Helen is a longtime journalist, a feminist and . . ." She hesitated, stammering. "And she's a l-l-l-lesbian . . ." She paused to adjust the microphone and asked, "Did you all hear that? She's a l-l-l-lesbian . . ."

My fear of losing my ties to the Asian American community never materialized. Rather, I discovered a new sense of freedom with my colleagues and my work. In a small way, my televised coming out was a statement that Asian Americans are everywhere in American life and belong in every aspect of national discourse. It was hardly a novel idea, but its time had come.

.   .   .

On the third floor of Honolulu's Richards Street YWCA in the late spring of 1993, a select group of Hawaii's leading Asian American advocates engaged in rapt conversation. Their meeting room overlooked the stately Iolani Palace. One hundred years earlier, Queen Lili-uokalani, Hawaii's last reigning monarch, resided at the palace and was preparing to issue a new constitution for the Hawaiian nation before her government was overthrown by Americans.

Weighing constitutional matters of another sort, the two dozen board members of the Japanese American Citizens League's Hawaii chapter were next door at the Y discussing the Hawaii State Supreme Court's May 1993 ruling that people of the same sex have the right to be married. A historic discrimination lawsuit had been filed in Hawaii two years earlier, seeking equal protection for gay men and lesbians under the Hawaii state constitution, which included the right to state-sanctioned, civil marriage. The Hawaii chapter's national board representative, Bill Kaneko, proposed that JACL support the lawsuit.

Why should we Asian Americans get involved in a controversy over gay rights or other issues that have nothing to do with us? asked one of the board members. He also noted that no other non-gay civil rights group was anxious to speak up on the issue, and even the gay and lesbian groups seemed ambivalent. Would the JACL board be representing its Japanese American membership, which they presumed to be mostly heterosexual, by taking such a position on gay marriage? Another board member said same-sex marriage and homosexuality were moral issues, not political ones, and supporting them would run counter to many members' religious beliefs, including his own.

Kaneko, a Sansei—third-generation Japanese American—stated his case. "When Japanese Americans were stripped of our constitutional rights and shipped like cattle to American concentration camps, few other Americans protested the injustice," he said. "If we stand by and watch in silence when another group is denied equal rights, we become no different from the people who watched Japanese Americans get sent away."

The Hawaii chapter of the JACL was in the forefront on many of the national group's civil rights stands. Earlier in 1993, the chapter came out in support of Native Hawaiian self-determination and persuaded the national board to do the same. The stand not only brought recognition from many Pacific Islanders but garnered an invitation to speak at the centennial of the overthrow of the Hawaiian nation—and JACL was the only non–Native Hawaiian group so honored. Arguing for a similar stance in support of same-sex marriage, the chapter president, Sansei Allicyn Hikida Tasaka, cited JACL's civil rights history.

With 24,000 members and more than one hundred chapters across the country, the Japanese American Citizens League was the largest civil rights group in the Asian American community. Founded in 1929, it was formed to encourage the political participation of American-born Japanese; later, it began to address racism and legalized discrimination against Japanese Americans. After the World War II internment, JACL began to take up social justice issues beyond its own community, especially those affecting other Asian Americans. In 1988, when Japanese Americans finally won a presidential apology and an act of Congress providing redress for the internment, community activists hoped to keep the civil rights momentum going. A new generation of leaders, the Sansei—like Kaneko, Tasaka, and many others—attempted to persuade an older and often more conservative JACL leadership to assert a bolder Asian American voice on national public policy concerns.

On the day that the chapter was to vote on same-sex marriage, board members listened closely to the recommendations of the issues committee, which had studied the Supreme Court's decision. My brother Hoyt Zia, an attorney who chaired the issues committee, showed how the arguments against same-sex marriage paralleled those made against interracial marriage. As late as 1967, miscegenation was still outlawed in sixteen states, until such laws were finally struck down by the U.S. Supreme Court that year. When the JACL board counted their votes, all but two directors supported the lawsuit for same-sex marriage. One of two dissenters immediately resigned from the board, citing a conflict with his religious convictions.

The other board members felt certain that the civil rights group must stand on its principles, no matter how controversial or seemingly distant from their ethnic membership base. With their vote, the Hawaii JACL members set in motion a process that would propel Asian Americans to the front lines of a national controversy—and threaten to split its own membership.

In the months following the Hawaii chapter's endorsement of same-sex marriage, Bill Kaneko, as JACL's national vice president for public affairs, brought the Hawaii chapter resolution in support of same-sex marriage to the national organization. He found enthusiastic allies among other chapters, national board members, and the staff of the national headquarters. There was a hopeful spirit for positive change in the sixty-four-year-old JACL, led by its first woman president, Lillian Kimura. Like Kaneko, the majority of the national board were Sansei and born in the baby boomer years.

After months of debate at the national board level, in May 1994 the national board of directors approved Kaneko's resolution to support same-sex marriage, 10 votes to 3, with 2 abstentions. The Japanese American Citizens League became the first non-gay national civil rights organization to support same-sex marriage.

The next day JACL's legal counsel to the national organization resigned, citing conflict with his religious views. The attorney was duly replaced, but a dissenting chapter called for the issue to be discussed at the national convention. Kaneko and the Hawaii chapter knew that they were going to have to fight an uphill battle.

As the debate took its tumultuous path through JACL, other Asian American groups watched closely, wondering how far an Asian American constituency was willing to move beyond obvious self-interest—and whether the strain of controversy might lead to a fracture. For the first time, Asian Americans and Pacific Islanders would lead the nation with a strong, clear stand on an unpopular and divisive issue.

Initial discussions in the Hawaii JACL chapter arguing for the same-sex marriage suit came a few months after the unprecedented ruling by the Hawaii State Supreme Court in May 1993. In its decision, the high court determined that the state discriminated by denying marriage licenses to gay and lesbian couples. The court said that state law was violated by denying "same-sex couples access to the marital status and its concomitant rights and benefits." The Hawaii court also relied on a 1967 U.S. Supreme Court case that said marriage is a civil right. The Hawaii court ordered that same-gender marriages must be allowed unless there was a "compelling state interest" against such unions, one of the toughest legal tests for a state to prove, generally involving evidence that public safety is at stake.

The Hawaii court's ruling was an unexpected shock that made news across the nation. "Ruling by Hawaii's Supreme Court Opens the Way to Gay Marriages" was the headline in *The Washington Post* on May 7, 1993. Two of the supreme court justices were Asian American: Chief Justice Ronald T.Y. Moon concurred with the opinion, while Justice Walter Heen dissented. The potential consequences of the decision were staggering. If the state of Hawaii allowed marriages to take place between lesbians and gay men, other states with less expansive constitutions might be forced to recognize the unions. The entire bodies of law, from family law and tax code to employment rights and estate law, could be thrown into disarray.

On the mainland United States, Hawaii is best known as the island paradise of idyllic beach vacations. Though the territory joined the United States in 1959, even today some confused mainlanders think of Hawaii as a foreign country rather than as the fiftieth star on the Stars and Stripes. But those familiar with the state are not surprised that the case for same-sex marriage took root there.

First, there is a consciousness for equality in Hawaii that was forged in peoples who had experienced being colonized and used as chattel plantation labor. In 1778, when English Captain James Cook first sailed into Waimea Bay on the island of Kauai, an estimated 400,000 Native Hawaiians populated the islands. But the islanders had no immunity against venereal disease, smallpox, and other deadly ills introduced by Europeans and Americans. Nor were the Hawaiians immune to the rapacity of Anglos for their land and natural resources. By the 1880s, fewer than 40,000 Native Hawaiians survived. 80 percent of the land was under the ownership of Anglo missionaries, and most Hawaiians were landless in their own land.

The high death rate and declining labor pool among the native people forced enterprising Yankee sugar plantation owners to import indentured laborers from Asia, Puerto Rico, and Europe. They created a systematic race-based hierarchy, with white Anglo-Saxon Protestants at the top, Portuguese overseers in the middle, and various Asian ethnicities—mainly Chinese, Japanese, Korean, and Filipino—vying with poor Hawaiians for room at the bottom. Asian laborers were commodities on purchase manifests that ordered "Fertilizer, Filipinos" and "Laborers, Mules & Horses." Within a few decades, Japanese, Chinese, and Filipino plantation workers and their descendants dominated the population.

Racial divisions were also exploited during World War II against the Japanese Americans in Hawaii. As the state's largest ethnic population, they were too crucial to Hawaii's economy to evacuate and imprison—though that possibility was entertained. Instead, Japanese Americans were restricted in their movements, removed from potentially sensitive jobs, and socially stigmatized. Like Asian Americans on the West Coast, people of other Asian ethnicities in Hawaii wore buttons saying "I'm Not Japanese."

Second, the desire to correct the inequalities that Hawaii's citizens had experienced became incorporated into the law. Over time, a vigorous labor movement in Hawaii challenged the racial hierarchy. As the descendants of Asian plantation workers and Native Hawaiians came to political power, the Hawaii state constitution evolved as a reflection of their strong commitment to equality. These experiences of living in a colonized condition, subjected to overt inequality and racism, drove the Asian American children of those plantation workers to become staunch supporters of equal rights for all. In 1972, Hawaii became one of the first states in the country to support a constitutional amendment guaranteeing equal rights for women. Hawaii's voters adopted the Equal Rights Amendment by a 6-to-1 margin to ensure that equal rights under the law would not be denied on account of sex. U.S. Representative Patsy Mink, a Japanese American and the first woman of color to be elected to the House of Representatives, was a co-sponsor of that amendment.

The mainly Asian and Pacific Islander American voters of Hawaii not only ratified the federal Equal Rights Amendment but decided to incorporate this and other equality concerns directly into their state constitution, which became more inclusive in its equal rights protections than the U.S. Constitution. Whereas the Fourteenth Amendment to the U.S. Constitution states that no person shall be denied the equal protection of the laws, in 1993 the Hawaii state constitution incorporated the additional provision that "No person shall . . . be denied the enjoyment of . . . civil rights or be discriminated against in the exercise thereof because of race, religion, sex or ancestry."

In 1993, after three local lesbian and gay couples sued for the right to marry, the Hawaii Supreme Court noted that same-sex marriage fell under the equal protection of the law, unless a "compelling state interest" proved otherwise: "By its plain language, the Hawaii Constitution prohibits state-sanctioned discrimination against any person in the exercise of his or her civil rights on the basis of sex." In its decision, the Hawaii court analyzed the U.S. Supreme Court's 1967 ruling against state laws that prohibited interracial marriages in the case of *Loving* v. *Virginia*.

When Mildred Jeter and Richard Loving—a black woman and a white man—were married in Washington, D.C., in 1958 and returned home to Virginia, they were promptly arrested and convicted of violating the state's miscegenation laws banning interracial marriage. In his sentencing decision, the trial judge wrote that Divine Providence had not intended that marriage extend to interracial unions: "Almighty God created the races white, black, yellow, malay and red, and he placed them on separate continents. And but for the interference with his arrangement there would be no cause for such marriages. The fact that he separated the races shows that he did not intend for the races to mix."

The court's arguments linking same-sex marriage to *Loving* v. *Virginia*, which tore down the legal bars to interracial marriage, was certain to strike a sympathetic local chord in Hawaii, where more than a third of state's population claims a mixed ethnic and racial heritage. Nearly everyone in Hawaii has relatives of another race. Among Native Hawaiians, interracial marriages are so common it is believed that no full-blooded Hawaiians will exist within another generation. Hawaii's more accepting attitudes toward people of different races has been a major factor in the high inter-marriage rate. It remained to be seen, however, whether such attitudes, rooted in the shared history and commitment to equality held by the diverse Asian American and Pacific Islander peoples of Hawaii, would extend to gay and lesbian marriage.

Given the historical context, it was fitting for the court case advancing gay and lesbian marriage to break through in Hawaii, but it was quite another matter for an Asian American group to take up the banner. By anyone's standards, same-sex marriage was not typically associated with Asian Americans.

Until recent years, being visible and out front on public issues has been atypical for Asian Americans. Historically, there were numerous legal and social barriers that inhibited an Asian American voice. For much of the twentieth century, immigrants from Asia couldn't become U.S. citizens and they were thus denied the vote; Chinese in California were legally barred from testifying in court on their own behalf. Such a limited voice could only lower expectations of fair representation in the public record and in the news. Asian American advocates had to overcome resistance to the idea that Asian Americans might have something to contribute to the struggle against hate crimes, to race relations, to civil rights, and to other matters of national concern.

This chronic condition had a two-pronged impact: for Asian Americans, it verified that their voices were neither expected nor desired; for others, it confirmed that Asians are a silent, insular minority with nothing to say.

Internalizing their invisibility, Asian Americans sometimes enforced a self-imposed silence, in a sense "closeting" the community, especially when issues are tinged with a perception of shame or stigma. For years, Asian women activists around the United States struggled to ignite a broad community response to issues of domestic violence and sexual assault. A handful of shelters and programs addressing the needs of Asian battered women were established in the 1980s in major cities, among them New York, San Francisco, and Los Angeles. Their progress was hindered by the lack of support from Asian American male leaders who saw such issues as "dirty laundry" that shouldn't be aired in public.

Occasionally, race and ethnicity have been used to squelch the airing of such "negative" issues in the Asian American community. For example, Dong Lu Chen, a Chinese American in New York, killed his wife in 1987 by pounding her head with a claw hammer. Chen, who suspected his wife was having an affair, claimed that violence against women was the norm in Chinese culture under such circumstances. The judge accepted his argument and sentenced Chen to five years' probation, the lightest sentence possible, saying that Chen "was driven to violence by traditional Chinese values about adultery and loss of manhood." The case outraged Asian American women, triggering protest demonstrations and considerable debate on the validity of "cultural defense" arguments. Asian American men, however, offered little comment.

The absence of an Asian American community outcry against domestic violence and other "dirty laundry" had the paradoxic effect of reinforcing the Asian Americans' general invisibility. Asian American social service advocates, for example, constantly battle the stereotype that Asian Americans have no problems requiring public assistance or attention, that they take care of their own.

Even well-established causes such as combating hate crimes become distasteful to a cautious Asian American community when there is a whiff of shame or stigma. In 1993, around the time that the Hawaii JACL chapter was debating same-sex marriage, Vietnamese American Loc Minh Truong was attacked by a group of teenage boys near a gay bar in Laguna Beach, California. Fifty-five-year-old Truong, a former refugee, was so badly beaten that authorities could not initially determine his race. His left eye came out of its socket and his skull was impaled by a rock. Truong was in critical condition for several days; police described the attack as one blow short of murder.

Such an egregious hate crime would normally rally support from

Asian Americans nationwide. But not this case. Truong's attackers were apprehended and pleaded guilty to attempted murder, felonious aggravated assault, and committing a hate crime. They admitted to saying to Truong, "You fucking faggot . . . we're going to get you!" and claimed that race was not a factor in the beating. Gay and lesbian activists, together with leaders from Asian American communities, rushed to Truong's support. As his family and the local Vietnamese community dealt with the shock of the attack, they also expressed their fears. The family asserted that Truong was not gay and did not want his name to be associated with gays.

The denials diminished the community's ability to condemn homophobic violence as well as anti-Asian hate crimes, regardless of Truong's sexual orientation. An opportunity for Asian Americans to be visible, to reach out and show a broader range of concerns, was lost.

The dry mountain air in Salt Lake City crackled with energy as more than eight hundred JACL members from across the United States assembled at the group's national convention. The publicized agenda of the August 1994 biennium included the showdown over the same-sex marriage issue. A heated floor debate was anticipated.

Asian immigrant communities have often been slow to adopt democratic procedures, particularly when the members come from countries with totalitarian dictatorships. The more Americanized Nisei second generation adopted a democratic and Western style of governance, founding JACL to promote American citizenship.

By 1994, generational divisions over JACL's direction became evident, following the conclusion in 1988 of the campaign for redress and an apology for the internment. Many Sansei who had worked on the redress campaign wanted to continue the momentum. "Among the Sansei, there was a definite feeling that, post redress, JACL should stay in the civil rights arena," said Carole Hayashino, a Sansei and the organization's associate director for more than ten years. "We made a lot of friends in the civil rights coalition through redress. We wanted JACL to be more of a cutting-edge organization."

Only blocks away from the convention, the towering presence of the Mormon Temple, spiritual center of the staunchly anti-gay Church of Jesus Christ of Latter-day Saints, was more than symbolic. The Utah chapter, some of whose members were Mormons, was leading the efforts to oppose JACL's support for same-sex marriage. The Salt Lake City JACL chapter, which was also hosting the national convention, submitted a proposal to be voted on at the national convention to rescind the national board's decision to support same-sex marriage. As an alternative, it urged JACL not to take a position on the issue.

The Sansei advocates for same-sex marriage knew the battle would be uphill. "We didn't expect to win," said Carole Hayashino. "We considered withdrawing the resolution when it looked like we couldn't gather the necessary votes. But we decided that it was important to air a full discussion of the principles behind support for same-sex marriage."

On Saturday, August 6, discussion of the resolution began. Reid Tateoka, of the Mount Olympus Salt Lake City chapter, introduced the motion to rescind JACL's support of same-sex marriage. "This issue and the position of JACL at present compromises members' religious freedom and religious beliefs," said Tateoka. Other Utah chapter members appealed for neutrality, fearing that divisiveness over same-sex marriage would fracture JACL or inflict further damage upon the organization's precarious financial condition.

In an emotional exchange that previewed the debate over same-sex marriage that would later envelop other states, JACL delegates expressed their concerns for and against the resolution. The advocates for the Hawaii position were well prepared for a controversial floor debate, with key speakers from around the country ready to give their three-minute testimony to the delegates. Bill Kaneko set the tone, pointing out that this issue was about government-sanctioned civil marriage, not religious recognition or freedom. "What we have here is a community that needs our assistance. Fifty years ago if people supported us we may not have been in the camps. Let's open our hearts and remind ourselves that we too are minorities."

Larry Grant, of the Salt Lake City chapter, articulated the concerns of many who opposed same-sex marriage. "Marriage is a right granted by the states of the United States of America that has its origin in religious practices, and the marriage covenant is not only a vow of fidelity between two people but is also an obligation to raise a family and to help society. I don't believe supporting same-sex marriages can accomplish that."

In contrast, septuagenarian Nisei Chizu Iiyama, a longtime JACL member of Northern California's Contra Costa chapter, applauded the Hawaii chapter for bringing the issue into the open. "Morality has often been used to hide underlying prejudices—my mother was one of the people who came to the United States as a picture bride, and they were accused of being immoral," she said, referring to the thousands of Japanese women whose initial match with husbands in the United States was via photograph.

A number of gay and lesbian JACL members came to Salt Lake City for the purpose of coming out to the crowded assembly, some for the first time. Tak Yamamoto, who had served as president of the San Fernando Valley chapter in Southern California, spoke of his desire to receive the benefits of marriage with his partner of twenty-seven years. "I am not asking for special rights, I'm asking for equal rights," he said. JACL's former national program director, Lia Shigemura, said, "It's very un-Japanese of me to come out and draw attention to myself as a lesbian. But I am doing so because many of you might believe that issues of lesbians and gays are not real Japanese American issues, because when we come out we are often forced to leave groups like JACL, our communities, and even our families."

In the assembly hall, the buzz of anticipation reached a peak when the chair recognized U.S. Representative Norman Mineta. Mineta, who was the first Japanese American to be elected mayor of a major American city, San Jose, was much beloved for his leadership in the decades-long battle in Congress to garner an official apology and redress for the imprisonment of 120,000 Americans of Japanese descent during World War II. As he stood at the microphone, the congressman did not mince his words. "I cannot think of any more dangerous precedent for this organization than to take a position on an issue of principle that is based on how it will directly affect those of Japanese ancestry," he said, naming groups such as the NAACP, the National Council of La Raza, the Anti-Defamation League of B'nai B'rith, and the National Gay and Lesbian Task Force that had supported redress for Japanese Americans.

A hush fell on the room as Mineta shared a little-known anecdote about the uphill battle to pass redress in Congress. "For all the support that we generated outside the Congress, redress did not begin moving until 1987." Up until then, Mineta said, the legislation stalled in the House Administrative Law Subcommittee because of its chair, Representative Sam Hall, Jr., of Texas. But in 1987, Representative Barney Frank of Massachusetts was elected subcommittee chair. When Mineta went to congratulate him, Frank replied, "Norm, my top priority is to get redress moving."

"Now, here's an openly gay member of Congress with only a very, very small Japanese American constituency," Mineta told the JACL delegates. "What did he do? He made redress his top priority. Why? Because he saw our civil rights as an issue of fundamental principle for this great country. Doing what is right is often controversial. Doing what is just is often unpopular. But if we are to remain a viable voice in the national civil rights movement we cannot back away from our commitments simply because the issue is difficult."

What had appeared to be an uncertain vote turned on Mineta's words. When the resolution was called, the vote was 50 to 38 against rescinding support for same-sex marriage, with 11 abstentions and 4 split votes. The Japanese American Citizens League reaffirmed its support of the same-sex marriage issue in Hawaii.

Cheers of stunned joy filled the room as Japanese Americans exchanged teary-eyed hugs. Members of the Hawaii chapter crossed the aisle to stand with the Salt Lake City chapter, urging a reconciliation within the organization. The JACL national council then moved on to other business, but the convention was transformed by the knowledge that the JACL's action held national import. The Sansei activists had won on the principle of standing up for the equal rights of what was perceived to be the concern of another community. By their stand, they won on another principle: that every American has a right to speak out on any issue, without needing to be asked or invited, because every issue has implications beyond immediate self-interest.

News of the vote quickly spread to other Asian American advocacy groups, whose leaderships wondered if they, too, would be forced to take on gay rights, still seen as unrelated to Asian American communities. Only a few months earlier, in February 1994, Chinese American gays and lesbians in San Francisco insisted on marching as a contingent in the city's internationally televised Chinese Lunar New Year Parade. Unlike New York's St. Patrick's Day Parade, whose Irish American organizers refused to allow Irish gays and lesbians to march, the Chinese American festivities proceeded without public incident.

The JACL position offered a new kind of Asian American attitude that confounded the old threshold. But except for the most politically aware Asian Americans, there was little consciousness of what transpired in Salt Lake City. The majority of Asian Americans, like everyone else, depended on mainstream news media for information. A few newspapers in cities such as San Francisco covered the unprecedented vote. Not surprisingly, reports of JACL's stand failed to inspire the curiosity that a similar stand by other racial and ethnic groups might have. Even in the gay and lesbian press, the remarkable victory for same-sex marriage appeared only as a small item in some newsletters. Missing was any attempt to convey the content and character of the issues Asian Americans wanted to bridge.

Asian American lesbians and gays, however, were ebullient. To receive recognition and validation from one of the oldest and largest Asian American organizations was more than they had hoped for. Within JACL, new memberships grew among younger Sansei Japanese Americans, including lesbians and gays. May Yamamoto, an active member of JACL's Los Angeles chapter who came out as a lesbian during the debate, became president of her chapter. Beyond JACL, a greater confidence in coming out and participating in Asian American community activities emerged among individuals as well as Asian lesbian and gay organizations.

The openness of JACL to lesbians and gays had an energizing effect on international same-sex networks. Globally, Asian gay and lesbian communities sparked with the knowledge that a national Asian American organization supported gay rights. Women from nearly every country in Asia organized their first international Asian lesbian conference. In Taiwan, a thriving gay and lesbian culture began to blossom, and even in the totalitarian People's Republic of China an underground movement of gays and lesbians was emerging. JACL's support of same-sex marriage didn't cause these international events to happen, but its message of Asian American community acceptance of its gay sons and lesbian daughters was one of hope to Asians around the world: that the extended family, the community, could accept them.

In Hawaii, the Salt Lake City vote gave a boost to the same-sex marriage effort, which was still being decided in the courts. Opponents of the lawsuit were gathering arguments to prove the necessity for the Hawaii state government to keep marriage for heterosexuals only. Soon ads began appearing in the daily newspapers, condemning homosexuality as immoral. For the five years between the Supreme Court ruling and the statewide election in 1998, Hawaii residents were treated to daily messages in newspaper display ads such as "Homosexuality surpasses all other vices in enormity," "Homosexual acts are intrinsically disordered," and "The goal of the promoters of moral aberration: destruction of the family." Several large church organizations, particularly the Mormons and Catholics, actively voiced their opposition to same-sex marriage in the heavily Christian state.

Mainland-identified gay groups such as the Lambda Legal Defense and Education Fund came to the assistance of the local Hawaii lesbian and gay couples who were plaintiffs in the marriage suit; Lambda was instrumental in mobilizing national support for the lawsuit. When the issue moved from the courts and into the political arena, the Human Rights Campaign Fund, a national gay and lesbian civil rights group, stepped in. But other mainlanders took an interest as well. Randall Terry, founder of the anti-abortion group Operation Rescue, decided to set up shop in Hawaii against same-sex marriage.

Coverage of the lawsuit in the mainstream media and in the gay and lesbian press glossed over the locus of the debate, Hawaii. The islands became a colorful and inconsequential detail, a footnote.

The growing controversy had its most direct impact on the sizable population of local lesbians and gay men in Hawaii. Five out of the six plaintiffs for same-sex marriage were born and raised on the islands, but in the close-knit island community it is particularly hard to be openly gay. Locals in Hawaii joke that they can divine someone's entire family history and background simply by knowing his or her high school and graduating class. When everyone can potentially know everything about your family within one degree of separation, coming out can threaten the equilibrium within one's entire extended family.

Even without the vocal outcry against same-sex marriage, many local gays and lesbians remain closeted or leave Hawaii's closeness for the mainland, rather than risk bringing unwanted attention to their family members. But the largely negative spotlight on homosexuality brought a disconcerting attention to the unacknowledged local gays, provoking even greater fear and secrecy in many. Their absence from the same-sex marriage debate helped perpetuate the impression that there are no local gay men or lesbians in the state.

In Hawaii, with the influence of its majority of Asian and Pacific Islander American communities, the family takes on a far more dominant role than in many other American cultures. The irony for local gays and lesbians is that their respect for the institution of the family is what motivated three local couples to sue for acknowledgment of their relationships through civil marriage. Similarly, the importance of family to Asian and Pacific Islanders played a large role in moving a "straight" organization like the Hawaii chapter of JACL to insist on the rights of all people to make a family. Yet, at the same time, concern for the extended family forced local lesbians and gays deeper into the closet at a time when their own right to create a family was at issue.

For Native Hawaiians, who were fighting a hundred-year-long battle for their sovereignty, the same-sex marriage debate had a very different context. It was difficult for Native Hawaiians to rally behind the marriage question, especially when studies predicted that tourism could increase by $4 billion a year if same-sex marriage were legal. The destructiveness of tourism development was a major factor in the loss of ancient sacred sites and the disruption of agricultural land and water. Anti-gay groups injected a homophobic element into the tourism concerns by planting fears of the state being overrun by gay white men on their honeymoons.

Yet same-sex relationships were once an accepted part of Native Hawaiian culture, centuries before Hawaii had a constitution. "When men were away for long periods on voyages or for battle, they had same-gender relationships. So did the women at home together; it was something that was accepted," said Ku'umealoha Gomes, of Na Mamo O Hawai'i, a Native Hawaiian organization of gay, lesbian, bisexual, and transgender people. "Is it any wonder that the missionaries were so threatened by us?" Extended families often included same-sex partners, and many of the ruling chiefs, including King Kamehameha, had male companions in their households. Legends of Pele, the creation goddess of Hawaii, ruler of fire and volcanoes, include tales of her female partner. It is said that some of the Hawaiian warriors who first greeted Captain Cook ashore asked his sailors to become their lovers. How the Europeans responded to the invitation is not known.

Missionaries, particularly Mormons, won many converts among Native Hawaiians, but a certain ambiguity remained. "In the Hawaiian community there is a distinction between sexuality versus marriage," said political consultant Norma Wong, who is Native Hawaiian. "A broad tolerance exists for other relationships and children born from those. There's no term for 'illegitimacy.' Marriage was a missionary thing, but family was something else, larger. This distinction has been a gray area in Hawaii for a long time, until this issue made it so black-and-white."

Because of their more expansive view of family, the same-sex marriage issue seemed irrelevant to many Native Hawaiians. Questions of Hawaiian sovereignty—the right to self-governance—over, and its impact upon, a host of issues, from ancient sacred lands to poverty and water rights, loomed as far more pressing. "If you were to ask the question in relation to our culture, it would not be 'What is traditional marriage?' but rather, 'What is property?' " said Kinaʻu Boyd Kamaliʻi, chairperson of Hoʻomalu ma Kualoa, a Native Hawaiian unity initative. "To us, property is about *aina*—land—and giving the ceded lands back to the Hawaiian people. If you sell our lands, you will lose the Hawaiian people. If you lose the Hawaiians, you lose Hawaii. So when you talk about tradition and traditional marriage, you have to peel back the layers to what is traditional."

But the Native Hawaiian concerns over land and culture were soon linked with the same-sex issue. Hawaii Circuit Court Judge Kevin Chang ruled that the state, the Mormon Church, and others appealing the original court decision had failed to provide a convincing justification for the state to discriminate against lesbians and gays. On December 6, 1996, he ordered the state marriage bureau to begin issuing licenses. For a fleeting moment same-sex marriages were legal in Hawaii, but it was only an illusion. The state immediately appealed his decision. The next day Chang stayed his order, pending appeal. Though Judge Chang had rendered the courageous ruling that same-sex marriage was legal under Hawaii's constitution, he evidently did not want to be the one to allow the first gay marriage to take place.

Having lost in the courts, same-sex marriage opponents pressured the state legislature to allow a ballot initiative calling for a state constitutional convention to change Hawaii's state constitution. The possibility of changing the constitution sounded an alarm to Native Hawaiians. For years, land developers searched for ways to chip away at Native Hawaiian rights to water and land and to gather in sacred places. Before a developer could divert water for a golf course, for example, plans would have to account for Hawaiian rights—rights that are guaranteed by the state constitution. A constitutional convention to bar same-sex marriage could open up changes in Native Hawaiian rights. "Once the Constitution is open for change, there is a domino effect on other rights, the rights of Native Hawaiian people," said Kuʻumealoha Gomes. "The same-sex issue is being used as a wedge to divide us; it will have a domino effect on other people's rights."

The fear wasn't imaginary. Developers joined with the same-sex marriage opponents to lobby for a constitutional convention. "There is a link as to why developers jumped on the same-sex issue," said Eric Yamamoto, professor of law at the University of Hawaii. "A 'yes' to change the constitution on marriage could provide momentum for a constitutional convention vote and open up a reconsideration of Native Hawaiian rights. The link was a practical one."

By the spring of 1998, the Hawaii state legislature—under pressure from conservative and religious lobbies—authorized two special questions to be added to the November ballot: one an unprecedented proposal to grant the state legislature the power to amend the state constitution to restrict marriage to opposite-sex couples; the other proposing a constitutional convention to allow for revisions or amendments. In the previous election, the handful of legislators who publicly supported the Hawaii Supreme Court's ruling were targeted and lost their assembly seats. Few politicians were willing to stand in the way of the heterosexual-marriage forces.

The fight over same-sex marriage spilled from the courtroom into the communities. The battle for the hearts and minds of Hawaii's people promised to be challenging. A connection between gay and lesbian rights and the lives of a mainly Asian American and Pacific Islander electorate had yet to be built. Many locals equated "gay" with *haole*—Hawaiian for white. Gay relationships were *ugi*, pronounced "oo-gee"—a local term meaning "yucky." The widespread description of gay and lesbian relationships as *ugi* was a clear expression of homophobia. Putting a local, human face on the issue would be especially difficult when so many of the local gays and lesbians were closeted.

JACL, through its Hawaii chapter and national convention four years earlier, had pushed open the door. At 22 percent of the state's population, Japanese Americans made up the largest single Asian ethnic group. Filipinos and Pacific Islanders were each about 15 percent; Chinese, 6 percent; and Koreans, 2 percent. But in Hawaii's complex ethnic dynamics, what might resonate with one Asian group was unlikely to reach other Asian Americans. Native Hawaiians and Chinese Americans had found their place in Hawaii's early, Caucasian-dominated political scene. But since the 1950s, Japanese Americans had come into political prominence, a situation not without tensions with other Asian American immigrant groups, particularly Koreans and Filipinos.

With the backing of the national JACL at Salt Lake City, a substantial national network and resources were potentially available to help reach other Asian American ethnicities about the same-sex marriage issue. But the proponents of JACL's same-sex marriage proposal were unprepared for the backlash that followed the vote.

Even before the convention vote in Utah, there were rumblings of dissatisfaction toward the national board and staff for advancing the same-sex marriage issue. A secret strategy meeting took place two months before the convention. Key editors and board members of JACL's newspaper, the *Pacific Citizen*, held a brainstorming session to use the power of the press to "show membership that this leadership is lost and wayward" because of its "arrogant and inappropriate" position on same-sex marriage. Their plans, recounted in a confidential memo, included an election strategy to replace the national leadership. While the national board's Sansei majority had mobilized for the marriage vote, a more conservative, second-generation Nisei board was elected at the Salt Lake City convention, outnumbering the civil-rights-oriented Sansei leadership. The new president vowed to steer JACL away from its "treacherous path."

Though the majority of the new board now in control of JACL was opposed to the organization's same-sex marriage stance, they could not reverse a vote taken by the national council. Instead, the fury of the opposition was directed at the Sansei staff members of JACL's national office. At a closed board meeting in December 1994, four months after the August convention, the new president and majority announced that a projected budget deficit was forcing them to lay off five of the seven staff members. By March 1995, the five Sansei staff were terminated, and the remaining two resigned. One by one, the third-generation leadership resigned in protest from the JACL national board, excising the civil-rights-oriented generation from JACL's national leadership.

It was not the first time the Japanese American community faced serious rifts over deeply felt principles. Schisms during the Japanese American internment over whether and how to "prove" one's loyalty to the United States had terrible consequences for every family. Depending on how the internees answered the loyalty oath, some were sent to harsher internment facilities, others to federal penitentiaries or even deported. Young Japanese American men who enlisted in the war effort proved their loyalty with bravery that resulted in the highest casualty rates of any other fighting units. More than fifty years after the war, anger and bitterness over this question still smolders.

The schism over same-sex marriage was markedly different. It was a principle that Japanese Americans chose to debate, not one that was thrust upon them. But other Asian American groups watched the JACL splintering with alarm. A new generation of leaders was advancing in organizations throughout the various Asian American communities. This younger generation hoped to extend the public policy interests and reach of Asian Americans. The bold move to support same-sex marriage not only pushed the envelope to its limits but punctured it. Now one of the leading—and one of the few—national Asian American voices was immobilized by the unexpected backlash. What could be characterized to a large extent as a generational showdown was a grim parable to other new generation leaders: the nail that sticks out might indeed be hammered down.

As the battle over same-sex marriage shifted to the electoral arena, local leaders stepped forward to organize the campaign against the constitutional amendment to ban same-sex marriage. Heading the coalition called Protect Our Constitution was Jackie Eurn Hai Young, a third-generation Korean American former Hawaii state legislator, and the first woman to serve as vice speaker of the Hawaii House of Representatives. While she was vice speaker, a bill was introduced to define marriage for heterosexuals only—and Young voted against it. When she ran for office again in 1996, her opponent campaigned on the marriage issue, defeating Young by 187 votes and adding her to the roster of Hawaii politicians felled by their support for same-sex marriage. Because of her record, the Human Rights Campaign Fund approached her about assisting with the campaign.

Young enlisted the support of leaders in the local Asian American and Pacific Islander communities, including several past presidents and board members of the Hawaii JACL chapter, which was still free to support the issue, since, at least on paper, JACL supported same-sex marriage. JACL's endorsement opened the door to the politically influential Japanese American community. A Protect Our Constitution ad campaign featured an array of prominent Japanese American leaders who came out strongly in opposition to the "traditional marriage" amendment, including Bishop Yoshiaki Fujitani of the Buddhist Church; Jean Aoki, president of the League of Women Voters; Albert Miyasato, former deputy superintendent of the Department of Education; and Major General (Ret.) Walter Tagawa. Their presence helped to broaden the local support. As individuals from the Native Hawaiian, Filipino, and Chinese communities came forth, so did the Hawaii chapter of the NAACP, and Wally Amos, creator of Famous Amos cookies. "The initials for Protect Our Constitution are POC, which coincidentally is an acronym for 'People of Color,'" said Ku'umealoha Gomes, who was openly lesbian and a coalition member. "It was important for us to put a local face on the campaign."

Al and Jane Nakatani, a well-known Japanese American couple from Maui who had lost two of their sons to AIDS, also joined the coalition's leadership. The Nakatanis were outspoken critics of homophobia, especially in the Asian American community. Despite the support that the Nakatanis and others gave to gays and lesbians and their right to marry, the coalition itself, unlike JACL, did not come out directly in support of same-sex marriage.

Those opposing same-sex marriage also presented a local face. The leadership of the Save Traditional Marriage coalition was local, presenting ads that portrayed two Asian-looking Ken dolls in wedding tuxedos. Another showed two Asian men rushing to embrace each other while leaving an Asian bride standing alone and dejected. They argued that common sense and morality dictate that marriage should remain between a man and a woman.

The Protect Our Constitution group appealed to the need to protect everyone's constitutional rights, calling on voters to defend the state constitution and Hawaii's aloha tradition of equality. "Never before have we amended Hawaii's constitution to specifically discriminate against one group of people," said Young. If that were to happen, POC suggested, the rights of all people would be threatened. What group would be next—women, workers, Native Hawaiians, other minorities, the elderly? An ad cited the Japanese American internment experience, showing an elderly man and two boys with numbered tags on their clothes, with a sign in the background saying "Japs keep out, you rats"; the ad's caption: "It must not happen again. To anyone ever."

Many Japanese Americans were moved by the link to internment. "When I heard the POC people talk about same-sex marriage and how it is intertwined with my cultural background and history, I felt both touched and empowered," said Terri Oshio, a third-generation Japanese

American who manages her family's banana farm on Oahu. "Talking about same-sex marriage in the context of discrimination, the internment, and constitutional rights gave me the courage to discuss gay issues with my parents." Oshio organized block parties and persuaded her parents' close-knit neighborhood to support the POC position.

More than a million dollars was spent by each camp on intensive media campaigns. The final vote tally ended where the initial opinion polls began: 70 percent of the voters were against same-sex marriage, 30 percent voted with those who supported same-sex marriages. The fear that the same-sex marriage vote would act as a wedge in the Native Hawaiian constitutional vote didn't materialize, as voters clearly distinguished between the two issues. In the end, the arguments in the Hawaii statewide debate were reduced to the same polarizing questions presented to the JACL national board and council—morality versus civil rights, as though the issue were one or the other. But the members of the JACL were a self-selected group, specifically concerned about protecting civil and constitutional rights, whereas the general populace of Hawaii was not. The appeal to prevent discrimination from happening to another group was not persuasive enough to extend to same-sex marriage. A consciousness formed out of the racial hierarchy of the plantations and the colonization of the islands could not overcome the influence of homophobia; not yet.

Hawaii's JACL members who had supported the same-sex marriage issue were disappointed. "I'm shocked and ashamed that this anti-gay bigotry is happening in Hawaii. What happened in the national JACL should have been a sign of how this debate would evolve," said Alan Murakami, an attorney with Native Hawaiian Legal Corporation and a board member with the Hawaii JACL chapter. "It's a sign that we have to do more to build bridges between the different cultures in Hawaii. What reached Japanese Americans didn't matter to other Asian Americans."

The evolution of the same-sex marriage issue in the Asian American and Pacific Islander communities held great significance for the nation on many levels. Culturally, the spotlight on Hawaii showed that the state's image as a cultural paradise and ethnic melting pot was flawed. In a report to President Clinton's Initative on Race Advisory Board, a Hawaii panel pointed out that, as other cities and states across the nation increasingly resemble Hawaii racially and ethnically, the Aloha State could be a harbinger for the rest of the country.

Politically, the evolution of the same-sex marriage issue in Hawaii offered lessons for the rest of the nation. "In Hawaii, same-sex marriage was a litmus-test issue for Democrats, the way abortion has been for Republicans," said William Hoshijo, executive director of the Hawaii Civil Rights Commission. "But Protect Our Constitution also showed that we could bring a wide range of forces together beyond Asian ethnic issues— labor, Native Hawaiians, civil rights advocates, clergy, professionals, civic groups. It's the most exciting coalition to come into being in Hawaii in a long time."

For Asian Americans, the debate was deeply symbolic. The protracted debate in Hawaii and in other Asian American communities brought the community's attitudes about gay and lesbian matters out in the open. Despite the defeat in a nasty and homophobic campaign, a remarkably visible group of Asian Americans and Pacific Islanders supported the constitutional rights of lesbians and gays. And while the backlash in JACL scored a coup against the Sansei civil rights agenda, a significant majority of its chapters voted to support same-sex marriage as a civil rights issue.

"JACL was a catalyst for the Asian American community," said Colbert Matsumoto, an attorney and former president of the Hawaii JACL chapter. "Their action forced us to talk about our prejudices and to recognize how we look at people who we think are different from us. It also forced us to reconsider our common bonds." As the diverse Asian American communities search for ways to come together, they have also begun to question the prejudice that exists within and among our communities.

Most important, JACL's act of interjecting an Asian American voice into a seemingly peripheral national controversy was revolutionary. It marked the coming out of Asian Americans on a major issue, as a matter of principle rather than in reaction. Their stand was a expression of entitlement to participate in every part of the American dialogue. That the subject was same-sex marriage opened a new arena of engagement in society. Asian Americans passed another milestone as they develop the ability and strength to go beyond ethnic issues—and to be seen as full participants in this democracy.

# · 10 ·

# Reinventing Our Culture

It was so rare to see a real Asian American on television when I was a kid that we had a family ritual when one was spotted. It constituted what I now call an "Asian sighting." A hoot went out: "Hey, come see this, look now!"

Real Asians didn't include Hop Sing, the Cartwright family's houseboy on the TV show *Bonanza*, or David Carradine, Jerry Lewis, or the numerous white actors who donned yellowface to play Asians. We only shouted when we saw reg-

---

*Japanese taiko drumming was once performed by males only (Bob Hsiang)*

ular Asian Americans like us, on the news, game shows, variety programs, or beauty pageants. It was a rare event.

We would then drop everything and make a frenzied rush to the tube to see who had entered that mysterious TV land where people of Asian descent were virtually nonexistent. My parents participated enthusiastically in the routine as well. They liked to assess for us kids the looks, ethnicity, demeanor, intelligence, and other vital signs of the real Asian, which they conducted in a manner as succinctly and passionately as a sports announcer. Most irksome was their habit of comparing us to the TV Asian. When an Asian beauty contestant competed for Miss World or Miss Universe, my father invariably turned to me and said, in all seriousness, "Helen, why don't you try for Miss World?" My brothers snickered and taunted in the background while I seethed in embarrassed fury.

One day I became one of those real Asians on TV. In 1972, I visited China as one of the first Americans to get into the country after President Nixon's historic visit. The TV game show *To Tell the Truth* asked me to be a contestant on the show, which had celebrities guess the real contestant from impostors after receiving clues about the real person. The show would cover my train fare to New York from New Jersey. I wouldn't get paid, but for every celebrity panelist who guessed wrong, I'd win $50. That was enough to entice me, the struggling student, and I hopped the train to New York. On the set, I met the two Asian American actors hired to play me: not only were they older than I, they were Miss World material. The available selection of Asian American actors must have been as sparse as the roles available for them to play. When it came time to pick the real Asian American college student who went to China, somehow the panelists all picked me.

On the scheduled air date, my whole family crowded around the television. Mom and Dad held back from doing their usual critique. At first we all watched in stunned silence, to see me as the Asian sighting. In those pre–videocassette recorder days, it was startling to see yourself on the screen. My three older brothers made wisecracks and my little sister and brother jumped up and down in excitement. Finally Dad said, "Your voice sounds different." Mom said I should have worn more makeup. They stopped foisting the Miss World pageant on me. So much for my television career. Most mind-boggling was the thought that my brief, shining moment on *To Tell the Truth* was an Asian sighting for other Asian American families across America.

Asian sightings are more common now, but they are still infrequent enough to create a thrill whenever real Asians appear on the screen, as martial artists, for example, or television reporters. We cheer to see a Chinese man, chubby and middle-aged, as the star of a television series, or an Asian American female character who is aggressively nasty, so un–Suzie Wong. We heave a sigh of relief when a movie like *Mulan* is released, using real Asian American actors' voices, and it is not "ching-chong," as one friend puts it. Each Asian sighting that breaks through the constricting stereotypes gives another reason to celebrate.

Of course, there's no way to predict how images created and brought to life by real Asians will be interpreted by non-Asians. I was struck by this as I sat in the audience during a "meet the cast" session that followed an outstanding performance of the play *Golden Child* by David Henry Hwang. The all-star cast of Tsai Chin, Randall Duk Kim, Kim Miyori, Julyana Soelistyo, and Ming-Na Wen took questions from the multiracial San Francisco theater audience. The Asian Americans in the audience wanted to know about the actors' experience of performing in a provocative work by an Asian American playwright.

The inquiries from non-Asians were completely different. Every one of the half-dozen or so non-Asian questioners wanted to know more about the practice of foot-binding, which was only one story element in the play. Is foot-binding still being practiced in China? (No, it ended in 1911, the period in which the play was set.) Did American missionaries persuade the Chinese to stop? (No, Americans can't take credit for that; the Chinese stopped by themselves.) What was the purpose of foot-binding? (Too complicated to answer briefly.) And there were a number of other foot-binding questions that the non-historian actors were not prepared to answer.

It was fascinating to observe the different perceptions unfold. The great curiosity about things Asian was evident, as was the desire to hear the perspective of Asian Americans. The challenge and opportunity facing Asian Americans is to make ourselves real to other Americans. When we accomplish that, Asian sightings will no longer matter.

.    .    .

On center stage in the comfortable auditorium of the Oakland Middle School in Lake Elmo, Minnesota, a distant suburb of the Twin Cities, a cheerful, blond twelve-year-old named Marnie opens the assembly. "We're having a Hmong speaker today. Tou Ger Xiong does it all," she says to the four hundred seventh graders. A muscular young man with an embroidered Asian beanie-type hat springs onto the stage and starts doing push-ups. *"Ngo-xiong?"* he asks. "What's up?" He gets the children to repeat the question in Hmong.

"How many of you know any Hmong people?" A few hands go up. "We are a four-thousand-year-old culture. We're the hillbillies of Asia. Heeee-haaaw! Or as we say in Hmong, Cheeee-haaaw!" The students enthusiastically repeat, "Cheeee-haaaw!" Xiong combines traditional stories, puppets, and embroidered Hmong outfits with rap music, hip-hop, and humor to perform the tale of how his family came to St. Paul from Laos.

"I left my country at the age of four/All because of the Vietnam War," raps Xiong, who was born in 1973 and came to Minnesota in 1979 after living in a Thai refugee camp with his family. "My family was moving from place to place/Running from the guns at a very fast pace./My people was dying, there and there./Dead women, children, everywhere./When I think about these tragedies/I thank God for my life and my family . . ."

In Minnesota, Hmong Americans like Tou Ger Xiong have been engaged in a long-term cultural struggle that goes beyond fighting stereotypes. They and other Asian American cultural workers in the Twin Cities and elsewhere are creating new images of Asian Americans and the culture that makes us uniquely American.

Xiong doesn't gloss over the hardships of adapting to life in America, nor does he skirt experiences with racism or Hmong youth gangs. Students laugh as he talks about his first encounters with a flush toilet and when he shares his reaction to the first white people he saw when he was a child: "I saw a tall, big ugly monster with a long nose and yellow hair—my mom told me, 'Don't go too close, he'll bite you.' " His listeners grow quiet as he talks about getting beaten up as a kid. "Other kids called me 'gook' or 'Chink,' and said, 'Go back to your country.' They beat me, kicked me, and spit on me. I wondered what was wrong with me—I didn't like being Hmong for a long time. How many of you have ever been called names? How many of you have been hurt by words?" he asks. Hands shoot up from all over in his multiracial student audience.

Xiong has taken his show to hundreds of groups across the country, from North Carolina to California, as well as Minnesota and Wisconsin, especially communities where the Hmong have settled; there were 90,000 in the United States in 1990. His raps to Hmong audiences try to bridge the gap between parents and grandparents, and their American-born

Hmong youth. "I make the elders laugh when I tell their traditional stories in rap style. But hip-hop is the universal language of youth. The kids are already wearing baggy clothes and listening to rap music about gangs and drugs and shootings. What I do is turn all that around with lyrics about appreciating yourself, respecting others and our people's four-thousand-year history of courage. When Hmong parents see their thirteen-year-old-kid-with-an-attitude laughing with them at the same jokes, it opens up ways to connect with each other."

His unselfconscious style engages Hmong and non-Hmong listeners alike, leading them in an empathic embrace. By the time he raps out his finale, the entire audience is rooting for him, shouting as part of the rap, "Go, Hmong boy, go!" Combining the cultural forms of hip-hop and Hmong storytelling, Xiong makes his message universal. "What I'm about is having one foot in each culture. It's not that I've lost something by being Hmong American. I gain by being part of both cultures."

Xiong's challenge is to translate the cultural practices and beliefs of his Hmong community into stories and forms that can be enjoyed by those who aren't Hmong. In Minnesota, that means reaching out to people whose cultural heritage derives mainly from Scandinavia and other parts of Europe.

"This is the story of all Americans, not just the Hmong," said Xiong. "Every cultural group has been through the same thing. But right now it's our time in history to go through the acculturation—letting go of some things and holding on to others."

Between 1975 and 1991, after the United States withdrew from Vietnam, more than a million Southeast Asian refugees and Amerasians—children of American GIs—arrived in the United States. Of these, 40,000 Hmong found homes in the Minneapolis–St. Paul area. Like the other Southeast Asian refugee groups who came to America, the Hmong were allies of the United States. The CIA had organized Hmong soldiers to fight a "secret war" for the United States in Laos against the Pathet Lao, a Communist guerrilla force that supported North Vietnam. One of the CIA's promises, the Hmong maintain, was to resettle the Hmong soldiers and families if the United States was defeated, since they would face certain retribution in Laos for aiding the CIA. After American troops withdrew from Vietnam, many Hmong soldiers continued fighting the Lao and the Vietnamese troops, but by 1979 an estimated 140,000 Hmong and Lao fled across the Mekong River into Thailand. Many lived in refugee camps for several years until they were relocated to other countries. Those who came to the United States were dispersed throughout the country to locations where sponsors, mostly church-related charities, accepted them.

By the mid-1990s, Minnesota's Hmong population reached 60,000, through secondary moves by Hmong from other states, additional immigration, and the Hmong farming tradition of having many children, making the Twin Cities' Hmong community one of the largest in the United States, second only to Fresno, California.

The Hmong had arrived in Minnesota as post–Vietnam War refugees after overcoming tremendous challenges, having experienced the horrors of war, starvation, and suffering through years of desperate flight in pursuit of safety. Hmong Americans in particular encountered difficulty adjusting to life in the United States. Unlike many of the Vietnamese, Laotians, and Cambodians who had fled from major cities, the Hmong were from the rural mountains of Laos, where they farmed and fished. Until the war, the lives of the Hmong had not changed much since they left the mountainous regions of southern China in the 1800s. Whereas Vietnamese tended to be better educated and more fluent in English, the majority of Hmong were illiterate, with few skills that could be transferred to the American economy. Consequently, a high percentage of Hmong Americans have remained on the welfare rolls. With 63 percent of Hmong Americans living below the poverty line in 1989, they are the poorest of all the Asian American ethnicities.

The Southeast Asians who came to Minnesota through refugee resettlement efforts dramatically increased the state's Asian American population, which was only 6,000 in 1970. According to the Council on Asian Pacific Minnesotans, about 23,000 Vietnamese and 7,500 Cambodians settled in the state in addition to the Hmong. At the end of the 1990s, the number of Asian Americans living in Minnesota had increased to about 113,000 people, spanning forty different Asian ethnic groups, out of a total state population of 4.6 million people. Asian Americans will soon surpass in size the African American community, the state's largest community of color. With rapid growth came inevitable culture clashes.

During the morning drive broadcast on June 9, 1998, the Twin Cities KQRS radio talk show host Tom Barnard and crew went on an extended riff about a thirteen-year-old Hmong girl in Wisconsin who allegedly killed her baby after giving birth in a YMCA bathroom. Barnard, a competitor of shock jock Howard Stern, made pointed digs at the girl, as well as at the Hmong way of organizing families by clans and the special diet of boiled chicken that Hmong women eat after childbirth.

"I think when you stuff a baby in the garbage can, you forfeit some of these rituals," he said. The broadcast included a recurring fake Asian character named "Tak," who made comments in a mock-Asian, pidgin English accent and joked that it would "take a lot of egg rolls" to pay the criminal fines for concealing a corpse. Barnard recommended that Hmong "assimilate or hit the goddamn road."

Hmong Americans were outraged by the comments. Their traditional culture and clan-based family system have been fundamental to Hmong Americans' ability to survive multiple migrations through China, Laos, Thailand, Vietnam, and the United States. But in their Minnesota home, the culture so essential to their cohesiveness under such oppressive conditions has come into sharp conflict with the American way. Neighbors sometimes looked askance at Hmong rituals for the New Year, funerals and other ceremonies, involving shamans—religious leaders—who make contact with the spirit world of the Hmong's pantheistic religion.

Hmong marriage customs in particular have run afoul of what is acceptable, if not legal, in the United States. In Laos, members of the same clan—those who have the same family name—cannot marry, but first cousins with different family names can; marriages are sealed with the bride price, money that is paid to the bride's family. Girls as young as twelve and thirteen years old are considered marriageable in the traditional culture; if the prospective bride refused her suitor, he could kidnap her, and once he paid the bride price to her family, she was considered his wife. During the early years of their resettlement, reports of kidnapping and rape by Hmong Americans made the news.

Upholding both the community's customs and the law has placed Hmong American leaders in difficult positions. "We are sometimes stuck in the middle," said Kao Ly Ilean Her, executive director of the Council on Asian-Pacific Minnesotans. "When the community is disregarding the legal age of consent and marriage of sixteen, how aggressively do we prosecute an eighteen-year-old man who marries a fourteen- or fifteen-year-old, in violation of the state law? We try to create policy that the community can live with, to get parents to realize that, for their children to be successful, they need to have an education. We're trying to get leaders to say that we as a community don't condone early marriages. We've learned that you can't force a culture to change. That could lead to additional tension and family violence."

Out of frustration with how their culture was being ridiculed, Hmong Americans, especially youth and college students of the 1.5 and 2.0 generations, came together in a loose coalition called Community Action Against Racism (CAAR). Africans and African Americans joined in the CAAR protest. They remembered insensitive comments by Barnard and his morning drive crew the previous year about the murder of a Somali cabdriver. CAAR set up shop at the offices of the Hmong American Partnership, where Hmong youth worked alongside other volunteers, stuffing envelopes and assembling information packets to reach out to other Minnesotans for their support and understanding.

After a month of letters and phone calls to the radio station without a constructive response, CAAR organized a demonstration. The Hmong American community was angered not only by the broadcast but by the patronizing attitude of station manager Amy Waggoner, who replied to letters of complaint by boasting of the station's fine record of community service.

By August, the anger spilled into the streets. Several hundred demonstrators, mostly Hmong and other Asian Americans, marched to the steps of the Minnesota State Capitol in St. Paul on a rainy morning. Tou Ger Xiong led the crowd in an impromptu chant in protest against radio station KQRS's popular morning drive program. "It's 1998," he shouted. "We're not going to stand for racism anymore. No! No more!" U.S. Senator Paul Wellstone spoke, and the protesters called on KQRS to apologize for its talk show program that mocked Hmong customs, as well as for incidents that offended other communities of color.

In the months following the broadcast, the protesters and the radio station were at a standoff. The station manager further provoked the Hmong by consenting to meet only if she could discuss, among other issues, the dictionary definition of "racism" versus "insensitivity." In her memo to CAAR about a possible meeting, she wrote: "The purpose of this meeting is to hold a civilized discussion so that various points of view can be heard. If you become hostile, the meeting is adjourned."

Indeed, hostilities were surfacing from other residents of the Twin Cities. When Brian Lambert, media critic of the *St. Paul Pioneer Press*, asked, "Why can't KQRS apologize for its Hmong fiasco?" he received heated calls from readers. A sampling:

- You know, I'm getting really sick of hearing about all this . . . Frankly, all these Hmongs, it's their fault. The way I look at it, we didn't ask them here. They came into our country illegally.
- This is America. There's something called the First Amendment. You can say anything to anyone at any time. If these people don't like it, they can leave.
- I'm sick of people coming into this country and whining about every little thing. Well, they're handed a check when they get off the ship or whatever. I don't understand. You're here. You have an opportunity to make a go of it. It's better than what you had, and you're whining.

The responses to Lambert's column were typical of the comments that Asian American protests evoke. But they only aggravated the pain of the Hmong American community, which found itself besieged by multiple tragedies, all casualties of the trauma of cultural dislocation.

Not long after the June 1998 talk show incident and the flare-up of racial tensions surrounding the thirteen-year-old Hmong girl who allegedly killed her newborn, the Hmong American community experienced other horrors. On September 2, a twenty-four-year-old battered woman, the mother of six children, ages five to eleven, strangled each of her children to death, then called 911 and mumbled, "I don't know why I killed my kids. I can't figure it out." Not even a month after that incident, a woman who had gone to her clan leaders at least six times for help with her physically violent marriage disappeared and was presumed dead; meanwhile, her husband committed suicide. In October, a thirteen-year-old runaway Hmong American girl was raped and killed by a group of white teenagers in a Minnesota park.

The spate of killings in the close-knit community brought renewed attention to the cultural attitudes about women in Hmong American society. "In Laos, under the clan system, women were expected to stay home, support the husband, manage the household and the kids," said Gaoly Yang, a founder of the Women's Association of Hmong and Lao, which developed services for the elderly—and a program to prevent domestic abuse. "But here, a man can't support the family by himself. Women have to work. It changes the traditional roles and creates problems in the home. But domestic problems and domestic violence are taboo to talk about outside the clan. The clan is the basic support network. If you go outside, you will be ostracized." Yang and the others in the women's association were. "Within the community, we were seen as wrecking the family, trying to 'Americanize' Hmong women to be independent, to think for themselves. From the outside, mainstream groups thought we were too passive and too soft on the issue, that we should get the women out of abusive relationships." Yang resolved the conflict by finding a mainstream women's shelter to take on the Hmong program.

Left untouched were the simmering cultural pressure points many Hmong American women are faced with. "The older generation can't just blend in with the melting pot," said Yang. "It's tied up with what is considered culture, of who you are and what your identity is. Can we have respect for both—women who are progressive and women who are traditional?" Discussions were deferred until the internal conflicts reached a tragic, crisis situation that brought them to the attention of the media. Even then, the community disapproved of anyone who talked openly about its problems with outsiders.

One woman who spoke up was Pacyinz Lyfoung, an attorney and executive director of Asian Women United of Minnesota, who made a rare public criticism of the community's attitude toward the incidents. In a pointed Op-Ed piece for the Twin Cities' *Asian American Press* in October 1998, she wrote, "Hmong women, even those who have achieved a higher level of education and are now pursuing professional careers, are very cautious about blatantly airing too strong opinions about Hmong women's issues, for fear of being branded radical feminists and disloyal to the Hmong community." Lyfoung linked the tragedies to the treatment of women in the Hmong community. Her agency found that the thirteen-year-old girl who was the subject of the KQRS protest had been raped. The twenty-four-year-old mother who killed her children was forced to marry when she was twelve, had made numerous domestic violence calls to the police, and had an order of protection. Lyfoung, a 1.5-generation Hmong American, charged that it was easier for both the Hmong American community and the mainstream society to focus on the racist comments of the KQRS host, and the terrible loss of six innocent children, than to confront the issue of gender violence in the community. Though Lyfoung's remarks drew censure for her critique of the Hmong community, they could be readily applied to every Asian American ethnic community, regardless of generation, class, or citizenship status.

The airing of such criticisms brings the fear that a community's culture, traditions, and values might come under blanket condemnation. Misinterpretation by outsiders can be so strong a threat that it effectively silences women and others about the community's "internal" problems. Such fears are not entirely unfounded: cultural clashes and misunderstandings involving Asian Americans have had dire consequences for the whole community.

The responsibility of identifying which cultural traditions to maintain ultimately falls on the generation that grows up straddling the traditional and the American cultures. When Mee Moua, an attorney and Brown University graduate, and Yee Chang, a former reporter with the *St. Paul Pioneer Press* and graduate of St. Olaf College, decided to get married, they wanted to celebrate in the traditional Hmong manner. Both Moua and Chang are of the 1.5 generation who came to the United States when they were young children. "We wanted everything, the Hmong wedding, the 'American' ring ceremony, we wanted all of the old and all of the new," said Moua.

For Hmong Americans, the "old" meant undergoing three days of nonstop negotiations between the families to set the terms by which Moua would leave her family and join Chang's. It also meant setting the bride price that Chang's family would pay Moua's. "Someone who hasn't experienced our rituals might be offended and say my parents sold me, but that's not the case," said Moua. "The terms of the negotiations were not so much about us but about setting a community standard for the value of a daughter that will govern future generations of marriages. Going through the process, I felt I had grown wiser." Every member of the extended family has a specific role to play in the marriage process, which also defines special relationships and mutual reciprocity that certain family members will maintain with the couple throughout their lives, and, potentially, at their funerals.

Moua and Chang routinely attend many of the ceremonial Hmong funerals as a way of preserving the cultural rituals. "We see ourselves as the ones who must record and document the traditions of our culture—we have to know who we are," said Chang.

In Minnesota, Hmong Americans are not alone in the cultural struggle to create space for real Asian Americans to articulate their own stories, to define the forms of real Asian Americans. Perhaps because the Hmong's adjustment to America was so public, it challenged the other more established Asian American communities to be more visible, even those whose own cultural bias has been to assimilate and reject cultural practices that makes them stick out in America. In contrast, the Hmong American community insisted not only on retaining most aspects of its culture but also on holding on to customs that were unacceptable or even illegal in the United States.

The area's changing Asian American population caught the attention of a tiny but close-knit community of Asian American artists, including writer David Mura, who live in Minnesota's Twin Cities, far from the cultural centers of Los Angeles, San Francisco, and New York. They began meeting informally in 1990, for mutual support. They then formed a group, calling themselves the Asian American Renaissance, a reference to the Harlem Renaissance. The Minnesota artists had visions of cabarets, fireside chats with artists, a literary journal, and an organization that could be a resource for budding Asian American artists.

The Asian American Renaissance began its quest with a national conference in 1992. For the first time, more than two hundred Asian American artists from all over the country came together to discuss their work and their common experiences of creating art in an Asian American context, while reaching for mainstream audiences and recognition. Such well-known Asian American artists as Brenda Wong Aoki, Jessica Hagedorn, Renee Tajima-Peña, Jon Jang, Walter Liu, Garrett Hongo, Li-Young Lee, and Marilyn Chin shared their own challenges. "The world may see me as an Asian American, or a 'Jap,' but that is not the way I live in myself," said poet Garrett Hongo.

After the conference, the St. Paul–based Asian American Renaissance became the incubator, training ground, and showcase for Asian American performing, literary, media, and visual art in Minnesota. By nurturing Asian American artists and art audiences, a number of Asian American institutions have emerged on the rich Twin Cities art scene: Theater Mu, Asian Media Access, Pom Siab Hmoob Theatre—a Hmong community theater. With these institutions came a climate that could encourage young artists like Tou Ger Xiong. "In Minnesota, we were starving for a way to see ourselves, to express ourselves in the midst of this Nordic presence," said Marlina Gonzalez, the executive director of Asian American Renaissance and a former curator at the Walker Museum in Minneapolis. "In New York and California, people are used to Asian American artists. We had a hunger, a famine for so long. We got support from the Minnesota arts foundations because we were novel, unique. It's up to us to keep it fresh."

Asian American artists are at the core of expressing the Asian American identity. But there are no simple definitions. "People ask us, what is Asian American art?" said Gonzalez. "Well, what is Asian American? It is something that is continually evolving. For Asian American Renaissance, it is pan-Asian in scope. It has to go beyond merely thinking of second-generation or third-generation sensibilities. It has to encompass a more inclusive pan-Asian global definition. Here in Minnesota we are existing within the pan-Asian diaspora. What do you qualify as Asian American art?"

Just across the Mississippi River, in Minneapolis, Theater Mu has also been expanding the notions of Asian Americans and their art. Formed in 1992 to "give voice to Asian Americans," it uses theater to "redefine the culture and the community in which we live." The theater's artistic director, Japanese Canadian playwright and taiko performer Rick Shiomi, came to Minnesota for a visit; he first thought it an impossible place to be an Asian American artist. He had staged his own acclaimed plays—*Yellow Fever*, *Rosie's Cafe*, and others—in the more established Asian American locations. His potential Asian American audience in Minnesota was markedly different, with former refugees comprising more than two thirds of the Asian American population, followed in number by Korean adoptees, primarily raised by white Minnesotans. Shiomi decided to stay, co-founding Theater Mu.

Shiomi's works at Theater Mu are noted for combining traditional Asian performance with Western forms. "With this political-cultural movement, we are creating our own particular culture, a hybrid that tells our own story," said Shiomi. "These explorations are as new and different for us as for everyone else." Their 1998 season featured *The Walleye Kid*, the story of a European American Minnesota couple who wish for a baby. While ice-fishing in one of the state's lakes, they catch a huge walleye, Minnesota's official state fish. Miraculously, their wish comes true when a Korean baby girl emerges from the fish. As the girl grows older, she has questions about her identity and takes a mythical trip to Korea. The play draws heavily on a mixture of Asian traditions—Korean drumming and dance movements are woven throughout, while the story is based on the Japanese folktale of Momotaro, the boy who was found in a peach.

The questions of identity and culture have become more faceted and complex as newly emerging populations of Asian Americans push against ethnic, racial, generational, and class boundaries. *The Walleye Kid*, a play about a Korean child discovered by white parents, offers a way of using culture to explore the emotional dynamics of a significant Asian American population that is finding its own cultural identity. The "Land of 10,000 Lakes" is home to an estimated 10,000 to 15,000 Korean adoptees. "We call it the Land of 10,000 Adoptees," said one Korean adoptee. An astounding 140,000 Korean-born adoptees have come to the United States since adoptions began after the Korean War ended in 1953, the living legacy of a nation impoverished by years of war and foreign occupation. An Oregon farmer named Harry Holt brought back eight orphans and Amerasian children; he and his wife later founded an adoption service specializing in international adoptions of Asian children, mostly from Korea. The peak year of Korean adoptions was 1986, when some 6,150 Korean children were adopted by Americans, comprising more than half of all foreign-born children adopted in the United States.

As more Korean adoptees have grown into adulthood in recent years, the arts have offered an outlet for them to explore their identities. Most were adopted by white families, dispersed throughout suburban America. Twin Cities' filmmaker and writer Me-K. Ahn was adopted at the age of two by a family in Minnesota. Ahn has been in the forefront of the growing number of Korean adoptees in the arts. She began her experimental film *Living in Half Tones* when she went back to Korea for the first time in 1992. "Because a lot of us don't know about our family histories, art is something that can help explain the unexplainable, what is mysterious in our lives. It's a way to bring some sort of acknowledgment of our experience—we lost families, language, culture." Though adoptions from Korea tapered off after 1988, each year about 1,000 children are adopted from China. Mostly girls, they numbered more than 15,000 by 1998. "We can share our experiences with the kids who are being adopted now," said Ahn.

In her documentary *Searching for Go-Hyang*, which recounts her and her sister's reunion with their family in Korea, filmmaker Tammy Tolle also exposes the verbal, physical, and sexual abuse that she experienced. Growing up, she was told that she was ugly and would have died or become a prostitute had she stayed in Korea. Adoptees say that it is not uncommon to be told such things. Tolle, who ran away from her adoptive home as a teenager, said in *AsianWeek* newspaper that she had met "quite a few" other adoptees who had been abused. Little research has been conducted to determine whether Asian children raised in non-Asian families are at greater risk for sexual abuse. The question of "Asian sexual exoticism" and the potential for sexual abuse wasn't raised by officials or the media when movie celebrity Woody Allen became sexually involved with Korean adoptee Soon-Yi Previn, whom Allen had presumably parented as the significant other of Mia Farrow, Previn's adoptive mother. Few questioned the implications that the relationship might have had for other adopted Asian children. Through film, Tolle was able to broach a subject that others never considered, perhaps spurring research into this area.

Even as Korean American adoptees interject their voices into the Asian American cultural mix, there is another emergent Asian American group coming to the fore in significant and increasing numbers—hapas, the mixed-race children of interracial couples. Hapas—the word means "half" in Hawaiian—are becoming particularly visible in the arts and entertainment media, with some identifying strongly as Asian American and others not at all. Still others are refusing to choose a particular lineage and are asserting all parts of their heritage. Anywhere from 4 to 12 percent of Asian Americans will claim a mixed-race heritage, depending how the question is asked, according to the *San Francisco Chronicle*. Hapa activists estimate that in 1990 as many as one in four, or about 500,000, Asian American children were hapa. Outmarriage rates for Asian Americans in Los Angeles County ranges from 11 percent for Korean Americans to 51.9 percent for Japanese Americans in 1989.

Actor Amy Hill, who played the grandmother on the first Asian American TV sitcom, *All-American Girl*, has a Japanese mother and a Finnish American father. When she first started performing in Asian American theater, Hill was told that she is not Asian enough. She is one of an increasing number of prominent mixed-race Asian Americans in the popular arts and media. Their ranks include golf master Tiger Woods; the *Today* show's Ann Curry; CNBC's Sydnie Kohara; actors Dean Cain, Keanu Reeves, and sisters Meg and Jennifer Tilley; playwright Velina Hasu Houston; martial artist Shannon Lee, Bruce Lee's daughter; Olympic fencer and Pan American Games gold medalist Peter Westbrook; and music professor and jazz artist Anthony Brown, among many others. Perhaps more than any group, hapas are forcing other Asian Americans to reconsider who Asian Americans are and what constitutes Asian American culture.

Sheila Chung, a board member for Hapa Issues Forum, a group that was founded in 1992 to provide a voice for people of partial Asian and Pacific Islander ancestry, relates much more to being Asian American than to being Korean American—the Asian side of her Korean Argentinian heritage. "I was politicized more as an Asian Pacific American than as a Korean," said Chung, who has to contend with the fears and the expectations of mixed-heritage Asian Americans. "People say that we're a 'cultural bridge,' or the other extreme, that we represent 'cultural degeneracy' and we'll dilute the culture. We're not monolithic any more than Asian Americans are monolithic. We just want mixed-race people to be embraced as a part of the Asian American community."

With their growing presence, hapas are bringing issues of prejudice and acceptance within Asian American communities into the light, challenging blood quantum requirements—the minimum qualifying percentages of Asian "blood"—for such community events as Cherry Blossom beauty pageants or sports leagues. It is often assumed that Asian interracial marriages are to whites, when in fact there are what the Hapa Issues Forum calls double-minority hapas, like Eric Akira Tate, who calls himself "100 percent black, 100 percent Japanese, and 100 percent hapa." Double-minority hapas are challenging the prejudice that they encounter. "In

Japan, being non-Japanese is one thing, but being black is another. You can't get any further down the pole than that," said Tate in a 1998 interview with *AsianWeek*. "Usually, if you're part black, the black community will embrace you, no problem. But the minute you say you're something else besides black, there's an issue. There's this feeling that you're trying to disclaim your blackness or that you're ashamed of it. My attitude is that I'm not going to let other people tell me who I am or what I should be." Golf star Tiger Woods, who is more than half Asian, came under fire from African Americans for asserting that he is "Cablinasian"—Caucasian, black, Indian, and Asian—while double-minority hapas criticized the hypocrisy of Asian Americans who embraced Woods but shunned non-celebrity Asian-black hapas.

More recently, a significant trend of Asian American outmarriage to other Asian American ethnicities has been documented. Larry Hajime Shinagawa of Sonoma State University and Gin Yong Pang of the University of California at Berkeley found that marriages between different Asian American ethnic groups, as well as with Latinos, have risen to 25 percent of all outmarriages; Asian interethnic marriages rose 200 to 500 percent between 1980 and 1990. According to Shinagawa and Pang, these inter-Asian marriages are evidence of a growing pan-Asian American identity.

As new and self-identified communities develop and seek their places in the Asian American community, they extend the boundaries of what it means to be Asian American and open up the range of Asian American culture. In the same way that the Hmong and other Southeast Asian Americans have forced more established Asian Americans to rethink their class biases, the Korean American adoptees and the hapas have enriched the Asian American mix with a new understanding of ethnic and racial diversity.

The evolution of new Asian American communities also complicates the notion of creating an Asian American identity with cultural imagery that can replace pernicious and simplistic stereotypes. If there was ever a "single" identity group that could be described as diverse, Asian Americans are it. With our constant growth and change, we are our own moving target. There is no monolithic Asian American culture; it would be more accurate to speak of Asian American cultures. Is it possible to create cultural symbols and expressions that can convey the richness and complexity of Asian Americans?

Asian American cultural workers have been confronting this question since the 1970s, fighting to create spaces on stage, in film and print, in studios and galleries. In those early days, there was a conscious effort to emphasize the American aspect of "Asian American" in both content and form. "In the early days of Asian American theater, we stayed primarily with Western dramatic or comedic forms that were Asian American in content—plays about racism that were expressions of our Asian Americanness," said Theater Mu's Rick Shiomi. "We stayed away from the traditional Asian forms because of the way mainstream exotifies us, like *The King and I*—'those curious and strange Asians.' The fear was that we would be made to feel more foreign."

The avoidance of traditional Asian forms by Asian American artists was not unique to the theater. In the visual arts, the style of political realism was heavily favored, as with the distinctive silk screen poster art of San Francisco's Kearny Street Workshop director, Nancy Hom. Folk-rock songs played on acoustic guitars were the style of the first self-defined "Asian American" singing group of Chris Iijima, Nobuko Miyamoto, and Charlie Chin for their 1973 album, *A Grain of Sand*. Their content established an Asian American identity that was very clear in their lyrics as well as their style:

> We are the children of the migrant worker
> We are the offspring of the concentration camp
> Sons and daughters of the railroad builder
> Who leave their stamp on Amerika.

Film and video activists created media centers in Los Angeles, New York, San Francisco, Seattle, and Boston in the 1970s because Asian Americans had no access to mainstream television and film production. Media activists adhered to certain precepts for their works: "The first was that being Asian American transcended the experience of being solely Chinese, Korean, or Japanese American," wrote Stephen Gong in *Moving the Image: Independent Asian Pacific American Media Arts*. "The second was a belief in the power of the media to effect social and cultural change . . . Many foresaw the opportunity of replacing negative media stereotypes with more authentic and affirmative images."

As Asian American cultural expression began to flourish, it was treated as a form of bastard art, of dubious origin without definition or identity—in contrast to works by Asians from Asia, which were more highly valued by mainstream aficionados as the "real" thing, uncorrupted by Western influence. Asian nationals gained access more readily to precious gallery space and recognition by critics and distributors than did Asian American artists. It would take another decade for Asian American cultural artists to gain some credibility—in the theater, in film, as visual artists and writers. "A window opened up in the late 1980s and early 1990s for Asian American visual artists to be recognized as artists and not just 'political' or 'low' art," said University of California at Berkeley professor Elaine Kim, an expert on Asian American visual art. "Since then, there has been a flowering of work, in greater numbers and range of material, showing our humanity in a way that isn't being done in the political arena."

Still, the notion of an Asian American culture was elusive. "An Asian American film may now be seen by millions," wrote filmmaker Renee Tajima-Peña, who produced *Who Killed Vincent Chin?* and *My America (. . . or honk if you love Buddha)*, in an unpublished paper. "What still remained from the 1970s was the sense that we as Asian American artists were building a pan–Asian American culture from scratch."

Over time, Asian American artists began to include Asian art forms in their work more consciously and less self-consciously, as the need to assert their full creative range and humanity overcame fears of being stereotyped. "By avoiding traditional forms, we were cutting ourselves off from one of our most powerful forms," said Shiomi. "It would be as if African Americans were to reject tap." But unlike the much larger and more established African American community, whose embrace made it possible for black artist Paul Robeson to continue performing after he was shunned by mainstream institutions and later exiled, Asian American artists have been unable to depend solely on the support of the Asian American community. Theater companies like East West Players in Los Angeles, Pan Asian Repertory Theatre of New York, Asian American Theater Company in San Francisco, Northwest Asian Theater Company in Seattle—and Theater Mu in Minneapolis—must struggle to survive by patching together an audience from an evolving population. When Asian American arts producers achieve a measure of success, they must contend with the siphoning away of talent, product, and audience to mainstream companies.

Yet those who market pan–Asian American stories, whether on stage, in film, or in books, continue to grapple with defining the Asian American identity. "After ten years in business, I still see an Asian American market, but it's not as large as I originally thought," said Sandra Yamate, founder of children's book publisher Polychrome Publishing of Chicago. "Instead, there are a lot of smaller Asian ethnic markets. Many who profess to being pan-Asian will still only buy books of their own ethnicity for their kids."

In Minnesota, because the Twin Cities' Asian American population has a relatively high proportion of first-generation immigrants who identify more closely with their own ethnicity than as Asian Americans, Theater Mu has had to find ways to appeal to particular communities. *The Walleye Kid*, for example, was promoted to Korean and Japanese American communities, as well as to Korean American adoptees and mainstream audiences. In another production, Theater Mu takes a Hindu story that is performed with traditional Indian dance and Japanese taiko drumming, in a Western theatrical form. The productions are collaborative ventures between Western-trained Asian American and traditionally trained artists.

"Our primary audience is Asian American; they are essential for us to tell our stories, to express our cultural artistic vision," said Theater Mu's Shiomi. "But they can never be our sole audience—we would never survive. Beyond survival, it is also imperative that we communicate who we are to the wider American audience. Of course, there's no guarantee what they'll take away with them about us. But we can't be so concerned about how the audience might reinterpret that we lose our own expression of who we are."

Dependency on mainstream audiences had raised heated controversies among Asian Americans over the authenticity of an artist's creative treatment of the culture. While mainstream art critics from outside the community questioned the purity of Asian American versus Asian art, so did critics inside the Asian American community, who equated commercial success with cultural fraud. The most public example of this argument was the stinging criticism of bestselling author Maxine Hong Kingston, who wrote *The Woman Warrior*, by writer Frank Chin, whose play *The Chickencoop Chinaman* is also a classic. To be commercially successful, the argument went, writers and artists must have pandered to Western fantasies of Asian culture. In other words, artists who achieved acclaim from the mainstream were, by definition, sellouts, exploiting Asian American images as stereotypic commodities. Mainstream media have contributed to the friction when individual artists are portrayed as representing the views of all Asian Americans.

Despite authenticity debates, distinctions between "pure" Asian art and Asian American hybrids are blurring as global influences affect both Asian and Western forms. Asian American artists, at the forefront of creating synergies between Asian and Western culture, are themselves influencing artists in Asia. For example, taiko drumming, a traditional Japanese musical form, became popular in the 1970s among Asian Americans of various ethnicities, not solely Japanese Americans. These Asian American taiko enthusiasts adapted the Japanese theatrical and ceremonial form into a contemporary form, turning what was a male-only art in Japan into music performed by Asian American women as well. A number of all-female and mixed-gender taiko drum dojos (schools) have been established among the approximately 150 taiko groups performing in North America, including Minnesota. The innovations of Asian American taiko drummers have reached Japan, where Japanese taiko groups have sought out Asian American interpretations of classical Japanese taiko. Asian Americans are providing creative inspiration to Asia as well as America.

In mainstream American culture, the influence of prominent Asian American artists is undeniable, particularly in architecture, classical music, and design. Minoru Yamasaki, I. M. Pei, Maya Lin, Yo-Yo Ma, Kent Nagano, and Isamu Noguchi are just a few of the celebrated artists. How much of their creative brilliance stems from Asian and Asian American influences is an open argument. Terms such as "balance, harmony, grace" and "technical precision" are often applied to Asian and Asian American artists, sometimes in a way that suggests they are masters of technique, not art. Other artists find themselves limited and defined by stereotyped views of Asian art.

To reach their status in popular culture, some Asian American celebrities have had to publicly fight overt racism. When Chinese American architect Maya Lin's design for the Vietnam Veterans Memorial was selected as the best from 1,420 anonymous entries, in 1981, an ugly controversy erupted in which many questioned the wisdom of awarding the design to an Asian American, who looked so much like the enemy. Even after overcoming antagonistic objections and finally building the memorial, Lin wasn't mentioned once at the dedication ceremony. But her design was vindicated by the families of the Vietnam veterans and veterans themselves who turned her memorial into a living monument. Lin readily acknowledges the Asian influence in her designs, which also include a memorial to the civil rights movement and other public works. Of her own ethnicity, she wrote in *Art in America* in September 1991, "If you ask, I would identify myself as Chinese American. If I had to choose one thing over the other, I would choose American. I was not born in China, I was not raised there, and the China my parents knew no longer exists . . . I don't have an allegiance to any country but this one, it is my home."

Artist, musician, and filmmaker Yoko Ono has faced intense hostility and derision ever since her marriage to Beatle John Lennon in 1969. "Maybe the way John nearly flaunted the fact that he loved me so much was part of the cause," she told *Interview* in 1989. "But Paul and Linda [McCartney] have been together for ages now, and he's still a popular person. All in all, though, if John had married a blond upper-crust English lady there would have not been the same sort of reaction . . . It was Asian-bashing, it's as simple as that."

When tennis star Michael Chang gained his upset victory at the 1989 French Open, he dedicated his win to the Chinese students who were demonstrating in Beijing's Tiananmen Square during the same period. During the tournament, Chang stated that he had consciously tried to break opponent Ivan Lendl's concentration. Sportswriters then attacked him for his "mental" game. When French newspapers referred to Chang's "vicious Oriental mind," and another paper called him "our little slant eyes," there were few objections on this side of the Atlantic.

Yet even with such overtly racist encounters, not many successful Asian Americans see themselves as a torch-bearers or role models for "their people." Unlike African American heroes such as boxer Joe Louis and runner Wilma Rudolph, or Latino baseball player Roberto Clemente and singer Gloria Estefan, or Native American Chief Wilma Mankiller and writer Sherman Alexie, who were very conscious of breaking down barriers for their communities, Asian Americans tend to see themselves as individual achievers. Often lacking is the awareness that others who came before helped pave the way for their personal success. This apparent historical amnesia may result from our large population of recent immigrants with no link to the past struggles for equality by Asian Americans and an entire civil rights movement of African Americans and others. Some Asian

American activists point to a lack of charitable tradition in Asian cultures, or the single-minded dedication to one's own family.

In the popular media, Asian Americans are still passing through the stage where simply "being there" may be enough for Asian American communities—for now. There are so few positive images that each prominent person is valued regardless of any reciprocal interest. Real images of Asian Americans may have their greatest impact on Asian American children. Children Now, an advocacy institute, surveyed the media perceptions of 300 each of white, black, Latino, and Asian children. When asked "How often do you see your race on television?" Asian American children were least likely to see images of themselves: 13 percent said they "never see their race," while 51 percent said, "Every now and then." By comparison, the African American and Latino children who say they see themselves "very often" or "often" are 78 percent and 49 percent, respectively.

Highly distinguished Asian Americans are a source of pride to their communities and a reminder to the rest of society of our contributions. Novelist Amy Tan's bestsellers paved the way for a generation of Asian American fiction writers. Physician and author Deepak Chopra is renowned for his teachings on holistic healing and Ayurvedic medicine. Fourth-generation Japanese American Kristi Yamaguchi's parents and grandparents were interned in concentration camps during World War II; her Olympic gold medal for figure skating has inspired many young Asian American athletes. *Time* magazine Man of the Year David Ho's innovations in AIDS research and treatment of people who have been marginalized in society have saved countless lives.

Network television anchor Connie Chung's success opened the doors for hundreds of hopeful young Asian American female TV reporters, in a way that network news correspondent Ken Kashiwahara's long career did not for Asian American male broadcasters—a difference that some attribute to the relative acceptability of Asian American women. Yet throughout much of her award-winning career, Chung publicly discounted her own Chinese American heritage and declined invitations to participate in Asian American community or professional activities, at a time when contemporaries such as Los Angeles television anchor Tritia Toyota were busy founding the Asian American Journalists Association. Emotions flared at the 1990 AAJA convention when Chung had to cancel her keynote speech—and her first scheduled appearance before the group:

she was roundly booed at a banquet whose eight hundred attendees included the country's top journalism executives.

But people and times do change. Connie Chung, for example, has become visibly involved in support for the journalists' association and other groups. With new generations coming forward to break down barriers, some are vocalizing their sense of responsibility to their ethnic community. Texas A&M All-American linebacker Dat Nguyen has spoken about the difference he can make in the attitudes of Texans to Vietnamese Americans, some of whom were shot at and reviled when they first came to the state as refugees. Even as her records top the *Billboard* music chart, pop star Jocelyn Enriquez has said publicly many times that she can never deny who she is as a Filipina. "My ultimate goal is to give back what I've learned as far as the industry and help out aspiring Filipinos," she said to *A. Magazine* in 1997. When Korean American football player Eugene Chung was drafted into the National Football League in 1992 by the New England Patriots, he had a larger goal in mind. "I think by having a chance to play in the NFL, it's going to do a lot for the Korean community. I'd like to be somewhat of a spokesperson for that . . . It will let the people know back in Korea and in the United States to be aware that we . . . are not meek people. The Korean American kids should know that Asians can do more than play Ping-Pong." As Asian American communities become more visible and less marginal in American society, it will also become more "acceptable" for Asian American celebrities to show their support.

Asian American faces in greater numbers and diversity are appearing with regularity in places that once seemed unlikely. In professional sports, they are seen on football fields, tennis courts, and baseball diamonds, in billiard halls, and winning Olympic medals in a widening array of sports. Asian foods are no longer looked on askance as the stuff of chop suey houses but are a vital element of haute cuisine. Asian religions like Buddhism and Hinduism, once limited to practice by Asian Americans in the United States, and then considered to be cultish, are now practiced widely by business leaders and celebrities such as Richard Gere. From Pokémon and *Mulan* to the adoption by European Americans of India chic from mehndi tattoos to bindis, the appeal of things Asian is bringing a certain level of acceptance of things Asian American.

New images of Asian Americans, from documentary realism to the experimental and fantastic, are erupting with volcanic energy from independent film and video artists. Asian American film has evolved as a reflection of the times. "Previous generations of filmmakers were looking outward with stories of the larger community, primarily using a documentary approach," said Janice Sakamoto, director of the Media Fund for the National Asian American Telecommunications Association. "A new generation of filmmakers is looking inward, to stories that are more personal. But the themes are the same—cultural identity, the generation gap, wanting to be American. There are homeland questions for the 1.5 generation. Films like *Three Seasons* by Tony Bui, a 1999 Sundance Film Festival winner, involve going back to countries like Vietnam or Cambodia, instead of going back to China. This new generation of talented and resourceful young Asian Americans is coming forward, in numbers never seen before, with big, artistic visions. They are more attracted to narrative and dramatic feature film, with an eye to the commercial theatrical markets."

The burgeoning success of Asian American–produced independent film and video has not gone unnoticed in Hollywood, where the potential is greatest for reaching mass audiences. Ang Lee's *The Wedding Banquet* grossed $7 million at the domestic box office and $17 million at the foreign box office. *Eat Drink Man Woman* grossed $7.2 million at the domestic and $17.2 million at the foreign box office. Wayne Wang directed *The Joy Luck Club*, the first commercially produced Hollywood film with an almost entirely Asian American cast, grossing $33 million at the domestic box office. Asian American actors who for years have struggled for realistic Asian roles have noticed a change.

"It used to be that the only roles available for Asian American actors were to play foreign characters, and we had to do an Asian accent," said actor Amy Hill, who has played various TV and stage roles and performs her own one-woman shows. "Now roles are coming up to play Asian Americans, and I'm asked to audition for roles without an accent. It's a new millennium—it's about time."

Attitudes change more slowly. In 1997, Korean American actor Steve Park, who appeared in *Fargo* and *Do the Right Thing*, wrote a "Mission Statement to the Hollywood community," decrying the "white, exclusionary culture" of Hollywood and its pervasive racism toward Asians and other people of color. Hollywood studio executive Christopher Lee, former president of motion picture production for Columbia Pictures, shared war stories with the Asian American Journalists Association in 1999. *The Joy Luck Club* was a bad idea, said one executive, because there were no Americans in it; there are no Asian leads, said another, because no Asians speak English well enough; since Hong Kong star Chow Yun Fat is a "Chinaman," he's not handsome enough to play a lead role, Lee was told. Then Lee observed, "This is a contact sport; you can get hurt. You have to pick yourself up and get back in the ring."

It remains to be seen whether a growing cadre of Asian Americans in the entertainment industry and their loose network, called Coalition of Asian Pacifics in Entertainment, can one day wield enough clout to alter Hollywood's characterization of Asians and Asian Americans. In the martial arts genre, such actors as Sammo Hung, Kelly Hu, Michelle Yeoh, and Jackie Chan have added a humanity to Asian characters that David Carradine's portrayal of Kwai Chang Caine could not. Nor are they relegated to "loyal sidekick" roles as Bruce Lee was. Yet there are still vast empty spaces where Asian Americans are missing—such as "true life" hospital dramas that have no Asian American health workers, or programs with no Asian characters situated in a city like San Francisco, which in 1999 was nearly 40 percent Asian American.

In the music realm, a new generation of Asian American artists and cultural workers has no intention of just "being there," but is outspoken and brash. These artists are starting record labels and producing sounds that are deliberately pan–Asian American. In Oakland, California, Jason Jong's band, Asian Crisis, fuses jazz with rhythms from Korea, Japan, India, and Vietnam. "Everyone in the group has a strong sense of the need for Asian American aesthetics," said Jong. "We're definitely trying to create a unique sound that's pan-Asian. We know we're creating our own audience because there is no strong defining Asian American aspect in popular or contemporary music." In 1999, Jong organized what may have been the first Asian American hip-hop concert.

An Asian American attitude is extending into every art form. Acting and performance troupes with overtly Asian American identities, such as 18 Mighty Mountain Warriors, Kai, The Mountain Brothers, Pinay, Peeling the Banana, and Korea Girl, are multiplying. Packed dance clubs play bhangra music, a blend of hip-hop with traditional Punjabi music and dance. Zines have names like *Secret Asian Man, Bamboo Girl, Slant,* and *hardboiled.* Web sites called Angry Little Asian Girl, Exoticize This!, Stir, and Jade are proliferating, vying with newsstand magazine titles *A. Magazine, Giant Robot, Yolk,* and the biweekly newspaper *AsianWeek.*

These artists are not afraid to challenge and poke fun at their Asian and Asian American cultural heritage. The lead performer in the band Superchink, Bert Wang, chose the name of the group to "reclaim" the word "Chink." While that's about as welcome to many Asian Americans as the use of the "n" word is to African Americans, Wang wants to make it empowering. In a show presented by the Asian American Theater Company of San Francisco called *Susie Wong Is Dead!*, Filipina American performance artist Wilma Consul transforms herself from a struggling fresh-off-the-boat immigrant to a transgender hooker, while Suz Takeda performs, preacher-style, in "The Church of Born-Again Asian Americans," a satire on the Asian American movement: "I learned how my ancestors were endlessly wronged throughout history. I looked around my classroom and for the first time in my life (Amen!) I was in a room of beautiful Yellow! (Glory, glory be!) Beautiful Yellow People! Yellow Like Pineapples, Yellow Like Lemons!! Beautiful Yellow People! . . . I began to crave bowls of hot rice!!"

As Asian American theater companies, publishers, filmmakers, and artists struggle for support of a continuously changing pan-Asian audience, *A. Magazine: Inside Asian America* has aimed its sights entirely on Asian Americans. When it premiered in 1990, potential advertisers asked Jeff Yang, the magazine's founder, if his Asian American readers would speak English.

"It's an exciting time to be Asian American," said Yang. "We're putting together the pieces, helping to build the foundation of a community and the arts. Asian Americans are even moving to the forefront of cultural cool. When other kids talk about seeing Jackie Chan in *Rush Hour*, Asian American kids can say, So what? I've been watching him since I was six years old. A pantheon of heroes is being made. What we do is pioneering, we're creating the canon, the playwrights. When I meet young people in college, I wonder—is this the young Shakespeare? We're writing our own culture at a time when culture is exploding."

Into the cool Minnesota autumn of 1998, the noisy protest against KQRS continued; local newspapers and TV stations provided ongoing coverage. Support for Community Action Against Racism swelled beyond the local Asian American community, including Korean American adoptees and hapas. The NAACP, church organizations, gay and lesbian groups, and others signed on with their support. As word of the issue made its way into Internet chat rooms and onto E-mail list serves, Asian American groups around the country offered their help. Los Angeles–based Media Action Network for Asian Americans, which monitors the entertainment media for fair, accurate, and balanced depictions of Asian and Pacific Islander Americans, offered suggestions from its own campaign against a Los Angeles radio station.

Throughout the boycott against KQRS, CAAR maintained four demands: a public apology; the removal of "Tak," the mock-"Oriental" character; air time for members of the Hmong community; and a station policy against on-air racist remarks. Talk show host Tom Barnard used his program to ridicule CAAR leaders. "This all started because of one fat chick . . . because her ego was bruised," he said on the air, referring to the CAAR organizer who first complained about the talk show. The station manager sent letters to advertisers claiming that the protests were good for business, because KQRS's listenership had increased. Meanwhile, CAAR's supporters called advertisers to boycott KQRS and Barnard's show. Audiotapes of the offending program and documentation of the station management's poor response convinced several corporations to drop their advertising with KQRS; among them were Norwest Corporation, Perkins Family Restaurants, Mall of America, Kinkos, US West, Texaco, and Mystic Lake Casino.

By October 16, 1998—more than four months after Barnard's initial broadcast about the thirteen-year-old Hmong girl who had allegedly killed her baby—ABC Radio, the station's parent corporation, stepped in to negotiate a resolution to the stalemate. It offered a series of community initiatives to end the protest, including a number of public service announcements featuring Asian teens to be produced by a local pan–Asian American media center, Asian Media Access; two thirty-minute radio programs featuring Asian American youth; a public service campaign addressing issues of racism; a broadcast journalism scholarship for Hmong or other Asian American students; and a minority internship program at KQRS. A full-page ad appeared in local newspapers with the banner "KQRS and the Morning Show staff apologize. We are sorry."

At their victory party, praise for CAAR and the Hmong youth came from both the Hmong and the American sides of their extended Minnesota community. Of their two main speakers, one was U.S. Senator Paul Wellstone, who encouraged CAAR to persist in its efforts to educate the public through the media and by continued organizing. The other was Hmong community elder and Lao war veteran Xang Vang, who extended his intergenerational congratulations to the youthful CAAR members.

Six months after the protest against the station began, on January 10, 1999, a two-part radio program entitled *Calling America Home* was broadcast on Minnesota radio station KQRS. As part of the agreement made by KQRS to address issues of racism in the Twin Cities, Hmong American college and high school students put together a program addressing prejudice and racism that Asian American youth face. Pakou Hang, talk show host and a senior at Yale University, opened the program with the statement "It is predicted by the year 2050, every ethnic group, including the formerly dominant Caucasian ethnic group, will be a minority."

After the long protest that began in reaction to defamatory slurs against their traditional culture, Hmong Americans in Minnesota have made significant advances in establishing their own voices and images in various cultural forms. At the same time, a rising generation of Hmong American women and men are revisiting the cultural traditions that will strengthen their community in America. They are joined by new communities of Asian American playwrights, musicians, poets, filmmakers, writers, and artists who are asserting their visions of Asian American culture.

# ·11·
# The Last Bastion

I still remember the scene in my fourth-grade class. Mrs. Granada was trying to teach a bunch of nine-year-olds the meaning of democracy. She asked us to explain the Boston Tea Party slogans that set off the Revolutionary War, "No taxation without representation" and "Taxation without representation is tyranny." More specifically, she wanted us to understand the meaning of "representation." Hands shot up, and one by one pulled back as the guesses missed the mark.

Exasperated, Mrs. Granada explained it like this. "Representation means having your say."

My own hand stayed down. Politics was one of my father's favorite topics, but he never mentioned representation. Mrs. Granada's explanation didn't quite make sense to me. In my family's traditional household, the best thing children could say was nothing. Mom was one notch up from the children, with say over

*Washington Governor Gary Locke, with First Lady Mona Lee Locke, among the cheering crowds at his family's ancestral village in Jilong, China, in October 1997 (Rod Mar/Seattle Times)*

us, but that was about it. Confucius didn't care much for women. Judging from the confused looks on the faces of the other kids, I guessed that they had some kind of Confucius in their homes. It was hard for us fourth graders to comprehend the purpose of a war fought over something we didn't have.

Inside my family, Dad had all the say. According to my schoolroom lessons, that meant he had all the representation, the power, and the taxation, too. As I grew older and learned more about representation, I realized how little say Dad had outside of our house. He had come to America before Chinese could become citizens and have the vote. Even though that law had changed, my parents didn't think about becoming naturalized, despite my father's avid interest in politics. I suspect they didn't believe that the say of two Chinese immigrants like themselves could mean very much.

One day when I was in my late teens, Dad got a surprise call from the Immigration and Naturalization Service. The caller said, you've been in this country for more than twenty years; why don't you become a citizen? My father looked at his six American-born Chinese kids seated around the dinner table that night and said to us, "Doesn't look like we're going anywhere—I may as well become a citizen."

To prepare for his citizenship test, he memorized the Constitution, the Bill of Rights, and the Declaration of Independence, documents that he already knew well. He memorized all the presidents, vice presidents, and secretaries of state, the dates of their terms, and with whom they served. It gave him great pleasure to grill his teenage kids at the dinner table, his bully pulpit. "Helen, do you know who the fourth vice president of the United States was?" "No," I'd mutter. Triumphantly he'd exclaim, "George Clinton, 1805–1809—in his *first* term." By the end of the meal he would declare that he was much smarter than any of his smart-aleck children, despite his white hair. He'd also use the occasion to tighten his discipline, since we were obviously not studying hard enough.

But outside our house, the idea of representation was being defined for me. The civil rights movement was fighting for representation of African Americans. Millions of young people—the baby boomer generation—were demanding to be heard. American women were rising up, seeking emancipation from the Western-style Confucianism toward women. Everybody wanted their say. In the parlance of the times, I could dig it.

For me to have a say was more complicated. To have your say means that you are being heard. To be heard would suggest that you are also seen. I never saw or heard any Americans who looked like me in the news. Never. It was as though we didn't exist. That sense of invisibility would wash over me at various times in my life—while waiting in line, at the airport, the bank, or the grocery store, when other people—most often, a white man in a business suit—would try to walk right over me. Over the years I have learned to make myself visible. Nowadays when someone tries to step over me, I yell back, loud and long, New York style. I am waiting for the right moment to say, like Barbra Streisand's Fanny Brice, "What am I, chop suey?"

All this came to mind when I was asked in 1995 to give the opening address to the Organization of Chinese Americans' Leadership Summit, a gathering of Asian American civic and community leaders from around the country. It was quite an honor, and I wanted to offer a leadership challenge to the gathering, which was taking place soon after the Justice for Wards Cove Workers effort had been defeated in Congress for a fourth time.

I decided to talk about how Asian Americans and Pacific Islanders could have our say, even when our Washington allies stab us in the back, as they did with Wards Cove. I talked about moving forward as a community by taking risks and going beyond the days when those who spoke up were investigated, imprisoned, deported, or otherwise stigmatized.

I said that Asian Americans and Pacific Islanders will never achieve equal partnership and equal power with other Americans as long as we are seen as the quiet voice of reason, the ones who always behave, the people willing to discuss and negotiate no matter how outrageously we are mistreated. I said that we needed to broaden our repertoire of what we displayed as leadership, to be less predictable and more creative in our tactics. That we ought to shake up friend and foe alike, to tolerate dramatic actions, and to welcome the emergence of Asian American leaders who could stir up passions in the manner of the Reverend Al Sharpton and such leaders of other communities. I asked them to imagine the scenario of an Asian American group dumping a truckload of rotten fish on the steps of Congress when it failed us for the fourth time on Wards Cove.

When I finished, there was polite applause from the staid audience. The OCA president escorted me from the podium, saying, "Thank you for that very disturbing speech."

It was not what they expected to hear. I decided to try out the same message again, this time to a younger crowd at the East Coast Asian Students Union conference on the occasion of its twentieth anniversary in 1998. This time I was more direct: "We have to stop being so fucking polite!" Instead of polite applause, there was shocked silence to hear a woman like their mothers say such a thing. I repeated my statement. This time, they cheered. They were already leading the way for all Asian Americans, through their new wave of outspoken organizing on their college campuses. This generation is determined to have its say, to be heard and seen and represented. After all, as I learned in the fourth grade, taxation without representation is tyranny.

.    .    .

In Governor Gary Locke's waiting room, under the domed edifice of the Washington State Legislative Building, it is impossible not to feel a sense of the extraordinary. On the walls of the imposing anteroom hang portraits of eighteen previous governors. Each larger-than-life figure looks remarkably like the next—pale complexions, of European heritage. The only variation in the theme is Dixy Lee Ray, who in 1977 became the state's first and so far only female governor.

Next door, in the governor's chair, is a man with unmistakably Asian features. In case that detail is somehow missed, he is surrounded by an assortment of modern-day chinoiserie. Above his head, a sixty-foot-long dragon kite dangles from the high ceiling, lording over the cavernous room and complemented by a decorative Asian fan and framed paintings in Chinese brushstroke-style calligraphy. Governor Gary Locke, the twenty-first governor of the state of Washington, is the first Chinese American to be elected as a governor in the United States, and the first Asian American to head a state on the mainland.

In Washington, where Asian Americans are less than 4 percent of the population, Gary Locke, the son and grandson of Chinese immigrants, was elected by a sweeping 56 percent of the electorate in 1996. Locke doesn't downplay his ethnic heritage—he points with pride to his past support for issues like redress for Japanese American internees, and has given prominent placement in his office to the photograph of the stately residence where his grandfather worked as a houseboy only a few blocks away.

Before running for Washington's highest office, Locke conducted test polls to see if his Asian ancestry might trigger a negative reaction among the voters. He found that a small percentage of people would never vote for any candidate who wasn't white. The remaining voters were his to win—and he never looked back. "The fact that I was Asian American never came into the campaign as an issue," said Locke. Some observers say that the majority of voters didn't think of him as an Asian candidate at all, and a few speculate that the image of the hardworking, smart Asian may even have helped. Locke says he doesn't believe being Asian American offered any advantages to his candidacy; rather, he credits timing, luck, and the fact that he knocked on more doors and shook more hands.

Two years after his inauguration as Washington's governor, Gary Locke still has trouble grasping his status as a role model and a symbol, not just to Asian Americans, but internationally, in Asia, and to his rural white constituents in eastern Washington. There, he and his family are seen as creating a new Camelot in the governor's mansion. They are the classic American immigrant story: the youthful forty-eight-year-old governor with his glamorous wife, former TV reporter Mona Lee, and two young children, Emily and Dylan, both born during his administration. Some say the Locke family has a Kennedyesque aura that may transcend race. "It's hard to believe, but a lot of folks in Washington don't see Gary as Asian at all," said then Seattle city council member Martha Choe.

While some of Locke's constituents may overlook his race, not so his fellow Asian Americans, particularly Chinese Americans, who would like to model themselves after him. To them, his ascendancy portends a new era for Asian Americans as leaders of and contributors to America. On the governor's wall, close to his Eagle Scout plaque, is a massive, framed calligraphed letter from "Nine Chinese Elders" of the state of Georgia, in formal language reminiscent of an imperial proclamation:

> Greetings: As good news spreads quickly through the Chinese American community, we here in Georgia have heard a report that you have been elected to office as the Governor of the great state of Washington . . . Like the old Chinese proverb about beans and melons, your good reputation is an indication that you have reaped what you have sown . . . Please consider the needs of your sizable and extensive Chinese American constituency nationwide, which looks up to you.

Political empowerment has been a stubborn hurdle for Asian American communities. Timothy Fong, professor at Holy Names College in Oakland, California, describes it as "the final frontier" in his book *The*

*Contemporary Asian American Experience: Beyond the Model Minority.* A dynamic political life has always existed within the confines of Asian American ethnic communities, but a toehold in mainstream electoral politics has been elusive. Most non-Asian elected officials rarely visit Asian American communities except in their familiar campaign posture: arm extended, palm open.

Why haven't Asian Americans advanced as much as Jews, or Italians, or other immigrants who also came at the beginning of the twentieth century? Culture is often cited, the lack of progress attributed to a cultural uninterest in politics, a clannish tendency to stick to themselves, and a willingness to accept "benevolent" despotic rule. The real answer is much simpler: Asian Americans lost at least three generations of political development because of federal laws that barred us from citizenship and full political participation. It was not until 1952 that all Asian Americans got the right to become citizens and to vote, when Congress finally struck down the last of the anti-Asian exclusionary citizenship laws.

Only since that milestone of citizenship was crossed did the first Asian American go to Congress, with the election of Dalip Singh Saund from Southern California in 1956. Three years later, after Hawaii was admitted to statehood, Hiram Fong and Daniel Inouye took their seats in the U.S. Senate, followed by Patsy Mink to the House of Representatives. In 1999, the list was still unacceptably short. In addition to the three Asian American members of Congress from Hawaii, only five others sit in the House, a number which includes the Pacific Islander nonvoting representatives from Guam and American Samoa. The organizations and networks, the know-how and the relationships so essential to creating a political presence have been evolving for a relatively short time. With each elected official, each visible community leader, new inroads are being made for others to follow.

In recent years, the path to political empowerment has been tortuous. By the late 1990s, with fears of the Soviet "evil empire" extinguished and the bugaboo of China resurrected, simply looking Chinese in certain quarters is enough to merit a scarlet "S" and a spy probe. Not so in Washington State, where the economy's heavy reliance on Pacific Rim trade may have turned Locke's Chinese heritage into an asset. Even before his inauguration ceremony, officials from bitter rivals Taiwan and the People's Republic of China were jockeying for the new governor's favor. On his first day in office, he met with envoys from Taiwan, while later that year he led a trade mission to China. Cheering crowds lined the road to his ancestral village, welcoming Locke and his family as heroes. "I was moved to tears when our motorcade went through the crowds," he said. "I'm very proud and touched that people would follow us from around the world and all over the country. It's so hard to fathom. I don't see myself as a trailblazer, I'm just an ordinary guy who likes to tinker with cars."

But tinkering didn't get Locke to the governor's mansion. He served as a state legislator for eleven years, including five years as chair of the powerful Appropriations Committee of the legislature. In 1993, he was elected chief executive of King County, which includes Seattle. It is the state's largest county and the thirteenth most populous in the nation. Locke's visible political presence inspired other Asian Americans to enter electoral politics, in the same way that others before him blazed his path. Kip Tokuda, former director of the Washington Council for Prevention of Child Abuse and Neglect, ran for the state house in 1994 in part because of Locke. "As an agency head, I had to come to the capitol to lobby," said Tokuda, now a state representative. "On a subconscious level, it made a difference to deal with this bright Asian American. It took me out of an adversarial environment to where I didn't have to fight to be seen or heard. It gave me the idea that I could run for office, too."

In Washington State, Asian Americans have been on a steady climb to seek and win elective office. Their rise is the product of many years of political evolution that can be traced to the 1940s and 1950s. In 1960, the Asian American population of Seattle was less than 3 percent, but there were already visible political leaders from the community. Back then, a Chinese American named Ruby Chow was elected to the Seattle city council. So was Wing Luke, a city council member who was so popular that he was a top contender for mayor of Seattle in the early 1960s, a dream left unfulfilled when he was tragically killed in a plane crash in 1965.

By 1999, Washington State's Asian Americans were ahead of all other states except Hawaii in political representation, with three state representatives and one state senator, in addition to the governor's seat. In Seattle, the state's largest city, three of the nine city council members were Asian American. Their achievement is enviable compared to other mainland states including California, New York, Texas, Illinois, and New Jersey, which all have more Asian American residents than Washington but far less to show. On the other hand, Washington's percentage of Asian Americans in the state population is higher than in every mainland state except California, which in 1997 was 12 percent, against Washington's 4 percent. Yet in 1999 California had only two Asian Americans in its state legislature, compared to the Evergreen State's four.

Washington's Asian American public officials are also unusually diverse. Among the five state-level officeholders, the four most numerous Asian American ethnicities are represented: Gary Locke is Chinese American; Kip Tokuda and Sharon Tomiko Santos are Japanese American; Velma Veloria is Filipino American; and Paull Shin, in the state senate, is Korean American. In 1999, Veloria and Santos were the only Asian American women to sit in any state legislature on the U.S. mainland.

The example established by the early, pioneering Asian American elected officials created opportunities for successive generations. "The mainstream got used to seeing Asian and Pacific Islander Americans in politics," said Martha Choe, who was serving her second four-year term as a Seattle city council member. "But we could only accomplish this by coalition building within the API [Asian and Pacific Islander] community and with other communities. With each APA [Asian Pacific American] candidate, the entire community has rallied, there's a real sense of pan-Asianness. We've always understood that, as a small minority in the state, we had to reach a wider constituency," said Choe. "The reaching out begins with our different Asian and Pacific Islander communities."

The communities are also reaching out politically. In 1996, three thousand Asian and Pacific Islander Americans went to the state capital to talk to their legislators about the impending federal welfare bill, urging them to treat immigrants and refugees fairly, in the face of cuts in vital benefits. As a result of their visits, Governor Locke and the legislators provided state aid to cover food stamps for poor immigrants. Ever since then, the Asian American community sends thousands to Olympia each year to show their political interest and build the relationship between the community and their elected officials.

The early Asian American political leaders used their positions to develop the next generation, a distinguishing hallmark of the Washington State Asian communities. One of those consistent political mentors is Ruth Oya Woo, a Japanese American Nisei who got a job as a receptionist for the mayor of Seattle in the early 1950s after being interned during World War

II. She spent many years as a campaign worker before she had an epiphany. "I realized that I had worked to elect all these white men. I wanted to get people elected who would do something for my community, who wouldn't treat us as suspects, to keep another internment from happening again."

The unassuming Woo, who runs a small licensing bureau in a South Seattle neighborhood strip mall, has used her expertise to guide the campaign strategies for almost every Asian American aspirant for elective office in the state of Washington, including Governor Locke. "We have to keep bringing young people into the political pipeline. When I meet students, I tell them, 'You're going to be the first Asian American Supreme Court justice,' " said Woo. Two of Woo's protégés have created their own programs to develop community skills and civic participation: state representative Kip Tokuda started a community institute to teach leadership skills, while King County District Court Judge Eileen Kato established a juvenile justice conference for Asian and Pacific Islander youths to learn about the law. Both have linked their work with national organizations: Tokuda's is modeled after the Leadership Education for Asian Pacifics' public policy institute, while Kato developed her conference through the Asian Pacific American Women's Leadership Institute.

Elsewhere in the United States, such essential political foundations are still being developed. In New York City, where Asian Americans made up 8 percent of the population in 1997, the diverse community had yet to come together to elect the first Asian American to the city council. While he was a member of the Los Angeles city council, Michael Woo (not related to Ruth Woo) was the highest-ranking Asian American elected official of a major U.S. city. But when he stepped down from the city council to run for mayor in 1993, no Asian Americans were in place to run for his vacant seat. His defeat cost Asian Americans more than the mayor's office: there was no longer an Asian American voice at the policy level of city government in Los Angeles, where Asian Americans then numbered 11 percent of the city, equal to the population of African Americans.

If Asian Americans are to advance politically, they must understand the importance of building a broad base of support both within and beyond the ethnic community, according to political scientist Don Nakanishi, director of the UCLA Asian American Studies Center. At the same time, they also run the risk of paying less attention to their ethnic base.

Asian Americans in Washington State tried to push Governor Locke to be more outspoken on national controversies affecting the Asian ethnic communities. Privately they speculated whether he was playing it safe with his white constituency. Similar comments have been made about other Asian American elected officials.

"When you look at the elections of Congressman Robert Matsui, former Congressman Norman Mineta, and Governor Gary Locke, the percentage of Asians in their districts is minuscule," said Nakanishi. "They weren't elected by Asian voters. But if you look at their political histories, they were encouraged to run by other Asian Pacific Americans, the core that helped them to get elected at the city council level. They're in the kitchen cabinet, and the core of volunteers—from JACL chapters, church friends, or union members—who go door-to-door campaigning out in the community. There's definitely an Asian American connection for these guys. At the same time, their political careers depend on their ability to develop a broad base—it's necessary preparation for the next political office."

It's not easy for Asian Americans to make themselves visible and politically relevant when they are still considered peripheral to white-and-black society. In Washington State, as in California, Asian Americans have surpassed African Americans in population. But a surprising number of people still view Asian Americans as aliens. In 1997 and 1998, members of Congress advanced dozens of proposals to strip legal permanent residents of their right to political expression, including barring them from participation in the electoral process by handing out flyers, for example, or making campaign contributions. While Congress was working to limit the political rights of Asian Americans and other immigrant communities in this way, poor Asian Americans in San Francisco's public housing projects faced harassment and violent attacks by poor African Americans, motivated in part by the notion that Asians were not entitled to receive public assistance and live in public housing.

At times both blacks and whites have viewed Asian American advances as coming at their expense, prompting resentment from both. A recent study on perceived group competition by sociologists Lawrence Bobo and Vincent Hutchings found that whites feel least threatened by blacks and most threatened by Asians. Meanwhile, a *Los Angeles Times* survey found that blacks identified Asians as the group they consider least trustworthy. Asian Americans are "intruders" in the white–black paradigm; it seems paradoxic that they are also anointed "honorary whites" because of their "model minority" status. Their presumed opposition to affirmative action postulates that they, like whites, are victimized by the advancement of blacks and Latinos. In the absence of clearly articulated Asian American views on such subjects, the opinions of others seeking to advance their own agendas are more readily imposed on and attributed to the Asian American community.

The battleground over affirmative action is a prime example of how the purported opinions of Asian Americans were bandied about by white and black pundits as a prominent part of the debate, while the Asian American community's voice was missing. A myth has evolved that most Asian Americans oppose affirmative action. It persists because Asian Americans make easy marks in the crossfire of black–white tensions, convenient surrogates to divert black frustration and white excuses. Though many individual Asian Americans may indeed oppose affirmative action, there are also a great many who support the policy and who have benefited from it.

The affirmative action myth was first promulgated in the media. An absence of supporting data didn't stop countless commentaries and reports from asserting Asian American opposition to affirmative action. On the eve of the elections that included a ballot measure on affirmative action in California, NBC network anchor Tom Brokaw speculated that Asian Americans might stay away from the polls because of the heavy emphasis on affirmative action and immigration. Even when the highly publicized nomination of Bill Lann Lee for U.S. assistant attorney general for civil rights was stalled because Lee had been an outspoken advocate for affirmative action, the contradiction with the presumed views of his Chinese American ethnic community was ignored.

There is no simple explanation for how the diverse Asian American communities respond to affirmative action in education, employment, and contracting, yet little if any effort has been expended to survey the varied multilingual, multiethnic community's perspectives. When all Asian Americans are assumed to share conservative white views, there is no need to bother. As a result, Asian Americans' views are underresearched and undersurveyed on this and other major policy issues.

But initial broad-based research studies have widely countered the assumptions. The first tri-region, multilingual exit poll on the question was conducted in 1996, commissioned by the National Asian Pacific American Legal Consortium (NAPALC) in conjunction with its affiliates in New York, Los Angeles, and San Francisco and conducted by Larry Hajime Shinagawa, chair of American Multicultural Studies at Sonoma State University. The survey's main purpose was to test the need for bilingual voting information, in addition to the issue-related questions. A total of 4,650-plus Asian American voters in several heavily Asian voting areas of California and New York were surveyed at the polls on a variety of questions, with information and translators available in several Asian languages. Nine hundred and fifty voters were surveyed in four communities of Southern California—Koreatown, San Gabriel Valley, South Bay, and Little Saigon—and more than 500 were polled at San Francisco and Oakland sites. In New York, more than 3,200 voters at 14 sites in Manhattan, Brooklyn, and Queens were questioned.

The results of the polling were startling. An overwhelming majority of Asian Americans opposed the 1996 California anti–affirmative action ballot initiative. In Northern California, 84.1 percent of the 500-plus Asian Americans polled voted against the anti–affirmative action measure. A similar pattern was found in Southern California, where 76 percent of the 950 Asian Americans polled voted no to ending affirmative action.

There were a number of other significant findings in the exit polling, which was intended more to identify concerns of immigrant, non-native-English-speaking Asian American voters than to highlight affirmative action or other specific ballot measures. "The primary reason we wanted to do the survey was to monitor the need for bilingual assistance at the voting booth," said Karen Narasaki, the executive director of NAPALC. "Bilingual assistance makes a difference. We see that in the numbers. This is a policy we need to defend to make sure that Asian Pacific Americans have a voice in the polls." Of the more than 4,650 voters polled, more than half in all three cities asked for and received Asian-language surveys to fill out. Access to Asian-language information was available in several Chinese dialects, Korean, Tagalog, Vietnamese, Japanese, Hindi, Urdu, Gujarati, Bengali, and Malayalam, as well as English. Previous polls conducted by mainstream organizations had all been conducted in English, thereby missing the views of the majority of Asian American immigrants, who may not feel comfortable answering a telephone survey in English.

In contrast to their image as conservative and apathetic, most of the Asian Americans voted to support affirmative action. Further, in all three regions, they heavily supported Bill Clinton, the Democrat, over Bob Dole, the Republican. In New York, 71 percent voted for Clinton, 21 percent for Dole. The San Francisco vote was 83 to 9 percent, and Los Angeles County, 53 to 41 percent, Clinton over Dole. This Democratic tilt broke sharply with polls taken at previous elections by mainstream pollsters that queried limited numbers of Asian American voters, and solely in English. Those polls found that a majority of Asian Americans polled supported George Bush over Michael Dukakis in the 1988 presidential elections, and Bush again over Clinton in 1992. Other research found that, besides those who affiliate with Democrats or Republicans, between 20 and 30 percent of Asian American voters are independent, unaffiliated voters who may act as a swing vote. In 1996, the multilingual polls suggested a leftward swing.

The exit poll's remarkable findings failed to attract media attention despite the extensive coverage on affirmative action. Reporters and people with little knowledge of the Asian American experience have a hard time believing that Asian Americans can support affirmative action when they seem to outperform everyone in the classroom. In the logic of self-interest, Asian Americans ought to keep every available slot for themselves. But many Asian Americans have also had painful encounters with discrimination in employment and business, which share the central core of the affirmative action debate. In the early 1980s, Asian Americans for Affirmative Action was organized by scientific and technical professionals of AT&T and Bell Laboratories because of workplace discrimination, becoming one of the first Asian American employee organizations in the country created to address job bias. The glass ceiling is a lively topic among Asian Americans. Disparities for Asian Americans in the workplace are well documented in research data, although this distress passes unnoticed by non–Asian Americans.

The evolution of the affirmative action myth offers strategic pointers to Asian Americans on the road to political empowerment, particularly in the electoral arena where perception can mean everything. Even on issues for which a consensus may not exist, Asian Americans must find the resources to define, characterize, and put forth views on key policy issues, as the Japanese American Citizens League did on the issue of gay and lesbian marriage. Unless Asian Americans define ourselves, others will do so to advance their own agendas, using Asian Americans as a shield or wedge on volatile race matters.

Race theorist Mari Matsuda issued this warning to Asian Americans in a speech to the San Francisco–based Asian Law Caucus in 1990: "For a variety of historical and cultural reasons, Asian Americans are particularly susceptible to being used by dominant society," said Matsuda, who teaches law at Georgetown University and is coauthor, with Charles Lawrence, of *We Won't Go Back: The Case for Affirmative Action*. "When Asian Americans manage to do well, their success is used against others. Internally, it is used to erase the continuing poverty and social dislocation within Asian American communities. Externally, our successes are used to deny racism and to put down other groups. Yes, we take pride in our success, but we should also remember the cost. I hope we will not be used to blame the poor for their poverty. Nor should we be used to deny employment or educational opportunity to others."

In the political trenches, Asian Americans have had to work particularly hard to dispel notions that their interests are identical to whites'. When the anti–affirmative action initiative known as I-200 was placed on the 1998 state ballot in Washington, Governor Gary Locke used his position as chief executive to stump for affirmative action, even though the measure to reverse affirmative action passed by a large margin, as predicted. Asian Americans like Locke have succeeded in navigating this difficult racial terrain by articulating clear political stances.

Over the years, Locke and a number of prominent Asian American leaders have worked closely with black, Latino, and Native American groups. Their multiracial coalition was rooted in Seattle's past; because of a history of redlining and housing segregation, people of color lived in the same neighborhoods and attended the same schools of South Seattle. Familiarity turned into political action when activists from those communities called for the hiring of minority construction workers for the Seattle Kingdome in the 1960s. The same coalition provided multiracial community support for Filipino American cannery workers in the Wards Cove case. In the electoral arena, that cooperation helped elect an African American, Norman Rice, to be mayor of Seattle from 1989 to 1997, and Gary Locke as governor in 1996.

When Gary Locke sought the Democratic Party nod in the gubernatorial race, his chief rival was Rice. Locke emerged as the clear victor, but there was always the danger that, as an Asian American, he might be seen as a usurper, particularly when the affirmative action and model minority imagery is so dominant. In an environment of racial myths, Asian American political leaders find they have a special responsibility to reach out to other communities of color. For example, in 1999, two Asian Americans—Kip Tokuda and Sharon Tomiko Santos—were elected to represent South Seattle's 37th Legislative District, the same district that launched Governor Locke's political career. The district, which is about 30 percent black, 30 percent Asian, and 10 percent Hispanic, had traditionally produced African American legislators. "More Asians doesn't necessarily mean better, and there was some concern in the district whether two Asian Pacific Islander representatives could serve the diverse needs of the community," said Tokuda, a longtime activist for children and family services. "That's why we need to advocate for issues that transcend all boundaries." Tokuda met regularly with his African American constituents to discuss strategies to get blacks and other people of color elected in white enclaves.

"People say about the legislature, where are the blacks? We ask that, too," said Washington Representative Velma Veloria, a Filipino American first elected to the state house in 1992. "Just because Asian Americans are in the legislature doesn't mean we can stop coalition building. We have been pushing forward Hispanic and African American candidates. And if the elected positions aren't there, it's our responsibility to find positions in other departments to make sure all voices are at the table."

Even with their progress, Asian Americans in Washington State still feel the sting of racism. Gary Locke recalls overt racist remarks by other legislators when he was a state representative, during debates over redress for Japanese American state employees who were fired en masse during World War II. King County District Court Judge Eileen Kato was no stranger to racial slurs from angry defendants. "I get called a 'fucking Jap' in court," said Kato. "I give them fair warning. If they don't stop, I fine them and hold them in contempt. It's thirty days in jail for contempt. I learned this from a Chinese American judge. He warned one guy three times—ninety days in jail. It's just deserts."

Sometimes the bias is subtle, an attitude rather than a slur. But attitudes can bolster or undermine political efforts. "When I do something that people think is out of context for an Asian, my colleagues come up and say, 'Wow, I can't believe you swore, you got in that guy's face!' " said State Representative Tokuda. "It really surprises people when they see me get tough, because so many still see me as the inscrutable, enigmatic Japanese. It's an image we need to change. But we also need to change as a people. We are opinionated— we need to be able to express ourselves and our political will."

In 1996, the political paths carved out in the course of fighting for redress, Wards Cove, and other issues were severely eroded when politically active Asian Americans around the nation became targets of racially charged investigations intended to uncover campaign finance abuses in the Clinton presidential campaign. The search quickly took on a partisan edge, and, as alleged illegal acts by a few Asian American fund-raisers emerged, conservative opinion leaders began to characterize their actions as an "infection . . . imported from China into the American political system."

Asian Americans community leaders were caught by surprise. UCLA's Don Nakanishi noted, "The 1996 elections were supposed to be the defining moment for Asian Pacific Americans in electoral politics. They were to be a celebration of a successful nationwide voter registration campaign that enfranchised thousands of new voters. Campaign fund-raising records were expected to be set by both Democrats and Republicans as they traveled along an increasingly lucrative circuit to mine the gold mountains of Asian America. And, maybe this time around, the President, in assembling a Cabinet that 'looks like America,' would appoint at least one Asian Pacific American. That's how the story was supposed to go."

In early 1996, Asian American political momentum gathered steam with a broad-based national "Get Out the Vote" campaign directed at the diverse Asian American communities. Young Asian American voters in particular were targeted. Spearheaded by the Organization of Chinese Americans, nineteen national Asian American organizations rolled out a national mobilization with a multilingual public service announcement that featured a *Who's Who* of Asian American show business celebrities, including Tamlyn Tomita, Russell Wong, Rosalind Chao, B. D. Wong, Ming-Na Wen, Dustin Nguyen, Jason Scott Lee, Amy Hill, Steve Park, Jenny Shimizu, Dean Cain, Mako, and Margaret Cho.

Besides the voter drive, Asian American political activists launched a vigorous fund-raising campaign intended to help win political recognition for the Asian American community by President Bill Clinton's Administration. Little did they know how much attention they would receive. It was later determined that a small number of the Democratic fund-raisers made numerous violations of campaign finance law, including the acceptance of funds from Chinese government officials. But in the course of the investigation of the illegal acts committed by a few, the entire Asian American community was subjected to a level of political stigma and racial profiling it had not experienced since the 1940s and 1950s.

Asian Americans had donated under $4 million, less than 0.2 percent of the $2 billion raised in soft money for the 1996 presidential race, but they became the sole focus of the many investigations and media probes into improper campaign fund-raising. Thousands of news reports tracked the activities of Asian Americans in politics and government, from municipal politicians to career civil servants; numerous congressional committees of the House and the Senate, as well as the FBI, the Democratic National Committee, and countless news organizations, investigated the lives of a relatively small universe of Asian American donors and political activists.

As the investigative steamroller pursued Asian American donors, a major Dole fund-raiser, Simon Fireman, was fined $6 million for violations—a fine that far exceeded the total money raised by Asian Americans. Sporadic coverage was given to Cuban drug money and to alleged money laundering by Thomas Kramer, a German who was not an American citizen, but these abuses received only cursory glances from the various governmental and news investigators.

For the next eighteen months, Asian Americans were subjected to a barrage of racial innuendos and slurs that questioned their loyalty to the United States, even suggesting they were "spies" and "influence peddlers" for China. Members of Congress, TV commentators, and newspaper editorial boards expressed their surprise, suspicion, and indignation that Asian Americans might set foot in the White House. To cite only a few examples: *Newsweek* invoked the "mysterious Asian-Americans," while Chris Matthews, a CNBC news show host and *San Francisco Examiner* Washington columnist, referred to Asian Americans as "all those strange characters from Asia." Senator Sam Brownback of Kansas faked a "Chinese" accent and said, "No raise money, no get bonus," and told the Washington Press Club Foundation, "Two Huangs don't make a right"—a reference to Asian American John Huang, a fund-raiser for the Democratic National Committee who was under investigation for alleged campaign finance activities and as a possible operative for China. Senator Robert Bennett of Utah referred to "classic activities on the part of an Asian who comes out of that culture and who embarks on an activity related to intelligence gathering." Even perennial candidate H. Ross Perot made cracks about the "foreign-sounding" Asian American names: "Wouldn't you like to have someone out there named O'Reilly? So far we haven't found an American name."

The intensity and swiftness of the political and media juggernaut stunned Asian Americans. Some of the community's most politically active leaders and organizations came under investigation, implicated by their Asian ancestry. The roundup was pan-Asian in scope—suspects included Americans with ancestry in Taiwan, Korea, India, China, Indonesia, and Thailand—all presumed to be potential spies for the People's Republic of China. Civil rights groups such as the Organization of Chinese Americans, numerous private citizens, and prominent members of high-profile groups such as the Committee of 100 were forced to defend themselves against veiled accusations. Yvonne Lee, a commissioner for the U.S. Commission on Civil Rights, was stopped and interrogated while buying a gift at the White House souvenir shop. A reporter for a national news organization asked U.S. Senate candidate Matt Fong, a fourth-generation Californian whose mother, March Fong Eu, was a U.S. ambassador, "If the United States and China became engaged in a conflict, where would your loyalties lie?"

When Asian American leaders protested the tenor of the news, they, too, were accused: a *Boston Globe* editorial called complaints of racial stereotyping "a shabby maneuver to avoid scrutiny." An editorial by *The Washington Post* declared that "the idea of 'Asian bashing' has been floated in [John Huang's] defense. This was then and still is a variant on what is otherwise often known as 'playing the race card,' . . . shaming those who are pursuing Mr. Huang's alleged violations of the law suggesting that they are acting out of racial bias"; in a meeting with the *Post*'s editorial board, the concerns raised by the directors of national Asian American organizations were met with scorn. The attitude of several news establishments was that if you criticize their coverage of Asian American donors, then you, too, must be guilty of wrong-doing.

Inside the Washington Beltway, people of Asian heritage turned into personae non gratae. Career civil servants, elected officials, representatives of community advocacy groups, political appointees, party loyalists, even college interns seeking experience in the nation's capital found themselves suddenly isolated and unwelcome political liabilities. Community meetings, organized by Francey Lim Youngberg, then executive director of the Asian Pacific American Institute for Congressional Studies, were held in several cities to discuss the avalanche of accusations. Professor Frank Wu of Howard University School of Law, an outspoken critic of the racial inquest, captured the sense of Asian Americans when he entitled his research paper on the subject "Have You No Shame?"

Neurologist Suzanne Ahn from Dallas, Texas, who described her family's cumulative donations to both Democratic and Republican parties as "in the six figures," said that she and her family members were interrogated by the FBI, the Democratic National Committee auditors, and the news media, who obtained their names from the DNC when the Ahn family refused to give their Social Security numbers. Ahn's sister-in-law, a Korean American, was accused in the media of being a foreign agent. "My God, I've got an FBI file now and all because I had given money and my family had given money to politicians who have turned out to be fair-weather friends and ungrateful hypocrites," said Ahn. "Now, I'm not saying that what [the fund-raisers] did was right or wrong, but when the white men violate a campaign rule, there is an investigation, there is a fine . . . There isn't this maligning of the whole race."

Los Angeles–based attorney Anthony Ching was told by the DNC investigators that his $5,000 contribution to Clinton's reelection campaign would be "invalidated" if he didn't cooperate, so he asked for his money back. That same day, he received another call from the DNC soliciting funds for Clinton's reelection inauguration. My brother Hoyt, who was a captain in the U.S. Marine Corps and went to Washington to work as a Clinton appointee, became a target of investigators and was accused of being a "China connection" by far-right publications such as *The American Spectator* because he spoke up against the investigations—and he is Chinese American.

For Asian Americans who trace their histories in the United States back a generation or more, there was a real sense of déjà vu. The willingness of people to associate Americans of Asian descent with spying, corruption, "dual loyalties," and other sundry un-American acts was reminiscent of the war hysteria of the 1940s, when all Japanese American families on the West Coast had their household cameras and maps confiscated and Japanese American farmers were accused of planting their crops in patterns that would aid Japanese airplanes in case of an air attack. The Asian Americans who came to the United States after the 1965 Immigration Act got a firsthand lesson in how quickly today's model minority could become tomorrow's demon despised.

Gary Locke won his election as governor of Washington during this investigatory fervor, a bright spot in an otherwise ugly political climate in America. Lists of contributors to Locke's political campaign were also scrutinized for Asian-appearing names. His campaign ended up paying $2,500 in fines to the state campaign commission for violations involving about $5,300 in cash donations that exceeded the $50 cash donation limit set by Washington State; for failing to deposit the money within the time allowed; and for failing to report the names and addresses of twenty-three donors on time. No charges of foreign influence peddling were made. The cost of the investigations into his contributors far exceeded the amount questioned.

"This whole campaign financing scandal has caused a lot of Asian Americans to hunker down and shy away from politics, and that's very unfortunate," said Locke. "Mistakes were made. We made mistakes and immediately self-reported and then still got lumped in with the issues nationwide. It's distressing, but you just have to keep moving on. The last thing Asian Americans can afford to do is to shy away from politics."

For more than a year, the racial drumbeat continued to pound out of Washington, D.C. Adding to the sense of siege were a number of high-profile acts of violence against Asian Americans. In the San Francisco Bay Area, for example, there was a rash of anti-Asian graffiti and hate violence in both public housing projects and well-to-do suburbs. At a Denny's restaurant in Syracuse, New York, on April 11, 1997, a group of seven Asian American college students who were kept waiting to be seated were attacked and beaten by white male Denny's patrons while the restaurant management and security stood by and watched. Two of the students, one of whom was a young woman, were beaten unconscious and had to be hospitalized. It was the most severe and violent racial incident at Denny's in the country, though it received far less attention compared to other complaints against Denny's.

In the staid middle-class suburb of Rohnert Park, California, a thirty-three-year-old Taiwanese American, Kuan-chung Kao, was gunned down on the night of April 28, 1997, in his driveway by police, as his wife and four-year-old daughter watched in horror. Kao was drunk and swinging a stick, which, to justify the shooting, the police said he held "ninja-style." The police handcuffed the dying man and threatened to arrest Kao's wife, a registered nurse, when she rushed to her husband's side to provide medical treatment. A broad coalition led by Victor M. Hwang of the Asian Law Caucus called for a federal civil rights investigation of the Rohnert Park police after local officials ruled the homicide to be justifiable.

Asian Americans realized they needed bold and incisive political action to derail the assaults and to give Asian Americans a sense that they could fight back against the national whirlwind. The days of playing it safe by lying low and weathering the storm were over. Two San Francisco civil rights attorneys, Edward M. Chen and Dale Minami, initiated a legal complaint to the United States Commission on Civil Rights on behalf of fourteen national Asian American organizations and four individual political donors, charging members of Congress and public officials, the Democratic National Committee, the National Republican Senatorial Committee, and the news media of systematic bias, stereotyping, and scapegoating of Asian Pacific Americans.

After months of discussions with numerous Asian American leaders, Chen and Minami issued fifty pages of documented charges at a news conference at the National Press Club in Washington, D.C., on September 11, 1997. Organizing a legal complaint that unified the outrage and concerns of the widely divergent Asian American community wasn't easy. Professor Ling-chi Wang, chair of the Department of Ethnic Studies at the University of California at Berkeley and founder of Asian Americans for Campaign Finance Reform, also brought attention to the role of Asian business conglomerates and governments and their attempts to influence Asian American communities. His campaign finance reform group supported the petition, a sign of the broad desire for a national Asian American response to Congress and the media.

As a result of the petition, on December 5, 1997, U.S. Commission on Civil Rights chair Mary Frances Berry conducted a national briefing to hear testimony on the charges. More than twenty Asian Americans and others from across the country gave testimony, marking the first time in more than a year of accusations that Asian Americans had the chance to state our case. As a journalist who monitored the media coverage of the issue, I made a statement detailing my own research for the petition. I found that the careers of dedicated civil servants were damaged, that idealistic college students seeking a Washington experience were being stopped and questioned as they gazed at the White House with other tourists. In my testimony, I noted—most disturbing to me about the media fairness issue—the lack of voice given to the Asian American viewpoint by the very institutions entrusted to protect free speech.

The hard-fought effort to bring an Asian American viewpoint to the public had an impact: the racialized tone of the congressional hearings and the news reports began to lessen—at least temporarily. Asian Americans won a small victory and gained a valuable education. Few would have predicted the momentum and ferocity of the campaign finance storm, or the tremendous effort it would take to counter its force. It was a dramatic reminder that money and promises of political influence alone could not substitute for strength that comes from political education and organizing at the grass-roots level.

The campaign finance investigation was the most public broadside aimed at the Asian American communities, but it wasn't the only serious threat at the end of the 1990s. Congress moved to cut off medical care, education, food stamps, and other vital services to immigrants who, for whatever reason, had not become citizens—including both legal and undocumented immigrants, neonates and elderly, regardless of how long they had resided in the United States. With almost 70 percent of the Asian American population foreign-born, Asian Americans were hit harder than most communities. Contrary to the model minority image, many Asian Americans were reliant on those supports. As the cutoffs of benefits and services became imminent, there were widespread reports of suicides and panic among elderly Asian Americans—legal, tax-paying permanent residents, many of whom had paid into the Social Security system for years.

Throughout 1997, Asian Americans leaders gathered in search of new strategies. At conferences organized by the Asian Pacific American Institute for Congressional Studies and the Organization of Chinese Americans, community leaders from around the country argued emotionally for more aggressive, visible action from the Washington-based Asian American groups. But Asian Americans were hampered by the lack of a national, grass-roots-driven advocacy organization like the NAACP or the National Organization for Women. To create a rapid response to community crisis, more than twenty Asian American groups and numerous individuals founded a new organization, the National Council of Asian Pacific Americans.

Suddenly there was a profusion of new Asian American organizations. Within the same year, 1997, several national Asian and Pacific Islander American organizations were created. The National Federation of Filipino American Associations united three thousand Filipino American organizations together under one umbrella. The Filipino Civil Rights Advocates (FILCRA) has injected a Filipino American presence into civil rights issues, with a prominent campaign to obtain full GI veterans benefits for Filipino Americans who fought in World War II, and to press for an end to sweatshop labor in the Northern Mariana Islands, a U.S. Commonwealth. The Korean American Coalition (KAC) opened a Washington, D.C., office to create national visibility for Korean Americans. Numerous other organizations organized and reorganized during this same period.

Across the country, Asian Americans sought new ways to mobilize their communities. In several Southern states from Florida to Texas, resurgent Asian Americans, complete with Southern accents, are asserting their presence. A pan–Asian American coalition in Houston, Texas, has become an effective voice in City Hall—with South Asian and Southeast Asian leaders as well as East Asian Americans. In Dallas, ethnic-specific Asian business groups dissolved and merged to form a single Asian American Chamber of Commerce. "Politics is local; we have to show the nexus between the national strategy and the local. We have to make the connection," said Warren Furutani, director of the Office of Asian Pacific Islander American Affairs of the California Speaker of the Assembly.

The new groups didn't hesitate to use vigorous, even militant, tactics. In one bold action, Filipino American World War II veterans, elderly men in their seventies, marched on Washington, D.C., in the July 1997 summer heat and chained themselves to the fence surrounding the White House, many proudly dressed in military uniform. They were calling on Congress to end its stalling and give 70,000 Filipino American World War II veterans the pensions and benefits that every other allied veteran who fought under U.S. command receives. The new organizations extended the reach of the national and local network of organizations. Pan–Asian American linkages were also established when Vietnamese, Lao, and Hmong American veterans of U.S. wars joined the Filipino Americans' efforts for equal veterans benefits. Their goals are the same: to receive the same respect as all other veterans who fought under the U.S. flag.

More groups and voices have also created more opportunities for conflict. In San Francisco, where 33 percent of the city's population is of Chinese descent, and about 40 percent Asian American, an upstart group of Chinese Americans who are part of the post-1965 immigration managed to upend city politics. Using Cantonese- and Mandarin-speaking radio stations and the Chinese-language press, the San Francisco Neighbors' Association mobilized 30,000 Chinese voters to support a 1997 ballot measure that nearly all of the city's power brokers opposed, including some Chinese Americans. According to A. Magazine, their tactics include personal attacks over Chinese radio against all who oppose them, allegedly calling Chinese clients of the Asian Law Caucus "human garbage" and accusing a Chinese American city supervisor of being a Communist for supporting tenants' rights. The insurgents' proven ability to get out the vote has brought them considerable political clout in the city and is radically altering Chinese American politics in San Francisco.

Another fractious conflict raged in the Vietnamese American community of Little Saigon in Westminster, California. A Vietnamese businessman hung a poster of Ho Chi Minh and a flag of the Communist government of Vietnam in his video store. For several months in 1999, up to 10,000 demonstrators protested outside his store—aging veterans in military fatigues; former political prisoners, hauling re-creations of P.O.W. "tiger cages" in tow to underscore the torture and imprisonment they suffered at the hands of the North; grandmothers carrying placards. Comparing the store display to waving a Nazi flag in a Jewish neighborhood, the angry, anti-Communist protesters became regular fixtures on the news. But the issue was not so clear-cut for most Vietnamese Americans, whose families come from both the North and South of Vietnam. Over the course of the protest, police arrested fifty-two people and spent more than $200,000 in overtime. Anti-Communist sympathy demonstrations were held in other cities with sizable Vietnamese American populations—San Jose, New Orleans, and Houston. After the video store closed down for unrelated reasons, protesters directed their anger at Tony Lam, a Westminster city council member who in 1994 had become the country's first Vietnamese American elected official, because he didn't show enough support for the protest.

Conflicts and all, the dynamic emergence of bold voices and new organizations and leadership marks the continuing evolution of the Asian American community. "At what point do you stop seeing yourself as a minority group that's too small to have divergent views?" asked Lillian Galledo, co-chair of FILCRA. "It is a sign of our growth and maturity to accept that we're all here to stay and we have common goals that we may approach in different ways."

At the start of the new millennium, Asian American students are a visible and vocal population on nearly every college campus, from the ivy-covered schools in the Northeast to public colleges and universities across the United States. The Asian American college population can be attributed in part to the high value that Asian Americans place on education for their children, combined with the demographics of the post-1965 Asian American immigration boom.

Asian American students constituted 6 percent of all American college students in 1999, but their sizable presence at the nation's top universities and programs made their impact seem much greater. Since the 1960s, there has been an explosive increase in the numbers of Asian American students, particularly after a federal investigation in the 1980s into complaints of more stringent admissions standards and quota limits for Asian Americans at elite schools such as Harvard, Princeton, Columbia, Brown, and Berkeley.

At the height of campus movements in 1969, Asian American students at Berkeley made up about 5 percent of the student body; in 1998, 41 percent of Berkeley's undergraduates were of Asian descent, compared to 31 percent white students. UC Irvine in Southern California topped the list with 58 percent of its student body Asian American. At some campuses Asian American students struggle to get even one course on Asian American topics, yet twenty-four schools offer full Asian American studies programs, thirteen have Asian American studies within another department, and ten offer regular Asian American studies courses. While most of these programs must struggle to continue, they are a concrete indication that the need exists and progress has been made.

With such numbers comes a tremendous potential strength that is also new and untested. Not only has the population of Asian American college students ballooned but so has the breadth of their concerns. Students are organizing and holding conferences on every conceivable issue and seeking recognition for their identities as they define themselves. The numerous mixed-race students, the children from the high proportion of Asian American interracial marriages, have asserted their presence and are altering the conversation of what it means to be Asian American. Korean adoptee students helped plan the first national conference of Korean adoptees and their families in 1999, reaching out to the 100,000-some Koreans who were adopted and mostly raised by European American families.

An upsurge in campus activism by Asian American college students offers the most exciting preview of the community's political future, as colleges and universities become the training ground for the new generation that is insisting on a place in society as Asian Americans. A new generation is storming the bastions over the same issues that pulled Asian Americans together as a American people three decades earlier.

In April 1999, Asian American students at the University of California at Berkeley joined with other students in a multiracial coalition to fight cutbacks in the very ethnic studies program created by student strikes at Berkeley and San Francisco State in 1968. Berkeley students began a hunger strike to protest the cutting of such courses as Chinese American history, Latino politics, and Native American history. During their peaceful hunger strike in the heart of the campus, more than one hundred students were arrested, including a number of Asian Americans. By the strike's ninth day, the university administration agreed to meet student demands to restore the ethnic studies program to its world-class reputation.

On May 3, 1999, at the University of Texas at Austin—just hours before the mass arrests at Berkeley—ten Asian American students were charged with criminal trespass and were arrested for refusing to leave a campus administration building. The students, members of the Asian American Relations Group, were seeking to speak with Judith Langlois, the interim dean of the College of Liberal Arts. Langlois had overturned the hiring of a director for the university's new Asian American studies program, which students had been seeking for five years. The following day, more than five hundred students rallied on campus to protest the arrests and to demand that the administration drop the charges against the students.

The student actions at Berkeley and UT Austin were the latest in a wave of campus activism for Asian American studies programs. A few years earlier, Columbia students staged a hunger strike to obtain Asian

American and Latino studies. Asian American students took over build-ings at Cornell and Stanford, held rallies at Harvard, and staged a hunger strike at Northwestern. For a two-month period in 1997, Asian American students at the University of Maryland at College Park held regular rallies and marches. At Mills College in Oakland, California, Asian American stu-dents at the all-women's school have been waging a long campaign to get Asian Americans and other professors of color added to the faculty and to obtain tenure for the few who have taught there.

At Princeton University, my alma mater, seventeen Asian American and Latino students took over the offices of the president at Nassau Hall in 1995, much as I had "occupied" the library during my first year to win recognition for students of color. In response to the Nassau Hall sit-in, the university promised that tenure-track faculty would be hired and regular courses on the Asian American and Latino American experiences offered. By 1999, the university still offered just one Asian American course per semester—not much of an increase over the number of courses that we mustered twenty-five years earlier. But in 1970 there were barely 40 Asian Americans on the campus, including faculty. In 1999, there were more than 400 Asian American students, about 14 percent of the student body.

One of Princeton's new crop of Asian American student leaders was William Huen, whose father, Floyd, was one of the Asian American strike leaders at Berkeley in the 1960s. This new generation has come around full circle, but with more political tools and sophistication than their parents had.

Many will take their energies back into the community. They might be among the young Asian Americans working on environmental justice with Laotian teenage girls in the Asian Pacific Environmental Network who live next door to chemical refineries in Richmond, California; leading street actions against posh boutiques and athletic shoe stores, in conjunction with groups such as Asian Immigrant Women Advocates, to expose designers, manufacturers, and retailers who rely on sweatshop labor; get-ting trained as organizers by unions or groups like the Center for Third World Organizing; becoming safer-sex educators for HIV/AIDS programs; creating innovative programs for such women's groups as the Asian Women's Shelter in San Francisco to teach survivors of domestic violence about homophobia and hate violence; and becoming involved in any number of other grass-roots community efforts. These young Asian Amer-ican leaders are stepping forward with a confidence and sense of their own self-worth and empowerment that their elders can only marvel at. They are the Asian American leadership for the new millennium.

Some will enter the arena of electoral politics, bringing the leadership and vision of Asian Americans to the mainstream and all Americans. When UCLA Asian American Studies Center director Don Nakanishi first began tracking Asian Pacific Americans in the electoral process in 1978, he could count only a couple of hundred names, mostly in Hawaii and California. "The list was so small I could Xerox and staple it at the top. Now there are more than two thousand elected and major appointed officials in over thirty states. Between 1996 and 1998 there was a 10 percent increase in Asian Pacific American candidates running for political office." The setbacks of 1996 and 1997 turned into a shared resolve to push forward on the political front.

By 1998, more than 300 Asian American and Pacific Islanders were elected to office in the United States and its territories, according to Nakanishi's *1998–99 National Asian Pacific American Political Almanac*. Not only were more Asian American and Pacific Islander candidates running for public office and winning, but candidates were also emerging from less represented communities, broadening the political leadership base of Asian Americans beyond Chinese Americans and Japanese Americans. In 1994, Ram Yoshino Uppuluri ran in the Democratic primary for a seat in Congress representing Tennessee. Uppurluri, whose father is Indian American and mother Japanese American, brought visibility to the growing numbers who have mixed pan-Asian ethnic heritage. In St. Paul, Minnesota, Neal Thao, a 1.5-generation Hmong American attorney, was elected to the Board of Education in 1998, becoming the first Hmong elected to political office in the United States.

In contrast to the days not long past when Asian Americans had to worry that they would be stigmatized for associating with other Asians, Governor Gary Locke stumped in neighboring Oregon for another Asian American candidate. In 1998 David Wu won election to the U.S. House of Representatives and became the first Taiwan-born American to be elected to Congress. Like other Asian American candidates, Wu ran on a campaign that appealed to Oregon voters of all backgrounds, not just the 2 percent who were Asian American. An Op-Ed piece entitled "Race Politics a Nonstarter for Asian Americans" ran in the *San Francisco Chronicle* in May 1999. It admonished Asian Americans not to get involved in race matters—using David Wu as a model. But Wu was not one to shy away from issues that might bring attention to his ethnicity. Shortly after taking office, he spoke on the floor of the House, boldly cautioning his colleagues against racial profiling when spy allegations were made against Chinese research scientists. Later, Wu introduced a bill asking for a "sense of the Congress that generalizing or stereotyping the actions of an individual to an entire group of people is not acceptable to Congress, and that Americans of Asian ancestry are entitled to all rights and privileges afforded to all Americans."

The renewed spy allegations that erupted in 1999 over Los Alamos scientist Wen Ho Lee, a Chinese American, may catalyze another surge in Asian American political activity. Many are angered over the mounting evidence that Lee was scapegoated and accused of the high crime of espionage because of his ethnicity, calling it a national disgrace that he and the estimated 200,000 to 300,000 Asian American researchers and engineers, including Nobel Prize winners and many leading American scientists, have had their loyalties, reputations, and livelihoods severely damaged. When Democratic presidential candidate Al Gore snubbed a national conference of Asian American political leadership in Washington, D.C., in May 1999 sponsored by the Asian Pacific American Institute for Congressional Studies, a number of Asian American political activists began discussing how to leverage their power independent of either political party. "The parties want to dance with us from a distance, so we're going to have to make our own music," said Vida Benavides, former director of public liaison for the Democratic National Committee.

Greater involvement and visibility of Asian Americans at political leadership levels cannot come soon enough. After an avowed neo-Nazi white supremacist shot and wounded several people at a Jewish community day care center in Los Angeles and then killed Joseph Ileto, a thirty-nine-year-old Filipino American postal worker, on August 10, 1999, shoddy treatment by politicians and news reporters compounded the Ileto family's pain. For several days after the rampage, news organizations around the country failed to report Ileto's name, ethnicity, and race or to consider the murder a hate crime, even though it was the fifth high-profile hate killing of an Asian American in 1999, and even when Asian American journalists pointed out the omissions in their newsrooms. At his own news event about gun control, with Joseph Ileto's family seated in the front row,

California Governor Gray Davis spoke only about the anti-Semitic nature of the attack, not once mentioning the slaying of the Asian American. President Clinton, in his statements on the hate crime, also failed to mention Ileto or the anti-Asian killing until the Ileto family told acting Assistant Attorney General for Civil Rights Bill Lann Lee how upset they were with the President. "Both the governor and the President said that their staffs didn't inform them," said Ismael Ileto, brother of the victim. It is unacceptable that those who represent all the people should be so ill informed about their Asian American constituents, and the solution is clear: Asian Americans need to be at every leadership table.

The 10 million Asian Americans, who made up nearly 4 percent of America at the end of the twentieth century, will double in size by 2010. We are the fastest-growing racial group in the country, and we have a young population, with median age of 31.2 years, 4.0 years younger than the median for the U.S. population as a whole, according to the United States Census Bureau. While some 11 percent of Asian Americans live in poverty, we also have the highest proportion of college graduates of any racial or ethnic group, at 42 percent. This compares with 25 percent for whites, 13 percent for African Americans, and 10 percent for Hispanics. We are a people who are looking forward.

Our demographics and achievements, trials and tribulations, tell a compelling story of a people who come together from markedly different backgrounds, without a common language or culture. Many have braved unspeakable horrors to join in this multiracial democracy. Out of numerous disparate, even hostile, Asian ethnicities, we have forged a sense of shared experience and common future as Americans—Asian and Pacific Islander Americans.

From the Vincent Chin case to the Los Angeles riots, from the salmon canneries of Alaska to the ballot boxes of Hawaii, from the stage and screen to the college campus, we are a people in constant motion, a great work in progress, each stage more faceted and complex than before. As we overcome adversity and take on new challenges, we have evolved. Our special dynamism is our gift to America. As we transform ourselves, so we are transforming America.

# ·12·

# Living Our Dreams

I was very fortunate to grow up amid tales of ghosts and demons, stories of the rich sights and smells of an ancient and thriving civilization that was unlike anything in my daily American life, yet so natural I could imagine this place called China without stepping outside my small New Jersey town. Mom sang lilting Chinese lullabies whose melodies and lyrics I could repeat but not comprehend.

When my father wasn't railing against Mao or Chiang or the U.S. government's Cold War policy toward China, he recited the poetry of Li Shangyin, whom he considered superior to Li Po and Tu Fu, the most celebrated poets of China, and finer than William Butler Yeats and Percy Bysshe Shelley, whose poems he also loved. He'd match theirs against Li's, stanza by stanza, in the tradition of Chinese poetry slams. Taking his

*The Zia family at my sister Humane's wedding in 1989. Standing, left to right: Haddon, Gee Han, Dad, the author, Humane, Kevin, Hoyt, Henry, Hugo (and baby Frank); seated: Auntie Betty, Mom, Leigh-Ann (and baby Emily), Camille, Dorothy*

favorite line from Shelley, "When winter comes, can spring be far behind?" he would discuss its merits compared to Li's couplet in Chinese: "Lotus leaves grow, spring sorrow blooms;/Lotus leaves wither, autumn sorrow advances." At those moments I would have gladly traded in my American accent and "good English" to understand the Chinese classics.

If I fell sick with fever, my mother came to my bedside with a large spoon and a dish filled with lukewarm cooking oil. I would yell, "No, not the Chinese treatment!" As I lay facedown with my back exposed, Mom dipped the broad edge of the spoon in the oil, then slowly and repeatedly scraped it hard along each of my ribs, until my back was a canvas of red zebra stripes. The process was as painful as it looked. I'd cry out, tears in my eyes, but within hours, my fever would break. Every time.

These special parts of my life were private, even secret—the bicultural, bisected Asian side of my upbringing that I didn't share with my outer, American world. Some things, like the "Chinese treatment," were likely to be misunderstood, even labeled child abuse. But my own inhibitions were unconscious and deep. My Chinese side was so personal that I actively blocked any risk of potential ridicule, embarrassment, and shame.

I became aware of this tension when I was twelve. For a brief time I had a pen pal, another twelve-year-old, from Edinburgh, Scotland. The Brainiac computer at the New York World's Fair matched us according to our age and interests. We exchanged the usual musings of preadolescent girls—school, vacations, the books we read, and pop music, probably the Beatles. I looked forward to her letters from Scotland with anticipation. After a few exchanges, my pen pal sent me pictures of herself and her family. Suddenly I had a problem. Of course she would expect pictures of me—and somehow I had neglected to mention that I was Chinese American.

I didn't try to hide my Chineseness from my pen pal—it wasn't something that seemed to matter, until the pictures. I took my cues from the world around me, the TV shows and movies I saw, the books and magazines I read. I had become a member of the Invisible Society of Asian Americans. With my pen pal, I made my Chinese self invisible. Her pictures forced me to decide how to share the news, a prospect that filled me with self-conscious dread. With my twelve-year-old's logic, I was certain that my pen pal would reject me, since, after all, she had wanted an American pen pal, not a Chinese one.

To spare myself from this imagined disappointment, I never wrote back. My decision made me feel cowardly and ashamed. I didn't want to make my Chinese self vulnerable, or to risk feeling less American than I already did. As a kid, I didn't know the meaning of internalized racism and self-hate, but I knew I didn't feel self-love.

I count myself lucky. I eventually discovered a community intent on asserting its Asian American identity and reclaiming its history and contributions to building America—a heritage that every American should know. This knowledge helped me to meld my Asian and American identities and to see that they were never really separate. I could now envision my future in a society that could include the ghosts and demons, songs and poems of my childhood.

The issue of what to keep private and internal to the community and what is appropriate to expose to the outside has not gone away. The potential for misunderstanding and more harmful consequences is still very real.

Not long ago, the question arose in an on-line members' E-mail discussion of the Asian American Journalists Association. Someone from Michigan posted an E-mail objecting to a statement made on a late-night TV talk show by an Asian American actor, Hawaii-born Kelly Hu, costar of the 1999 hit TV show *Martial Law*. The talk show host pulled out a can of Spam, a staple in Hawaii. He ragged on the questionable animal parts that make up the canned meat product, in a predictable gag about foods that Asians eat. He dared Hu to eat some. The actor scoffed back. "Come on!" she said. "I come from a people who eat monkey brain."

The E-mail posting, critical of Hu's reference to eating monkey brains, triggered diverse reactions. Some felt the criticism was an overreaction, that Asian Americans need to lighten up and laugh at our own stereotypes. A journalist from California wrote back, noting that many Americans are too willing to use such casual comments as weapons of contempt, evidence that we don't belong in America. A writer from Honolulu referred to a time in Hawaii's recent past when Asians Americans of different ethnicities could laugh at each other, with each other; those times had given way to greater sensitivity and sophistication, she said, but in the process some of the naturalness and spontaneity had been lost.

My reaction was mixed. I added my own grist to the on-line mill, writing, in part:

*These days I am wishing that we Asian Americans could be less self-conscious and more open and outspoken about ourselves, who we are really, as perhaps Kelly Hu was doing. To fight the stereotyping, I wish that AAJA and our community could speed up this glacially slow process of getting more and more Asian American voices of all kinds out there. If stereotyping is seeing people in one dimension, then our best solution is to blast out the full, rich multidimensional picture.*

*When I was a child, my mother talked about eating monkey brains. Not her, a Shanghainese, but the Cantonese. She said that a long time ago, the Cantonese served the monkeys at special tables with little holes through which the tops of their heads protruded. Now, I have no idea if this is true, or if it was a Shanghainese-Cantonese thing, but it was a part of my family folklore.*

*Two years ago, my partner Lia and I were on a China South-eastern Airlines jet to Chongqing. They had an in-flight magazine, in Chinese and English. Lia turned to the food section and found a recipe for "Ambrosial Puppy Stew." We looked at each other in disbelief and read on. Yes, it explained which puppies were tastiest (yellow ones) and, yes, how to cook them. It upset me, not just because of poor Spot, but also because I had spent much of my adult life screaming "We don't eat dogs!" at rude bozos. Yet, illustrated and in color, in English and Chinese, indeed some of us do.*

*Everyone has similar stories about strange, maligned food from their own cultures—haggis, steak tartare, chitlins, maggot cheese, head cheese, and so on. Would I share my examples of Chinese extreme cuisine on TV? Probably not, unless there was an opportunity to give the full context—an unlikely scenario on TV. And that's too bad, because if we can't understand and try to appreciate each other's sustenance, then how will we ever really know one another?*

I have to confess that I was conflicted about including this "insider" discussion here. As I mulled this over, the memory of my pen pal came flooding back. Will Asian Americans be forever censoring ourselves, fearful of how we might be reinterpreted and misconstrued by "outsiders"— other Americans? When will we feel safe enough to project our whole selves? If not in the benign context of my own book, when? The path ahead, blazed by so many bold and daring Asian Americans whose words and deeds have carved a place in America for us, is clear. To be seen, we must make ourselves visible, showing blemish as well as beauty.

Greater visibility also brings the responsibility of holding others accountable for their characterizations, so that the blemishes of individuals aren't applied to an entire people, whether the transgression involves unusual food or improper campaign fund-raising or working in high-security jobs. Unfortunately, there is no dearth of examples—innocent, ignorant, or malicious—that illustrate the disturbing willingness of otherwise intelligent people to suspend common sense when it comes to Asians.

One article that I've kept to remind me of this point ran on January 20, 1984, in the *Detroit Free Press*. The story, "Peking Headlights Get the Green Light," was reported by a member of the Knight Ridder foreign staff about Beijing's decision to make cars use headlights at night, instead of parking lights. The article contained the following lines: "Most Chinese are still not comfortable with the car. There is no word for automobile in Chinese."

Now, China has had cars on its soil from the time that the Model T rolled off the assembly line. Even I, a culturally deprived ABC, knew the Chinese word for car. I sent the following note, which was printed in the letters to the editor column:

> *Shame on the* Detroit Free Press *for running this ridiculous article which perpetuates the notion that Asian people are peculiarly different from the rest of the "civilized" world. Yes, the Chinese have a word for car. It is* qi-che *in Mandarin. The Chinese also build cars, as the writer must have known. There are words for train (*huo-che*), plane (*fei-ji*), buses, and even rockets (remember, the Chinese invented them). It is unfortunate that someone who is ignorant of China and the Chinese language is writing about one-fourth of the world's population.*

The paper's executive editor then, David Lawrence, sent me a personal note:

> *Dear Helen Zia: Your point is excellent and I'll share it with others here. That paragraph, pure and simple, should not have run. I'm*

*glad you took the time to point it out. When you spot such and point them out to us, you do us a favor. We do learn from our mistakes.*

It is a source of great frustration to Asian Americans, particularly those of us who are journalists, that modern-day American journalism is still replete with news of the "strange and exotic Asians" ilk. At first glance, such coverage may seem harmless, like the November 1998 article in *The New York Times*, "Lost, and Gained, in the Translation," about American movie titles that get distorted in foreign-language translations, particularly in Asian countries. "George of the Jungle" in Chinese supposedly became "Big Dumb Monkey Man Keeps Whacking Trees With Genitals"; "Batman and Robin": "Come to My Cave and Wear This Rubber Codpiece, Cute Boy." And "Barb Wire," starring Pamela Anderson Lee: "Delicate Orbs of Womanhood Bigger Than Your Head Can Hurt You." I laughed when I read the story and wondered out loud how it could possibly be true. Sure enough, *The New York Times* had to retract the story—the translations were a hoax and the writer took the bait. Of course, mistakes happen. Then again, the same writer authored one of the more stereotype-laden editorials about Asian Americans and Chinese Americans during the campaign finance scandal. Could there be a connection, an inclination or predisposition to look at things Asian in a certain light? Many Asian Americans think so. I do.

Where is the line between the "strange and exotic" and the "Asian Invasion/Yellow Peril"? The most harmful and malicious reports cover the whole spectrum of racialized commentary. As congressional Republicans prepared to attack Clinton and his China policy by highlighting alleged security breaches by Chinese American scientist Wen Ho Lee, *The Washington Post* ran a story on March 21, 1999, headlined, "Chinese Spy Methods Limit Bid to Find Truth, Officials Say." The story did not directly quote a single official, but instead noted:

*China's spying, they say, more typically involves cajoling morsels of information out of visiting foreign experts and tasking thousands of Chinese abroad to bring secrets home one at a time like ants carrying grains of sand. The Chinese have been assembling such grains of sand since at least the fourth century BC, when the military philosopher Sun Tzu noted the value of espionage in his classic work,* The Art of War.

Students of history will recognize that the allusion to "ants" harks back to Cold War justifications to drop nuclear bombs on China, whose people were likened to insects, ready to swarm into other countries. History buffs will also recall that bitter rivals Athens and Sparta were locked together in the Peloponnesian Wars around the time that Sun Tzu was writing his classic; surely Western civilization had discovered the art of espionage by then. Indeed, the Bible makes several references to spies—centuries before Sun Tzu. But according to the "experts," the cultural predilection of Chinese toward espionage turns all Chinese Americans and visiting Chinese nationals, from students and tourists to business representatives and diplomats, into potential spies for China.

If sophisticated journalists and political leaders find it so easy to abandon good judgment and accept uncritically such strange and exotic absurdities, or to take that downhill spiral into the Asian Invasion and Yellow Peril journalism, what are Biff and Buffy likely to think? That their Asian American neighbors are rummaging through their garbage, sending every grain of sand "home"? Or that their missing pet has made it onto my dinner table? Some will reach those unfortunate conclusions, just as clever pundits and talk show hosts will exaggerate stereotypes without regard to how they are contributing to the racial harassment, taunting, and even acts of violence committed against Asian American schoolchildren and anyone who is "different." All Americans have an interest in a fair society that upholds its promise of equality and justice. At the same time, it is the special task of the Asian American population to put America on notice that we will not accept racial prejudice and discrimination against any people, including our own.

Such flash points come for Asian Americans at the dawn of a new century, when American prosperity is high and competition with Asia is low. It is a time when emergent Asian Americans are reaching out boldly to other communities to share our dreams and to learn about theirs. Fundamentally the dreams are the same, for freedom and family and the next generations. It is the vision that has sustained Americans from every shore. The next time tensions with Asia rise and the rhetoric grows ugly, perhaps Asian Americans will be working with people from other communities on constructive solutions, as Americans all.

Ruth Oya Woo, the mentor to so many of Washington State's Asian

American political candidates, asked me, "What will it take for Asian Americans to get there, to be a part of this American dream?"

I had no simple answer. But we've pushed open the door and moved inside. We're out of the shadows and into the light. With 10 million of us at the dawn of the millennium, there's no "back" to send us to. History, demographics, and our determination are on our side. What we have learned can't be taken away. We will be full partners in the future of America.

I see the evolution in my own family. My parents started out in America with little more than their dreams and convictions. They raised six children, scratching out a living. Of their six children, there's a corporate manager, an entrepreneur, a writer, and three attorneys, one of whom—my sister—is also an engineer. All the lawyers are public servants who entered the law as idealists hoping to make a difference. I—the writer—am the underachiever of the group, having ended my formal education at a bachelor's degree.

Auntie Betty's son Pete, my cousin the commercial airline pilot who is half Danish and half Chinese, likes to exclaim, "We're just like the United Nations." I've heard many other Asian American families say the same thing. My extended family, besides being Chinese American, includes Japanese-Okinawan American, Japanese American, Malaysian Chinese, Italian American, Scottish-German-Italian American, Filipino American, African American, Puerto Rican, and Jewish American. In the younger generation, there are scholars, athletes, and everything in between. One of my second cousins is seven feet two inches tall; he plays professional basketball in overseas leagues. And, most astonishing to me, some of my nieces and nephews refuse to eat Chinese food. I have to tell cousin Pete that, actually, we're just like the United States.

My father is buried in Burlington County, New Jersey, not far from where I grew up, in a cemetery overlooking the highway he drove on nearly every day to deliver our homemade pink and blue baby novelties. Before his stroke, we asked him to tell some of his stories on videotape. They are familiar stories. His voice broke, as it always had when he recounted the tragic deaths of his mother, brother, and sister-in-law at the hands of the Japanese army. He spoke once again of the Chinese voyager who might have discovered America, exclaiming, "If only Cheng Ho had turned left instead of turning right!"

We asked Dad what he thought about his six American-born Chinese kids. Without hesitation he declared, "You're all too American! If I could do it all over again, I would raise you to be more Chinese." It was just like him, ever the critical Asian American immigrant parent whose kids could never achieve enough. My siblings and I, now adults with another generation of ABC children, just sit and roll our eyes, fidgeting at Dad's taped words, the same way we did when we were children at the dinner table.

Inside, I smile. I believe my mother when she says that Dad was proud of what his children had accomplished—though he would never tell us so himself. That he had high hopes for his many grandchildren. His dreams and those of the Asian Americans who came before him stay within each of us. They are the memories of where we've come from, the lessons of what we've been through, and the visions of roads we have yet to walk in this land called America. They are our dreams, Asian American dreams.

# Bibliography

Ablemann, Nancy, and John Lie. *Blue Dreams: Korean Americans and the Los Angeles Riots.* Cambridge, Mass.: Harvard University Press, 1997.

Ancheta, Angelo N. *Race, Rights, and the Asian American Experience.* New Brunswick, N.J.: Rutgers University Press, 1998.

Bandon, Alexandra. *Asian Indian Americans.* Parsippany, N.J.: New Discovery Books, 1995.

Bulosan, Carlos, et al. *On Becoming Filipino: Selected Writings of Carlos Bulosan.* Philadelphia: Temple University Press, 1995.

Chan, Jeffrey P., ed., et al. *Aiiieeeee: An Anthology of Asian American Writers.* New York: Penguin, 1997.

Chan, Sucheng. *Asian Americans: An Interpretive History.* Boston: Twayne Publishers, 1991.

Chan, Sucheng, ed. *Hmong Means Free: Life in Laos and America.* Philadelphia: Temple University Press, 1994.

Chang, Edward, ed., et al. *Los Angeles Struggles toward Multiethnic Community: Asian American, African American and Latino Perspectives.* Seattle: University of Washington Press, 1994.

Cheng, Lucie, and Edna Bonacich, eds. *Labor Immigration Under Capitalism: Asian Workers in the United States Before World War II.* Berkeley, Calif.: University of California Press, 1984.

Chow, Claire S. *Leaving Deep Water: The Lives of Asian American Women at the Crossroads of Two Cultures.* New York: Penguin, 1998.

Choy, Philip P., ed. *The Coming Man: 19th Century American Perceptions of the Chinese.* Seattle: University of Washington Press, 1995.

Churchill, Thomas. *Triumph over Marcos.* Seattle: Open Hand Publishing, 1995.

Daniels, Roger. *Asian America: Chinese and Japanese in the United States since 1850.* Seattle: University of Washington Press, 1988.

DasGupta, Shamita Das, ed. *A Patchwork Shawl: Chronicles of South Asian Women in America.* New Brunswick, N.J.: Rutgers University Press, 1998.

Endo, Russell; Stanley Sue; and Nathaniel N. Wagner, eds. *Asian-Americans: Social and Psychological Perspectives.* Palo Alto, Calif.: Science and Behavior Books, 1980.

Eng, David L., and Alice Y. Hom, eds. *Q & A: Queer in Asian America.* Philadelphia: Temple University Press, 1998.

Eng, Phoebe. *Warrior Lessons: An Asian American Woman's Journey Into Power.* New York: Pocket Books, 1999.

Espiritu, Yen Le. *Asian American Panethnicity: Bridging Institutions and Identities.* Philadelphia: Temple University Press, 1992.

———. *Filipino American Lives.* Philadelphia: Temple University Press, 1995.

Fadiman, Anne. *The Spirit Catches You and You Fall Down: A Hmong Child, Her American Doctors, and the Collision of Two Cultures.* New York: Farrar, Straus and Giroux, 1997.

Fawcett, James T., and Benjamin V. Carino, eds. *Pacific Bridges: The New Immigration from Asia and the Pacific Islands.* New York: Center for Migration Studies, 1987.

Fong, Timothy P. *The Contemporary Asian American Experience: Beyond the Model Minority.* Upper Saddle River, N.J.: Prentice Hall, 1998.

Fong-Torres, Ben. *The Rice Room: Growing Up Chinese-American—From Number Two Son to Rock'n'Roll.* New York: Plume, 1995.

Friday, Chris. *Organizing Asian American Labor: The Pacific Coast Canned-Salmon Industry, 1870–1942.* Philadelphia: Temple University Press, 1994.

Gall, Susan, and Irene Natividad, eds. *The Asian American Almanac.* Detroit: Gale Research, 1995.

Gong, Stephen. *Moving the Image: Independent Asian Pacific American Media Arts.* Los Angeles: UCLA Asian American Studies Center and Visual Communications, 1991.

Hagedorn, Jessica Tarahata, ed. *Charlie Chan Is Dead: An Anthology of Contemporary Asian American Fiction.* New York: Penguin, 1993.

Hamamoto, Darrell Y. *Monitored Peril: Asian Americans and the Politics of TV Representation.* Minneapolis: University of Minnesota Press, 1994.

Hatamiya, Leslie T. *Righting a Wrong: Japanese Americans and the Passage of the Civil Liberties Act of 1988.* Stanford, Calif.: Stanford University Press, 1994.

Hing, Bill Ong. *Making and Remaking Asian America through Immigration Policy, 1850–1990.* Stanford, Calif.: Stanford University Press, 1993.

Hong, Maria, ed. *Growing Up Asian American: Stories of Childhood, Adolescence & Coming of Age by 32 Asian American Writers.* New York: Avon Books, 1995.

Hongo, Garrett, ed. *The Open Boat: Poems from Asian America.* New York: Anchor Books/Doubleday, 1993.

Horton, John. *The Politics of Diversity: Immigration, Resistance and Change in Monterey Park, California.* Philadelphia: Temple University Press, 1995.

Houston, Velina Hasu, and Roberta Uno, eds. *But Still, Like Air, I'll Rise: New Asian American Plays.* Philadelphia: Temple University Press, 1997.

Hsia, Jayjia. *Asian Americans in Higher Education and at Work.* Hillsdale, N.J.: Lawrence Erlbaum Assoc., Publishers, 1988.

Hune, Shirley. *Pacific Migration to the United States: Trends and Themes in Historical and Sociological Literature.* Washington, D.C.: Research Institute on Immigration and Ethnic Studies, 1977.

Irons, Peter H. *Justice at War.* Berkeley, Calif.: University of California Press, 1993.

Jennings, James, ed. *Blacks, Latinos, and Asians in Urban America: Status and Prospects for Politics and Activism.* London: Praeger Press, 1994.

Jo, Yung-Hwan, ed. *Political Participation of Asian Americans: Problems and Strategies.* Chicago: Pacific/Asian American Mental Health Research Center, 1980.

Kang, K. Connie. *Home Was the Land of Morning Calm: A Saga of a Korean-American Family.* Reading, Mass.: Addison-Wesley Publishing Co., 1995.

Kim, Elaine, et al. *Making More Waves: New Writing by Asian American Women.* Boston: Beacon Press, 1997.

Kim, Elaine H., et al. *East to America: Korean American Life Stories.* New York: New Press, 1997.

Kitano, Harry H.L., and Roger Daniels. *Asian Americans: Emerging Minorities.* 2nd ed. Englewood Cliffs, N.J.: Prentice Hall, 1995.

Knoll, Tricia. *Becoming Americans: Asian Sojourners, Immigrants, and Refugees in the Western United States.* Portland, Oreg.: Coast to Coast Books, 1982.

Kwong, Peter. *The New Chinatown.* Rev. ed. New York: Hill and Wang, 1996.

Lawrence, Charles R., and Mari J. Matsuda. *We Won't Go Back: Making the Case for Affirmative Action.* Boston: Houghton Mifflin, 1997.

Lee, Joann Faung Jean. *Asian American Experiences in the United States: Oral Histories of First to Fourth Generation Americans from China, the Philippines, Japan, India, the Pacific Islands, Vietnam, and Cambodia.* New York: New Press, 1992.

Lee, Josephine D., et al. *Performing Asian America: Race and Ethnicity on the Contemporary Stage.* Philadelphia: Temple University Press, 1997.

Lee, Robert G. *Orientals: Asian Americans in Popular Culture.* Philadelphia: Temple University Press, 1999.

Leonard, Karen Isaksen. *The South Asian Americans.* Westport, Conn.: Greenwood Press, 1997.

Leong, Russell, ed. *Moving the Image: Independent Asian Pacific American Media Arts.* Los Angeles: UCLA Asian American Studies Center and

Visual Communications, Southern California Asian American Studies, 1991.

Lieberson, Stanley, and Mary C. Waters. *From Many Strands: Ethnic and Racial Groups in Contemporary America*. New York: Russell Sage Foundation, 1988.

Lim, Shirley Geok-Lin, et al. *Reading the Literatures of Asian America*. Philadelphia: Temple University Press, 1992.

Liu, Eric. *The Accidental Asian: Notes of a Native Speaker*. New York: Random House, 1998.

Lott, Juanita Tamayo. *Asian Americans: From Racial Category to Multiple Identities*. Walnut Creek, Calif.: AltaMira Press, 1997.

Lowe, Lisa. *Immigrant Acts: On Asian American Cultural Politics*. Durham, N.C.: Duke University Press, 1996.

Mangiafico, Luciano. *Contemporary American Immigrants: Patterns of Filipino, Korean, and Chinese Settlement in the United States*. New York: Praeger Press, 1988.

Marchetti, Gina. *Romance and the "Yellow Peril": Race, Sex, and Discursive Strategies in Hollywood Fiction*. Berkeley, Calif.: University of California Press, 1993.

Matsuda, Mari J. *Where Is Your Body? And Other Essays on Race, Gender and the Law*. Boston: Beacon Press, 1996.

Min, Pyong Gap, ed. *Asian Americans: Contemporary Trends and Issues*. Thousand Oaks, Calif.: Sage Press, 1995.

Nakanishi, Don T., and Bernie C. LaForteza. *The National Asian Pacific American Roster, 1984*. Los Angeles: Asian American Studies Center, University of California, 1984.

*National Asian Pacific American Political Almanac and Resource Guide*. 8th ed. Los Angeles: UCLA Asian American Studies Center, 1998–99.

Ng, Franklin, ed. *The History and Immigration of Asian Americans*. New York: Garland Publications, 1998.

Njeri, Itabari. *The Last Plantation: Color, Conflict, and Identity: Reflections of a New World Black.* Boston: Houghton Mifflin, 1997.

Okihiro, Gary Y. *Margins and Mainstreams: Asians in American History and Culture.* Seattle: University of Washington Press, 1994.

Ong, Paul; Edna Bonacich; and Lucie Cheng, eds. *The New Asian Immigration in Los Angeles and Global Restructuring.* Philadelphia: Temple University Press, 1994.

San Juan, Epifanio, et al. *From Exile to Diaspora: Versions of the Filipino Experience in the United States.* Boulder, Colo.: Westview Press, 1998.

San Juan, Karin Aguilar, ed. *The State of Asian America: Activism and Resistance in the 1990s.* Boston: South End Press, 1994.

Saxton, Alexander. *The Indispensable Enemy: Labor and the Anti-Chinese Movement in California.* Berkeley, Calif.: University of California Press, 1971.

Shah, Sonia, ed. *Dragon Ladies: Asian American Feminists Breathe Fire.* Boston: South End Press, 1997.

Shankar, Lavina Dhingra, and Rajini Srikanth, eds. *A Part, Yet Apart: South Asians in Asian America.* Philadelphia: Temple University Press, 1998.

*The State of Asian Pacific America: A Public Policy Report, Policy Issues to the Year 2020.* Los Angeles: LEAP Asian Pacific American Policy Institute and UCLA Asian American Studies Center, 1993.

Tachiki, Amy; Eddie Wong; and Franklin Oda, eds. *Roots: An Asian American Reader.* Los Angeles: UCLA Asian American Studies Center, 1971.

Takahashi, Jere. *Nisei/Sansei: Shifting Japanese American Identities and Politics.* Philadelphia: Temple University Press, 1997.

Takagi, Dana Y. *The Retreat from Race: Asian American Admissions and Racial Politics.* New Brunswick, N.J.: Rutgers University Press, 1992.

Takaki, Ronald. *Strangers from a Different Shore: A History of Asian Americans.* Boston: Little, Brown and Company, 1989.

Tsuchida, Nobuya, ed. *Asian and Pacific American Experiences: Women's Perspectives.* Minneapolis: Asian/Pacific American Learning Resource Center, 1982.

Tuan, Mia. *Forever Foreigners, Or, Honorary Whites: The Asian Ethnic Experience Today.* New Brunswick, N.J.: Rutgers University Press, 1998.

United States Commission on Wartime Relocation and Internment of Civilians. *Personal Justice Denied: Report of the Commission on Wartime Relocation and Internment of Civilians.* Seattle: University of Washington Press, 1997.

Weglyn, Michi Nishiura. *Years of Infamy: The Untold Story of America's Concentration Camps.* Seattle: University of Washington Press, 1996.

Wei, William. *The Asian American Movement.* Philadelphia: Temple University Press, 1993.

Wong, Diane Yen Mei, et al. *Making Waves: An Anthology of Writings By and About Asian American Women.* Boston: Beacon Press, 1989.

Wong, K. Scott, and Sucheng Chan, eds. *Claiming America: Constructing Chinese American Identities during the Exclusion Era.* Philadelphia: Temple University Press, 1998.

Wong, Shawn, ed. *Asian American Literature: A Brief Introduction and Anthology.* New York: HarperCollins College Publications, 1996.

Yamamoto, Eric K. *Interracial Justice: Conflict and Reconciliation in Post–Civil Rights America.* New York: New York University, 1999.

Yang, Jeff; Dina Gan; Terry Hong; et al. *Eastern Standard Time: A Guide to Asian Influence on American Culture, from Astro Boy to Zen Buddhism.* New York: Houghton Mifflin, 1997.

Yung, Judy. *Unbound Feet: A Social History of Chinese Women in San Francisco.* Berkeley, Calif.: University of California Press, 1995.

Zia, Helen, and Susan Gall, eds. *Notable Asian Americans.* Detroit: Gale Research, 1995.

# Acknowledgments

I am indebted to so many who introduced me to their communities, campuses, workplaces, and friends and families, opening their souls as well as their record files to me, offering their wisdom so that I might share their tales with others. As my research took me across the country, many kind people made their homes and hospitality available, as well as their ideas and experiences. My humble thanks go to the hundreds of individuals who agreed to be interviewed for this book, unfortunately too numerous to mention here. All have my deep and heartfelt appreciation.

Colleagues from the Asian American Journalists Association helped me in innumerable ways, with suggestions, leads, enthusiasm, and, most important, friendship; in particular, Jeannie Park, Jon Funabiki, and Sandra Oshiro have never hesitated to lend their wisdom and support. My family of editors at *Ms.* magazine constantly inspired me; Robin Morgan long ago urged me to authorship, while Gloria Steinem, Marcia Gillespie, Mary Thom, and other present and former editors encouraged me. The Journalism and Women's Symposium gave advice and counsel from its special network of journalists, writers, and editors. I was also privileged to have the feedback of June Jordan, Sandy Close, Ann Okahara, Lynne Ogawa, and Joan Lester at the early stages of developing *Asian American Dreams*.

This book and most of what is known about Asian Americans is rooted in the research, scholarship, and hard work of those in the field of Asian American studies, notably those affiliated with the Association of Asian American Studies. I am indebted to its members and its coordinator, Anita Affeldt. Professors Evelyn Hu-DeHart, Elaine H. Kim, Ling-chi Wang, and K. Scott Wong were especially generous with their knowledge. Wei Chi Poon, curator of the Asian American Studies Collection of the Ethnic Studies Library at the University of California at Berkeley, and Bea Dong of the Eastwind Books of Berkeley (www.ewbb.com), patiently advised me. Research for this book also depended on the open doors of numerous public libraries, notably the main branch of the Oakland (California) Public Library.

The Asian American ethnic and community news media, the true chroniclers of our communities, let me rummage through their morgues. In particular I thank Dean Wong, Bob Shimabukuro, and Eric Hsu of the *International Examiner* in Seattle; Richard Springer of *India West*; Ashok Jethanandani of *India Currents*; Kapson Yim Lee of the *Korea Times* English Edition; and the archives of *AsianWeek*.

Nanette Fok, Sandra Yoshizuka, and Donald Young of the National Asian American Telecommunications Association kindly allowed me to review tapes from NAATA's extensive catalogue of Asian American film and video; independent videographer Christopher Chow offered video recordings from his personal library. I am also grateful for the timely research assistance of Momo Chang, Tamina Davar, Carlos Gallegos, Audee Kochiyama-Holman, Ellen Okazaki, Mary Schaefer, Alethea Yip, and the law offices of Minami, Lew and Tamaki.

American Citizens for Justice co-founders James Shimoura, Roland Hwang, and Harold Leon always made themselves available when my memory dimmed on details of the Vincent Chin case. My special appreciation to Daphne Kwok and the Organization of Chinese Americans, whose doors were always open to me; Leigh-Ann Miyasato and Bob Sakiniwa, both formerly of the Japanese American Citizens League Washington office, and Patty Wada of the JACL national office; Deborah Ching with the Los Angeles Chinatown Service Center; Seattle city council member Martha Choe and her staff; and KaYing Yang of the Southeast Asia Resource Action Center. All were most generous with their time, documents, and office space. The Inland Boatmen's Union of the Pacific and its regional director Richard Gurtiza paved the way for me to visit the salmon canneries of Alaska.

I am grateful to many Asian Pacific American women and men whose dedication to their communities is an inspiration. Martha Lee, the visionary founder of the Asian Pacific American Women's Leadership Institute, and its network of amazing women shared their high spirits and expertise with me. So did the many dynamic women of the National Asian Pacific American Women's Forum; at their founding conference I had the good fortune to connect with author Phoebe Eng, who took considerable time away from writing her book, *Warrior Lessons*, to share her insights, wisdom, and friendship with me.

Several book chapters benefited from the thoughtful readings and comments of talented writers Sally Lehrman, Teresa Moore, and Venise Wagner. Scholars Ji-Yeon Yuh, professor at Northwestern University, and Himanee Gupta, a Ph.D. candidate at the University of Hawaii, both former journalists, applied their critical analysis to certain chapters. I am also grateful to Farrar, Straus and Giroux copy editor Elaine Chubb for her thorough and meticulous review.

My siblings were my cheerleaders, advisers, and confidants; brother Hoyt and sister-in-law Leigh-Ann read some chapters; youngest siblings Humane and Haddon gave helpful input; brothers Hugo and Henry sent me love and encouragement, as did my dear friend from the Chrysler stamping plants, Robert Duiguid. During the long stretches of researching and writing, my life was full with the love and positive spirits of numerous friends, especially the support of writer and playwright Diane Yen-Mei Wong.

Amid this bounty, I am truly fortunate to have as my literary agent Sydelle Kramer, who from the start believed in what I had to say, offering consistent excellent advice and patiently helping me shape my ideas for this book.

I could never have imagined working with such a wonderful editor, Elisabeth Kallick Dyssegaard. Her enthusiasm and her unfailingly wise and good-humored guidance were a rare and special gift. As she took up the joy and indignation of these stories, at times she seemed to be turning Asian American.

My deepest gratitude belongs to my parents. My father, Yee Chen Zia, encouraged me to write from the time that I could hold a crayon. My mother, Beilin Woo Zia, with her unconditional love, imparted her special empathy and caring for others. I only wish that my father were alive to read this book and to offer his criticisms.

Most of all, I thank my life partner, Lia Shigemura, who read every word of this book's many versions with good cheer and genuine excitement, adding her special insights with encouragement, understanding, and loving care.

# Index

ABC News, 91, 183

Abercrombie, Neil, 157, 158

Abraham & Straus, 84–85

Ackerman, Gary L., 210

actors: Asian American, 111–12, 114–30, 134–35, 276–77; white, in yellowface, 110, 113–14, 119, 122–25, 130, 252

Actors' Equity, 112, 119, 123–25, 127–29, 131; Committee on Racial Equality, 119–20

Adams, Brock, 155–60

adoptions of Korean children, 265–66, 279, 306

Advani, Anuradha, 204

affirmative action, 153; Asian American attitudes toward, 291–94; in theater, 129

AFL-CIO, 125, 158

African Americans, 46, 50, 52, 72, 205, 228; actors, 120, 123, 128, 129; artists, 270; athletes, 273; autoworkers, 56; in civil rights movement, 45, 47, 68, 70; enfranchisement of, 26; hapas, 267–68; in Hawaii, 36, 249; Korean Americans and, 85–89, 92–98, 100–8, 118, 171, 173–84, 187, 192; in Minnesota, 257, 259; pan-Asian groups and, 221, 223; politics and, 289–91, 294, 295; in post–Civil War South, 36; at Princeton, 16, 18, 20; sentencing of, compared to whites, 60; taxi drivers and, 201; on television, 274; and Vincent Chin case, 70–71, 73, 74, 78, 79; violence against, 74, 86; Wards Cove workers supported by, 151

Afro-Caribbeans, 85, 87, 92–93, 97, 108

Ahn, Me-K., 265–66

Ahn, Suzanne, 299

*Ah Sin* (Harte and Twain), 114, 130

Akaka, Daniel, 155, 157

Alaska, 38; salmon canneries in, 142–65

Alaska Cannery Workers Association (ACWA), 147

Alexie, Sherman, 273

Alien Land Law (1920), 30

*All-American Girl* (television series), 267

Allen, Woody, 266

*A. Magazine*, 115, 222, 278, 304

Amerasians, 51, 256

American Airlines, 211

American-Arab Anti-Discrimination Committee, 75

American Bar Association, 160

American Citizens for Justice (ACJ), 67–80

American Civil Liberties Union (ACLU), 72

American Communist Party, 19–20

American Federation of Labor, 35, 37–38

American Homecoming Act (1987), 51

American Players Theatre, 121

*American Spectator, The*, 299

Amos, Wally, 249

Angry Little Asian Girl (Web site), 277

anthropophagia, 129

anti-Communism, 10, 44–45, 76, 148, 149

Anti-Defamation League of B'nai B'rith, 68, 124, 240

antimiscegenation laws, 34, 232, 235–36

antiwar movement, 13–14, 17–18

Aoki, Brenda Wong, 263

Aoki, Guy, 134

Aoki, Jean, 248

Apna Ghar (South Asian women's group), 214

Aptheker, Herbert, 20

Arab Americans, 69

architecture, 272

Arizona, internment of Japanese Americans in, 42

Arkansas: Chinese plantation workers in, 36; internment of Japanese Americans in, 42; Vietnamese refugees in, 51

Army, U.S., 63; 442nd Nisei Regimental Combat Team, 43; Western Defense Command, 41

*Art in America* (magazine), 273

artists, Asian American, 263–66, 269–73; mixed-race, 267

*Art of War, The* (Sun Tzu), 316

Asian American Chamber of Commerce, 303

Asian American Defense and Education Fund, 48

Asian American Heritage Festival (New York), 100

Asian American Institute, 216

Asian American Journalists Association (AAJA), 89, 99, 126–27, 230, 274–75, 277, 313, 314

Asian American Law Students Association, 75

Asian American Legal Defense and Education Fund, 104, 126, 220

*Asian American Panethnicity* (Espiritu), 81

Asian American Political Alliance, 48

*Asian American Press*, 261

Asian American Renaissance, 263–64

Asian American Resource Center, 48

*Asian Americans* (Lott), 208

Asian Americans for Action, 48

Asian Americans for Affirmative Action, 294

Asian Americans for Campaign Finance Reform, 301

Asian Americans for Equality, 48

Asian Americans/Pacific Islanders in Philanthropy, 207

Asian American Student Associations, 48

Asian American studies programs, 48

Asian American Theater Company, 122, 270, 278

Asian Crisis (band), 277

Asian Immigrant Women Advocates, 307

Asian Law Caucus, 48, 81, 301, 304

Asian Media Access, 264

Asian Pacific Alliance for Creative Equality (APACE), 120, 126, 134

Asian Pacific American Heritage Month, 98

Asian Pacific American Institute for Congressional Studies, 299, 302, 309

Asian Pacific American Labor Alliance (APALA), 158, 160

Asian Pacific American Legal Center, 81, 179, 189

Asian Pacific Americans for a New Los Angeles, 192

Asian Pacific American Women's Leadership Institute, 119

Asian Pacific Environmental Network, 307

Asian Pacific Planning Council, 190

Asians for Justice, 78

*AsianWeek* (newspaper), 266, 268, 278

Asian Women's Shelter (San Francisco), 307

Asian Women United of Minnesota, 261

Asiatic Exclusion League, 32

Association of American Physicians from India, 208

Association of Asian/Pacific American Artists, 126

Association of Indians in America, 201

Astaire, Fred, 113

AT&T, 294

athletes, 268, 273, 274, 275

Atonio, Frank, 149, 155

Aubrey, Larry, 174

automobile industry, 55–58, 62, 72–73, 75

Azuma, Julie, 96

*Bachelor Father* (television series), 115

Baehr, Nina, 227

Bakewell, Danny, 178

Bald, Vivek Renjen, 218

Ball, Don, 78

ballots, bilingual, 64, 292

*Bamboo Girl* (zine), 277

Bangladeshis and Bangladeshi Americans, 199, 201, 203, 206

Bannai, Lori, 50

Barnard, Tom, 257–59, 279

Barnes, Christopher, 132–33

*Because They Thought He Was . . .* (Echeverria), 81

Bell Laboratories, 294

Benavides, Vida, 309

Bennett, Robert, 298

Bentley, William, 24

Berk, Alvin, 97

Berry, Mary Frances, 301

Bhutanese, 200

Bible, the, 317

bilingual ballots, 64, 292

Bill of Rights, 282

bindis, 90, 275

Bing, Ah, 38

Black Power movement, 47

Black-Korean Alliance (BKA), 174–78, 180–81, 183, 192

Blackmun, Harry A., 151, 152

Black Women for a Better Society, 69

Blatner, Jeff, 153, 164

Bloomingdale's department store, 84

Blue Shield insurance company, 48

boat people (Vietnamese), 51

Bobo, Lawrence, 290

*Bonanza* (television series), 115, 252

Boone, Richard, 114

Boston: community activism in, 228; pan-Asian movement in, 78

*Boston Globe, The*, 298

Boston Museum of Fine Arts, 116–17

Boublil, Alain, 113

Bradley, Tom, 175, 179

Brando, Marlon, 114

Brazil, anthropophagia in, 129

*Breakfast at Tiffany's* (film), 114

Breslin, Jimmy, 98–100, 102

Bridges, Kim, 80

Brindle family, 150, 154

Britain: colonialism of, 25; investments in U.S. of, 90; South Asians in, 200

Brokaw, Tom, 291

Brooks, Jack, 159

Brotherhood Crusade, 178, 179

Brown, Anthony, 267

Brown, Lee, 102

Brown, Ron, 190

Brownback, Sam, 297

Brown University, 305

*Brown v. Board of Education* (1954), 45

Buchanan, James, 24

Buddhists, 12, 41, 248, 275

Bui, Tony, 276

*Burlington County Times*, 22

Burroughs Corporation, 70

Bush, George, 151, 153, 293

Byun, Chong Duck, 104

cabdrivers, *see* taxi drivers

Cabreros-Sud, Veena, 132

Cain, Dean, 267, 296

California, 38, 236; anti-Asian violence in, 77, 91, 301; automobile industry in, 58; Court of Appeals, 34; driving out of Chinese from, 27–28; Filipinos in, 34–35; gold rush in, 25–26; Hmong in, 257; Indians in, 32, 33, 200; internment of Japanese Americans in, 42, 43; Japanese in, 29; Koreans in, 173; labor movement in, 36; land ownership prohibitions in, 30; migrant agricultural workers in, 144, 145; politics in, 286–88, 290–92, 304–5, 308; Vietnamese refugees in, 51, 52; *see also* Los Angeles; Oakland; San Francisco; San Jose

California, University of: at Berkeley, 25, 30, 47–48, 185, 200, 268, 270, 301, 305–6; at Davis, 115; at Irvine, 305; at Los Angeles, 48, 208, 289, 308; at Riverside, 175, 187; at San Diego, 81

*Calling America Home* (radio program), 280

Cambodians and Cambodian Americans, 191–92, 194; during Los Angeles riots, 188, 191; in Minnesota, 257; poverty among, 207; refugees, 51, 204, 206, 257; violence against, 78, 91

campaign finance scandal (1996 presidential race), 296–302

Campeau Corp., 85

Canada: Chinese in, 73; Indians in, 31–32

Cao, Tuan Ana, 101, 102, 104

Caoile, Gloria, 154, 156

Carnegie Mellon University, 81

Carradine, David, 114, 242, 277

*Carry the Tiger to the Mountain* (Lee), 80–81

Carson, Robert (Sonny), 86, 97, 98, 100, 101

Case, Clifford, 141

Castle & Cook, 147

Catholics, 243

*Cats* (musical), 112

CBS News, 42, 89

Census Bureau, U.S., 41, 310

Center for Third World Organizing, 307

Central Intelligence Agency (CIA), 256

Central Pacific Railroad, 27

Chan, Eddie, 62

Chan, Jackie, 277, 278

Chan, Liza, 64, 65, 68, 69, 72, 74, 79

Chan, Sucheng, 26

Chang, Edward T., 174, 187–88, 192

Chang, Kevin, 245

Chang, Man Feng, 74

Chang, Michael, 273

Chang, Soo, 94

Chang, Tisa, 126

Chang, Yee, 262–63

Chao, Rosalind, 296

*Charlie Chan Is Dead* (Hagedorn), 135

Chavez, Cesar, 38

*Cheat, The* (film), 114

Chee, Ah, 62

Chen, Dong Lu, 237

Chen, Edward M., 301

Chen, Lily Lee, 184

Cheng Ho, 23, 318

Chiang Kai-shek, 66, 76, 167, 311

Chicago: Indian Americans in, 215–17; Japanese Americans in, 96; pan-Asian movement in, 75

*Chicago Tribune*, 215–17

*Chickencoop Chinaman, The* (Chin), 271

Children Now, 274

Chimurenga, Coltrane, 87

Chin, Charlie, 80, 269

Chin, David Bing Hing, 63

Chin, Frank, 271

Chin, Lily, 63–65, 74, 76, 80

Chin, Marilyn, 263

Chin, Soo-Young, 132–33

Chin, Stephen C., 160, 161

Chin, Tsai, 254

Chin, Vincent, 58–61, 63–67, 69–81, 92, 169, 180, 203, 219, 229, 310

China, 76, 140–41, 286–87; and British imperialism, 25; and campaign finance scandal (1996), 297, 298; civil service system in, 13; Communist revolution in, 5, 10, 44–45, 196; coverage of Vincent Chin case in, 73; Cultural Revolution, 140, 196; foot-binding in, 254; gays and lesbians in, 242; Japanese occupation of, 5, 8, 167–69; nineteenth-century educational mission to U.S. from, 24; Nixon in, 140, 141, 253; Tiananmen Square protests in, 273; U.S. policy toward, 316–17; in Western reference books, 22–23; in World War II, 5, 39

Chinatown Service Center (Los Angeles), 188, 190

Chinese American Citizens Alliance, 28

Chinese American Educational and Cultural Center (Detroit), 66

Chinese and Chinese Americans, 3–20, 32, 41, 82–84, 94, 142, 172, 191, 192, 236, 311–19; African Americans and, 100–1, 103; in Alaskan salmon canneries, 144, 145, 150; anti-Communism and, 44–45; artists, 272–73; barred from immigration, 5, 28, 200; in California gold rush, 25–26; in campaign finance scandal (1996), 298; citizenship for, 26, 28–29, 40; in civil rights movement, 47; Detroit community of, 61–62; domestic violence among, 237; driving out of, 21, 27–28, 38; employment options for recent immigrants, 196–98; FBI

surveillance of, 10–11, 45; in films, 115–16; first in U.S., 24; gay and lesbian, 241, 242; government offices held by, 46; in Hawaii, 234, 246, 249; immigration quota for, 40–41; Japanese attitudes toward, 29–30; Korean Americans and, 33, 96, 184, 194; labor movement and, 36, 37; land ownership prohibited for, 30; during Los Angeles riots, 188; in Mexico, 24; middle-class and elite, 204, 205; as model minority, 46; parent–child relationships among, 166–69, 227–29, 281–82; in politics, 284–88, 291, 295, 304, 308; railroads built by, 9, 23, 27, 36; restaurants run by, 56, 62, 64; slaves replaced in Caribbean colonies by, 25; smuggling rings and, 206; South Asians and, 201, 203–4; spying allegations against, 309, 316; in student movement, 146; on television, 274–75; violence against, 23, 26, 58–61, 63–67, 76, 90, 91, 301; during World War II, 39–40, 44

Chinese Association for Human Rights in Taiwan, 75

Chinese Consolidated Benevolent Association, 61, 75, 103

Chinese Equal Rights League, 28

Chinese Exclusion Act (1882), 28, 29, 144

Chinese for Affirmative Action, 48

Chinese Hand Laundry Alliance, 75

Chinese Progressive Association, 75

Chinese Six Companies, 28

Ching, Anthony, 299

Ching, Deborah, 188, 190

Ching family, 11–12

chinoiserie, 116–17

Cho, Margaret, 296

Cho, Sumi, 132

Chock, David, 74

Choe, Martha, 285, 288
Chong, Bill, 87, 89, 96
Chopra, Deepak, 274
Chow, Ruby, 287
Chow Yun Fat, 277
Choy, Christine, 79, 80
Chrysler Corporation, 56–58, 72, 75, 229
Chung, Connie, 274–75
Chung, Eugene, 275
Chung, Sheila, 267
Cincinnati: African American–Korean
    American conflicts in, 96; federal civil
    rights trial in, 79–80
Cirrus Logic, 205
citizenship, 238, 282; by birthright, 28–30,
    38, 42; denial of, 26, 28, 30–33, 43, 236;
    dual, 139; lifting of restrictions on, 40,
    45, 286
City College of New York, 101
Civil Liberties Act (1988), 50, 153, 159
Civil Rights Act (1991), 152–59
Civil Rights Commission, U.S., 119, 301
civil rights movement, 4, 13, 45, 144, 232,
    236, 273; in nineteenth century, 28; pan-
    Asian activism in, 47–50; same-sex
    marriage as issue for, 233, 238, 240, 243,
    251; and university admissions, 15; see
    also specific organizations
Civil War, 22
Claiming America (Wong and Chan), 26
class action discrimination lawsuits,
    147–52, 159, 162, 163
Clemente, Roberto, 273
Clinton, Bill, 160, 293, 296, 297, 299, 310,
    316; Initiative on Race of, 81, 186, 250
Clinton, Hillary, 199
CNBC, 267, 297
Coalition of Asian Pacifics in
    Entertainment, 277
Coast Guard, U.S., 52

Coffey, Shelby, 183
Cohen, Richard, 164
Cold War, 311, 317
Colorado: internment of Japanese
    Americans in, 42; Koreans in, 173; see
    also Denver
Colorado, University of, 25, 212
Columbia Pictures, 276
Columbia University, 305, 306–7
Columbus, Christopher, 23
Colwell, Racine, 69, 78, 79
Commerce Department, U.S., 190
Commission on Civil Rights, U.S., 119
Committee Against Anti-Asian Violence
    (CAAAV), 91, 92, 99, 104, 131–32,
    203–4
Committee of 100, 161, 298
Communists, 14, 44–45, 149, 191, 304;
    American, 19–20; Chinese, 5, 10, 44,
    140, 196
Community Action Against Racism
    (CAAR), 259, 278–80
Confucianism, 11, 13, 17, 19, 166, 168, 187,
    282
Congress, U.S., 52, 141, 142, 302, 308; anti-
    Communism in, 10; Asian Americans
    in, 45, 46, 50, 286, 290, 309; and
    campaign finance scandal (1996), 297,
    301; Caucus on India and Indian
    Americans, 210; and Filipino American
    World War II veterans, 303–4;
    immigration restricted by, 31, 35; and
    redress for Japanese American
    internment, 232, 240; and Southeast
    Asian refugee crisis, 51; and Wards Cove
    case, 152–62, 283; see also House of
    Representatives, U.S.; Senate, U.S.
Conqueror, The (film), 114
Constitution, U.S., 282; Fourteenth
    Amendment, 28, 235

construction trades: discrimination against minority workers in, 147, 148, 294; integration of, 228

Consul, Wilma, 278

Contemporary American Theater Festival, 80

*Contemporary Asian American Experience, The* (Fong), 285–86

Continental Congress, 24

Conyers, John, 69

Cook, Capt. James, 234, 244

"coolie" labor, 25

Cornell University, 307

Council on Asian Pacific Minnesotans, 257, 258

*Courtship of Eddie's Father, The* (television series), 114

Crichton, Michael, 134

Crips gang, 176

Crocker, Charles, 27, 36

Crossroads International, 133

Cuba, importation of Chinese laborers to, 25

Cultural Revolution (China), 140, 196

Cummins, Judith, 73

Cuomo, Mario, 99, 105

Curry, Ann, 267

Dachau concentration camp, 43

Daly, Tyne, 123

Dancel, Genora, 227

Danforth, John, 153, 155, 157

DasGupta, Sayantani, 213

DasGupta, Shamita Das, 213–14

Daughtry, Herbert, 102

Davar, Tamina, 203

Davis, Gray, 309–10

Davis, Joe, 72

December 12th Movement, 86, 87, 89, 99, 104

Declaration of Independence, 282

deLeón, Dennis, 98, 108

Democratic Party, 46, 293, 294, 308, 309; and civil rights legislation, 153; in Detroit, 77; fund-raising by, 296, 299; in Hawaii, 251; National Committee, 297–99, 301; and "Yellow Peril" movement, 28; and Wards Cove case, 152, 155, 156, 159, 161

Denny's restaurant chain, 300–1

Denver, violence against Chinese in, 21, 28

DePaul University, 132

Desai, Bhairavi, 198–200, 202–4, 218

design, 272

Detroit, 55–81, 229; automobile industry in, 55–58, 62, 72–73, 75; murder of Vincent Chin in, 58–61, 63–67, 69–81

Detroit Chinese Welfare Council, 61–62, 64, 66

*Detroit Free Press*, 60, 315

*Detroit Metro Times*, 57

*Detroit News, The*, 60, 61, 78

Detroit Roundtable of Christians and Jews, 68

Detroit Women's Forum, 69

Dewhurst, Colleen, 114, 120, 123

DeWitt, Gen. John, 41

Dickinson, Angie, 113–14

Dingell, John, 58

Dinkins, David, 92, 97, 98, 100, 101, 104–8, 122–23

Disney Corporation, 115, 117

documentary films, 79, 80, 270, 218, 266, 270, 276

*Dogeaters* (Hagedorn), 135

Dole, Bob, 153, 155, 293, 297

Dole Corporation, 147, 148

domestic violence, 214, 229, 237, 260–62, 307

Domingo, Nemesio, Jr., 146–48, 152

Domingo, Nemesio, Sr., 146, 148
Domingo, Silme, 139, 146–49, 165
Donahue, Phil, 73
Dotbusters, 90–91, 221
*Do the Right Thing* (film), 276
*Dragon Seed* (film), 114
driving-out time, 21, 27–28
drumming, 252, 272
D'Souza, Selma, 215–16
Du, Billy Heung Ki, 176
Du, Joseph, 176
Du, Soon Ja, 176–82, 185, 186
Duggan, Dennis, 89
Dukakis, Michael, 293
Duke, David, 153
Duke Power Company, 150
Durant, Will and Ariel, 22
Dutton, Charles, 123

East Coast Asian Students Union, 283
East West Players, 121, 126, 270
*Eat Drink Man Woman* (film), 276
Ebens, Ronald, 59, 69, 75, 77–80
Echeverria, Consuelo, 81
Edwards, Don, 157
18 Mighty Mountain Warriors
   (performance troupe), 277
Eisenberg, Alan, 120, 123
elites, Asian American, 204–6
Emmons, Gen. Delos, 41
employment practices, discriminatory, 48,
   78, 119; in Alaskan salmon canneries,
   142–65
*Encyclopaedia Britannica*, 8, 22
Enriquez, Jocelyn, 275
entrepreneurs, 204–5
environmental activists, 307
Equal Rights Amendment, 235
Espiritu, Yen Le, 81
Estefan, Gloria, 273

Eu, March Fong, 298
Eugenio, Claro, 139
Exoticize This! (Web site), 277

*Face Value* (Hwang), 125
Fairbanks, Douglas, 114
*Fargo* (film), 276
Farrow, Mia, 266
Federal Bureau of Investigation (FBI),
   10–11, 41, 44, 45, 70, 74, 141, 297, 299
Federation of Indian Associations, 215, 221
Felissaint, Jiselaine, 92–93, 106
Fewel, Jean Har-Kew, 133
Fiji, immigrants from, 206
Filipino American Community Council,
   66
Filipino Civil Rights Advocates (FILCRA),
   303, 305
Filipino Federation of Labor, 37
Filipino Labor Union, 27
Filipinos and Filipino Americans, 9, 16, 29,
   38, 41, 49, 133–34, 191, 192, 229; actors,
   129, 131; in Alaskan canneries, 142–52,
   154, 155, 159–65, 294; artists, 275, 278;
   barred from immigration, 5; in civil
   rights movement, 47; citizenship for, 40;
   in Detroit, 62; discriminatory
   employment practices against, 48; in
   Hawaii, 234, 246, 249; immigration
   quotas for, 40–41; Korean Americans
   and, 96; in labor movement, 37–38;
   during Los Angeles riots, 188; middle-
   class and elite, 204, 205; in politics, 288,
   295; in student movement, 146; and
   Vincent Chin case, 67, 74, 77; violence
   against, 309–10; white nativist prejudice
   against, 34–35; during World War II, 39,
   40, 44, 148, 303–4
films, 269, 276; Asian actors in, 114–18,
   254, 276–77; documentary, 79, 80, 218,

266, 270, 276; Hindi, 212; portrayals of
Asians in, 112–14, 117, 134
Finucane, Matt, 160
Fireman, Simon, 297
First Korean Church of Brooklyn, 102
fishermen, Vietnamese, 52
Florida, Vietnamese refugees in, 51
*Flower Drum Song* (play and film), 114,
117, 121
Foley, Thomas, 157–59
Fong, Hiram, 46, 286
Fong, Kam, 118
Fong, Matt, 298
Fong, Timothy, 285–86
food, Chinese, 56, 82–83, 314
foot-binding, 254
Ford Motor Company, 70
Forsythe, John, 115
Forum of Indian Leftists (FOIL), 204, 218
France: colonies of, 25; in World War II, 43
Frank, Barney, 240–41
Frankel, Max, 98
*Frank Leslie's Illustrated Newspaper*, 21
Fraser, Doug, 72–73
Freeman, Morgan, 123, 128
French Open tennis tournament, 273
Friday, Chris, 146
Fujitani, Yoshiaki, 248
Fung, Margaret, 104, 126
Furutani, Warren, 189, 303

Galledo, Lillian, 305
Gandhi, Mohandas K., 223
Gatchalian, Ray, 133–34
Gates, Bill, 210
gays, 132, 221, 230, 279; right to marry of,
227, 230–51, 293; violence against,
237–38
Gee, Emma, 47
General Motors, 24, 70; Tech Center, 74

George, Mrs. (teacher), 12–13
*George* magazine, 199
Georgetown University, 294
Gephardt, Richard, 157–59
Gere, Richard, 275
Germany: investments in U.S. of, 90; in
World War II, 43
*Giant Robot* (magazine), 278
GI Bill, 44
Gish, Lillian, 113
Giuliani, Rudolph, 199, 202, 218
glass ceiling, 119
*Golden Child* (Hwang), 120, 254
*Golden Venture* (ship), 206
gold rush of 1848, 25–26
Gomes, Kuʻumealoha, 244, 245, 249
Gompers, Samuel, 35–36, 38, 73
Gong, Lue Gim, 38
Gong, Stephen, 269
Gonzalez, Marlina, 129, 264
*Good Earth, The* (film), 114
*Good Woman of Setzuan, The* (play), 114
Gore, Al, 309
Gotanda, Philip Kan, 111–12, 121, 126, 135
*GQ* magazine, 132
*Grain of Sand, A* (record album), 269
Grant, Larry, 239
Greater Detroit Taiwanese Association, 66
Greeley, Horace, 28
*Griggs* v. *Duke Power Company* (1971),
150, 151
*Gunsmoke* (television series), 114
Gupta, Himanee, 214
Gurtiza, Richard, 162, 163
Guyana, immigrants from, 206

Hagedorn, Jessica, 135, 263
Haitians, 92, 97
Hajratwala, Bhupendra, 212–13
Hajratwala, Minal, 212–13

Hall, Gus, 19–20

Hall, Sam, Jr., 240

Hamamoto, Darrell, 115

Handa, Robert, 58

Hang, Pakou, 280

Hapa Issues Forum, 267

hapas, 266–68, 279; in politics, 308; in student movement, 306

*hardboiled* (zine), 277

*Hard Copy* (television series), 120

Harlins, Latasha, 176–78, 180, 184

Harper, Jim, 78

Harte, Bret, 114, 130

Harvard University, 187, 193, 305, 306

Harvey, Steven, 74

hate crimes, 308; anti-Asian, 58–61, 63–67, 69–81, 90–92, 101–4, 132, 134, 178, 203, 219–22, 229, 236, 300–1; anti-gay, 237–38

*Have Gun Will Travel* (television series), 114

Hawaii, 38; annexation by U.S. of, 31; Asian plantation workers in, 36–37; Chinese in, 5; Civil Rights Commission, 251; Filipinos in, 35; House of Representatives, 248; Japanese in, 30; politics in, 286, 308; same-sex marriage in, 227, 230–51; statehood for, 45–46, 234, 286; State Supreme Court, 231–33, 235, 242, 246; during World War II, 39, 40

Hawaii, University of, 177, 214, 246

Hawaiians, Native, 234, 236, 245–46, 249; same-sex relationships among, 244–45

Hayakawa, Sessue, 114, 117

Hayashi, Dennis, 156

Hayashino, Carole, 238, 239

Hayes, Helen, 113

Hearst newspaper chain, 41–42

Hecco, Joseph, 24

Heen, Walter, 233

Hegel, Georg Wilhelm Friedrich, 22

Henderson, Wade, 164

Hepburn, Katharine, 114

Her, Kao Ly Ilean, 258–59

Herzig, Aiko, 50

Herzig, Jack, 50

Heston, Charlton, 124

Hill, Amy, 267, 276, 296

Hinduism, 32, 213, 275

Hirabayashi, Gordon, 50

Hispanics, *see* Latinos

HIV/AIDS, 307

Hmong American Partnership, 259

Hmong and Hmong Americans, 51, 52, 254–63, 268, 278–80; in politics, 308; poverty among, 207; traditional marriages of, 258–63

Ho, David, 274

Ho Chi Minh, 304

Holt, Harry, 265

Holy Names College (Oakland), 285

Hom, Nancy, 269

homosexuality, *see* gays; lesbians

Hongo, Garrett, 263

Ho'omalu ma Kualoa, 245

Hoover, J. Edgar, 10, 41, 45

horticulture, Asian American contributions to, 38

Hoshijo, William, 251

House of Representatives, U.S., 24, 45–46, 153–54, 157–61, 235, 286, 297, 308–9; Administrative Law Subcommittee, 240; Committee on Immigration and Naturalization, 35; Judiciary Committee, 159; Rules Committee, 157

Houston, Velina Hasu, 267

Houston (Texas), 304

Howard University, 299

Hu, Kelly, 277, 313, 314

Huang, John, 298
Hu-DeHart, Evelyn, 25
Huen, Floyd, 307
Huen, William, 307
Human Rights Campaign Fund, 243, 248
Hung, Sammo, 277
Hutchings, Vincent, 290
Huynh, Thong Hy, 52
Hwang, David, 70, 71
Hwang, David Henry, 112, 116, 120, 121, 125, 126, 130, 254
Hwang, Ronald, 69
Hwang, Victor M., 81, 301

Iacocca, Lee, 58
Ice Cube, 177
Ichioka, Yuji, 47
Idaho, internment of Japanese Americans in, 42
Iijima, Chris, 269
Iijima, Kazu, 48
Iiyama, Chizu, 239
Ileto, Joseph, 309–10
Illinois: Koreans in, 173; politics in, 287; see also Chicago
Imam, Saddique, 209, 211, 212
Immigration Act (1917), 32
Immigration Act (1924), 31, 34
Immigration Act (1965), 62, 68, 145, 174, 179, 196, 200, 205, 300
Immigration and Naturalization Service (INS), 16, 282
India: British imperialism in, 25; during World War II, 40
India Abroad (newspaper), 214
India Abroad Center for Political Awareness, 222, 223
Indians, American, see Native Americans
Indians and Indian Americans, 29, 38, 41, 198–206; barred from immigration, 5; in

campaign finance scandal (1996), 298; in Canada, 31–32; "chic," adoption by European Americans of, 275; citizenship for, 32–33, 40; elective offices held by, 45; first in U.S., 24; intergenerational clash in values among, 211–15; labor movement and, 36; land ownership prohibited for, 30, 33; during Los Angeles riots, 188; middle-class and elite, 204–6, 208–11, 218; in politics, 308; Sikhs, 32, 33, 200; slaves replaced in Caribbean colonies by, 25; taxi drivers, 198–204, 215–19; violence against, 90–91, 219–22
India West (newspaper), 214
Indo-American Center (Chicago), 216
Indo American Democratic Organization, 215, 216
Indo-Caribbeans, 220, 221
Indochina Migration and Refugee Assistance Act (1975), 51
Indonesia, 298; refugee camps in, 51
Inland Boatmen's Union (ILWU Local 37), 146–49, 162
Inouye, Daniel, 46, 155, 157, 286
Intel, 210; Science Talent Search, 207
International Longshoremen's and Warehousemen's Union (now International Longshore and Warehouse Union; ILWU), 146–49, 157, 158
Interracial Justice (Yamamoto), 177
Interview (magazine), 273
In These Times, 88
Irish Americans, 241
Irons, Peter, 50
Italian Americans, 31, 69, 86
Italy, investments in U.S. of, 90

Jackson, Jesse, 76, 87
Jade (Web site), 277

Jang, Bong Jae, 82, 92, 94, 97, 102–7
Jang, Jon, 80, 263
Jang, Pong Ok, 94, 105–6
Jansen, Marius, 18
Japan: automobile industry in, 57–58; bubble economy of, 85; China occupied by, 5, 8, 167–69; coverage of Vincent Chin case in, 73; emigration policies of, 28–30; establishment of relations between U.S. and, 24; investments in U.S. of, 90; Korea occupied by, 33, 34, 39, 185; in World War II, 5, 8, 10, 39, 69
Japanese American Citizens League (JACL), 45, 32, 216; civil rights legislation advocated by, 153; and electoral politics, 290; and pan-Asian movement, 48; and same-sex marriage, 231–33, 237–42, 244, 246–51, 294; and Vincent Chin case, 66, 75; and Wards Cove case, 156, 160, 161; and World War II internment, 43, 159
Japanese and Japanese Americans, 29–30, 89–90, 94, 142, 169, 172, 191, 192, 200; African Americans and, 96; in Alaskan salmon canneries, 144–45, 150; in antiwar movement, 48; arts and, 271; and automobile industry, 58; citizenship for, 30–31, 45; in civil rights movement, 47; first in U.S., 24; 442nd Nisei Regimental Combat Team, 43; gay and lesbian, 240, 242; in Hawaii, 234, 246, 248–49; Korean Americans and, 33, 96, 194; labor movement and, 36, 37; land ownership by, 38–39; during Los Angeles riots, 188; outmarriage among, 267; in politics, 24, 46, 288–89, 308; at Princeton, 16; South Asians and, 201; in student movement, 146; and Vincent Chin case, 67, 74, 76; violence against, 78; war brides, 7; during World War II,

9, 10, 16, 39–44, 49–50, 69, 96, 117, 146, 159, 172, 184, 232, 234, 238, 240, 247–50, 274, 284, 288–89, 295, 300
Japanese and Korean Exclusion League, 32
Japanese Mexican Labor Association, 35
Jaswa, Raj, 209
Jefferson, Thomas, 27
Johnston, George, 134
Jones, Jennifer, 113
Jong, Jason, 277
Joy Luck Club, The (film), 115–16, 276, 277
Justice Department, U.S., 70, 79

Kai (performance troupe), 277
Kalayil, Ann, 215–17
Kamali'i, Kina'u Boyd, 245
Kamehameha, King, 244
Kaneko, Bill, 231–33, 239
Kang, K. Connie, 190
Kao, Kuan-chun, 301
Karlin, Joyce, 180
Karloff, Boris, 114
Kashiwahara, Ken, 274
Kato, Eileen, 289, 295
Kaufman, Charles, 60, 65, 69, 72, 74
Kawakami, Rod, 50
Kearney, Denis, 35
Kearny Street Workshop, 269
Keating, Charles, Jr., 85
Kennedy, Edward M., 152, 153, 155, 157–61, 163–64
Kennedy, Joseph, II, 157
Keshavan, Narayan, 210
Khmer Rouge, 51
Khmu (Laotian people), 51
Kim, Bong Hwan, 180–81, 186, 187
Kim, Charles, 38, 193
Kim, Do, 187, 188, 193
Kim, Elaine, 270
Kim, Harry, 38

Kim, Hwa Ja, 166

Kim, Jae Yul, 169–71, 185–86, 193–94

Kim, Nina, 169, 171, 185

Kim, Randall Duk, 121, 254

Kim, Sung Soo, 87, 89, 107

Kimura, Lillian, 232

King, Martin Luther, Jr., 45

King, Rodney, 169, 176, 177, 181, 183, 184

*King and I, The* (musical and film), 121, 269

Kingston, Maxine Hong, 271

Klein, Joe, 99

Knight Ridder newspaper chain, 315

Kochiyama, Yuri, 96

Kohara, Sydnie, 267

*Kongnip Sinmun* (newspaper), 33

Koppel, Ted, 91, 183

Korea: Japanese occupation of, 33, 34, 39, 185; U.S. military presence in, 95

Korea Girl (performance troupe), 277

Korean American Association of Illinois, 75

Korean American Coalition (KAC), 192, 303

Korean American Grocers Association (KAGRO), 177, 186, 187

Korean American Small Business Service Center, 87, 107

Korean American Women's Association, 77

Korean Produce Association, 105, 107

Koreans and Korean Americans, 29, 33–34, 49, 118, 169–72, 200, 208, 229; adoptees, 265–66, 279, 306; arts and, 271; athletes, 275; boycott of businesses owned by, 85–89, 92–108, 173, 229; Breslin's attack on, 98–99; in campaign finance scandal (1996), 298; citizenship for, 40, 45; in Detroit, 62; in Hawaii, 234, 246, 248; impact of Los Angeles riots on, 169–94; labor movement and, 37; middle-class and elite, 204, 205; outmarriage among,

267; in politics, 288; South Asians and, 201, 203–4; and Vincent Chin case, 67, 74, 77, 80; violence against, 90, 118–19, 171, 178, 179; during World War II, 40

Korean Society of Greater Detroit, 66, 77

Korean War, 10, 12, 44, 79, 265

Korean Youth Cultural Center (Los Angeles), 180, 186

*Korea Times*, 172, 175, 179, 182, 184, 189

Korematsu, Fred, 50

KQRS radio station, 257–62, 278–80

Kramer, Thomas, 297

Kroll, Jack, 130–31

*Kudzu* (comic strip), 90

Ku Klux Klan, 52

Kumu Kahua repertory company, 121–22

*Kung Fu* (television series), 114

Kwan, Nancy, 114

Kwoh, Stewart, 81, 179, 189, 190, 192

Kwok, Daphne, 156, 160

Kwong, Peter, 100–1, 103

labor movement, 35–38, 97; in Alaskan salmon canneries, 139, 146–49, 162, 163

Lagon, Patrick, 227

Lam, Tony, 305

Lambda Legal Defense and Education Fund, 132, 243

Lambert, Brian, 260

land ownership prohibitions, 30, 33; circumvention of, 38–39

Langlois, Judith, 306

Lao and Laotian Americans, 51, 204, 207, 256–57

*Last Plantation, The* (Njeri), 178

Latinos, 69, 228, 273; actors, 120; Asian Americans' marriages to, 169, 172, 185, 192, 194; politics and, 294, 295; at Princeton, 16, 18, 307; on television, 274; Wards Cove workers supported by, 151

Lau, Henry, 91
*Laugh-In* (television series), 117
Lawrence, Charles, 294
Lawrence, David, 315–16
Le, Ngoan, 206
Leadership Conference on Civil Rights, 153, 158, 160, 164
Leadership Education for Asian Pacifics, 48, 119
League of American Theatres and Producers, 127
League of Nations, 22
League of Women Voters, 248
LEAP Asian Pacific American Public Policy Institute, 208
*Lectures on the Philosophy of History* (Hegel), 22
Lee, Ang, 276
Lee, Bill Lann, 291, 310
Lee, Bruce, 118, 267, 277
Lee, Cherylene, 80
Lee, Chol Soo, 49
Lee, Christopher, 276–77
Lee, Chung, 175, 178, 183, 192
Lee, Cynthia, 60
Lee, Edward, 182
Lee, Jason Scott, 296
Lee, Josephine, 130
Lee, K. W., 39, 172, 184–85, 187
Lee, Li-Young, 263
Lee, Mary, 113
Lee, Michael, 74
Lee, Shannon, 267
Lee, Wen Ho, 309, 316
Lee, Yvonne, 298
Lendl, Ivan, 273
Leni-Lenape Indians, 22
Lennon, John, 273
Leon, Harold, 78
Leon, Joyce, 78

lesbians, 132, 221, 228–30, 279; right to marry of, 227, 230–51, 293
Lester, Sheena, 177
Letterman, David, 199
Levin, Michael, 101
Lewis, Jerry, 251
Liff, Vincent, 121, 122
Liliuokalani, Queen, 230–31
Lim, Mable, 67
Lim, Ray, 67
Lin, Maya, 272–73
Lincoln, Abraham, 24
Li Po, 311
Li Shangyin, 311–12
Liu, Mini, 91
Liu, Walter, 263
*Living in Half Tones* (film), 266
Locke, Gary, 281, 284–90, 294–95, 300, 308
Locke, Mona Lee, 281, 285
Loo, Jim Ming Hai, 91
Lord, Jack, 118
Los Angeles, 96; anti-Asian violence in, 119; Asian American actors in, 126, 129; Board of Education, 189; pan-Asian movement in, 75; Police Department (LAPD), 176, 182; politics in, 289, 292, 293; riots in, 46, 169–94
Los Angeles County Human Relations Commission, 174–77, 179–80, 182, 189
*Los Angeles Sentinel*, 173, 177
*Los Angeles Times*, 35, 41–42, 177, 183, 184, 189, 190, 208, 290
Lott, Juanita Tamayo, 208
Louis, Joe, 273
Louisiana: Chinese plantation workers in, 36; Filipinos in, 24; *see also* New Orleans
*Loving* v. *Virginia* (1967), 235
Lu, Lisa, 115
Luce, Henry, 40
Lugosi, Bela, 113

Luke, Keye, 118
Luke, Wing, 287
Lyfoung, Pacyinz, 261–62
Lynch, Bill, 98
Lyu-Volckhausen, Grace, 105

Ma, Yo-Yo, 272
McCarran Internal Security Act (1950), 45
McCarthy, Nobu, 126
McCarthyism, 10
McClatchy, V. S., 31
McCray, Fred, 102–3, 106–7
McDermott, Jim, 157, 158, 160
Mackintosh, Cameron, 112, 119, 120, 122–24, 126–30
MacLaine, Shirley, 114
McLaughlin, Lindsay, 157
McWhirter, Nikki, 60
*Madama Butterfly* (Puccini), 113, 115, 116, 130
*Madame Butterfly* (film), 114
Mahaffey, Maryann, 73
Maharaj, Chandra, 220
Maharaj, Rishi, 219–22
Mako (actor), 296
Malaysia, refugee camps in, 51
Malcolm X, 96
Maldivians, 200
Man, Pang, 78
Manavi (South Asian women's group), 214
Mankiller, Wilma, 273
Manzanar internment camp, 42
Mao Tse-tung, 76, 140, 196, 311
Marcos, Ferdinand, 49, 148, 149
marriages: arranged, 30, 212–14, 240; interracial, 33, 34, 194, 200, 232, 235–36, 266–68, 306, 318; outmarriage, 268; same-sex, 227, 230–51, 293; traditional Hmong, 258–63
Marro, Anthony, 100

martial arts genre, 277
*Martial Law* (television series), 313
Maryland, University of, 307
Massachusetts: Chinese factory workers in, 36; Southeast Asian refugees in, 52; *see also* Boston
Mast, Terri, 149
Master Race (racist group), 90
Mathew, Biju, 218, 219
Matsuda, Mari, 294
Matsuda, Minn, 48
Matsui, Robert, 50, 155, 157, 161, 290
Matsumoto, Colbert, 251
Matthews, Chris, 297
Mazumdar, Sucheta, 209
*M. Butterfly* (Hwang), 116, 121
Media Action Network for Asian Americans (MANAA), 134, 279
mehndi tattoos, 275
Mehta, Monica, 210
Melillo, Joseph, 227
*Menace II Society* (film), 118
Meredith, Burgess, 114
*Metropolitan Detroit* (magazine), 57
Mexicans and Mexican Americans: in Alaskan salmon canneries, 145; intermarriage of Sikhs and, 33, 200; in labor movement, 37
Mexico, Chinese in, 24
MGM-UA, 118
Michigan: anti-Asian violence in, 77; Court of Appeals, 74; Indian Americans in, 212; *see also* Detroit
Microsoft Corporation, 210
middle class, Asian American, 206, 208–9
Midwest Asian American Center for Justice, 80
Mien (Laotian people), 51
Milken, Michael, 85
Mills College, 307

Minami, Dale, 48, 50, 301

Mineta, Norman, 24, 50, 155, 157, 164–65, 240–41, 290

Ming, Marisa Chuang, 78

Ming dynasty, 23

Mink, Patsy, 46, 155, 157, 158, 235, 286

Minnesota: Asian American artists in, 263–65, 271, 272; Hmong in, 52, 254–63, 278–80, 308; Koreans in, 173, 265–66

Misérables, Les (musical), 112, 130

Mishra, Debasish, 222

missionaries, 234, 244

Mississippi, Chinese plantation workers in, 36

Miss Saigon (musical), 109, 112–13, 115, 119–32, 134–35

Mitchell, Lee Arthur, 178

Mitsubishi Corporation, 89, 90

Miyori, Kim, 120, 126, 254

model minority myth, 46–47, 117, 118, 152, 205, 213, 302

Mody, Navroze, 91, 221

Monitored Peril (Hamamoto), 115

Montalban, Ricardo, 114

Monthly Detroit, 57

Moon, Ronald T.Y., 233

Moon, Sun Myung, 88

Mormons, 238, 243–45

Mother Jones magazine, 210

Moua, Mee, 262–63

Mountain Brothers, The, 277

Moving the Image (Gong), 269

Ms. magazine, 197, 198, 229

Muhammad, Ruby, 108

Mulan (film), 115, 117, 254, 275

Multicultural Collaborative, 192

Muni, Paul, 114

Mura, David, 263

Murakami, Alan, 250

Murkowski, Frank, 154, 155, 157, 161

Murray, Patty, 160

Murrow, Edward R., 42

musicians, Asian American, 80, 269, 272, 275, 277, 278

Muslims, 32, 203

My America (. . . or honk if you love Buddha) (film), 270

Myamoto, Nobuko, 269

Myasato, Albert, 248

NAACP, 175, 176, 240, 249, 279, 303

Nachman, Jerry, 99

Nagae, Peggy, 50

Nagano, Kent, 272

Nakanishi, Don, 289, 290, 296, 308

Nakatani, Al, 249

Nakatani, Jane, 249

Na Mamo O Hawai'i, 244

Narasaki, Diane, 150

Narasaki, Karen, 160–62, 292

Narika (South Asian women's group), 214

National Asian American Telecommunications Association, 276

National Asian Pacific American Bar Association (NAPABA), 48–49, 156, 160, 161

National Asian Pacific American Legal Consortium (NAPALC), 81, 219, 292

National Association for the Education and Advancement of Cambodian, Laotian and Vietnamese Americans, 206

National Association of Black Journalists, 99

National Association of Hispanic Journalists, 99

National Council of Asian Pacific Americans, 303

National Council of La Raza, 240

National Federation of Filipino American Associations, 303

National Football League, 275

National Gay and Lesbian Task Force, 240

National Institute for Occupational Safety and Health, 202

*National Journal*, 164

National Lawyers Guild, 72

National Network Against Anti-Asian Violence, 179

National Organization for Women (NOW), 303

National Science Foundation, 208

National Women's Political Caucus, 198

Native Americans, 8, 22, 273, 294; Alaskan, 142, 147, 148, 150, 151, 156

Native Hawaiian Legal Corporation, 250

Native Sons of the Golden State, 28

Naturalization Law (1790), 32

Nazis, 43

NBC News, 291

NEFCO–Fidalgo Packing Company, 147, 148

Nepalese, 200

Newark (New Jersey) riots, 46

*New Chinatown, The* (Kwong), 100

New England Fishing Company, 146–48

New England Patriots football team, 275

New Jersey: anti-Asian violence in, 90–91, 221; Chinese factory workers in, 36; Newark riots in, 46; politics in, 287

*New Jerusalem* (play), 125–26

New Orleans, 304

*Newsday*, 89–90, 98–100, 104, 135

*Newsweek*, 130–31, 297

New York Asian Women's Center, 229

New York City, 229; anti-Asian violence in, 77, 90–91, 101–4, 132, 219–22; Asian American actors in, 114–30; boycott of Korean American businesses in, 85–89, 92–108, 173, 184; Breslin's attack on

Koreans in, 98–100; Chinatown in, 5, 82–84; Commission on Human Rights, 96, 129; Japanese investment in, 89–90, 92; Mayor's Community Assistance Unit, 98; pan-Asian movement in, 75; Police Department (NYPD), 91, 93, 94, 98, 203; politics in, 289, 292, 293; after stock market crash of October 1987, 84–85; sweatshops in, 197–98; Taxi and Limousine Commission, 202, 203, 218; taxi drivers in, 198–204, 217–19

*New York Daily News*, 202

*New York* magazine, 199

*New York Post*, 99, 124

New York Shakespeare Festival, 125–26

New York State: anti-Asian violence in, 300–1; Asian American Advisory Council, 105; Division of Human Rights, Crisis Prevention Unit of, 87, 89; politics in, 287; *see also* New York City

New York Taxi Workers Alliance, 198, 199, 202–4, 215, 218, 221

*New York Times, The*, 73, 90, 92, 98, 100, 114, 121, 122, 124, 205, 217, 218, 220, 316; *Magazine*, 46

Nguyen, Dat, 275

Nguyen, Dustin, 296

*Nightline* (television program), 91, 183

Nisei, *see* Japanese and Japanese Americans

Nitz, Michael, 59, 69, 77–80

Nixon, Richard M., 140, 141, 253

Njeri, Itabari, 178

Noguchi, Isamu, 89, 272

nontraditional casting, in theater, 127–29

North Carolina, anti-Asian violence in, 91–92

Northwest Asian Theater Company, 122, 270

Northwestern University, 100, 307

Northwest Labor and Employment Law
    Office, 147–48, 152, 163
Nostrand-Fulton Korean American
    Merchants Association, 87
Novell Corporation, 205

Oakland: African American–Korean
    American conflicts in, 96; fires in,
    133–34
Oakland Tribune, The, 125
Oh, Angela, 183, 186–87
Ohio, Koreans in, 173; see also Cincinnati
Ohio State University, 133
oil crises, 57–58
Oland, Warner, 114
Olympic Games, 274, 275
On Leong Merchants Association, 61, 62, 75
Ono, Yoko, 273
Operation Rescue, 243
Oregon, 38; Indians in, 32; migrant
    agricultural workers in, 145; politics in,
    308–9
Organization of Asian Women, 99
Organization of Chinese Americans
    (OCA), 48, 298, 302–3; civil rights
    legislation advocated by, 153; "Get Out
    the Vote" campaign of, 296; Leadership
    Summit, 283; and Vincent Chin case, 75;
    and Wards Cove case, 156, 160
Organization of Chinese American
    Women, 66
organized crime, 62
Organizing Asian American Labor (Friday),
    146
"Oriental" styles, adopted by Western
    artists, 116–17
Oshio, Terri, 249–50
Osman, Saleem, 203
outmarriages, 267, 268; see also marriages:
    interracial

Oyama, David, 126
Ozawa, Takao, 30–31
Ozawa v. United States, 30

Pacific Citizen (newspaper), 247
Pacific Overtures (musical), 121
Pakistani Americans, 3–4, 206, 216, 217,
    222; intergenerational clash in values
    among, 212; taxi drivers, 199, 201,
    203–4, 218; violence against, 221
Pallas (ship), 24
pan–Asian American movement, 47–49,
    52, 57; arts and, 264, 270–71; after Los
    Angeles riots, 184, 190–92; politics and,
    303; South Asians in, 201, 217, 220–23;
    and Vincent Chin case, 66–67, 74–77;
    see also specific organizations
Pan Asian Repertory Theatre, 122, 123,
    126, 270
Pang, Gin Yong, 268
Papp, Joseph, 125
Park, Krystene, 187
Park, Steve, 276, 296
Park, Tae Sam, 179
Part, Yet Apart, A (Shankar), 201
Patchwork Shawl, A (DasGupta), 213
Pathet Lao, 256
Patil, Suhas, 205, 210
Pearl Harbor, bombing of, 39, 41
Peeling the Banana (performance troupe),
    277
Pei, I. M., 272
Peloponnesian Wars, 317
Pennsylvania: Chinese factory workers in,
    36; Vietnamese refugees in, 51; see also
    Philadelphia
Pennsylvania, University of, 211
Penthouse magazine, 133
performance troupes, 277
Performing Asian America (Lee), 130

Perot, H. Ross, 298

Peru, importation of Asia laborers to, 25

*Phantom of the Opera, The* (musical), 112, 130

Philadelphia, Hmong in, 52

Philippine Heritage Foundation, 156

Philippines: independence granted to, 35; Marcos regime in, 49, 148, 149; refugee camps in, 51; as Spanish colony, 24; U.S. annexation of, 34, 142; during World War II, 39, 40

Piche, Lloyd, 91–92

Piche, Robert, 91–92

Pickford, Mary, 114

picture bride marriages, 30, 240

Pierce, Franklin, 24

Pinay (performance troupe), 277

Pokémon, 275

politics, Asian Americans in, 281–310; affirmative action and, 291–94; and campaign finance scandal (1996), 296–302; elective office holders, 284–90, 294–96, 305, 308–9; student activists, 305–8

Polychrome Publishing, 271

Pom Siab Hmoob Theatre, 264

pornography, images of Asian women in, 133

Portuguese, 36, 37, 234

poverty, 207; Hmong, 257; Native Hawaiian, 245

Pregil, Antoinette, 227

Previn, Soon-Yi, 266

Princeton University, 14–20, 305, 307; Third World Center at, 18

professionals, immigration of, 205

Protect Our Constitution (POC) coalition, 248–51

Pryce, Jonathan, 113, 119, 120, 122–24, 127–29, 131

Public Theater (New York), 125, 134

Puccini, Giacomo, 113

Puerto Ricans, 36, 234

Purdy, Patrick, 91

Quackenbush, Justin, 163

Queens College (New York), 208

Quinn, Patrick, 123

Radio Korea, 182

railroads, building of, 9, 23, 27, 36

Rainer, Luise, 114

Raja, Rizwan, 217–18

Rangaswamy, Padma, 216

Ray, Dixie Lee, 284

Reagan, Ronald, 74, 150, 151

Reeves, Keanu, 267

Refugee Act (1980), 51

refugees, 50–52, 91, 204, 206–8, 256–57

Rekhi, Kanwal, 205, 210

Reno, Robert, 89

Republican Party, 46, 316; and civil rights legislation, 153; in Detroit, 77; fund-raising by, 296, 299; in Hawaii, 251; National Senatorial Committee, 301; and Wards Cove case, 155, 161, 162; and "Yellow Peril" movement, 28

Resorts International, 85

Reynolds, William Bradford, 74

Rice, Norman, 294–95

Rider University, 218

Ridley-Thomas, Mark, 175

riots, 46, 169–94

*Rising Sun* (Crichton), 134

Rivers, Tony, 132

Robinson, Edward G., 113

Rocher, Rosane, 211–12

Rockefeller Center, Japanese investment in, 89–90, 92, 184

Rodney King riots (Los Angeles), 169, 171–73, 181–93

Rodrigues, Tammy, 227

Rohmer, Sax, 117

Roldan, Salvador, 34

Rooney, Mickey, 114, 117, 130

Roosevelt, Franklin D., 41, 42

Roosevelt, Theodore, 145

*Rosie's Cafe* (Shiomi), 264

Rudolph, Wilma, 273

*Rush Hour* (film), 278

Rutgers University, 213

Sa, B. J., 105, 107

sa-i-gu, 172–93

*St. Elsewhere* (television series), 120

St. Paul Board of Education, 308

*St. Paul Pioneer Press*, 260

Sakamoto, Janice, 276

Sakhi (South Asian women's group), 214, 215, 221

salmon canneries, Alaskan, 142–65

Salonga, Lea, 129, 131

Salt Lake City, Japanese Americans in, 238–41

same-sex marriage, 227, 230–51, 293

Samoan Americans, 149

San Francisco, 290; anti-Communism in, 45; pan-Asian movement in, 49, 75, 76; Police and Fire Departments of, 48; politics in, 292, 293, 304

*San Francisco Chronicle*, 266, 308

*San Francisco Examiner*, 297

San Francisco Neighbors' Association, 304

San Francisco State University, 47–48, 306

San Jose, 24, 304

Sansei, *see* Japanese and Japanese Americans

Santos, Sharon Tomiko, 287, 295

*Saturday Evening Post, The* (magazine), 116

Saund, Dalip Singh, 45, 286

Save Traditional Marriage coalition, 249

*Sayonara* (film), 114

Schroeder, Patricia, 157

Scott, Tyree, 152

Seaman Furniture Co., 85

*Searching for Go-Hyang* (documentary), 266

Seattle: politics in, 285, 287, 294, 295; Third World workers' movement in, 147

*Secret Asian Man* (zine), 277

Sedler, Robert A., 72

Selma-to-Montgomery civil rights march, 45

Senate, U.S., 45–46, 153–61, 286, 297, 298; Committee on Labor and Human Resources, 160–61

Sengupta, Somini, 220

sexual abuse of adopted children, 266

sexual harassment, 19, 159, 237; racialized, 132

*Shanghai Express* (film), 114

Shankar, Lavina Dhingra, 201

Sharpton, Al, 283

*Shasta Republican*, 26

Shelley, Percy Bysshe, 311, 312

Shigemura, Lia, 240

Shimizu, Jenny, 296

Shimoura, Jim, 69

Shin, Min Chul, 95

Shin, Paul, 288

Shinagawa, Larry Hajime, 268, 292

Shinto, 41

Shiomi, Rick, 264–65, 269–71

Sikhs, 32, 33, 200

Simon, Howard, 72

Simon, Paul, 157

*Simpsons, The* (television series), 199

Singh, Jane, 200

Sinha, Sumantra Tito, 220–22

*Sixteen Candles* (film), 118
*Slant* (zine), 277
slaves, Asian laborers as replacement for, 9,
    25
Soelistyo, Julyana, 254
Sonoma State University, 268, 292
South Africa, opposition to apartheid in,
    Asian Americans and, 97
South Asian Lesbian and Gay Association,
    215, 221
South Asians, *see specific nationalities*
South Asian Students Alliance (SASA),
    222–23
South Asian Youth in Action, 221
Southeast Asians, *see specific nationalities*
Southern California, University of, 133
Southern Christian Leadership Conference
    (SCLC), 175, 176
Spain, American colonies of, 24
Spanish-American War, 34, 142
sports stars, 268, 273, 274, 275
Sri Lankans and Sri Lankan Americans,
    200, 206, 222
Stanford University, 307
*Star Trek* (television series), 117, 134
State Department, U.S., 141
Stein, Alma, 106
Stern, Howard, 100, 258
Stevens, John Paul, 152
Stevens, Ted, 153, 155
Stir (Web site), 277
Stockton (California) school shootings, 91
*Story of Civilization* (Durant), 22
*Strangers from a Different Shore* (Takaki),
    25, 37
Strobel, Chris, 164–65
student activism, 15–20, 47–48, 146,
    222–23, 283–84, 305–7
sugar plantations in Hawaii, 36–37
Sul, Yong Hwan, 182

Sundance Film Festival, 276
Sunoo, Brenda Paik, 184, 189
Sunoo, Jan Jung-Min, 176, 182
Sun Tzu, 316, 317
Superchink (band), 278
Supreme Court, U.S., 16, 28–33, 45, 142,
    150–55, 201, 232, 233, 235–36
*Susie Wong Is Dead!* (performance piece),
    278
Suzuki, Pat, 114
sweatshops, 197–98, 307

Tagawa, Walter, 249
taiko drumming, 252, 272
Taiwan, 286–87, 298; gays and lesbians in,
    242; and Vincent Chin case, 73
Tajima-Peña, Renee (Renee Tajima), 79,
    263, 270
Takaki, Ronald, 25, 37
Takeda, Suz, 278
Takei, George, 117, 126, 134
Tamils, 222
*Taming of the Shrew, The*, 123, 128
Tan, Amy, 115, 274
Tang, Henry, 161
Tang, Joyce, 208
Tariq, Javaid, 195, 198, 200, 203, 218,
    219
Tasaka, Allicyn Hikida, 231, 232
Tate, Eric Akira, 267–68
Tateoka, Reid, 239
taxi drivers, 198–204, 206, 215–19
*Taxi-vala/Auto-biography* (documentary),
    218
Taylor, Anna Diggs, 78, 79
*Teahouse of the August Moon, The* (play
    and film), 114
television: Asian Americans on, 252–54,
    274, 276; portrayals of Asians on, 112,
    115, 117, 252

Tennessee, politics in, 308

Terry, Randall, 243

Texas: Koreans in, 173; politics in, 287, 303; Vietnamese in, 52; *see also* Houston

Texas, University of, 306

Texas A&M University, 275

Thai Dam (Laotian people), 51

Thailand, 298; refugee camps in, 51, 255

Thao, Neal, 308

*That Was the Week That Was* (television series), 117

theater: Asian American, 80–81, 121–22, 126, 254, 264–65, 269–71, 278; nontraditional casting in, 127–29; portrayals of Asians in, 112–15, 119–32, 134–35

Theater Mu, 264–65, 269–71

The IndUS Entrepreneurs (TIE), 204–5, 207, 209, 211, 223

*Thief of Bagdad, The* (film), 114

Thind, Bhagat Singh, 32–33, 201

Thomas, Clarence, 153

Three Obediences, Confucian order of, 11, 13

*Three Seasons* (film), 276

Thurmond, Strom, 45

Tiananmen Square protests, 273

Tilley, Jennifer, 267

Tilley, Meg, 267

*Time* magazine, 39–40, 44, 274

Tith, Sovann, 191

*Today* show, 267

Togasaki, Minoru, 76–77

Tokuda, Kip, 287–89, 295, 296

Tolle, Tammy, 266

Tomita, Tamlyn, 126, 296

Tong, Kam, 115

Tong, Sammee, 115

tongs, 61–62

*To Tell the Truth* (television series), 253

tourism, Hawaiian, 244

Toy, Vivian S., 220

Toyota, Tritia, 274

Toyota (corporation), 24, 184

transcontinental railroad, 9, 23, 27

Trinidad, immigrants from, 220

Truong, Loc Minh, 237–38

Tu Fu, 311

Tule Lake internment camp, 43

Turner, Lana, 113

Twain, Mark, 114, 130

Twentieth Century-Fox, 134

Tydings-McDuffie Act (1934), 35

Umeki, Miyoshi, 115

Underwood, Cecil H., 81

Unification Church, 88

United Auto Workers (UAW), 56, 72–74

United Cambodian Community Agency of Long Beach, 191

United Construction Workers Association, 147

United Farm Workers, 38

*United States* v. *Bhagat Singh Thind*, 33

Uppuluri, Ram Yoshino, 308

*U.S. News & World Report*, 46, 205

Utah, Japanese Americans in, 42, 238–41, 247

Vang, Xang, 280

Vann, Albert, 87, 89

Varadarajan, Tunku, 217

Veloria, Velma, 287, 295

Veterans of Foreign Wars (VFW), 148

video artists, 269, 276

Viernes, Gene, 139, 146–50, 160, 163, 165

Vietnamese and Vietnamese Americans, 192, 201, 229; athletes, 275; middle-class and elite, 204, 205; in Minnesota, 257; politics and, 304–5; refugees, 50–51, 204,

206, 257; shrimpers and fishermen, 208; violence against, 52, 77, 78, 91, 101–4, 237–38

Vietnam Veterans Memorial, 272

Vietnam War, 12–14, 17, 18, 47, 48, 50–51, 92, 117, 255–57

*Village Voice, The*, 100, 103, 199

violence: anti-Asian, *see* hate crimes: anti-Asian; domestic, 214, 229, 237, 260–62, 307

visual arts, 269–70

Volkswagen, 70

Voting Rights Act (1992), 164

Waggoner, Amy, 259

Wakabayashi, Ron, 189

*Walleye Kid, The* (Shiomi), 265, 271

Wang, Bert, 278

Wang, Ling-chi, 301

Wang, Wayne, 276

Wards Cove Packing Company, 146–52, 154–64, 283, 294, 296

Washington, Craig, 157

Washington, George, 23, 24

Washington, D.C.; African American–Korean American conflicts in, 96; anti-Asian violence in, 118–19; Asian American lobbying groups in, 153, 156, 158–61, 164, 303; during campaign finance scandal (1996), 299, 300

Washington, University of, 146

Washington Council for Prevention of Child Abuse and Neglect, 287

*Washington Post, The*, 233, 298, 316

Washington State, 38; driving out of Chinese from, 28; Indians in, 32; migrant agricultural workers in, 145; politics in, 284–90, 294–96, 300, 317–18; *see also* Seattle

*W.A.S.P., The* (magazine), 114, 116, 117

Watanabe, Gedde, 118

Watts riots, 46

Wayne, David, 114

Wayne, John, 114

Wayne State University, 72

Web sites, 277–78

*Wedding Banquet, The* (film), 276

Wellstone, Paul, 259, 280

Wen, Ming-Na, 115–16, 254, 296

Westbrook, Dennis, 177

Westbrook, Peter, 267

Westinghouse Science Talent Search, 47, 207

Westminster (California), 304–5

West Virginia, dialogue on race in, 81

*We Won't Go Back* (Lawrence), 294

Wheat, Alan, 157

*Who Killed Vincent Chin?* (documentary), 79, 80, 270

Williams, Harrison, Jr., 141

*Will Rogers Follies, The* (musical), 130

Wilson, Woodrow, 22

WNET public television station, 131

Wojciechowski, Gene, 215, 216

*Woman Warrior, The* (Kingston), 271

women: and intergenerational clash in values, 213–15; sexual exploitation of, 132–33; violence against, 214, 229, 237, 260–62, 307

Women's Association of Hmong and Lao, 261

Wong, Anna May, 114

Wong, B. D., 112, 116, 119–26, 129, 130, 296

Wong, Eddie, 76

Wong, Jai Lee, 174, 177, 181, 187

Wong, K. Scott, 26

Wong, Martha, 160

Wong, Norma, 244

Wong, Russell, 296

Wong, William, 125

Wong Kim Ark, 16, 28–29

Woo, Elaine, 184

Woo, Michael, 184, 289

Woo, Parker, 69

Woo, Ruth Oya, 288–89, 317–18

Woods, Tiger, 267, 268

Workingmen's Party (California), 27, 35

workplace discrimination, class action
    lawsuits on, 147–52, 159, 162, 163

*World of Suzy Wong, The* (play), 121

World War II, 6, 10, 22, 39–44, 49–50, 69,
    89, 96, 117, 234, 295, 300; Asian
    American GIs in, 40, 43, 44, 63, 148,
    247–48, 303–4; China during, 5, 39;
    internment of Japanese Americans
    during, 10, 42–44, 50, 146, 159, 172, 184,
    232, 238, 240, 247–50, 274, 284, 288–89

writers, 270, 271, 274

Wu, David, 308–9

Wu, Frank, 299

Wyoming, internment of Japanese
    Americans in, 42


Xiong, Tou Ger, 254–56, 259, 264


Yale University, 24, 280

Yamaguchi, Kristi, 274

Yamamoto, Eric, 177, 246

Yamamoto, May, 242

Yamamoto, Tak, 240

Yamasaki, Minoru, 272

Yamate, Sandra, 271

Yang, Gaoly, 261

Yang, Jeff, 278

*Yankee Dawg You Die* (Gotanda), 111–12,
    135

Yasui, Minoru, 50

*Year of the Dragon* (film), 118

Yeats, William Butler, 311

Yee, Henry (author's brother), 3, 6, 7, 12,
    167, 311

Yee, Henry (Detroit restaurateur), 60–62, 64

Yee, John, 6–7

Yee, Kin, 61, 62, 64, 65, 74, 75

Yee, Paul, 103

yellowface, 110, 113–14, 119, 122–25, 130,
    134–35, 252

*Yellow Fever* (Shiomi), 264

"Yellow Peril" movement, 27–28, 35

Yellow Power movement, 47

Yeoh, Michelle, 277

Yi, Young Kyu, 179

*Yick Wo* v. *Hopkins* (1896), 28

Yin, Monona, 91

*Yolk* (magazine), 278

Young, Andrew, 223

Young, Jackie Eurn Hai, 248

Young, Loretta, 113

Youngberg, Francey Lim, 299

Yuh, Ji-Yeon, 98–100

Yung, Victor Sen, 115

Yung Wing, 24


Zia, Beilin Woo (author's mother), 3–9, 11,
    55–56, 82, 83, 110–11, 166–69, 195–97,
    281, 311–12

Zia, Haddon (author's brother), 168, 311

Zia, Hoyt (author's brother), 3, 12, 168,
    232, 299, 311

Zia, Hugo (author's brother), 3, 168, 311

Zia, Humane (author's sister), 168, 311

Zia, Yee Chen (author's father), 3, 5, 7–11,
    22–23, 55–56, 82, 83, 110, 166–69, 282,
    311, 318–19

zines, 277